PEE WEE

Serial Killer or Homicidal Maniac

A Novelized True Crime Story Volume II

GRADY QUERY

authorHOUSE®

AuthorHouse™ LLC
1663 Liberty Drive
Bloomington, IN 47403
www.authorhouse.com
Phone: 1-800-839-8640

Published by AuthorHouse 9/15/2014

ISBN: 978-1-4969-1922-9 (sc)
ISBN: 978-1-4969-1923-6 (hc)
ISBN: 978-1-4969-1921-2 (e)

Library of Congress Control Number: 2014910885

CONTENTS

This volume is dedicated to my astonishing wife, Lisa, and to my grandson, Austin. I am forever grateful to Lisa for her help and for the joy she brings me each day. To Austin I am indebted for his enthusiasm and optimism. His academic excellence is an inspiration.

VOLUME II

In Volume I the atrocities committed by the tiny criminal Pee Wee Gaskins are described in detail. His childhood and his many years of incarceration which began in reform school at age thirteen and graduated to the toughest penitentiary in South Carolina are covered in that volume. During his many confinements Pee Wee was beaten and sexually abused. His unpredictable reaction was to adopt extreme violence as his trademark and to evolve from the weakest to the most powerful inside the prison walls. He committed his first murders within the prisons and then continued an onslaught against those whom he perceived to be a danger to him and those that he considered to have betrayed him, whether lover or felon accomplice. During the period of his murderous rampage, he killed again and again as he strove to destroy those involved in interracial relationships. Gaskins was obsessed with the need to employ his violent solution to what he believed was an abomination that he believed required him to act.

At the conclusion of Volume I Pee Wee Gaskins, his crony Walter Neely and the much younger Knoy Judy had each been taken into custody in separate arrests by police. Gaskins and Neely were being held as "Safekeepers" on Death Row at Central Corrections Institution in Columbia, South Carolina and Judy was in the Florence County Detention Center in Florence, South Carolina. All were charged with murder arising out of the discovery of six bodies near Florence and all three were being held without bond. While no schedule had been announced the prosecutor in Florence had announced to the media that he intended to try all three men at the earliest possible date.

CHAPTER FORTY NINE

Retaining Counsel

James Knoy Judy was arrested in Charleston in the first week of December in 1975 by SLED agents, Florence County Sheriff's deputies and North Charleston Police Officers. He was taken directly to the Florence County Detention Center where he was booked and placed in a cell by himself. Young Judy was astonished when arresting officers informed him that he was being arrested for murder as a co-defendant of Pee Wee Gaskins.

Knoy's sister, Tina, called Grady Query who was the only lawyer she knew from him representing a friend of hers. He was a young lawyer, but he was fully ensconced in an extremely active trial practice. He had asked the Clerks of Court for Charleston, Berkeley and Dorchester counties to appoint him to any criminal cases that required an appointed lawyer. The three counties had common borders and businesses both legitimate and illegitimate generally crisscrossed all three.

Tina asked him to go to Florence County where her brother was being held. She was not certain of the charges against him but knew that it was associated with the bodies that were announced across the front pages of the newspapers. Query agreed to make an initial appearance but cautioned her that he was not agreeing to the full representation since so little was known about the charges and circumstances.

In Florence County, Query had only a few minutes to speak to the bronze skinned young man, with shoulder length black hair and full mustache before the brief hearing. Query advised the young defendant that his sister had asked him to come, and that he would advise the court that the family would probably be retaining him or some other private attorney, but that he had not yet agreed to take the case. Query told Judy that he would try to contact officers investigating the case and learn anything that he could and even try to visit the location of the graves before going back to Charleston.

The trial judge shook his head for a moment as Query and Judy appeared before him. Not many years older than Judy, Query was just slightly taller and his hair was of the same blue black color and only a few inches shorter than the shoulder length hair of Judy. It was the time of long haired hippies protesting war and demanding rights for women and blacks. Young lawyers brandishing locks below their ears and over their collars were viewed as having made a brash statement to the court, even before they spoke. Judge Harwell, however, had seen Query in court and the experienced judge knew that he could expect the young advocate to be polite and professional but also stubbornly determined. He knew Query would have an unyielding insistence on obtaining every benefit to which his client might be entitled. The judge quickly acknowledged Query's limited appearance and advised Judy of his rights. With Query's acquiescence, the judge postponed any consideration of bond and moved on to the next matter at hand.

After court Query headed immediately for Prospect. A stop at a country store gained easy information about the location of the graves accompanied by the caution that the police wouldn't let anyone near the place. Query was pleasantly surprised when he arrived at the vast array of police vehicles and was politely escorted to the Sheriff after announcing his representation of Judy.

The consensus among law enforcement was that the three graves represented the extent of burial sites and most urged abandoning further searches, absent more information. Rumors, however, abounded and the North Charleston contingent was insistent that there should be searches of additional areas associated with the Gaskins man since they had information about other missing persons.

The search for additional graves did in fact continue in Prospect. The young girl, Kim Ghelkins, was still missing and rumors spread that yet others were missing who had some connection to Pee Wee Gaskins. Query was ultimately permitted by Tom Henderson and Sheriff Barnes to enter the cordoned search area and examine the graves where work continued.

The bodies from those graves would ultimately be identified in the following weeks as those of Dennis Bellamy, John Henry Knight, Diane Bellamy Neely, Avery Howard, Jessie Judy, and Johnny Sellers. At a second meeting, Query advised the young defendant that any bond set would be unaffordable and that the solicitor would no doubt file additional charges if bond appeared likely.

Shortly before Christmas, Query traveled with his wife and two small children to Charlotte, North Carolina, to visit his family and then to Albion, Michigan, where they would spend the remaining holidays with his wife's parents. His Michigan visit would be for only a few days since he was scheduled as "first up" in the upcoming term of criminal court in Charleston for a murder trial. The term would begin soon after the New Year.

Early in January, the seventy year old father of Knoy Judy set out to find a lawyer for his son. The holidays had been unbearable. He knew only that his youngest son had been arrested and charged with murder. Knoy had been picked up from their home by a frightening array of police officers and sheriff's deputies who were heavily armed. They had entered their little home with weapons brandished and some wore bullet proof vests with POLICE stenciled in bright yellow letters. His son was being held without bail in Florence, South Carolina. The newspapers and television had been filled with stories about the three graves, the search to confirm the identities of the six people buried - two to each grave, and the speculation that more graves would be found.

Though short on experience, the elder Judy was not without imagination. Faced with the perplexing dilemma of selecting an attorney to defend his son's life, Mr. Judy loaded his wife of thirty years, the mother of their four children, into his pickup truck and drove straight to the Charleston County Courthouse. He had been told that court was in session and that there would be trials in progress. Sessions were not continuous during that era. Civil and criminal court alternated utilizing both of the two courtrooms available in the historic Charleston Courthouse.

Walking into one of the two main entrances located on opposite ends of the building, Mr. Judy inquired of the first person they encountered about the location of the trials. He was directed to the third floor where the main courtroom was located. Purely by happenchance, it was a week during which criminal court, known in South Carolina as the Court of General Sessions, was in session. Mr. and Mrs. Judy slipped quietly through the large double doors and took seats on the last long wooden bench. A trial was in progress and both parents were soon totally engrossed in the proceedings. They were astonished to learn that one of the lawyers was the young lawyer his daughter had asked to go to Florence to find out the nature of the charges against his son, Knoy, and that they were trying a murder case.

The case at bar involved a particularly brutal murder during the commission of which a very attractive, sexy twenty-two year old blonde had lured a man in his sixties from his open air market into a wilderness area outside of Charleston by promising him pleasures beyond his imagination. According to the testimony, it was well known in the North Charleston community, in which the market was located, that the operator closed up alone and carried substantial amounts of cash in his pockets without stopping to make night or weekend deposits at a bank.

The Judy's sat patiently through the testimony of police officers who had responded to the call when the lifeless body of the elderly grocer was found floating in a small pond miles from the North Charleston city limits. They heard the precise, coldly, technical description of the autopsy given by the Medical Examiner from Charleston County who concluded that death was by drowning but that there was also a concussion that had resulted from blunt trauma to the back of the head with an unidentified object. The Medical Examiner testified that the blow to the head had preceded death and may have been sufficient to render the victim unconscious.

Three men in their twenties were accused of conspiring with the girl to rob the old man and of actually carrying out the robbery and murder along with her. The girl had agreed to plead to a charge less than murder and to testify against the others. Query appeared to the Judy's to have assumed the leading role among the three defense attorneys. He was making most of the objections and arguing various issues to the court. Query poked through the testimony of the Medical Examiner on cross examination getting little information of a helpful nature except a final concession that he had no way, based upon what he had available to him, to ascertain whether the blunt trauma injury to the head of the victim was from a blow having been

4

struck by an assailant or was merely from a fall against a hard object. That small victory was soon forfeit when the young, robber woman fleshed out the scene of mayhem that had occurred when her compatriots had raced into the clearing where she had lured the victim.

The story was now being related in gruesome detail by the young woman who had admittedly led the old man to his deathtrap. She told it with little emotion except to sob theatrically when she explained how she had not expected any harm to come to the man. She appeared detached and her answers to the questions of the prosecutor were colorless and well rehearsed. The plot that she described had involved her lover and two male friends. She said that the group often partied together drinking and using drugs.

The attractive woman said that her boyfriend had come up with the plan to get the man's money and with the help of his two friends he had talked her into it. She said the boyfriend gave her marijuana to make her high on the night they were to do it and told her that no one would be hurt.

The comely young woman said that she had been attired in her shortest cut-off dungarees and a sheer tee top that she had worn without a bra to make her breasts obvious through the thin material. Her attire was specifically intended to lure the old man who was known to have an eye for young women who shopped in his store. At close of business on a Saturday evening, when they believed that it was very likely that his pockets would be bulging from the proceeds of the market, the girl was to make her approach to him. She had gone to the market on several occasions and lingered after her shopping was complete, making little remarks that were at first flirtatious and then later nothing short of salacious. By her third visit she was openly discussing her promiscuous leanings and telling the aging proprietor of her fascination with older men.

On the fateful Saturday night she said she arrived at the market about twenty minutes before closing and openly approached the owner about spending an amorous evening with her in the country. They rode in the man's truck to an isolated area where she told him it would be particularly nice for them to lie down on the bank of a small pond and watch the full moon reflecting off the slick, black surface of the water. Unbeknownst to the much beguiled victim, they were followed by her three companions.

As she testified the prosecutor, officially titled Solicitor in South Carolina, nodded frequently in agreement and encouraged her to expand or repeat certain key aspects of her story. He guided her as often as possible to testimony that she had no intention of causing physical harm to the old man and was shocked by the assault and murder. This was in order to justify her deal and the solicitor's decision to make the deal.

The attractive, young criminal was now clearly aligned with the police and the prosecution. She was their star witness and, in return for her cooperation and testimony, she had been promised a probationary sentence after her plea to Accessory after the Fact of Murder. It carried a maximum sentence of ten years and is essentially defined as rendering assistance after the commission of a crime. Clearly, this was a much less serious offense than the one she had actually committed. She would only be allowed to enter that plea after her testimony at the trial of her co-defendants, all of whom were being tried for murder with the state seeking the death penalty. It was one of the many deals with the devil that prosecutors and police make where it seems that there is no other way to solve a crime or obtain a conviction.

Unfortunately, prosecutors and police officers involved in such deals often try to improve the image of their witness. Sometimes it is merely an attempt to emphasize any positive facts about the witness in order to make a better impression on the judge and jury. But, it is not unusual for them to become so invested in the witness that they begin to reveal information to the witness that allows the witness to improve on the testimony. In the same context, the tough law enforcement officers become so enthralled with the process that they actually start to believe everything the witness says and to accept excuses for any past criminal involvement of the witness, including the crime of the moment. In this case, the sexy beauty of the young woman made it even easier for the all male police/prosecution team to excuse her involvement in the brutal murder and to tout her as a champion for bringing the other defendants to justice.

She, on the other hand, fed off of their sympathetic attention and employed her well honed skills as a con artist. She picked up on any intimation about her role as a victim and began with each re-telling to minimize her own involvement and to maximize that of her codefendants.

"I had been shopping at his market for a while," she testified. "He would always come over to talk to me as I looked around and when I was ready to leave he would always add something. Just an apple or an orange, saying 'Try this, they're really good,' she continued."

"Before long he would ask me to wait while he closed and have a beer with him. He would lock the door and we'd just stand around and have a beer. He would empty the cash register while we drank and always made a point of showing me what a big chunk of cash he was taking out with him," she continued. "On those nights he wouldn't even charge me for the groceries."

"I told my boyfriend about the big rolls of cash and he came up with the plan for me to get the old gentleman out in the country and get his pants off so they could grab them and get his money. Just like we had planned, I got him to go out to the little pond with me and when we got there I started sort of dancing around and he asked me to take off my shirt. I told him we should just go swimming. And he said, like, "Oh yeah!" So we both stripped and went into the water. When we were in up to our waist I started hugging and kissing him to keep his full attention and the boys came running out of the woods to grab his clothes."

"They were rummaging through his pockets while he was still naked in the water with me, but he was much faster than any of us had expected. He turned and splashed through the water and was on them before they could even empty his pockets. He must've been strong, too. He grabbed Carl and just threw him aside going after Grant. I yelled to Grant to watch out and just as Grant stood up, Tom hit the old man with a limb so hard that blood flew from his head and he fell straight down. Then they threw him into the water and we ran to the car."

Grady Query's client, Tom, had denied being part of any robbery until after the girl's testimony. During the break, after being sternly admonished by his attorney:

"If you know anything about what she is saying, you had damn well better tell me now," this said as the young attorney leaned to within inches of his client in the tight confines of the holding cells used by attorneys to confer with clients.

"If you help me, I can hurt her on cross examination. If you don't, you're sending me to a gunfight without a gun. You have got to help yourself before I can do anything to help you."

The young man, his voice quaking with emotion, then conceded that he had been part of the plan and had in fact been at the scene of the murder. He denied that he had struck the blow that rendered the victim unconscious and insisted that it had, in fact, been the boyfriend of the witness.

"She's not telling the truth," he stammered. "This whole thing was her idea. We were all over at their house drinking one night. She had stopped at the market on her way home. She couldn't stop talking about the big roll of money the old man had and his thousand dollar watch. She said he took the money home every night and she had a plan for us to get his money. She was going to get him out in some woods at a little lake and get naked with him on a blanket, we'd run down and threaten them and take his money. Grant would start to rape Janet because she was his girl anyway. Then one of us would say he heard a car, and we would run off. Jan would start to cry and then go back to town with the old man. She'd ask him not to call the cops because her husband would find out about her going with him into the woods and about the rape."

"Grant was the one that decided to kill the old man. I have no idea why. He just started beating him with a big stick and then threw him into the pond. When he didn't drown and tried to swim away, Grant went into the water and held him under until he stopped making bubbles. We all knew for sure he was dead when Grant came out of the pond."

Returning to the court, Query began to question the witness. Subjected to cross examination, the young female criminal found it more difficult to keep her story together. As she waivered, it became more and more apparent that the plan had not given much consideration to the fate of the victim once his cash was in the hands of his assailants. Only a fortuitous turn of events had led to the victim and the seductress wading into the water after disrobing. She admitted that the men had, in fact, intended to grab the man, wrest his money from him and begin a fake assault on her. They were to interrupt the apparent rape on the pretense of hearing a vehicle. It was necessary to the plan that they leave the girl as a supposed victim since the real victim could identify her and knew that she lived in the general area of the market.

She also admitted, contrary to her original testimony, she had not come forward as a result of any feelings of guilt, but only when she was told that she had been identified by a customer from the market as having been there on the night of the murder. She had been told that she was a prime suspect and could only extricate herself from the threat of the death penalty if she cooperated and testified against the others. Query suggested that during this negotiation, she had gleaned that it would be very important to establish that she had no prior knowledge that the victim would be killed. He suggested that she had made that fact an important component of her statements and testimony. Although she denied this, the thought was now with the jury.

"And so, it was at the time that the police told you that you could get a deal and do no jail time, that you remembered that the old man was not to be harmed, isn't that correct?"

"No, I thought we were just going to get his money. It was supposed to look like I almost got raped."

"What was going to happen if he put up a fight?"

She paused for a long time and then said, "I didn't ever think about that possibility."

"You mean you didn't care. When you left him there in that water, you had no idea whether he was alive or dead, isn't that correct?" The defense lawyer persisted.

"I was just scared," was her weak and barely audible reply.

"So frightened that you and your boyfriend and the other two men went to a bar and spent a hundred dollars on drinks and then you went home where everyone drank more. And then to further relieve your overwhelming remorse, you and your boyfriend went into the other room to have sex while your two friends continued to drink in the kitchen. Is that how terrified you were about what had happened out there where you took that man?" Query boomed his voice a crescendo, reaching a level barely acceptable in the courtroom and obviously tinged with anger and disgust.

She next conceded that she had denied any involvement in the crime when questioned by police on two different occasions and, that when she finally admitted having knowledge of the victim's death, she told police that the entire group had gone to the lake together. She admitted to telling them that a shoving match had taken place between her boyfriend and the victim when the victim began to feel her breasts while they were all swimming together. She had alleged that the skirmish occurred on the edge of the water and that the victim had fallen, striking his head on a cypress root and had then rolled away in the pond where they were unable to find him in the dark water. She admitted to having made this revelation only after a second confrontation with police and when police told her that a customer at the market had identified her as the girl who left the market with the victim.

After cross examination of the young woman, whose recklessness with the truth seemed apparent, Query requested another recess to confer with his client. Judges are usually generous in granting such requests realizing full well that conferences at such crucial stages of a trial often involve decisions on the part of defendants to change their plea to guilty. The entry of a plea of guilty by a defendant in a trial involving a single defendant obviates the necessity of continuing the trial which releases the jury and virtually eliminates the potential for an appeal. In trials with multiple defendants, the judge is always conscious of the possibility that a legal error regarding one defendant can affect the entire trial and necessitate a re-trial for all of the defendants. Judges are always cognizant of the cost and inconvenience of second trials of the same cases with criminal dockets already crowded.

"We need to act right now, Tom," Query admonished his young client. "We made some progress against her just now. She's not the state's little sweetheart anymore. That jury knows that she is a little slut and that she probably set all this up. They know that she has already lied to the police at least three times. The solicitor isn't going to be too happy about resting his entire case on that little liar, but he'll do it if he has to. While we've made her a liar, we still haven't changed the fact that she says the man was killed and that you killed him. Once the solicitor finishes his case he, might not talk to us. You have to give me your OK to go to him now, but we need to offer to plead and testify to avoid the death penalty."

"Yeh, you've been right all along. I shoulda' made a deal when you first told me to. Can you still get me manslaughter? I didn't kill the man, I swear it. Grant did that and me and Carl had nothing to do with it except bein' there."

"I doubt they'll still take manslaughter, but I'll ask. Are you sure you didn't know he was going to be killed?"

"No way, nobody wanted him killed except that crazy son of a bitch, Grant, and his crazy bitch, Janet. The plan Carl liked was just get him in the car, stop the car, drag him out, rob him and her, and run. Like I told you, it was her idea of getting him out rollin' around on the ground with her, then jump him and take his money and pretend to start to rape her and then run off and leave them both. Grant even said he would really rape her just to make it look real. Do it right there in front of the old man and then run off. Janet liked that plan. She said nobody would ever believe that it was fake. That it would really be a turn on for Grant to actually do her, and her pretending, just like in a movie, and all of us watching and pretending we were next."

"What went wrong?" asked the lawyer.

"When we ran up on them, they were out in the water. They were naked and his clothes were right up there on the bank. All we had to do was grab his money and run. Instead, Grant ran down to the water and yelled at him to give him his watch or he would rape the girl. He had some kind of fancy pilot's watch that Janet was always talkin' about. Cost a thousand dollars she said. Instead the old man came flyin' through the water right at him. Grant picked up a limb, the size of a baseball bat, and hit him in the head with it. Busted his head open. Then Janet took the watch off of him and came in and started getting dressed. The old man was just lyin' there in the edge of the water bleedin'."

"Janet started yellin', 'He's swimming off, Grant. He's swimming away. Get him, Grant. Get him,' Tom continued."

"Sure enough he was easing his way out into the lake slow and easy like. Grant tore into the water and hit him again in the head with the stick and then he grabbed him by the neck and pushed him under. The bubbles kept coming up from where his head was and then there was one last big burble-burble and there weren't no more bubbles. Grant pushed him further out in the water and then waded in to shore."

"We all got in the car and Janet drove. Grant and Janet just kept talkin' about how he just kept bubblin'. Carl and I weren't saying nothing. We just sat quiet knowing that something terrible had just happened. Grant put on some shorts and a T-shirt that he had in the car and we went to the Anchor Bar. Carl and me, we wanted to go home but Janet said she wanted some liquor and some music. We went in and Carl and me just sat there and had one drink after another just lookin' at each other and not sayin' nothin'. Grant and Janet were dancin' and drinkin' and he was feelin' her up on the dance floor in front of all the sailors. She would dance over and dance in front of the sailors and rub her breasts with her hands and then laugh at them and dance away."

"When she finally got tired of teasin' them poor sailors, we had spent a hundred dollars of the money. We stopped at the seven eleven and got some quart bottles of Schlitz Malt Liquor and went to their house. We went into the kitchen and opened the beers. After a few minutes Janet got up and said, 'Come on, Grant, you were supposed to screw me out there in the woods so you owe me a good one.' They got up and went to the bedroom. At the bedroom door she stopped, turned toward us and squeezed her titty through her t-shirt and then stuck out her tongue at us and went into the bedroom."

"I really think we were still in shock. We just drank our beer, went in the living room and fell asleep sitting up on the couch. I would've never gone out there for that old man to get killed, Mr. Query. I ain't like that. I've done plenty wrong but it was stealin' and smokin' pot and doin' some speed. I ain't ever robbed or hurt anybody. We was just gonna grab his money and go. I admit I was gonna go along with the fake rape but that was just so the old guy wouldn't think Janet was in on it. That's the truth, that's every bit of it."

Query went to the solicitor and advised that his client wished to plead guilty and testify for the state. He cautioned, however, that his recitation of the facts would be quite different from that of the lovely, young Janet. After a substantial argument between Query and the solicitor, Tom was finally allowed to plead to manslaughter. In the process, the solicitor allowed Query to confront Janet outside the courtroom. With the solicitor present he pressed her on the accuracy of Tom's story. Ultimately, she conceded that his version was, in fact, accurate although she denied that she had pointed out the movement of the victim in the pond, and laid that burden at the feet of poor hapless Carl. She agreed that she would correct her testimony and identify her boyfriend, Grant, as the one who had actually killed the old man.

Query then went to Carl's attorney and laid out Tom's testimony and his deal with the state. Carl agreed to plead and testify as well. Both would receive a thirty year sentence for voluntary manslaughter. Carl would also receive twenty five years for Armed Robbery to be served concurrently. He still had only a thirty year sentence but the additional charge had been tacked on because he only agreed to cooperate after Tom had made an agreement with the prosecution. It was the rule of the game; first in got the best deal and the rest had to line up.

The trial continued against Grant, now with three witnesses testifying to his cold blooded murder of the old merchant. But yet another bizarre turn awaited. When Tom had completed his testimony and the court had recessed for the day, the trial judge, who was from another circuit but assigned to Charleston for several months of criminal court, called Query to his chambers. He was just a year on the bench but was ambitious. Starting court early and finishing, late he was known for his severe sentences.

"Grady, do you know this lawyer representing this boy that's left in this trial?"

"Yes sir, Your Honor."

"What's he know about murder trials? The solicitor tells me he offered this boy a plea to murder and he would take the death penalty off the table. He said the boy turned it down and the solicitor didn't think the lawyer pushed him to plead. This jury is going to get this case tomorrow or the next day and they are going to give that boy the chair. He probably deserves it, but I've never sentenced a man to death and I don't particularly want to start with this one. He's mean as a snake, but he's only nineteen and that woman was leading him around by his dick through this whole thing. What do you know about this lawyer, can you talk to him?"

"Well, Judge, he's a patent attorney. He was appointed to this case like the rest of us."

"What do you mean he's a patent lawyer? How many trials has he done?"

"None, Judge, just some pleas."

"What in the hell is he doing in a death penalty case?"

"He says that he likes to keep his name on the appointed list so that he gets a chance to be in court once in a while. His name just came up next on the list and he was appointed to this case."

The case preceded the formation of a full time public defender's office in Charleston County and much of the indigent defense was provided by the appointment of attorneys who were members of the local bar. Those with no criminal experience could opt out but if they did not withdraw their names they would be appointed from time to time. In reality, a small group of attorneys who agreed to accept virtually unlimited appointments were appointed to the majority of the cases. When a number of serious cases with multiple defendants occurred close in time, that pool was quickly exhausted and each defendant was entitled to have a separate attorney.

"You go talk to that boy in the lock-up, put some sense in his head. Tell him this jury is going to send him straight to the electric chair as quick as I tell them they can vote on it," ranted the irate judge.

"I can't talk to him, Judge, he's represented," Query replied.

"Call the lawyer, get him up here, tell him I told you to talk to that boy. Hell, get him in here and I'll tell him," the judge roared.

This was all somewhat shocking for a young judge who was becoming known as one of, if not the, toughest sentencing judge in the state. Query went to the young defendant after getting permission from his attorney. Thirty minutes later the boy told his own attorney that he wanted to accept the plea. Speaking to his attorney and Query, he related exactly the same story as that told by the other two young men. In another thirty minutes he entered his plea and was sentenced to prison.

"And there to be held for the rest of your natural life, and that sentence is consecutive to the twenty-five years for armed robbery and the thirty years for kidnapping," were the final words in the sentence imposed by the judge. As startling as they were, they did not include the alarming phraseology of a death sentence.

At every break Mr. Judy had made inquiry of various spectators who appeared to him to be carefully observing the proceedings. Ultimately, he decided to focus on an elderly couple he had learned were daily visitors to the courthouse. He learned that the couple came there each morning of a court session and selected among the matters to be contested, the one case of greatest interest to them. And then they watched every minute of the trial. The old man would explain that it was much more interesting than television and gave them a feeling of knowing what was going on in the community. In response to an inquiry, an elderly bailiff would confirm to Mr. Judy that the couple were astute observers and well versed on the proceedings and the people of the courts.

Mr. Judy told the couple that he was considering hiring Query to represent his son who was in some trouble.

"Yes sir, you get that young Mr. Query. He's a fighter. He fights for every one of his clients and he's not afraid to stand up to the solicitor or the police or even the judge when he is in the right," the elderly couple offered in sympathetic advice having learned of Mr. and Mrs. Judy's determination to find a good attorney for their son.

"Oh and he's so polite. He's always nice to everyone and when we have a question, he will take the time to explain something that happened or tell us why the judge ruled a certain way. He really cares about people," added the wife.

"But it's the fight he likes. That's what I think brings him down here. You can see it when the trial starts. He's like a little banty rooster lookin' over his yard and waitin' for another rooster to challenge his territory. And he knows his law. You can watch, when he makes an objection or an argument to a judge you can watch 'em sit up and listen. He told us that the appeals court can send a case back if the judge makes a mistake and the judges have to be careful when they realize you are making a good argument on the law of a case. But the jury, he says nobody can correct their mistake. You got to win their hearts on the first try. He's says if you can't make them love your client, you gotta make them hate the other side even if it's the police. And, if you give them enough to work with, they'll almost always come to the right conclusion."

"Now there are plenty of other good lawyers around here and we'll be glad to give you their names and point them out, but you can't go wrong with that one. He had a judge tell him last term that if he asked a certain question one more time he was going to lock him up for contempt. Query told him they were in a real mess. He said 'Judge, I've sworn to represent my clients to the best of my ability, so I've got to ask the question, and now you've promised to put me in jail if I do what I took an oath to do. I have to put the question on the record, Your Honor, so the Supreme Court can decide whether I was entitled to ask it. When I do, you're going to lock me up. Doesn't seem quite right, Your Honor.' The old judge took a break and took the lawyers back in his chambers. When he came out, he told the court reporter that Mr. Query was going to give her his question and his client's answer in writing to be put in the record and they could move on to the next witness. The whole courtroom was buzzin' 'til they worked that out. Lawyers were comin' in here from up and down the street to watch the standoff. The judge was "Bullet Bob" Hayes, a WWII decorated war hero and everyone knew he might do it. Most of us also knew Query wasn't going to back down."

"Thanks y'all. I think I'm gonna want to talk to him before I talk to anybody else. I think this thing for my boy might be a bad fight," said Mr. Judy as he took his wife's arm to leave the courthouse.

Query's office was located on historic East Bay Street; specifically it was next door to the massive and spectacular Customs House with its mammoth columns and magnificent wide granite steps. The office building was built in 1859 as a two story office warehouse combination to serve the maritime business for the wharves located down Cumberland Street at the rear of the building. The Office was grey stucco over brick. An ornate stucco facade, typical of its era, adorned with tall, heavily corniced four pane windows rose from the flagstone sidewalk. Adjacent to the outside entrance, a twenty-six by eighteen inch bronze plaque proclaimed in polished letters over blackened background "O. Grady Query, Attorney and Counsellor at Law", honoring his mentor's preference for the older English spelling of counselor.

A single granite step entered a short portico to the rich polished redness of heart of pine doors standing twelve feet high. Six feet past the door, a stairway of the same rich wood led upward to an interior door of similar appearance upon which a filigreed brass plate announced simply: Law Office.

On the single granite step, undoubtedly uncomfortable at only a few inches in thickness, Query found the man he would come to know and always address as Mr. Judy. He was sitting on the cold hard stone. He was attired in what Query would learn was the standard daily garb for the elderly man; tee shirt, zip up cotton jacket, khaki pants and white canvas Keds.

"I've been here since six thirty," said the man who appeared to be sixtyish to young Query. "I knew you wouldn't be here that early but I couldn't sleep and I didn't want to miss you," the old man said quietly but fervently. His hazel eyes were bright and quick and his skin was tanned hard from much time in the sun, but with a pleasant bronzed look. Pure white hair cropped short but not in the military skinned sides capped the diminutive man who emanated an intensity that was corporeal.

"How do you do, Sir? I'm Grady Query. Is there something I can do to help you?" the lawyer replied. He carefully observed the man before him and the man's demeanor and appearance immediately stirred warm memories of Query's grandfather who had meant so much to the young lawyer through his childhood and adolescence.

"I need you to represent my son. The old couple that watches all the court cases, I can't think of their names, they say you're the best. Will you do it?" the father shot forth without further ado.

"I guess I'll need to know a little more about what it involves," Query responded.

"He's charged with murder; charged in those murders up in Florence. Charged with all of those bodies they found buried up in Florence. He's in the Florence jail. My daughter, Tina, she got you to go up there to talk to him. He never killed anybody, Mr. Query. He's been in some trouble, drugs and stuff, but he'd never kill anybody, Mr. Query. He's a good boy down deep, cares about people. He didn't kill anybody. I know it and I need you to prove it. Can you do it? Can you help him? I'll pay whatever it takes. We ain't got much but I've got my house that's paid for and we'll get the money somehow."

"Let's just slow down now. I'll be glad to look into it. Tell me your name and your son's name, please, sir."

"I'm James Judy and my son is Knoy Judy."

"Tell me your son's name again, please. I saw a James Judy in Florence."

"Yes, that's him, James Knoy Judy. We call him Knoy. It's pronounced Ca noy, spelled K N O Y."

"Please come on up and let me get some information."

Query knew the man was referring to the graves found in Florence County that were the subject of News and Courier headlines and his curiosity was peaked. How on earth were these remote Pee Dee murders linked to these gentle people in Charleston? He could not help but wonder. After a short interview, Query advised that he had told Knoy that he would try to find out all that he could about the charges and the circumstances under which he was being held. Query told Mr. Judy that he would continue to investigate and get back to Mr. Judy as soon as possible. Mr. Judy insisted that he would return at twelve to find out what Query had learned. Query objected that it might take longer than that to get any meaningful responses to his inquiries, but he finally acquiesced to the insistent Mr. Judy's plan.

At twelve noon Query reported to the ever prompt Mr. Judy, who was now accompanied by his wife. He told the couple that Knoy was still incarcerated in the Florence County Detention Center on the charge of Accessory to Murder and that no bond had been set in the case. The allegations were that he was somehow involved in the multiple homicides that had filled the graves hidden in a remote part of Florence County. Early news stories linked the murders to Donald Henry (Pee Wee) Gaskins of Charleston who was originally from the Prospect community where the graves were discovered by law enforcement officials. Query advised them that although bond could be set by a magistrate on the accessory charge, he had already been told that as soon as the request for a bond hearing was made, a new charge of murder and kidnapping would be filed, thereby requiring that bond be set by a circuit court judge in the Court of General Sessions.

He advised them their son met the legal criteria for bond. That is to say, there was not likely to be any solid evidence from the state that he was a risk to flee or that he presented a danger to the community. The state, however, would simply present over and over that there were multiple graves; the seriousness of the charge alone raised a risk of flight and that the allegations of multiple murders, regardless of the tenuous link to this defendant, raised the issue of danger to the community.

Query agreed to travel back to Florence some two hours away and meet again with Knoy Judy. This, he promised, would at least assure their son of the support of his family and allow him to form his own opinion of the idea of being represented by the long haired young lawyer from Charleston in the most serious battle of his life. Query drove to Florence that night for the first real meeting with Knoy since hearings scheduled on the following days would preclude his going during daylight hours.

CHAPTER FIFTY

The Client Interview

Upon arrival at the detention center, Query was admitted and shown to a conference table directly in front of the tower that controlled the various barred electric gates to different areas of the jail. There, he had the first meaningful encounter with young Knoy Judy. The blacker than black hair that bespoke his mother's full blooded Cherokee Indian lineage was betrayed by long sideburns and Fu Manchu mustache that made him appear more Hispanic. After some assurances that the meeting in no way obligated Judy to retain Query but rather was to assure him of his family's support and the availability of assistance, Judy's frightened countenance gave way to a brilliant smile of childlike warmth. Black eyes beseeched, seeking comfort, and then relaxed in open acceptance of the offered assurances about his family's determination to get an attorney for him.

In the following days the attorney met with Mr. and Mrs. Judy again. The fee quoted was ten thousand dollars and expenses. Query told them that he could help them find a good attorney in Florence and that would save a lot on expenses. Mr. Judy advised that he owned a vacant lot next to his home and that they had decided that they wanted Query to represent their son. They had decided to sell the lot to pay the fee and did not want to consider any other options. Query went back to Florence a day and a half later and told Knoy that he was being hired to represent him if he agreed. Young Judy confirmed that he wanted Query to represent him and expressed regret that it was such a financial burden on his family.

Query advised against seeking a bond hearing until it was clear that all charges had been filed. Knoy agreed, reluctantly, conceding that he could understand that going through the motions without any realistic hope of bond would not be wise.

At that point, attorney and client entered into their first discussion of the facts of the case, both from the standpoint of matters revealed by the police in charging documents or comments, news coverage and the client's actual knowledge. Query had learned through discussions with police and from the newspapers that one of the victims had been identified at least tentatively as Knoy's wife or ex-wife by the name of Jessie Judy. He had also discovered that Knoy had worked with Gaskins, the obvious central character, and that Knoy had even lived in the same house with Gaskins for a short period of time. Another of the victims was said to be Johnny Sellers, Jessie's lover. More directly, a witness had placed a dark haired, dark skinned individual that the police believed was Knoy in the presence of three people matching the description of Jessie Judy, Johnny Sellers and Gaskins. They had been seen at a country store between Charleston and Lake City on the approximate date of the disappearance of Jessie and Johnny.

"Knoy, you need to understand that what you tell me is privileged. I cannot be required to reveal anything that you say to me, that is known as the attorney-client privilege. That privilege allows you to talk to me about anything that I need to know to help you and prepare your defense. The thing that you cannot do is tell me that you are guilty of something and then later take the stand and say that you didn't do it and give testimony that is different from what you said to me in admitting your participation in a crime. At this point, I don't want you to tell me whether you are guilty of anything. I just want to know about the people who are involved and how you know them. Later, we will get to what you want to tell me about anything you have done and we will determine whether that constitutes a crime and what defenses we have."

Knoy began his story. He told of having been married to the beautiful, wild Jessie and the circumstances of their having become acquainted with the strange little man known as Pee Wee Gaskins. He explained that a few years back he had been unemployed and that Gaskins, who was living near his apartment, had befriended Knoy and his young wife and had offered to help Knoy get a job. Gaskins had gone even farther when he learned of their eminent eviction by telling the couple that they could have a bedroom in his house until they were back on their feet. Gaskins had assured the young couple that his wife would appreciate Jessie's help in the house and that his recommendation was certain to secure a job for Knoy. As promised, Gaskins got Knoy a job with the roofing company where Gaskins was a supervisor and the young couple moved into the Gaskins house. He rode to work with Gaskins every day. Pee Wee's wife was kindly toward them and they ate dinner together, the wives cooking there at the house on most evenings. Knoy related that Jessie became bored there. He said that she preferred a much faster lifestyle.

Knoy said Jessie liked to go the bars and clubs at night. Pee Wee and his wife, Sandy, never went to the clubs and Pee Wee frequently left the home alone at night saying that he did part time work as an auto mechanic and handy man. As a result of Jessie's displeasure with the sedate life, Knoy and Jessie moved back to their own apartment as soon as possible, but Knoy continued to work with Gaskins and they were frequently in his house. Gaskins' house was sort of open to all comers, according to Knoy's description, with any number of people in and out on the weekends. Pee Wee and the other men were frequently working on their own vehicles or doing light mechanic work for others at the house. Knoy said that he found the roofing work unbearable in the summer heat and began to drink too much and to use marijuana daily. His drugs and Jessie's appetite for the club life exceeded his earnings and he was soon participating in petty thefts with acquaintances from the Gaskins' house, all of whom seemed to have a penchant for petty crime.

Knoy continued his story saying that his drug use escalated to involve the use of downers more and more often. He said that he would sometimes fall back on an old high school vice of huffing glue when he couldn't find or afford painkillers or tranquilizers on the street. Huffing or sniffing glue involved emptying a tube of airplane glue in a small paper bag, covering one's nose and mouth with the bag and breathing in the volatile fumes until a semi-conscious state of delirium was achieved. The drugs and glue together with more marijuana and alcohol soon led to absences from work that cost him his job or at least reduced him to a casual laborer called in only on bigger jobs. He sold small quantities of marijuana to supply his own use and Jessie soon left him to move back in with Gaskins. He went there often and made frequent entreaties for her to return but to no avail.

He said Gaskins was tolerant of his visits as long as he was sober and sent him away if he was not, but he never suggested that Knoy might be welcome to join Jessie at his house. Knoy assumed that Jessie had moved back into the vacant bedroom that they had shared. He assumed that Gaskins coolness toward him was the result of Jessie having told Gaskins about the drugs and glue, habits that he knew full well Gaskins did not tolerate.

Ultimately, he was shocked when Jessie informed him that she and Gaskins were being intimate and that he was no longer welcome to call on her. When he asked about the whereabouts of Pee Wee's wife, Sandy, Jessie told him that Pee Wee had given Sandy to Walter. She said Sandy was happy living with Walter and that left Gaskins free to do as he chose, including sleeping with Jessie instead of with Sandy.

"We're all happy here," she had informed him, "Sandy and Walter live in the trailer and we're in the big house. Pee Wee doesn't want you coming here anymore. He says you're a dope head and that can only bring trouble."

Knoy said that as a result of that turn of events he seldom went to that house. From that time on, his main contact was on the occasions when Gaskins came by to say that there was work at the roofing company or work on a car that was familiar to Knoy. On at least two occasions, he and other cronies of Gaskins had stolen items that they took to Gaskins for assistance in selling them. According to Knoy, Gaskins had connections in Charleston, Sumter and Lake City for disposing of stolen goods at good prices. He went on to say that most of the minor criminals who came to Gaskins' home appeared to be afraid of Gaskins.

Knoy said he then met a beautiful, young woman who grew up in Charleston, ran away to California and had moved back to Charleston. The two of them became lovers almost immediately and then began living together. Knoy said that Donna did not share Jessie's craving for the late night life in the clubs and that she influenced Knoy to stay away from the glue and hard drugs. He said they smoked marijuana and drank beer but nothing more. Donna had two children by different fathers and, according to Knoy, she was a kind and caring mother. Donna and Knoy had a baby in the first year they were together.

Knoy said that when he began living with Donna, he had taken the first opportunity at work with Gaskins to ask him if he had any objection to their coming to his house on the weekends. Gaskins told him that he didn't want Knoy to date the nice girl he described because of his drug use, but he would not interfere if that was what she wanted. Knoy assured Gaskins that his relationship with Donna was important to him and that he was not using drugs. He told Pee Wee that he drank some beer but didn't drink just to get drunk as he had in the past.

Gaskins told him that they were welcome at the house anytime as long as he was sober. According to Knoy, they were there frequently and did other things with Pee Wee and Jessie, who Pee Wee now identified as his girl, and also with Walter and Sandy, who now seemed definitely to be together.

Sometime after this close relationship of the strange little group began, Knoy said that Jessie left Pee Wee to live with Johnny Sellers. Knoy knew little about Sellers, did not like him and never went anywhere with Sellers. Knoy said Pee Wee continued to allow Jessie and Johnny to come to the house. Pee Wee apparently had a background of some kind with Sellers, but also seemed to treat him with a certain coolness that Knoy assumed was related to Jessie. Jessie, according to Pee Wee, was the best woman that Pee Wee had ever known. Knoy said that he was surprised at Pee Wee's tolerance of Sellers and his relationship with Jessie but had the feeling that Pee Wee put up with Sellers just to have Jessie come around.

Knoy admitted that he then fell back into old habits of using drugs and drinking too much. He related with obvious despondency that Donna had left him and gone to live in the Gaskins' house. For a long time, he said he went there to see her and his child and it was apparent that she had her own room and lived privately in the house. Later, however, she became involved with Pee Wee and he even began to refer to Donna as his wife. Knoy said that he was still allowed to come there to see his child.

Knoy said that he had not been afraid of Gaskins and that Gaskins had not given him any reason to fear him except the strange deference that all of those who had known Pee Wee for years seemed to show to the little man. Knoy said that he took a different view of Gaskins after a Saturday afternoon when a rather large number of people were around the house. In addition to Gaskins, Donna, Sandy, Knoy and Jessie, there were Sandy's younger sister Wanda, Gaskins' friend Walter Neely and Walter's estranged wife, Diane, and Diane's brothers, John Henry Knight and Dennis Bellamy. Other friends of Gaskins and his wife and child were also there on the porch and in the yard. Knoy said these gatherings were essentially big cookouts and that while Gaskins encouraged everyone to have fun; he did not tolerate drugs, drunkenness or profanity in front of the children.

Knoy recalled that Dennis Bellamy had been very drunk that day and had continued to drink throughout the afternoon. The more he drank the more profane he became and the more aggressive he became in his approaches to the women who were there. Gaskins reminded Bellamy that he was very strict about profanity in his home. The normally gregarious little host chastised Bellamy several times for his cursing and told him to stop putting his hands on the women.

According to Knoy, Gaskins suddenly rushed from the porch into the yard with a large pistol in his hand. He grabbed Bellamy by the shirt and began beating him in the head with the pistol. When Bellamy sank to his knees and then fell over in the yard, Gaskins had continued to hit him with the gun, chiding Bellamy that he had asked him several times to stop cursing and now had no choice but to do what he was doing. Knoy said it was perhaps most amazing that while beating the man nearly to death Gaskins had never raised his voice and was almost plaintive as he spoke to the bleeding man. Knoy was much more wary of Gaskins after that occurrence.

Becoming impassioned once again Knoy said, "In short, if they think I killed Jessie because she left me, that's crazy. I was living with Donna after Jessie and I broke up. Donna was great for me and I was the happiest I had ever been when I was living with her. I didn't care about Jessie being with Johnny. I didn't care where she was period. I screwed up and got really involved with drugs and sniffing glue and Donna left me and went to live with Gaskins just like Jessie did. I really straightened out after she left. I started living with my folks and working every day, but Donna said that she was not going to go through that again and that we were through. Before long Gaskins was saying that Donna was his wife. If I had any reason to kill anybody, it would have been Gaskins." I've never hurt anybody, Mr. Query. I've done some drugs. I've even sold some drugs. I've stolen some things. I'm charged now with stealing some boat motors, which I did. I've got a charge for breaking into a place to steal some batteries that a guy agreed to buy from me for his tractor repair business and I'm charged on that. But I don't know anything about anybody getting killed."

"I thought Jessie and Johnny had run off because he had a bunch of serious charges against him. He's done time. His public defender had already told him he was going up again and I thought they had just taken off. I didn't know Avery Howard or Diane or Johnny Knight or even Dennis well enough to even know that they were missing."

Query told Knoy that he understood that the search for bodies was still ongoing and that he would meet again with any of the investigators that would talk to him and try to find out more about why the search was continuing.

For the next few weeks there was no official information released but stories of Gaskins driving a hearse with shovels in the back and of having told people of his private graveyard ran through the rumor mills and surfaced in news stories. The news finally broke, the story that two North Charleston detectives had conducted an intense investigation for months into the disappearance of a young girl and that the investigation had ultimately focused on Pee Wee Gaskins and his cohort, Walter Neely. They had eventually gone to Florence and Williamsburg counties with Neely and he had led them to the graves in Prospect. Except for the romantic and marital connection with Jessie, no more information surfaced about Knoy and he was usually mentioned in terms of "and Knoy Judy of Charleston, who is believed to have been the husband of one of the murder victims, Jessie Judy, was also charged."

After the meeting Query began spending every available minute, including weekends, in Florence, Prospect and North Charleston talking to anyone who was involved in the case or to anyone that knew Gaskins, Neely, Judy or any of the victims. Several times he went to the prosecutor's office in Florence but was told that they would not release any information and would take every action possible to prevent Knoy Judy or any of the defendants from being released on bail.

SECTION 4

CHAPTER FIFTY TWO

Prosecution Begins

The Solicitor in Charleston had an open file policy allowing defense attorneys to come to his office and see essentially the entire case file. It was the Charleston Solicitor's theory that full disclosure led to the prompt resolution of cases, usually by guilty plea, or if there was to be a trial, he believed that his position was not made any weaker by the attorney for the defendant having had the information at an early date.

At his first meeting with the young Assistant Solicitor, Dudley Saleeby, Query was assured by him, "Oh yeah, open file policy. No need for a lot of motions, just come on in and I'll show you what we've got. Hell, right now I haven't even seen it. Just give me a little time to wrap my head around it."

"Sure, I can understand that you guys are getting hit with an avalanche of information from all directions," Query responded. "Six bodies, rumors of others missing and a laundry list of people, suspects and victims with world class criminal records; I'll keep checking back with you. Just let me see it when you get it."

"Will do. I'll call you or if you're up here check with me. Stuff should start to be available pretty soon."

But when Query next talked to the young assistant, who was his contemporary, he was told that the Solicitor was handling everything himself and that Saleeby was not allowed to disseminate any of the information that they were receiving from the various agencies. He said that he had, in fact, been admonished to have no communication with Query or the other attorneys in the case unless the solicitor told him to.

Query than requested a meeting with the Solicitor, Kenneth Summerford. That meeting set the tone of the case.

"Look son, this is going to be a death penalty case and it's the biggest case in South Carolina. You'll get information from this office when a judge says you can get it and not before," the Solicitor drawled in vintage Pee Dee country southern.

He was a tall slender man with mostly grey hair and the rugged look of the popular Dodge City television Marshal, Matt Dillon. His emotions were easily deduced by the mottling that would immediately appear over his face when there was the slightest resistance to his consistent "my way or the highway" approach.

Public Defender, Monk Hinnant, was appointed to represent Gaskins and Query went to meet him to discuss the cases against their clients. Reminiscent of the Rumpole of the Bailey character, Monk was a large, slightly rotund man always attired in coat and vest. He had a delightful baritone voice that rang through the courtroom, a southern drawl for sure, but with a rolling eloquence instead of the harsh country twang and drumbeat on the consonants so familiar in the area. His mirthful smile was a window to his delightful humor.

"This will be rough going," Hinnant quickly advised without the slightest hesitation in spite of the fact that he was meeting Query for the first time. Both knew each other by reputation since a term of court seldom passed in either of their circuits when they were not involved in some phase of a murder defense or some other serious criminal case. With battles against the unequal application of the death penalty going on around the nation, attorneys regularly involved in such cases within the state were generally known to each other even though they had not met.

"Summerford is a mean spirited prosecutor. He'll bully you and push you around and he is driven mainly by his ambition. If he thinks it will help him to chew your man up, he's not likely to pay much attention to whether your client happens to be guilty or innocent. Don't rely on what he tells you and don't give him anything based on his promise unless he puts it in writing."

That first afternoon Monk introduced Query to the Downtown Deli, a sandwich spot a few blocks from the courthouse and detention center that served slightly oversized draft beers in frozen mugs. It became their informal headquarters and the owner and a couple of regulars were their sounding board to get a layman's reaction to the events of the day. Once trials were in session, these discussions were an outlet from the frustrations of dealing with the overbearing prosecutor.

"I'm still hopeful that I can get Kenneth to look at the possibility that my man may have had no involvement whatsoever and is being sucked into this entirely because of his past relationship with one of the victims."

"Well good luck on that one, my friend," was Monk's immediate retort. They brought Manny Lee Law in here full of so much Thorazine that his jaw hung slack. He sat there with his chin on his chest and his head lolling from side to side while they convicted him of murder and sentenced him to death. Now Manny was a murderer. He killed two people and chopped them up; I don't know what he knew about right and wrong when he killed those old people, but I don't think he ever had a clue about what was going on in that courtroom."

South Carolina adheres to the McNaughton Rule on the issue of an insanity defense. In short, the rule requires only that a person be able to distinguish whether his actions, or the consequences of his actions, are right or wrong at the time of the commission of the crime. It is, however, also required in South Carolina that a defendant have the capacity to participate in his own trial and assist his attorney in his defense. Monk was convinced that the court had wrongly concluded that Manny Lee Law possessed that capacity at the time of his trial.

"My God, Grady, they had a state doctor going into his cell in the morning and giving him a shot of Thorazine while the guards restrained him. That was just so he could be present in the courtroom without talking out of his head and yelling out all sorts of incoherent ramblings. He is a dangerous character. Hell, he's the only man I've defended in all these years that I didn't go in the cell with. I just took my little chair and sat down right outside the bars, not that I could talk to him anyhow. He was spending his time seeing and talking to things a lot stranger than me. But just the same, he's insane, he's a raving lunatic. He belongs in the state hospital and then if he ever came back to earth they could try him, but not in the condition he was in at trial."

The next morning brought yet another stark revelation to the front pages of South Carolinas leading newspapers. A hunter had discovered what he thought were human remains in a small depression, deep in a forest near the Pee Dee River. Exhumation of the depression had revealed the body of a young Caucasian woman and the body of an infant child.

When the bodies were identified as those of Doreen Dempsey and her two year old daughter, Michele, the connections between Pee Wee Gaskins and Dempsey were soon made known to police through interviews and by information called into the various agencies by Doreen's family and people who had known them.

Query drove directly to Florence to determine, straight from the horse's mouth, whether his client had any connection to Doreen Dempsey. He was greatly relieved when young Judy adamantly denied having ever heard the name. When he got back to Charleston, Query went to the home of Mr. and Mrs. Judy and they confirmed that they had never heard of anyone by that name. They said that they had never heard Gaskins or any of Knoy's friends talk about anyone who met the description of the woman and her child who had been described as racially mixed.

After returning to his office, Query received a call from Paul Cantrell, a young Charleston attorney in general practice that was definitely on the up and coming list. Cantrell advised that he and Chris Staubes, another well respected young attorney, had been retained by the family of Walter Neely, Pee Wee's long time associate. Cantrell said that his client, Neely, was also charged in the Prospect murders. Query went to Cantrell and they discussed what little they knew about the evidence that might support the charges against their respective clients.

Within a few days, all three of them met with Hinnant in Florence to plan their strategy for the preliminary hearings and the bond hearings that would be the first proceedings in the case. South Carolina law requires that bonds in capital cases be set by Circuit Court judges whereas other bonds are set by Magistrates. Recognizing the complexity of the multiple murder cases and the likelihood of a tremendous burden on the court system, a special judge was assigned to the cases that were emerging from the discovery of the bodies in Florence County.

Judge Dan M. McEachern (pronounced McCann) was a stern man, slight in build and stature, with years of experience as a county judge. County Courts were courts of limited jurisdiction established to handle cases involving controversies below ten thousand dollars in civil cases and criminal cases for which the maximum penalty did not exceed ten years.

These were cases over which the Courts of General Sessions (criminal) and Common Pleas (civil), as the trial courts of highest jurisdiction had concurrent jurisdiction, and the work of the county courts greatly reduced the burden on the dockets of the higher courts. Judge McEachern was appointed as a Special Circuit Court Judge for the purpose of trying the cases against Gaskins, Neely and Judy.

Since the county court in which he presided had limited jurisdiction, Judge McEachern had no experience in death penalty cases but he had applied all of the same rules of criminal procedure and dealt with all of the issues of state and federal constitutional protections in the cases that were tried before him in the Florence County Court. From the first appearances by Query on behalf of Judy, by Cantrell and Staubes on behalf of Neely, and by Hinnant on behalf of Gaskins, Judge McEachern established that he intended to maintain firm control of the courtroom. Any histrionics on the part of the attorneys would be dealt with swiftly and severely. He seemed patient and thorough in allowing full arguments on any valid points of law or procedure. Query and Cantrell thought he seemed clearly predisposed to rule in favor of the state and the police in anything other than the most compelling situation. Most of his rulings may have appeared favorable to the prosecution, and his overall demeanor was pro-prosecution, but this was not inconsistent with many of the South Carolina judges who were tough sentencing and law enforcement oriented. The four defense attorneys felt that on any close call, the tie would always go to the solicitor.

Mordant comments accompanied the judge's ruling on Query's argument for a bond for his young client.

"Sit down, Mr. Query. I understand that your client's family loves him, and that they are certain that he will appear in court as required, and that he is not a danger to anyone, but I'm looking at a case involving the murder of six people and the solicitor says he is going to seek the death penalty. I have to assume that anyone facing the death penalty is, by definition, a flight risk. Let me hear from these other defendants and I'll give you a chance to add anything that you have in addition to what you have submitted to me in writing and the argument that you have made this morning."

After brief arguments from the other lawyers and similar "enough said" from the judge, the judge issued his brief ruling: "I'm going to deny bond for all three defendants at this time, but I will allow you to renew your motions at a later date."

"If there are going to be any Preliminary Hearings in these cases, they will be held by me in this court. I may decide to hold the preliminaries for all defendants together, but we'll cross that bridge when we know which defendants have requested a preliminary."

This was a departure from the ordinary procedure where the Preliminary Hearing would be held by a magistrate. The Preliminary Hearing requires only that the state show that there is probable cause for the charges and that the matter should be bound over to the Court of General Sessions where the solicitor makes further decisions about whether or not to go forward for an indictment and proceed with the prosecution of the case. The defense cross examines witnesses for the state, usually limited to investigating officers, but the defense is not permitted to offer any evidence since the only question is whether or not the prosecution has enough evidence to continue to the next stage.

Query, Staubes and Cantrell began scrambling to interview witnesses and to simply identify, beyond just their names, the victims whose bodies had been discovered in the Prospect community. Because the date of death of the victims, and even the question of whether any or all of the victims died at the same time were unknown or unanswered, the standard types of investigation involving alibis or the whereabouts of one's client on a certain date were simply not available. Efforts were directed primarily to obtaining information about the backgrounds of the victims and their connections or relationships, if any, to the defendants.

The Preliminary Hearings were, in fact, consolidated for all three defendants. In spite of longstanding requests by all defendants, the preliminaries, which are normally held within thirty days of the request, were not held until April twenty-eighth of 1976, four months after their arrests. The hearing was held in the main courtroom the morning following the Coroner's Inquest which had been held on the night before in that same courtroom. The Solicitor presented brief testimony from deputies of Florence County at both hearings.

The sheriff's deputies recounted information that had been gleaned by various investigators that linked Gaskins to each of the victims. He was said to have known and had a romantic relationship with Jessie Judy and was possibly a jilted lover jealous of Johnny Sellers, who was identified as Jessie's paramour. Gaskins and Dennis Bellamy were said to have long standing mutual bad feelings. John Henry Knight was the younger brother of Dennis Bellamy. Diane Neely was the estranged wife of Walter Neely. Avery Howard was her paramour with whom she was living with, again with bad feelings among the triangle of lovers. Neely was allegedly Gaskins' closest friend and companion.

The association between Neely and his estranged wife, Diane, was obvious and Neely's close association with Gaskins was in itself damning, particularly since it included the fact that Gaskins and Neely had been cellmates at CCI, the legendary high security penitentiary. The lengthy and often violent criminal histories of the two were introduced as well.

Knoy Judy was linked to the grisly crimes because Jessie Judy was his estranged wife. A witness interviewed by one of the deputies was said to have described seeing a dark haired, dark skinned man, which matched the description of Knoy Judy, in the company of a small man who seemed to match the description of Gaskins and a couple matching the description of Jessie Judy and Johnny Sellers. The prosecution refused to identify the witness. [1]

This testimony was coupled with preliminary reports from the medical examiner indicating evidence of gunshot wounds to the skull of John Henry Knight and Dennis Bellamy, to the back and head of Johnny Sellers, and knife markings consistent with stabbings found on some of the ribs or skeleton of Jessie Judy and Diane Neely and Avery Howard. This evidence was quickly found sufficient to establish probable cause for the case to be bound over to the Court of General Sessions for trial on the various murder charges against each of the defendants.

---

[1] The attorneys would learn many months later that the witness was actually the former mother-in-law of Johnny Sellers. Not only would she have recognized Sellers but had also known Pee Wee Gaskins for many years. She had also met Jessie Judy when Johnny visited his children. She did not know the identity of the younger dark haired man.

Gaskins was indicted on all eight murders by the Grand Jurors of Florence County on May 3, 1976. Walter Neely was indicted for the murders of the six people that were found buried in Prospect. James Knoy Judy was indicted in the murders of Jessie Judy and Johnny Sellers.

The solicitor's office had the right to determine, at that point, which of the cases would be called for trial. Solicitor Kenneth Summerford chose to call first the case against Gaskins for the murder of Dennis Bellamy whose body had been found interred in a common grave with his younger step brother, John Henry Knight.

Summerford made it clear at a meeting with all of the lawyers that he had no intention of accepting pleas from any of the defendants and would vigorously pursue the death penalty for each of them. Subsequently, when little other evidence surfaced against Knoy Judy, Summerford called Query to his office. He told Query that he would consider allowing Knoy to plead to "common law murder" in return for Judy's testimony against Gaskins and Neely. Common law murder was so called because it referred to the crime of murder based on the old common law. That is, crimes that did not have to be defined and prohibited by statute but which were so to speak inherently wrong and considered crimes under the Common Law of England which formed the foundation of our legal system. Murder, rape, assault and battery and larceny are examples of common law crimes. A conviction or plea to common law murder would carry a penalty of life in prison with eligibility for parole after service of at least ten years.

"Kenneth, this boy is telling me he had no idea any of these people were dead or even missing, and that he certainly had not participated in harming them or murdering them. Of course, I'll tell him what you have offered, but I think if you will look at what we can produce it bears out what he is saying."

"I don't need anything else to look at. We have plenty to convict him; I'm just giving him an opportunity to help himself. The offer is good for twenty-four hours," said the solicitor.

"Come on, Kenneth, I have to come back from Charleston and I have to get his parents involved. He isn't going to make any decision without talking to his father. How about helping me set it up with the detention center to have a meeting with him and with his father present? That is very difficult for me to set up without your help or help from the sheriff."

"That's your problem. Call the sheriff if that's what you need to do. He runs the jail. I'll leave the offer open for a week."

Sheriff William "Billy" Barnes was an all business lawman. Elected sheriff in a large county at a young age, he began to modernize the department and increase the efficiency of his considerable force of deputies. South Carolina sheriffs typically hold office for long periods of time and wield tremendous political power within their county. Barnes, therefore, had a reasonable expectation of a long run in a position of significant power. The ambition of the young sheriff was tempered by integrity and a genuine respect for the legal system that he had sworn to uphold. He stated, at any opportunity, his belief that Gaskins and the other defendants were responsible for the deaths of the eight people buried in his county and pledged that he would use all of the resources of his department to see that they were convicted and imprisoned or executed. He was equally quick to assure that he would do everything within his power to see that they were afforded every right to which they were entitled, and that he would work with defense counsel to see that they had ample opportunity to meet with their clients and work with them in preparation of their defense.

County sheriffs are also in charge of the jail or detention center and Barnes had the authority to arrange the visit Query was requesting even though the arrangement would normally have been made on the basis of an agreement with the solicitor. Good to his word, Barnes quickly arranged for Query to meet with Knoy and to allow Knoy's parents to be present at the meeting. Query was somewhat surprised when Barnes also listened intently to his protestations that his young client had been wrongly accused and that the quasi-identification of someone similar in appearance to him accompanying Gaskins and others was a very shaky link.

"I can understand why that's bothering you and I guess you have your work cut out for you, if that witness is as shaky as you seem to believe. My job is to gather all of the available evidence and to arrest the people that evidence points to. The actions of my department are based on the evidence that we have. After that, it's up to you guys to fight it out and prove what evidence is good and what's not. I don't ever get upset when someone is not convicted, unless my deputies failed to do something. I can promise you that we'll continue to investigate every aspect of this case and we will continue to develop evidence, and if we can find evidence that the solicitor can use to bury your guy, then that's how it will be. On the other hand, if we find something that points to someone else or that shows that your guy was not involved, you can be sure I won't hold that back. That's not how I do business."

"I hear that you've been out in the Neck talking to people," the sheriff continued. "You be careful out there. That's rough country and there are some people out there that are just plain mean. They tend to take care of their own and they don't want anyone else poking around – including the government. You can run into someone out there who has nothing to do with this case, but if he thinks you are going to stir something up that affects whatever he is into, you can get hurt over something and not even know what it was."

"Thanks, Sheriff. You're right about my not knowing the territory, but I've got to talk to the people that know Pee Wee and that might know something about who or why he or someone else wanted all of these people dead. The Neck seems to be where most of those people are. Actually, they're around Spruill and Reynolds Avenue in North Charleston as well and I doubt whether the people in the Neck could possibly be any worse than the criminal element in the north area of Charleston, but I do appreciate the warning."

"Just watch yourself and if you get in a bind call us, we'll be there. We don't like even lawyers getting killed in our territory," the sheriff laughed and picked up the phone to give instructions to the jail about the arrangements for the visit by Query with Knoy Judy and his parents.

The visitation was at a table in an open area near the control room. The table was located far enough away to provide adequate privacy, but by placing it in the open area, the visit was not impeded by a dividing screen or glass and in a show of genuine compassion the guards made no objection to hugs from the distraught mother and father. After a few minutes of expressions of parental concern and assurances from Knoy that he was getting along all right, Query went straight to the issue of the offer from the prosecution.

"The solicitor is offering Knoy a plea to Common Law Murder. That means that there would be no exposure to the death penalty. The sentence would be Life in Prison and parole is possible after ten years."

Mrs. Judy began to cry and Mr. Judy immediately began to ask questions about jury trials and justice for innocent people.

"You are absolutely right, Mr. Judy. If Knoy has done nothing wrong and the system works the way it is supposed to work, he will be found not guilty by a jury and that will be the end of it. Most of the time it, works just the way it is supposed to work. I truly believe in our system, I believe that it is the best in the world, the best ever thought of, but that still doesn't make it perfect, and when the death penalty is possible, then if there is a mistake it might not be corrected."

"I can't do that, Mr. Query. I can't say that I killed somebody when I don't know anything about it. I swear to you, I didn't even know some of those people and I didn't know some of the ones I did know were missing. I haven't seen Jessie in more than a year. Everyone thought she and Johnny ran off to keep him from going to jail. We also assumed that his mother knew where they were. This is not right; I haven't even seen Pee Wee in months. Can we get a jury? Can you tell them I wasn't anywhere close to here, that I don't even know where Prospect is? Tell them I had never been to Florence until they brought me to this jail."

"Of course we'll do all of that, Knoy, but people are going to be looking for someone to convict. There are six people dead and buried in the woods at this little crossroads and if they can show that Gaskins did it, then anyone that they can connect to him in any way, is going to be in real danger of getting convicted by association," advised Query. I'm not trying to talk you into this, but I have to tell you that it has been offered and I have to be sure that you understand what the risk is. Summerford says the offer is only good for a week, but he won't stick to that. He knows his case against you is weaker than the others and he'll take a plea whenever he can get it."

"Okay, tell him we're not ready to accept but we'll keep thinking about it," offered Mr. Judy.

"No, I think I'll tell him that I'll see him in hell before we plea to a murder that we didn't commit. Let's make him know that he's in for a real fight, if he's going to keep us in this. By now he's checked around enough to know that when I say we're going to fight, then it's going to be a fight. It won't be pretty for him, especially not if he's trying to stretch a weak case into a death penalty conviction," answered Query.

"That's what I want to hear," said Mrs. Judy, who, except for her initial sobs, had been completely silent. "I want to know that you are going to fight for my boy. I want to know that you are going to make that Summerford pay for what he is doing to my boy," the blood of Cherokee warriors now hot in her veins, her voice rose as she spoke, and her face went from fear to solemn resolve.

The following morning Query was in Kenneth Summerford's office when the solicitor arrived.

"He's not going to plead, Kenneth. I'll have my initial pre-trial motions to you tomorrow and we can see if there are things that we can agree to."

"I can answer that for you right now. There ain't a damn thing that we can agree on and I'm going to personally see your boy in the electric chair," he roared. "I tried to give you a chance. You're a young lawyer with a reputation as a good trial lawyer. Now, I'm going to roll over you, embarrass you, and put your boy on death row. You won't have such a hot shot reputation when I'm finished with you."

"What if I can show you that it's highly unlikely that he was involved or that he couldn't have been here when it happened?"

"Tell you the truth, I was going to have a hard time selling my law enforcement people on this plea anyway. They've come up with an eyewitness statement that puts your boy at the murder. If he'd taken that deal they would have been madder than hell," the solicitor shot back.

"Solicitor, I promise you there are some things that raise serious questions about Knoy Judy having anything to do with the murders of any of these people and I'd just like for you to see what I have and consider it in deciding where to go with his case."

"I don't want to see a damned thing you've got. You can show it to a jury. I'm thinking I might just call his case first. Put your little hippie doper on death row for his wife's murder and then get on with the other two for the rest. Might come back then and see if I can tie Judy to any of the rest of them. Maybe get him a second death penalty. Get ready, son, this ain't gonna be all chummy like you Broad Street lawyers down in Charleston," continued the solicitor.

"I'll be ready, Ken. I guess it's good to know from the beginning that you have no interest in justice or in who is guilty. Keeps you from getting confused, I guess. Who made this new mystery statement about my client?"

"No mystery to it. One of Gaskins women said she was there and saw your boy kill his wife or her boyfriend or help Gaskins do it. You'll get a copy. I haven't even read it. One of the officers was just telling me about it this morning. I'm not holding out on you, I just can't keep all of these different women straight at this point. Seems like another one turns up every day, and half of them are or were Pee Wee's wives."

Two days later Summerford summoned Query, Cantrell and Staubes to his office. Summerford met them in his reception area with an armed uniformed deputy. He had the three of them ushered to a small conference room and left there to marinate for almost thirty minutes before Summerford finally graced them with his presence.

"I've brought y'all here to go over something once and once is all," he began. "I always try to help young lawyers and you boys seem like ambitious young lawyers who want to get somewhere in this business. I don't know what the hell y'all are doing in this case. Can't be enough money comin' in from these losers. Somebody said you were goin' to do a book, Paul, maybe that's the angle. Anyway, my reason for calling you up here is to keep you boys from getting into some trouble that you can't get yourself out of. I just want to warn you that I know about it, and that I don't want to turn y'all in to the grievance people. I'm trying to help you."

"What the hell are you talking about, Kenneth?" said Query. "If you think that we have committed some ethics violation then report it. In case you haven't read the canons, you're obligated to report us if you know that we have committed some violation and it's a serious violation on your part if you fail to report us."

"Kenneth, you can tell me precisely what the nature of your accusation is or I'm leaving," Cantrell replied much more formal in his speech than Query.

"I'll go beyond that," the normally quiet and passive Staubes virtually growled at the older man, "I'll report to the ethics committee that you have alleged some serious violation of the canons of ethics and that you refuse to disclose it to us. I'll ask for a complete investigation including whether or not you have committed a violation by failing to report us."

"Well I'm just trying to give you a chance. Young lawyers make mistakes. They get over zealous. I understand how that happens with young lawyers. Well, I've got a confirmed report and, I mean, I've even

41

spoken to the witness myself so it's not in doubt. You fellas have gone out and talked to a witness, talked to Gaskins' daughter and asked her what she was going to say. Asked her to go back and look at a calendar and make sure she is right about when things happened. That's subordinating perjury. That's serious. That's not just an ethics violation, that's a crime. I'm just tryin' to help you young lawyers and give you a chance to straighten this out. I want your word that you won't talk to anymore witnesses. I'm going to step out and give y'all a minute to talk about it and I'll be back for your answer," upon which the tall lanky solicitor stepped out of the room closing the door behind him.

"What in the hell is he talking about, subordinating perjury?" asked Paul.

"He's trying to say suborning perjury," said Query. "Everything he does is a bullying tactic, that's why he doesn't care enough to even try to recall the right term. As a matter of fact, there is a very recent appellate court decision that says we are ethically bound to attempt to talk to all witnesses in a criminal case and that failing to do so can constitute ineffective representation."

"Yeh, I remember reading that in the advance sheets," Staubes chimed in. "Let me call my office and I'll see if I can get us a cite for the case."

When Summerford returned Query spoke for the group, "We're out of here. This lame attempt at intimidation is over. Let me assure you that we will be talking to every witness that will talk to us just like the Supreme Court says we are required to do. You might read your case law and you'll have a little better understanding of the process. That's the trial process, not the railroad process that you seem to be more familiar with. And by the way, subordinate means to place under or behind in order; seems like that's what you should do with perjury. The word you're looking for is suborn. Thanks for the help though, Kenneth. I don't know what young lawyers would do without Good Samaritans like you."

With that, the three attorneys left and headed for Monk Hinnant's office several floors down in the same building. As they rode the elevator down, they were not quite as exuberant as their remarks might have made them appear.

Having heard the three recount the attempt at intimidation from the prosecutor, Monk offered, "That's him, bully and push and shove, it's all he understands. He's a far cry from a great trial lawyer but he has a very clear understanding of the power of his office. He knows very well that he can stick a defendant with a much worse conviction than he deserves if he's sure he has enough to prove the lesser offense, and he uses that to bully people into pleas that are harsher than they deserve. He loves to try cases that would have been pleas if he had only made a reasonable offer. Both sides know that it's a sure conviction, but the defense has to try it because he hasn't offered anything less than the defendant would get after a jury trial. It gives him a chance to grandstand and announce a victory that was inevitable as though he had just tried the case of the century. Even when you can convince the jury to convict your client of the lesser offense, he can still say he got a conviction."

"Sometimes I get the feeling that you aren't one of his greatest fans," joked Query.

"I've just been at this too long to put up with that kind of crap. Hell, he's pulled the same kind of crap on me that he pulled on you guys this morning. We work in the same courthouse and in the same courts before the same judges week after week and he acts as if I'm some subversive character hell bent on the destruction of our community. I work hard at this Public Defender stuff. This is only part time. If I were smarter, I guess I'd just spend all of my time in my private practice and just walk over here at court time and shove the poor defendants who can't afford private counsel through the grist mill without any regard for their rights or for what constitutes a just result. But, you know my assistant, Johnny DeBerry, and I have just decided we're not going to cave in like that. We fight the cases that need to be fought and we scratch and claw for the constitutionally guaranteed protections that make our courts function. I don't mean to get on the soap box but, you know, if you start to let them crush the rights of these people who can't afford to fight back, then it's just a matter of time until they start to step on the rest of us."

"Well, I guess you know you are preaching to the choir," replied Cantrell, "but we certainly are of the same mind. It's easy to agree that someone wrongfully accused should be afforded the rights necessary to establish his innocence, but it is awfully hard to get people to accept the fact that the protection of the rights of the most guilty son of a bitch out there is where you write in stone the protection of the innocent."

The damning eyewitness/codefendant statement about which Summerford had spoken to Query had been given by Pee Wee's wife, Sandy. The statement gave a detailed account of having accompanied Gaskins, Knoy Judy, Jessie Judy, Johnny Sellers and possibly Walter Neely into the woods where the graves were found. Summerford still did not give Query a copy of the statement, but instead gave an oral summary claiming that the actual statement was still in the hands of investigators and would be provided as soon as it was available. Sandy told a story of cold blooded murder, perhaps not too far from the truth in so far as the ultimate consequence, but in all likelihood, nowhere close to the truth in so far as the parties who were involved or the exact manner in which the murders were accomplished.

At the time of the murders Sandy was living with and romantically involved with Walter Neely and he was either present or not present according to the version of the statement one was hearing or reading. She described a chilling scene in which Gaskins had taken Johnny Sellers from the car in which Gaskins, either with or without Neely, had driven the group to the field near the graves. In the edge of the woods, she said Gaskins ordered Sellers to run for his life and then directed Knoy Judy to hold a big five cell flashlight on Sellers as he ran. She said that Gaskins then shot Sellers squarely in the center of his back as he ran in the beam of the light. She said that Gaskins then stabbed Jessie Judy. The statement was devoid of the details of the burial, the location or the roles of the various participants or even where or how Jessie Judy was stabbed to death. Her description of the route taken to the site of the murders was not close enough to be in the same county.

CHAPTER FIFTY THREE

Formal Proceedings

May 17, 1976, the defendants, Gaskins and Neely, were formally arraigned before the Honorable Dan M. McEachern, Special Judge, in the Florence County Court of General Sessions using the traditional stilted language.

If you answer to the name of Donald Henry Gaskins, raise your right hand. (Defendant complies) Put it down. The Grand Jurors of the County of Florence, State of South Carolina, present that you, Donald Henry Gaskins, did willfully, deliberately and premeditatedly, with malice aforethought in Florence County, on or about the Tenth day of October, Nineteen Seventy-five, kill one Dennis Bellamy, by means of shooting the said Dennis Bellamy with a gun, and that the said Dennis Bellamy, did die in Florence County as the proximate result thereof on or about the Tenth day of October, Nineteen Seventy-five, against the peace and dignity of this State. How say you, Donald Henry Gaskins, of the felony wherein you stand indicted, guilty, or not guilty?

Defendant: Not guilty.

Solicitor: How will you be tried?

Defendant: By God and my country.

Solicitor: May God send you a good and true deliverance. Are you ready for trial?

Defendant: Three days.

Solicitor: All right, Sir. If you answer by the name of Donald Henry Gaskins, raise your right hand....[2]

And so it continued for eight indictments after which Walter Neely was similarly arraigned for the six murders involving the victims buried in Prospect. Query sat at counsel table with the attorneys for Neely and Gaskins and mused about the determined effort made by the two uneducated men, who each required several armed guards to escort them to and from the courts, as they spoke their cumbersome lines, determinedly following the script laid out for them. These men, who as a way of life, regularly broke virtually every law imaginable, were suddenly doggedly determined to try to conform to the rigid formalities of the courtroom as they played out an ancient drama speaking words that came from a different era.

Hinnant and DeBerry for Gaskins, and Staubes and Cantrell for Neely, then argued to the court that they had not been provided information that might be favorable to the defendants or information that was exculpatory in nature, as required by the familiar Brady vs. Maryland decision of the U.S. Supreme Court. Query joined in the motions of the other defendants but Judy was in Columbia undergoing psychiatric evaluation and Query argued the motions on his behalf when his case was called for trial.

Solicitor Summerford stanchly refused to say with certainty which of the cases he intended to call on the following Monday or even whether he would try Gaskins and Neely separately or together.

Hinnant urged that the decision in the Brewton case required that he be given any statement made by a co-defendant prior to trial, if the defendants were to be tried together. When it appeared that the judge might actually require the solicitor to comply, the solicitor announced that Gaskins would be tried separately but still refused to say on which murder or to give his list of witnesses.

All five attorneys argued vigorously and provided numerous affidavits, news clips and video tapes in support of their motions for a change of venue based on excessive pre-trial publicity which they argued would prejudice any potential juror. The judge promised to read everything that

---

[2]   All italicized sections are actual quotations from the official transcript of record from the court.

was submitted and instructed them to re-convene the following morning at nine a.m. Query asked that a pending motion of his be heard at that time.

The next morning, the solicitor finally confirmed that he would call Gaskins to trial on Monday for the murder of Dennis Bellamy. He argued that he was not required to provide his list of witnesses until jury selection began and refused to provide the criminal records of any witnesses the state intended to call. He argued that he was not required to provide the criminal records until he made a final decision about which witnesses he would call. He denied having decided who would be called as witnesses. He also maintained that he was only required to turn over such records and copies of statements that were actually in his possession. He denied having the statements or the records. A statement to the court that could have only been true in the narrowest sense, that is to say that it may have been true that he did not have them in his personal possession at that particular moment in time.

The judge did not require him to do any of these things and found that neither statute nor case law required the solicitor to do so at that time. He then ruled that he would question the jurors to determine whether a change of venue was necessary.

Query asked, on behalf of all of the defendants, that the entire pool of potential jurors be sequestered from the court during questioning of individual jurors about pre-trial publicity and their general qualifications.

Summerford countered that there were not adequate facilities to accommodate the entire pool in a secure situation outside the courtroom. Cantrell strongly insisted that inadequate facilities could not excuse the denial of due process and the judge ultimately agreed and instructed the clerk to make the necessary arrangements.

The attorneys were allowed to make a motion in chambers regarding contact with witnesses whom they argued vehemently, urging that they were ethically bound to attempt to interview all witnesses and that the solicitor was having deputies threaten those witnesses with prosecution if they talked to them. The solicitor assured the judge that no threats had been made and that he would make sure none were.

Query then asked to have one motion heard that pertained only to his client, James Knoy Judy.

Query: We have one other motion, Your Honor. (Copy handed to the court)

The Court: Mr. Summerford, have you got a copy of this motion and affidavit?

Solicitor: No, sir.

Saleeby: Yes sir, Your Honor, I got that yesterday afternoon.

The Court: Well, he simply says in effect that he wants to have access to the defendant in the office of the Public Defender, in this building.

Query: That's correct, Your Honor.

The Court: He says for the purpose of a polygraph examination —that he wanted to do that or for the purpose of having a conference with him or whatever else he wanted to do.

Solicitor: We would very definitely have to contest that motion, Sir. It would put us in the position of being at the mercy of the defendant, if we permitted such to go on, Sir. In other words, what I am stating to the Court that this defendant, through a relative, a friend, or even his attorney, could make certain statements and this matter would come before the public by the news media. The results of it —I think we would tend to set a precedent that would be a loophole around your necks forever. And we think it would be highly improper under these circumstances. We would very vigorously contest this.

Query: Your Honor, this matter, as the proposed order and the motion indicate is strictly for the use of counsel. Clearly Mr. Summerford's implication is that I would disclose certain things to the press. As I see it and as your Honor would see from the press clippings that you reviewed, the only statements that have been made to the press have been made by Mr. Summerford. Your Honor, of course, we base the motion solely on the Sixth Amendment right of the defendant, and the application thereof through the due process clause of the Fourteenth Amendment. However, I would state for the Court that there are precedents in the various Circuits of this Court for orders identical to that one. I feel that —(interruption)

The Courts: I don't —Mr. Summerford, I think he's got a right, of course, to confer with his client, and his client has got a right to the effective assistance of counsel. There is no question about that.

Solicitor: We don't argue that, Sir.

Query: Your Honor, I think that's my decision. The proposed order, Your Honor, is an order that was signed by Judge Eltzroth in a murder case where the polygraph was opposed for use of counsel by the prosecution. Your Honor, we are simply asking that it be made available in the conference room. And I don't think the prosecutor has any right to inquire as to what takes place in that conference.

The Court: I think he is entitled to it, Mr. Summerford. I think he is the lawyer, and he is the judge of what he is going to do to defend his client. And I don't think the Court can restrict him. Of course, it could restrict him from doing something that was unlawful. But as far as restricting him from doing something that would otherwise be lawful, I don't think it can be done.

The solicitor continued to argue that there was no reason for the polygraph and Query continued to insist that the solicitor had no right to inquire about or to interfere with his defense of his client.

The Court: All right. Well have you got —do you want to submit any authorities on this question?

Solicitor: Yes, sir.

The Court: Well, there is no pressing reason to decide this issue at this moment now I take it.

Query: If the Solicitor's position is that my client is not going to trial on Monday, then there is no pressing reason, Your Honor. But if he is not going to tell me that until Monday, then I think there is a pressing reason.

Solicitor: No, sir, I am going to tell you today I am not going to trial on Mr. Judy on Monday.

The Court: Well, Mr. Summerford, you submit whatever authorities you want to me on this issue, and I will hold it under advisement.

Query asked that his client be allowed to visit with his family in that he had just been returned from two weeks in Columbia for psychiatric evaluation and had not been able to have visitors during his evaluation. Judge McEachern asked the sheriff to make appropriate arrangements, if possible. The mother and father of Knoy Judy were allowed to visit with their son for thirty minutes that evening as long as Query was present. Query remained in Florence until late that evening so that the visit could occur.

On Monday morning, Hinnant began an argument alleging prejudice to his defense of Gaskins resulting from his incarceration in Columbia.

The Court: Other than the length, what else do you contend for?

Hinnant: The manner in which he was held, Sir, standing unconvicted, untried, presumed innocent under our law, and held in solitary confinement on death row in the penitentiary.

The Court: Well, you had access to him didn't you?

The judge ruled that access had been sufficient and that no prejudice to the ability of the lawyers to prepare had resulted.

Hinnant voiced a final complaint alleging that despite demands for bond hearings, preliminary hearings, and production of evidence against the three defendants, an inquest was not had until April twenty-seventh, Nineteen Seventy-six, at seven-thirty P.M. in that very courtroom. The following morning a preliminary hearing was held for all defendants in the same courtroom. Less than a month later, the death penalty case of one of the defendants was to be called. Hinnant maintained that he had still not received copies of statements and other materials that the prosecution was required to produce.

Monk Hinnant renewed his motion for a change of venue and submitted affidavits from attorneys regularly engaged in the practice of criminal law in Florence County, as well as numerous affidavits from people in the Prospect area, and copies of media coverage. The affidavits averred that it would not be possible to find jurors in the community whose ability to consider only the evidence properly presented in court would not be affected by the vast amount of publicity.

Judge McEachern ruled that the evidence submitted by Hinnant and DeBerry was not sufficient to prove that a jury could not be selected in that county and he further ruled that he would question jurors called for the trial of the case and if it was evidenced by that questioning that an unbiased jury could not be selected, he would change the venue. He conceded that in the event that it became necessary to change the venue, such change would be made to a county outside the Twelfth Judicial Circuit. If a change of venue was required, jurors from the adjacent counties would be similarly tainted and therefore preclude trying the case anywhere in the circuit.

Hinnant and DeBerry submitted an extensive list of questions in their proposed *voir dire* relative to the change of venue. Judge McEachern declined to ask the specific questions but rather decided to ask his own questions of the prospective jurors in order to determine the extent of their exposure to pre-trial publicity, personal knowledge of the facts of the case, personal relationship or acquaintance with either the victim, the victim's family, or the defendant or his family, or a close relationship with any law enforcement officer involved in the investigation, and the effect of any of those factors upon their ability to serve as an impartial juror untainted by that exposure.

It was a daunting task because the trial judge had to elicit information from each prospective juror about newspaper, TV or other information that the juror had heard or read about the case. It was also a procedure that was totally unfamiliar to him. Questioning each juror about his knowledge of the case as a result of media coverage and any preconceived notions about the guilt of the defendant that resulted, proved much more complicated than he had expected and he proved to be particularly inept at putting the questions without making his own contaminating comments. He began by referring to media coverage of the Prospect Cases and then asked about stories or conversations about the bodies found in Prospect and finally degenerated to a reference in one instance of asking a juror whether he had heard: "something about a bunch —several bodies being found down in the lower part of the county near Johnsonville."

It was obvious that the judge was not glossing over these concerns but rather was struggling with how to adequately identify the case and the publicity without having the very inquiry taint the prospective juror. The judge found a sort of casual colloquy with the prospective juror to be most effective while defense counsel continued to urge that the formal, somewhat ritualistic, approach of asking the very specifically worded *voir dire* questions submitted by counsel was the only method that complied with the statutory and constitutional requirements.

The concern of the defense attorneys was that the information being given to jurors by the judge, in order to discern whether previous exposure to news about the case, might well have been more damaging than anything the juror had actually been exposed to prior to the trial.

The first juror called stated that his brother worked for the Florence County Sheriff's Office as a dispatcher but incredibly denied having received any information about the case except through the national TV news.

Judge McEachern: All right. Do you have any relations that are police officers?

Juror: I have a brother who works with the sheriff's department as a dispatcher.

The Court: All right, Sir. The Florence County Sheriff's Department?

Answer: Yes, sir.

The Court: All right, Sir. Do you feel now that you could give this defendant a fair and impartial trial based on the law and the evidence?

Answer: Yes, Sir.

The Court: All right, it appears to me that his juror is Qualified. What says the state?

The prosecutor answered in the traditional manner to indicate acceptance of the juror by the prosecution: "Present him."

Hinnant argued that the juror should be stricken for cause because of the affiliation of his brother with the very agency that had investigated the case and arrested the man on trial, but the court refused and the defense was forced to use one of the coveted strikes that they were entitled to use without giving any reason.

Finally, twelve jurors and an alternate were selected over the continued objection from DeBerry that such an inordinate number of jurors had answered affirmatively to questions regarding their inability to render a fair verdict without consideration of preconceived notions about guilt based upon the pre-trial publicity, community sentiment, rumors, or any other connection with the parties, or the elements of the case, that the court should only conclude that pre-trial publicity had so affected the general public of the region that it would be impossible for them to disabuse their minds of that information and consider only the evidence presented in court.

Jury selection was completed and the judge inquired of the attorneys as to whether or not there were any other matters to be taken up by the court before beginning the trial. Hinnant and DeBerry pointed out that, pursuant to their motions, the court had ordered the solicitor to provide them with any evidence in their possession that would be exculpatory or tend to prove that the defendant was not guilty.

The defense attorneys advised that SLED Agent Tom Henderson had testified during the preliminary hearing that one of the witnesses for the state had given as many as four different statements that conflicted in a number of ways. Surely, the mere existence of the conflicting statements would be exculpatory argued DeBerry. The judge opined that the defense should be entitled to statements of potential witnesses but avoided a direct order for the production of the conflicting statements.

CHAPTER FIFTY FOUR

Trial

Nevertheless, the jury having been selected and sworn, the trial of the case began in the usual manner with the judge addressing the jury briefly and then the Clerk of Court administering the oath to the jurors in the traditional language: "You will well and truly try and a true deliverance make between the State of South Carolina and the prisoner at the bar whom you shall have in your charge, and a true verdict render according to the law and evidence, so help you God."

The prosecution then made an opening statement during which Summerford promised to present evidence to convince the jury, beyond a reasonable doubt, of the guilt of the defendant, Donald Henry Pee Wee Gaskins, of the cold blooded murder of Dennis Bellamy. He told the jury that the state would show that Gaskins had taken Dennis Bellamy into the woods near Prospect with the intention to kill him, and had then and there shot him with a gun until he was dead.

Monk Hinnant opened for the defense. He asked the jury not to reach any conclusions until they had heard the entire case and cautioned them that there was more than one explanation for the evidence that the state would produce. Most importantly, he said, that they would learn that there was someone else who had many reasons to kill Dennis Bellamy and that Gaskins had none. He urged them to remember their oath and to hold the state to the burden of proving each and every element of the case beyond a reasonable doubt.

"Donald Gaskins comes before you cloaked in the robe of the presumption of innocence and the state bears the burden of stripping away that cloak with proof beyond a reasonable doubt. The defendant has no burden to prove anything and he can rely solely upon that presumption of innocence. When you find that the state has failed to carry that burden and has not completely stripped away that presumption of innocence, you must find the defendant 'Not Guilty' as I know you will," Hinnant finished.

Dr. Joel Sexton was called as the first witness and identified himself as the Medical Examiner for the County of Charleston and Professor of Forensic Pathology at the Medical University of South Carolina where he was available to the rest of the state as a medical examiner when requested. He testified in part as follows:

Answer: I was carried to an area in a wooded area by the law enforcement division from Columbia, and shown a site that had been previously partially exhumed —a grave that had been previously partially exhumed, and at our instructions, the exhumation had proceeded only far enough to detect that there was a body there. Upon arrival of myself and Dr. Brissey, and a medical student that was with us to help us conduct the investigation, we proceeded to further exhume the grave to find what was in the grave site. The reason for this was the fact that a body found in a grave of this sort sometimes may be partially decomposed, and some of the tissues may be lost in transit, or in the actual exhuming process, as well as some pieces of evidence. So we very carefully, with the help of the State Law Enforcement Division personnel there, exhumed this grave site with the supervision of the Coroner and the Sheriff and the other law enforcement personnel from the Florence area. We carefully removed the dirt so as to see what was in the grave site, so that we could then remove the body, or bodies, in a fashion so as not to lose anything that may be beneficial in determining the cause and manner of death. On exhuming the grave site, it was noted that there were two bodies in the grave, both of whom were males, both of whom were clothed, except for shoes. It was noted that neither of the two bodies had shoes. It was noted that the —one of the deceased, who was a Dennis Bellamy, had on socks. The other deceased who was later identified as a John Henry Knight, did not have on socks —had neither socks nor shoes. In addition, on digging out the grave, it was noted that the grave was a reasonably shallow grave. The bodies were less than a foot and a half from the surface, lying on their right side, the body of John Henry Knight was lying facing the back of Dennis Bellamy. They were both lying head to head. John

Henry Knight's arm was under Dennis Bellamy's body, under his chest region, and both bodies were touching one another. There was no dirt between that portion where they came in contact with each other. It was noted at the time that there was a gunshot wound present in the head of each individual, and by metal detectors it was noted that there were metal fragments present, or at least some metal object present in the head, chest and abdominal region —lower abdomen region of Dennis Bellamy —of the body which was later identified as Dennis Bellamy. At that time we simply labeled the bodies, A-1 and A-2, with Dennis Bellamy being labeled A-1 and John Henry Knight being labeled A-2. We carefully removed the dirt from around the grave site, photographed the scene and then carefully moved the bodies into plastic containers so that we could carry them to a suitable site for autopsy, being very careful at this time to make sure that any of these metal objects that were noted by metal detectors, were later found, or went with the body. And in the case of Dennis Bellamy who had these three areas where there was metal located, these three areas were still present when the body was in the body bag. I don't think of anything else pertinent about the grave site scene at this time.

Summerford elicited further testimony from the doctor in which he opined that the absence of any dirt between the two bodies indicated to him that it was most probable that they were buried at the same time as did the positioning directly next to each other. He also stated that it was likely that John Henry Knight's body was placed in the grave first since his arm was under the body of his half brother, Dennis Bellamy.

The pathologist then described the partial decomposition of the bodies.

Answer: Primarily, the decomposition was in the area of soft tissues around the facial regions, the anterior part of the neck, and superficially on some parts of the chest of Dennis Bellamy, on the upper part —the part closest to the surface of the ground, on the left side here was a little decomposition where some of the skin was actually missing. And what this entail there is actually no loss of anything other than the skin and flesh on the superficial part of the face, neck and part of the chest on one side.

Later, he continued to describe how the bodies were carefully cleaned of remaining dirt and the bodies in the body bags x-rayed to search for metal.

The bodies were then undressed and the clothing washed and examined for evidence of indications of damage that could have occurred in the course of injury to the body. The bodies were than x-rayed for evidence of fractures or other anomalies that might be useful in identification. He explained that dental records could be used but in these cases he observed that several fingers on the hands of each of the bodies had tissue on the tips that had not been destroyed by decomposition. He was therefore able to remove skin from the tip of the thumb of each of the deceased to obtain a fingerprint for comparison of the friction ridges with known prints. He said that the skin had been loosened by decomposition and so it could be simply slipped off of the finger. He said an officer from a local police agency brought prints of Bellamy and Knight and compared them to the prints he had obtained by inking the skin and rolling a print by placing the skin on his own finger, pressing it against the ink pad and then transferring the print by pressing his finger to a fingerprint card as though he was placing his own fingerprint on the card. He stated that he had worn surgical gloves during the process. Comparing the prints that he made in that manner to those brought by the police allowed him to identify the two victims.

He further confirmed the identification by comparison to existing medical records at MUSC. Dennis Bellamy had an old gunshot wound to the lower abdomen. Records showed that fourteen years before doctors had left the bullet in him near the sacral region of the spine. X-rays confirmed the bullet was still in place in the same area. John Henry Knight had broken his left arm just above the wrist. Again old and new x-rays confirmed the identity.

The pathologist continued:

Answer: Well, after we cleansed the bodies thoroughly externally, and examined them to find injuries, then we went into the bodies to pick up these bullets — to retrieve them at autopsy, so that they could be compared ballistically. ...let me mention that there were three gunshot wounds that occurred on or about the time of death in the case of Dennis Bellamy, and the one bullet that was still in place in the abdomen — a .22 bullet that was there from years before. And it was encased in bone, and did not show any hemorrhage. But the three wounds that were-occurred on or about the time of death, were located two in the head, one entering from the back of the head at approximately this location and proceeding to the front of the head, being found directly behind the left eye, in this region...

There were three gunshot wounds, two of the head, and one of the chest. The two of the head, I numbered arbitrarily from the top of the head downward, and I numbered No. 1, the one that entered on the forehead, at approximately this point—at approximately this point at about the hair line, and it travelled across the head to this point, which is slightly lower than the point of entry, striking a bone that it partially fractured at this point, and then ricocheting back towards the back of the head, being found in the back of the head. And that was one bullet.

...The one I labeled No. 2 entered the back of the head at approximately this point on the back of the head, and went forward pretty much horizontally through the head, stopping in front of the eye on the opposite side. But it went from back to front, starting slightly to the right of the midline, and coming to rest slightly to the left of the midline. And it was also recovered from the brain.

...The one I labeled No.3 entered the upper chest approximately at this point, passed to the right—I'm sorry—passed to the left, almost exiting on the left side at about the same height in the back, but to the left of the point of entry, and was found in the body bag under the body where it had almost dropped out of the body because it had almost completely exited the skin at that point. This one had passed through the heart and through the lung in passing across the chest.

Summerford: All right, Sir, Thank you, Sir. Now Doctor could any one or all of these injuries that you have referred to, could any one or all of these caused death?

Answer: The two that would have been more rapidly fatal—there were actually two that could have been rapidly fatal. The one of the heart could have been rapidly fatal, more so than the one of the back of the head. However, the one of the front of the head that went across the brain, went through a vital area of the brain. So it also could have been rapidly fatal. So it could have either been the gunshot wound of the head or the gunshot wound of the heart that could have caused death.

Dr. Sexton identified the three bullets each contained in a separate vial and they were entered into evidence. He offered his opinion in response to questioning that the two individuals had been dead at least a matter of about six weeks based upon the state of decomposition, the burial in shallow earth, and the cold temperatures during at least a part of that time. He repeated his estimate, expanding it slightly to surmise that the bodies had been in the ground between six and ten weeks, give or take two weeks.

He explained that not all gunshot wounds to the head rendered one unconscious but that the gunshot to the forehead had passed through a vital area of the brain referred to as a ventricle, which he explained is actually a fluid filled area of the brain. Any force striking a fluid is transmitted throughout the fluid equally, he explained. This fluid compartment in this location is in continuity with the base of the brain and that area controls impulses to and from the lungs and the brain and the person would have been rendered unconscious.

The direct examination continued.

Summerford: All right, Sir. Now did you have the occasion to perform an autopsy on the other body that you found and subsequently identified as Johnnie Knight, Sir?

Answer: The only gunshot wound that was noted on John Henry Knight's body was one that entered a little lower than the one I mentioned a moment ago, on the back of the head, passing from the back of the head on the right side at this point, nearly horizontally, but slightly upward, towards the front of the head, exiting at this point right about the side of the eye. It entered the back of the head, slightly to the right, passing nearly horizontally across the head, and coming out at the point to the left of the left eye. This passes at a little lower angle than it did in the case of Dennis Bellamy, and actually came in contact with the brain stem, with the base of the brain that I referred to earlier. And so it would have been an immediately fatal type shot and would have rendered the person most probably immediately unconscious.

Further testimony in response to questions indicated that the decomposition of the skin in the area of the head wounds was such that no skin remained for the pathologist to examine for particles of burnt powder that would have indicated a shot fired in close proximity to the victim. Regarding time of death, he offered that because rigor mortis would not have been expected to occur for five or six hours he said that it was likely that the bodies had been buried in a flaccid condition within hours of their death so that they lay naturally as though in sleep. He stated that his findings were consistent with death having occurred on October 10, 1975.

The doctor was then shown a number of plastic evidence bags containing articles of clothing and asked to separate them and designate which clothing was removed from each of the bodies. He identified brown checkered or striped pants as those of Bellamy. In response to the solicitor's question as to why the clothing remained in plastic bags, he stated that despite thorough cleansing the clothing still had an odor that resulted from the decomposition of the body. This testimony drew a gasp from a juror who then appeared embarrassed.

Next he identified a brown, gold and white striped shirt as that of Bellamy. The defense objected vehemently citing a case that excluded "the waving of the bloody shirt" as inflammatory and intended solely to arouse the anger and passion of the jurors. The shirt was allowed into evidence in spite of the objections. The boxer shorts were also identified and admitted over the same objection.

A red and gold colored athletic jersey bearing the number 88 was admitted along with the pants that had been removed from John Henry Knight. Monk Hinnant made adamant objections to the admission of this clothing as having no probative value in the case involving the death of Dennis Bellamy and urged that they were being offered only to prejudice and inflame the jury. His objections were overruled.

Sheriff William Barnes was next called and he began by identifying pictures of the location two miles from Prospect and approximately four miles from Johnsonville on Highway 341 with pictures showing the turnoff into the land and across the field for a quarter mile, and then the grave site some twenty-five yards into the woods.

Roy Lee Knight was then called and he identified pictures of his half brother Dennis Bellamy and his brother John Henry Knight. He also identified the clothing that had been admitted through Dr. Sexton as those of Knight and Bellamy and finally identified a pair of shoes, which had not been previously shown to the defense, as belonging to Dennis Bellamy.

He testified that he last saw both of his brothers on October 10, 1975. He said they were both living in the same home with him and his father and mother on that date.

A friend of Dennis Bellamy confirmed the identification of the clothing and testified that Bellamy was wearing that clothing and the shoes on the last day that he had seen him on October tenth.

Mrs. Ethel Knight, the mother of Dennis and John Henry, testified through tears and outbreaks of crying about the clothing. She cried openly when she confirmed that the athletic shirt was that of her teenage son, John Henry Knight, and that it was his favorite shirt. She stated that she had last seen both of her sons on October tenth.

A young man, Britt Davis, testified that he had seen Johnny Knight on October 10, 1975, at Joe's Tackle Shop where Johnny was shooting pool when he was joined by Dennis Bellamy and Walter Neely. He testified that the three of them left together right after dark, at about six-thirty or seven o'clock. He testified that he was certain of the date and that it was a Friday night because he left to go to the North Charleston Chicora football game at about the same time, and that he remembered it well because it was the first time Chicora had won in about seventeen years.

Shirley Anne Evans, the twenty-four year old daughter of Pee Wee Gaskins, was called as the next witness. She testified that she was married to Howard Evans and that she had four children.

Shirley Anne did not appear to be on the bright side. She answered questions hesitantly and with a slow drawl. She testified that Gaskins was her daddy, that he had come to her house on October 10, 1975, with Walter Neely in Pee Wee's 1968 Chevrolet (pronounced Chiv'r'lay). She said that another man and a boy had come in a separate vehicle, a Ford Mustang. She identified the picture of Dennis Bellamy and the sports jersey with number 88 on it as having been worn by the younger of the two. She said he was in his teens, about fifteen and that the other man looked like he was in his late twenties.

She said that the two men, whom she had not seen before, went with her daddy to his trailer and that Walter was sitting on the steps of her trailer with her husband. She said that she went briefly to her daddy's trailer where she heard her daddy call one of the men Denny or Dennis and that he told her they were there to sign some papers. She said that all four left together in the Chiv'rlay after a short time.

She testified that Belton Eaddy, who assisted Pee Wee in selling stolen cars and other items, had come to her house the following Saturday and that he had taken the Mustang. According to her, the key had been left with her and she had put it in the car and told Belton where it was when he came for the car.

She testified that after the bodies were found she gave permission to Deputies Cox and Shupe of Florence County to search the trailer, responding to questions from the solicitor that she had a key to the trailer, cleaned it for her daddy and kept some of her children's clothing in the trailer. The solicitor had elicited this testimony to establish her authority to consent to the search.

Tom Henderson, the lead investigator from SLED, testified regarding the arrest of Pee Wee Gaskins in the Sumter area in November. The arrest had been made before any bodies were found pursuant to warrants issued for Contributing to the Delinquency of a Minor and for Grand Larceny of a Motor Vehicle. He continued that Florence County Deputy Shupe and other deputies had searched the trailer belonging to Gaskins after obtaining a search warrant. That search warrant he said was based on information about the missing thirteen year old, Kim Ghelkins, who had been seen frequently in the company of Gaskins and who was reputed to have visited at the trailer on more than one occasion. The search revealed clothing belonging to the young girl and the warrant was issued for Gaskins arrest. During the search the deputies observed numerous vehicles around the trailer, some of the vehicles appeared to be hidden in the brush or forest. One of the vehicles came up on a check of stolen vehicles and the other warrant was issued, continued Agent Henderson.

Henderson testified that he and other SLED agents, along with the Sheriff of Sumter County, Byrd Parnell, his chief Deputy, McJunkin, and other Sumter County deputies had intercepted Gaskins in a taxicab on his way to the bus station with a one-way ticket to Tupelo, Mississippi. He testified further that since Gaskins was placed under arrest, it was necessary to do an inventory of his personal possessions which included a package that contained a .32 Beretta pistol and a 30/30 Model 94 Winchester Rifle along with the bullets for the guns.

Continuing to testify Henderson would swear that the guns were both loaded. The guns as well as additional .32 caliber bullets found in the pocket of Gaskins were offered into evidence as was the bus ticket.

The guns were admitted into evidence over the objection of the defense that a search warrant should have been obtained prior to searching the package as part of the inventory of Gaskins' personal effects at the time of his arrest since the package was safely in the hands of the police. The judge overruled the objection and the bullets and the bus ticket were also entered as exhibits.

Shirley Evans, the daughter of Gaskins, was recalled by the solicitor and shown the Berretta pistol which was now in evidence.

Solicitor: Mrs. Evans, I'm going to ask you to look at State's Exhibit No. 17, and again, see if you can identify that for me?

Answer: That's my daddy's gun.

Solicitor: Did he have a name for that gun?

Answer: That was his baby.

Solicitor: His baby? All right, did he ever carry it with him?

Answer: Yes, sir. All the time.

Solicitor: All the time. Would he ever loan that gun to anybody that you know of?

Answer: Not as I know of.

Solicitor: Not as you know of. And you say he called that his baby?

Answer: Yes, sir.

Solicitor: All right, where did he carry it on him?

Answer: Most of the time in his pocket.

Solicitor: Have you ever seen your daddy without this gun in his pocket?

Answer: He mostly had it. Every time I've ever seen him he has always had that gun in his pocket.

Solicitor: All right. Now, I'm going to ask you if you will, please Ma'am, to go back to the night of October the Tenth, when you testified about these two men coming there. Do you recall whether or not you saw that gun that night?

Answer: I believe it was in daddy's pocket.

The witness went on to testify that her mother was Mary Avant, the first wife of Gaskins. She stated that since her baby had been born, her mother visited with her often. She described again the close proximity of the trailer that she had called her daddy's trailer to her own. She said that her daddy's trailer was no longer there that it had been sold to Detective Ray Shupe by her grandmother.

Monk Hinnant asked on cross examination why she had not testified about the gun at the Preliminary Hearing or at the Coroner's Inquest.

"Nobody didn't ask me," was her response.

The State next called a Mr. Thomas Wright who testified that he lived next door to Pee Wee Gaskins for two years in Charleston. In rather bizarre testimony he stated that while the two of them were in Gaskins yard and Gaskins was working on his car, Gaskins had told him, more or less out of the blue, that he had a private graveyard in Florence County and that when he had to get rid of someone he buried them there using a pick and shovel that he kept in the trunk. Wright said that he walked by the open trunk and looked inside to see if it was true and saw the pick and shovel.

The solicitor did not elicit any testimony that explained the reason for this gratuitous and utterly macabre statement by Gaskins. In attempting to discredit the witness, the defense had little success, but may have inadvertently filled in the blank for the prosecution when Wright volunteered during the cross examination that he had attempted to have an affair with Gaskins' wife and that Gaskins had threatened him. Although that testimony may have explained why Gaskins would infer that he had killed and buried others, it also established a possible reason for Wright to testify falsely against Gaskins.

Ira Byrd Parnell, the young SLED forensic expert, was next called to the stand.

Answer: ...I have been an employee of the State Law Enforcement division for four years, three years of which I have been in the firearms lab. I made approximately three thousand comparisons of my own or observed those comparisons made.

Solicitor: All right, Sir, under whose direction did you receive your training?

Answer: Lt. Cate, Lt. DeFreeze and Agent Anderson.

Solicitor: Who is the head of that department?

Answer: Lt. Cate. He has been with that department for twenty-seven years.

Solicitor: I'll ask you, Mr. Parnell, to compare ballistics with the science of fingerprints. Is it just as accurate as fingerprints?

Answer: It is just as accurate, yes, sir.

Solicitor: All right. Do you recall, or were you present at any time when they exhumed the body of one Dennis Bellamy from a grave site, Sir?

Answer: Yes, sir, I was there.

Solicitor: Now I'll ask you, Sir, if you had the occasion to receive and I'm goin to refer you to State's Exhibits 1, 2, and 3, and ask you, Sir, if you have ever seen these exhibits, Sir?

Answer: Yes, sir, these are the bullets that I received from Dr. Sexton in Charleston.

Solicitor: I'm going to hand you State's Exhibit No. 17, and ask you, Sir, if you've ever seen that?

Answer: Yes, Sir, I received this weapon from Agent Tom Henderson of SLED.

Solicitor: Have you had the occasion to run ballistics tests on that weapon?

Answer: I test fired it.

Solicitor: Did you follow the body of Dennis Bellamy to Charleston and did you see these three bullets removed from the body of Dennis Bellamy?

Answer: Yes, sir, I did.

Solicitor: What weapon fired those three bullets?

Answer: These three bullets were fired from the weapon I received from Tom Henderson.

Solicitor: Is that the same weapon that has a marking of Donald Gaskins on it, Sir?

Answer: It is the same.

The state rested after the testimony of the young agent. Surprised by the sudden end of the prosecution's case, the defense asked for sufficient time to have Dr. Sexton return to appear as the first witness for the defense after lunch.

The Court: Well you'll just have to call another witness then. Call some other witness and let's get on.

Mr. Hinnant: We have planned the defense to call him as our first witness.

The Court: Well, there is no particular magic in one witness testifying in front of another, Mr. Hinnant. Haven't you got one witness you can put on the stand?

Mr. Hinnant: We'd like to set our order of witnesses, your Honor.

The Court: Well, I'd like to have the Court operate, Mr. Hinnant.

Mr. Hinnant: I understand that, your Honor. We expected the State to rest at noon at the earliest.

The Court: I'm not responsible for your expectations. Now, I want you to get a witness and let's get started on this thing. I will wait for ten more minutes, and you are going to have a witness.

Fifteen minutes later the defense called Marie Marlowe who was questioned on direct examination by Johnny DeBerry.

DeBerry: Where do you live?

Answer: I stay in a trailer over in Johnsonville.

DeBerry: How long have you known the defendant?

Answer: About a year this past January.

DeBerry: Did you ever hear Thomas Wright try to go out with Pee Wee's wife, Sandra Gaskins?

Answer: Yes, sir, I heard him ask her for a date and he asked her to come and live with him. He told Pee Wee that he would like to be with her.

DeBerry: Would you tell me where you were on Friday night the tenth day of October, 1975?

Answer: Well, I got off work. I was working at Marlowe's Manufacturing in Florence. And my mama was supposed to meet me at the fair with my two kids. I had got off work at four-thirty and my mother was supposed to meet me on the fair with my kids. And well me and Sherry —we got off from work.

DeBerry: Now who is Sherry?

Answer: Sherry Lee. She works with me. We went to the fair and met my mother and I got my two kids and went and played around for awhile. And it was late that night, about ten or ten-thirty, she took them and carried them home. We stayed there for awhile and then about twelve we went to Lake City when we left the fair. We went to Sam's Club in Lake City and they were closing when we got there, and Sandy and Donna they were at the dance club.

DeBerry: Who was there? What were their names?

Answer: Sandy and Donna. Sandy Gaskins and Donna Gaskins. And we all got in the car together, in the Chevrolet —the sixty eight Chevrolet. And we come back to Florence to the Eldorado Club, and we stayed there until it must have been about four o'clock. We left to go home, and as we were going in to Mr. Gaskins trailer at Ropers Crossroads, we saw the pickup was coming out —the white pickup.

DeBerry: Whose Pickup is that?

Answer: It's Pee Wee's.

DeBerry: And what did you do next?

Answer: We went on to the trailer and Pee Wee was there in the house. And we asked him where was the truck and he said that Walter had had it —was driving it. And so me and Sherry we let the couch down.

Solicitor: We object to the hearsay.

DeBerry: Your Honor, this is not hearsay. We are not offering this testimony for whether Walter was actually in the truck but merely for the fact that Donald Gaskins said that Walter was in the truck.

Solicitor: It's still hearsay.

The Court: It sounds like hearsay.

DeBerry: Not when it's not offered to prove the underlying fact, your Honor.

The Court: I'll allow it.

DeBerry: That was Pee Wee's truck.

Answer: It was. He drove it when he wasn't driving one of his other cars.

DeBerry: Do you know Walter Neely?

Answer: Not that well. He acts funny sometimes.

DeBerry: What do you mean?

Answer: Well, he just didn't act right.

DeBerry: Were Pee Wee and Walter friends? Did Walter use his truck?

Answer: They were friends. He used Pee Wee's things. He would come and go at the trailer whether Pee Wee was there or not.

DeBerry: Is this Pee Wee's gun?

Answer: Yes, sir.

DeBerry: Do you know where he kept it?

Answer: Sometimes he would keep it in the pocket of the truck. And he had a rifle or something 'nother on a rack in the truck too.

DeBerry: Do you know of anyone else that had access to Pee Wee's truck and his gun of your own knowledge?

Answer: Well, if I wanted to drive it, I could drive it, and Sherry, if she wanted to drive it she could drive it. Well all of his friends could drive it if they wanted to. The key was on the wall in the trailer.

Marie Marlowe would testify that about the thirteenth of October, she and Sherry moved into the Gaskins trailer where they lived until the last day of November. She said that they thoroughly cleaned the trailer and moved any clothes that were there to one closet near the kitchen. She testified vehemently that the shoes in evidence, identified as those of Dennis Bellamy, were not anywhere in the trailer. She testified that when she and Sherry moved out, Pee Wee was in jail and that she saw Walter in Charleston on the first day of December and that he was not in jail.

She finished her testimony by describing having seen Dennis Bellamy only on occasion in March of 1975. She said that he was beaten and bloody and that he was in the company of Walter Neely who was also beaten and bloody. She was barred from offering hearsay testimony about whether or not they had been in a fight but the implication was clear.

Solicitor: Where did you meet Gaskins?

Answer: Sam's Club.

Solicitor: And when did you move into his trailer?

Answer: About the last of January, 1975. Me and Sherry. She moved out in February. I stayed a few months; moved back home with Mama; moved back again in May for awhile and then back home and then back to the trailer in October.

Solicitor: Where were your children?

Answer: With my mother.

Solicitor: Now when you moved back to your mother's the first time in March, you then moved to Charleston didn't you? And you lived in Pee Wee's trailer down there in Charleston until you moved back to the trailer up here in May, didn't you?

Answer: Yes.

As cross examination continued, Marie denied having an intimate relationship with Gaskins and testified that while she lived in his trailer in Charleston, Gaskins lived in the house with his wife Sandy and their child, and that Marie cooked for them because Sandy couldn't cook.

Solicitor: Well, now when did Pee Wee start living with Donna?

Answer: I'm not sure. I was living with my mother at that time. We were gathering tobacco and stuff.

Solicitor: But you know that they lived together after he lived with Sandy?

Answer: Yes, sir.

During the remainder of cross, Marie revealed that during the times that she lived in Pee Wee's trailer in Charleston, she didn't work except to cook for Pee Wee and Sandy, that all of her expenses were paid by Pee Wee, and that she drove one of his cars the entire time. She admitted that at some point Pee Wee and Sandy stopped living together and that Sandy and Walter had gone together to Pennsylvania to visit her mother, and that although Pee Wee started living with Donna, Marie had remained there.

Marie testified that she was nineteen, had first moved to the Gaskins trailer in Charleston when she was eighteen years old where she was given the use of the red Ford Mustang. She also used a gold Plymouth Duster at Ropers Crossroads but she learned that it was stolen when she was stopped by police after Gaskins arrest. She had two children. She said that she had her first child when she was fourteen, a second when she was fifteen, and a stillborn child when she was sixteen. She left her husband about two years before she met Gaskins.

Marie continuously denied any sexual liaison with Gaskins and asserted that she had a boyfriend, J.L. Feagin, during that time. Feagin and Gaskins were charged and indicted together for a burglary in Florence County that occurred at about that time. She admitted to frequently traveling to and from Charleston and Ropers Crossroads with Gaskins in the same or separate vehicles but denied being involved in transporting either stolen vehicles or other stolen material for him.

Marie said that she and Sherry had lived in the trailer at Gaskins' house in Charleston and that Gaskins lived in the house with Sandy and Sandy's sister, Wanda Snell. She had previously admitted that Donna had come to stay there. All of the women were about the same age with the exception of Wanda who was fourteen or fifteen.

Gaskins smiled from time to time and displayed a general look of satisfaction as the solicitor pressed the issue of the number of women living with and apparently dependent upon Gaskins.

Sherry Lee reiterated in large part the testimony of Marie Marlowe. She gave the same details of the night of October tenth at the fair, Sam's Club and the Eldorado Club until four-thirty A.M. and then sleeping in the trailer at Ropers Crossroads. She was pressed by Summerford on Marie's relationship with Gaskins.

Solicitor: All right. Now let me ask you this: did Marie Marlowe the lady that testified just before lunch, didn't she sleep with Pee Wee Gaskins?

Answer: I didn't see her sleep with Pee Wee Gaskins.

Solicitor: Now do you deny under oath that you told Sheriff Barnes and Agent Tom Henderson in December of Nineteen Seventy-five, at the grave site in Prospect community, that Marie Marlowe slept with Pee Wee Gaskins, and you saw it with your own eyes? Now do you deny that under oath?

Despite her continuing denials, Summerford created a substantial issue regarding Marie's bias in favor of Gaskins based on their intimacy and he had, in all likelihood, established the same questions in the minds of the jurors about the nature of Sherry's relationship with Gaskins. Sherry was twenty-one when she lived in the Gaskins' trailer in Charleston and had moved away when she married in the spring of that year. She moved to Gaskins trailer in Prospect when she separated from her husband in October of 1975. At the time of her testimony in May of 1976, she was again living with her husband.

Sherry revealed that she and Marie had worked one or two nights in a club in Charleston as "bunny girls" sometime after she moved away from Charleston but was not specific about the time or place.

Another long colloquy occurred between the bench and the defense regarding the calling of the next witness. The judge became more insistent that any witness present in the courthouse should be called immediately while the defense argued that they had a right to call the witnesses in the order that they believed best presented their case. This debate became more interesting when it turned out that a witness that the defense had been attempting to locate, and had asked the sheriff's office to serve with a subpoena, was said to have been present in the sheriff's office the previous evening. Gaskins said he happened to see the man, Wade Stone, in the offices of the sheriff as Gaskins was being prepared for transportation back to the Darlington County Jail, some ten miles away.

The defense also complained that Deputy Glen Ard of the Williamsburg County Sheriff's office, a key player in the investigation, had been present in court during the state's case but was now missing. The defense said that he was not on duty and was not responding to calls from defense counsel's office or to messages left with the Williamsburg Sheriff's office. There could be little doubt that he was attempting to avoid being called as a witness.

Finally Dr. Sexton was called back to the stand, this time by the defense. He testified about the size of the feet of the deceased which he described in his autopsy as six and a half C. He said the shoe size was an approximation and could vary by one whole size.

In contemplation of calling the defendant, Donald Henry Gaskins, the defense presented him outside the presence of the jury in order to have the Court make a determination as to what part of his criminal record could be brought out by the state on cross examination.

The Court: Just convictions, now.

Assistant Solicitor Saleeby: 1/8/52, Assault and Battery of a High and Aggravated Nature. June 21, 1957, Murder, accessory after the fact. July 7,1959, National Motor Vehicle Transportation Act, three years. 12/19/68 aggregated sentences carnal knowledge of a child and escape. September 24, 1973, Violation of the explosives control act of 1970.

Hinnant argued that the record from which the assistant solicitor was reading was not a certified record and that there were errors. Summerford attempted to rebut the argument, urging that he intended to use the record only as a basis for cross examination, but he also tried to convince the court that the record that he had obtained was reliable. Hinnant pointed out that the reference to a 1968 conviction, for which a six year sentence was indicated, was impossible in that Gaskins was actually paroled in 1968 and that the only conviction since that parole was one for possession of dynamite for which he received a suspended sentence with probation to run with his remaining parole. Judge McEachern was convinced that the questioning based on the record, upon which the solicitor was relying, should be allowed in spite of that glaring inaccuracy.

Gaskins was advised by the judge that he had the right not to testify and that he would instruct the jury that his failure to testify could not be held against him and that he could rely upon the presumption of innocence, that he had no obligation to offer any evidence and that the burden lay solely upon the state to prove his guilt. The judge further instructed that if he did not testify, his criminal convictions could not be introduced against him.

Gaskins indicated that he understood his rights and that it was his desire to testify. He testified that during the week of October fifth through the tenth, he had traveled to Prospect on Tuesday or Wednesday night with John Henry Knight and Wade Stone. He said that they drove separately because he was buying a car from Knight. He said Knight and Stone drove that car up while Pee Wee went up alone in his Ford pickup. He said that Knight signed a bill of sale for him and that his daughter came to the trailer while they were there. He said that they left immediately and drove back to Charleston together where he dropped Knight at his mother's house and then drove Wade to his own house. This testimony was to explain the testimony of his daughter about having seen Gaskins at his trailer with two men filling out some papers.

Gaskins testified that on Friday night, October 10, 1975, he came to Ropers Crossroads accompanied by his wife, Donna, and his former wife, Sandy. He said that he again came in the white 1966 Ford pickup and that Donna and Sandy had driven the blue Chevrolet. The two women had come in order to go to Sam's Club for the square dance that night. Pee Wee said that he did not go to the club and stayed at his daughter's trailer next door until about nine-thirty in the evening at which time he went back to his trailer. He said that he undressed and was lying on the couch waiting for Sandy and Donna to return and for Marie Marlowe and Sherry Lee to come as well. He said that he was also hopeful that a woman, who frequently visited him at his trailer, would come by while the other women were at the club.

Gaskins said that just as he was lying down on the couch, there was a knock at his door. He said he called for the visitor to come inside with high expectations but was surprised to see Walter Neely come through the door. Monk Hinnant asked Gaskins if Neely was also charged with the murder of Dennis Bellamy, and then established that Neely was also charged with the murders of John Henry Knight, Neely's estranged wife, Diane, Bellamy Neely, and Avery Howard. Gaskins then described Neely's relationship to each of those people. Bellamy and Knight were the brother and half-brother of Walter's wife, Diane, and Avery Howard had been Diane's lover with whom she was living at the time of the murder.

He described the bad relationship between Walter and Dennis Bellamy which included a fight where Neely was beaten by Bellamy with a pipe so badly that he was not recognizable and had to be hospitalized. Gaskins then described the funeral of the child of Diane and Walter, who had been burned to death in the bath tub, while in Diane's care. Gaskins testified about Walter's anger and hurt over the death of his child. He said that Walter blamed Diane for the child's death. He described the child's injuries that had been shown to him by Walter's mother at the infant's funeral. He said that she showed him the injuries in order to anger him and convince him to assist Walter in seeking revenge because the police had refused to prosecute Diane.

Gaskins said that on the night of October tenth, when Walter came into his trailer, Walter asked to borrow his truck. He said that he regularly loaned things to Walter, even to the extent that if Pee Wee was not at home, Walter would simply take the keys from their regular place and use the truck. He said on that night he gave Walter permission to use the truck just as he usually did. Walter took the keys from where they were hanging and left in the truck. He also testified that his Berretta pistol was in the glove compartment and his rifle and shotgun were in a gun rack above the truck seat.

Further testimony from Gaskins indicated that Neely frequently came to the Prospect area, had access to the trailer owned by Gaskins, and knew the countryside well having hunted there with Gaskins. Finally, Gaskins volunteered that Neely had been admitted to the state hospital as a result of the breakdown he suffered over the death of his child.

On cross examination Summerford asked about the relationship between Neely and Gaskins. Gaskins confirmed that Neely had lived off and on in a trailer owned by Gaskins that was located behind the Gaskins' house on Calvert Street. He asked Gaskins to confirm that his former wife, Sandy, had moved into the trailer with Neely when Gaskins began living with Donna Carullo, the woman that he now identified as his wife, Donna Gaskins.

Summerford: He came to your trailer that night?

Gaskins: That's right.

Solicitor: By himself?

Answer: Yes, sir, by his self.

Solicitor: Walter Neely told me he was driving a nineteen sixty-nine blue truck, with Dennis Bellamy and John Henry Knight in it.

Answer: They were outside. At the road about seventy-five yards from my trailer. You couldn't see it from my trailer. There was vines and trees between it.

Solicitor: Do you know of any reason why your daughter would make a statement against her own father that wasn't true?

Answer: Yes, sir, I do. Because she had been threatened that if she did not, that her children would be taken away from her.

Changing gears, Summerford turned to earlier testimony regarding Neely in Charleston.

Solicitor: And you looked on the back of the dead child?

Answer: Walter Neely's mother turned it over and showed it to me.

Solicitor: Turned the child over?

Answer: Turned the child over and showed me the back of its body where it was all peeled off and red and everything.

Solicitor: In the coffin?

Answer: In the coffin. She took me in there and showed it to me. And Diane wouldn't sign no report to have it —to show cause of death on it.

Solicitor: All right. You are trying to give us the impression now that Walter Neely was shipped off to the State Hospital and was crazy. Is that what you are trying to convey to this court?

Answer: I can't give a qualified answer on whether he's crazy or not. All I know is that his mother did have him sent to the State Hospital.

Solicitor: You know he stayed one week?

Answer: I can't deny he didn't stay ten minutes, because I know the last time I saw Walter Neely he was in the patrol car going to the hospital.

Solicitor: You are not trying to give us the impression now that Walter Neely was crazy, are you?

Answer: No, sir, I'm not trying to give you that. He was funny.

Solicitor: Well why did you testify to it then?

Answer: I said he was funny. He didn't act normal.

The solicitor returned to the issue of Walter being charged with the death of Diane Neely, pointing out that Neely had actually been charged as an accessory and that Gaskins was also charged with her death but not as an accessory. He then changed direction again.

Solicitor: Who are you married to, sir?

Answer: I am married to Sandra Lee Gaskins, Williamsburg County January the first, nineteen seventy.

Solicitor: All right. Did you know that she had been married before? Did you know she had never been divorced before?

Answer: I know that she had been married before. She was not legally married.

Solicitor: How old is she?

Answer: I don't know exactly the paper said twenty-five.

Solicitor: All right. Well you heard the statement made that all of the women that you are fooling around with, Sherry was the oldest one, twenty-three.

Answer: I don't get what you mean fooling around with.

Solicitor: You know very well what I'm talking about. Never mind, we withdraw it. Now, but you don't deny that you lived with Donna?

Answer: Donna lived in the house with Sandy and I.

Solicitor: All right. And you don't deny that she went by the name of Donna Gaskins?

Answer: I'd like to see some proof where she has proven her name was Donna Gaskins.

Solicitor: And she —you never heard her referred to as that?

Answer: Her name is Donna Carrullo.

Solicitor: She was living with you, wasn't she?

Answer: She was living in the house there at Calvert Street.

Cross examination continuing, Gaskins confirmed that he bought a Ford Mustang from John Henry Knight and sold it to Belton Eaddy after fixing the starter on Saturday, October eleventh.

The solicitor asked incredulously:

Solicitor: And that's the car that you bought from Johnnie Knight, a fifteen year old young boy?

Answer: Right.

Solicitor: And he had the bill of sale for it or the certificate of title?

Answer: No, sir.

Solicitor: And Johnny Knight went back to Charleston that same night?

Answer: I took him back and I went back on Friday with Donna and Sandy.

Solicitor: And Friday night no one but Walter came to your house while Donna and Sandy were at Sam's Club?

Answer: Right.

Solicitor: And after Walter borrowed your truck when did he come back?

Answer: Between four and five.

Solicitor: How long did he stay?

Answer: I would say maybe eight o'clock, Sandra and Donna went back to Charleston and he went back to Charleston with them.

Solicitor: Now what happened to Marie and Sherry?

Answer: They was laying across the bed in the back of the trailer.

The solicitor than turned to a discussion of the gun, challenging Gaskins about the gun being in the glove compartment. Summerford asked when it was put in the truck and where Pee Wee ordinarily carried it. Gaskins replied that the gun was always kept in the glove compartment and never carried on his person. He said having his name on it was in case it was lost or stolen and denied having ever called it "his baby", saying that his daughter "just flat lied." He did admit, in earlier testimony, he had referred to it as a pocket gun in saying that he had three guns in the truck, a shotgun, a rifle and a pocket gun.

Gaskins further testified that he cleaned the gun every Thursday and that he kept it loaded.

Gaskins: My gun —the first time I realized it had been shot was the next Thursday.

Solicitor: All right. So you re-loaded it then?

Answer: I put six additional bullets to that after I had cleaned it.

Solicitor: Now your testimony is that you left it in the compartment, or the glove compartment of that truck from that weekend until Thursday without taking it out?

Answer: No, sir. No, sir.

Solicitor: When did you take it out?

Answer: It came out every evening when I came to my house. I would take it out and carry it in and put it in the top drawer in the bedroom.

Solicitor: In Charleston?

Answer: That's right.

Solicitor: And you never checked it to see if anything was wrong with it?

Answer: Well, I didn't think it had been shot.

Solicitor: I see. Now, but you loaded it?

Answer: I loaded it that Thursday night.

Solicitor: Did you ask Walter Neely why he had used your gun then? Is that what you are trying to convey for us?

Answer: No, I didn't ask him. He have used my guns before and shot them and I never asked him. He would go hunting. He would take my shotgun and go on the railroad tracks and down to the woods and shoot. I never asked him how many shells he'd shoot, or anything else. I had no reason to.

Solicitor: All right, Sir. Well, why were you going to Mississippi when you were arrested?

Answer: I was going down there looking for a girl named Kim.

Solicitor: Going down there looking for a girl named Kim?

Answer: That's right. I had information that she was at Route1, Sotille, Mississippi.

Solicitor: You weren't planning on coming back? You bought a one way ticket.

Answer: I was going to come back to Charleston not to Sumter.

Solicitor: If you were going to look for Kim why was it that you were taking a loaded pistol and a 30/30 rifle?

Answer: That was with me at all times.

Solicitor: At all times?

Answer: Wait a minute let me explain.

Solicitor: All right.

Answer: I had a red sixty-nine Ford that I had drove to Florida and back. I decided I wouldn't leave my rifle in there, or the pistol in there at that time in case somebody come by there and broke in the car. And so I had it, carrying them with me. I had stored them away —stored them away in a box. They was not on me in person whatsoever.

The solicitor next referred to a document and asked Gaskins if he had told a Barbara Cook Watts that he could knock her husband off. After objections by the defense, the solicitor argued that he should be able to impeach the witness by asking him about being a hit man. The court did not allow it and the defense moved for a mistrial because the jury had heard the question. The motion was denied.

Summerford revisited the testimony about the activities of Sandy Gaskins and Donna Carrullo on that day in October, asking again whether Gaskins had referred to both of them as his wife and questioning Gaskins about a wedding ceremony with Donna Carrullo which Gaskins denied somewhat obliquely by continually asserting that he had no marriage license for a marriage to Donna.

Gaskins continued to maintain that Sandy and Donna had gone to the square dance at Sam's Club and that he had stayed around his trailer, his daughter's, and the house of her father in law, all of which were located in close proximity to each other on the Evans farm. He stated again that he had gone to his trailer and to prepare for bed when Walter Neely arrived unexpectedly. Summerford continued to probe.

Summerford: But you didn't work at Sam's Place that night did you?

Answer: I had been quit Sam's Place quite a long time.

Summerford: All right, Sir. Mr. Gaskins, do you deny that on the Tenth of October, nineteen seventy-five, that you took Johnnie Knight and Dennis Bellamy behind your old home where you lived in a field?

Answer: Yes, sir, I deny that.

Summerford: Do you deny that you took them back there?

Answer: I deny it. Yes, sir.

Summerford: Do you deny that you took Johnnie Knight and asked him to look at a tree up there that was good to pull a motor out of an automobile?

Answer: Yes, sir, I deny that. Johnnie Knight knew that I had a portable chain hoist that when I got ready to pull a motor out if it was down side the highway, I could set it up right side the highway if I wanted to pull a motor out of a car and pull it out right there.

On redirect, Hinnant established that Shirley Evans, contrary to her earlier testimony that day, had testified at the preliminary hearing that the signing of a document witnessed by her in Pee Wee's trailer had been on a Wednesday not on Friday the tenth of October.

Summerford then attacked another area of Gaskins' testimony as the judge allowed, yet another, examination that the defense objected was outside the context of testimony permitted in reply. According to the rules of evidence and procedure, reply testimony is limited to matters raised during cross examination.

Solicitor: Mr. Gaskins, were you trying to evade the law in November nineteen seventy five?

Answer: I was looking for Kim. I wasn't trying —yes in one sense I was. But I was trying to find Kim to where I could get back to Charleston where she could verify that I hadn't contributed to her disappearance.

Solicitor: Did you have a nineteen sixty-nine Ford Torino?

Answer: I did.

Solicitor: Did you park that in the neck and cover it over with bushes?

Answer: I did.

Solicitor: Did you have anything in that car?

Answer: I have already stated to the jury here that I had a twelve gauge shotgun in that car. I had tools and all in there. A chain hoist and wrenches.

Solicitor: And you left those in the car?

Answer: They was locked up.

Solicitor: Where were the keys?

Answer: In my pocket.

Solicitor: Well when did you decide to bring this car down to Florence County into the neck and hide it?

Answer: I drove that car from Charleston down on Wednesday night —let me get the exact date and all and I'll tell you. (Witness referring to notes) On November the twelfth I left Charleston and went to Jacksonville, Florida. Left Jacksonville, Florida and came back to Florence, went on down to Prospect where I left the car. I went to Lake City and back to Charleston.

Solicitor: All right let me ask you this: you said there was one shotgun, or two?

Answer: There was one six shot shotgun in there and one single shot shotgun.

Solicitor: And both of those were loaded?

Answer: Possibly they may have been.

Solicitor: And didn't you have five sticks of dynamite in that car?

Answer: Yes, sir.

Solicitor: And you had seven electric blasting caps?

Answer: Eight I think.

The defense called Deputy Glen Ard who had testified at both the Preliminary Hearing and the Coroner's Inquest but who had not been called by the state in the trial. Ard had appeared only after the defense complained to the court that he would not respond to their calls.

Hinnant: Deputy Ard, did you have occasion to investigate this particular case or incident?

Answer: Yes, sir.

Hinnant: What is your official position?

Answer: Deputy Sheriff of Williamsburg County.

Hinnant: Who took you to the grave site, Sir?

Answer: Walter Neely.

The defense had called Ard solely to have the jury know that Neely had taken the authorities to the graves. The solicitor sought to recover the ground they had gained.

Solicitor: Now when you took Walter Neely to the grave site, did he appear to be familiar with that area?

Answer: No he did not.

Solicitor: And did he point out to you where the grave was?

Answer: No, sir, he did not.

Solicitor: Could he do it?

Answer: No, sir.

The defense called Gaskins' employer who testified about the reliability of Gaskins, confirmed the use of mattocks in roofing work, and that Gaskins frequently loaned his truck to Walter Neely. He also testified that he did not believe that Walter was "normal". At the conclusion of his testimony, the defense rested.

SLED Agent Tom Henderson was recalled by the State.

Mr. Saleeby: You are still under oath?

Answer: Yes, sir.

Saleeby: Have you been in Court during the conduct of this trial?

Answer: Yes, sir.

Saleeby: Did you hear the witness, Sherry Lee, testify and deny that she told you that Marie Marlowe slept with the defendant, Donald Henry Gaskins?

Answer: Yes she did.

Saleeby: And what did she tell you?

Answer: She told me that she had seen Marie Marlowe sleeping with the defendant, Donald Gaskins.

Mr. Saleeby: I believe you testified that you were present and participated in the arrest of the defendant, Donald Henry Gaskins in Sumter County.

Anwar: Yes, I did.

Saleeby: Was that on November the twentieth of nineteen seventy-five?

Answer: It was.

Saleeby: At the time that he was arrested did anyone throw him to the physically to the ground?

Answer: No, sir.

Saleeby: After he was taken to the Sumter Sheriff's Department was he advised of his Constitutional Rights?

Answer: He was told that he had the right to remain silent. Anything that he said could and would be used against him in a court of law. He was told he had the right to an attorney; that if he could not afford an attorney, the state would appoint one for him. We told him that he did not have to answer any questions if he did not wish to. And that any time during the questioning that he wished to stop answering questions or wished an attorney that one would be given to him, or he could stop asking questions —answering questions.

Saleeby: Was he asked if he understood those rights?

Answer: Yes, sir.

Saleeby: What was his reply?

Answer: He said that he understood his rights fully, that he had been told his rights before.

Saleeby: All right. Did you ask him why he had a bus ticket to Tupelo, Mississippi?

Answer: He said he was going down there to —he either had a job waiting on him, or he was going down there to get a job.

Saleeby: Did he ever say anything to you about going to Tupelo, Mississippi, to help find a girl by the name of Kim Geltman, from Charleston?

Answer: No, sir.

Saleeby: Now, Mr. Henderson, let me ask you during the course of your investigation of this case, you had occasion to ride and transport Mr. Gaskins from here to other parts of this state, particularly to Columbia?

Answer: Yes, sir, numerous times.

Saleeby During the course of your transportation, has he ever made any statements to you without being questioned by you?

Answer: Yes, sir.

Saleeby: Has he engaged in conversation with you?

Answer: Yes, sir. He said that women —he had a lot of women —women were always plentiful to him. And I asked him, I said: Is that the reason you gave Sandy to Walter? And he says: Yes because —something to the effect that I had no more use for her and Walter wanted her, so I gave Sandy to him.

Saleeby: All right. Now, Mr. Henderson, I'll ask you if you were here yesterday when Mr. Gaskins testified that he never made that statement to you at any time?

Answer: Yes, sir, I heard him say that.

Saleeby: And did he make the statement to you on a trip from Columbia to Florence?

Answer: Yes, sir, he did.

Shirley Ann Evans was recalled by the solicitor.

Summerford: Mrs. Evans, I believe we established when you testified on direct testimony on behalf of the state that you are the daughter of the defendant, Donald Henry Gaskins, is that correct?

Answer: Yes, sir.

Summerford: Now, Mrs. Evans, a statement was made to the effect that the reason that you testified against your father was that you were threatened that your children would be taken away from you if you did not testify against your father. I'll ask you if you've ever received any such threat?

Answer: There's not but one person has mentioned anything about my children. And that was the day that man right there come down to my house, and

Summerford: What man, right where?

Answer: That fat man right there that keeps pulling his pants up.

Mr. Hinnant: I ain't gonna accept service on that.

Summerford: Now you're telling me the only man that has ever told you that was this man right here, Mr. Hinnant?

Answer: He come down there and asked me had there been any threats about taking my children. And I said No Sir my testimony is free, voluntarily and no threats at all.

Summerford: What is your true feeling towards your father?

Answer: I love my daddy.

Summerford: All right, would you tell a story against him?

Answer: No sir, not if I knowed it was a story I would not say nothing against my daddy.

Summerford: All right Ma'am. Your witness.

Mr. Hinnant: Mrs. Evans do you know Mrs. Christine Prosser —Marie Marlowe's mother?

Answer: Mrs. Peanut Prosser. Peanut that's all I know.

Hinnant: Did you ever make a statement to her that you were scared to death you were going to lose your children because of this?

Answer: No sir, I did not.

Hinnant: But you know her and you have been to her house?

Answer: Yes, sir, I have been to her house with Marie Marlowe.

The defense rested and the attorneys made final arguments. Assistant Solicitor, Dudley Saleeby, argued first for the state. His argument addressed the roles of the judge and jury, explaining that the jury determined the facts of a case based on the law as it was explained to them by the judge. He urged that while the jury or even he might disagree with the law, or the death penalty, that they should not be influenced by the penalty that could result from application of the law to the facts. He told them that the law was exclusively the province of the judge, and that they had to accept the law as the judge explained it to them, and that they, the jury, were the sole judges of the facts as they determined them to be.

The assistant solicitor went on to argue that the jury and everyone else involved was there in court because of the two men found buried in Florence County, who had been shot to death. He told them that they had a duty to those two men who could not be there, and to their community, to return a verdict based on the facts presented in the court and not on sympathy or supposition. He told them that they should bring back a verdict that found the defendant guilty of premeditated murder.

Monk Hinnant next argued for the defense saying that the state's case was based solely upon circumstantial evidence. He urged that there was no direct evidence, such as a witness, who could say that he saw the defendant or anyone else shoot the victim. He addressed the jury in the finest style of the southern courtroom orator, literally hooking thumbs in his vest pockets at times as he strode back and forth in front of the jury box. His voice varied from a roaring baritone to barely a whisper as he sought to capture the attention of the jurors. He pontificated on the burden of the state to prove the facts, upon which it sought to rely the burden to prove those facts, not only beyond a reasonable doubt, but where reliance was solely upon circumstantial evidence to prove those facts to the exclusion of any other reasonable hypothesis.

He was suddenly and unexpectedly interrupted by the judge:

The Court: Wait a minute, Mr. Hinnant. We've got somebody who is absolutely fascinated by your argument. See if you can get that —find him a little more comfortable place.

Hinnant: What's that, that's Mr. Gaskins little son? What's wrong?

Spectator: It's an allergy he's got.

Mr. Hinnant: That's Mr. Gaskins little boy.

The Court: All right, go ahead, Mr. Hinnant.

Hinnant again returned to his description of the burden that must be borne solely by the state, asking the jury to accept nothing less than sufficient evidence to convince them that, even if the defendant was a close relative, they would be so convinced of his guilt that the proof would exclude any explanation other than guilt.

He then reminded them of the discrepancies about the size of the shoes and the testimony that relying upon rigor mortis to determine the time of burial could lead to either of two conclusions. Either the body was buried within hours before rigor mortis occurred or more than three days after death when rigor mortis is released. He urged that Walter Neely had taken the law officers to the graves and that it had been well established that he had a motive to want to harm Dennis Bellamy whereas none had been proven as to Gaskins. All of which certainly constituted another plausible explanation according to Hinnant.

John DeBerry completed the argument for the defense. He began by defining common law murder as the intentional killing of another man that was not willful, deliberate and premeditated. He told the jury that by reaching that verdict, the defendant would be found guilty but would be sentenced to life in prison rather than to death. He dwelt on the weight of a decision that would result in the death penalty and the unanswered questions that existed in the case which should give pause to consideration of a penalty that could not be corrected. Clearly, the purpose of his argument was to convince the jury to look for a compromise that would result in a finding of guilty but that would spare the life of his client.

As to the facts, DeBerry, like Hinnant, stressed the likelihood that Walter Neely would have killed the men against whom he had substantial grudges, and that he was much more likely than Gaskins to have buried the bodies where they could be discovered near the Gaskins' home. He finished with the proposition that shooting someone with a gun that could be easily traced directly to Gaskins would be the perfect way for Neely to divert attention from himself. He reminded the jury that Neely was a convicted felon who had served time in the penitentiary, a man to whom these obvious things would be known.

The order of the arguments is established by law in South Carolina and Kenneth Summerford made the final argument to the jury. Summerford spent the first portion of his argument reminding the jury that they had elected him as their solicitor some eight years ago. He then praised himself for his fair-mindedness and told the jury of his evenhanded approach to prosecution. He even assured the jury that if the defense had experienced any difficulty in obtaining information from any law enforcement agency, he would have stepped in to deliver it himself.

Next, turning to the facts of the case, he pounded the identification of the gun by forensics. Reminding the jury that identification of the murder weapon had been made by comparison of the test fired rounds from the Berretta, marked with Gaskins' name, to the bullets taken from the body of Dennis Bellamy. He recalled for them the damning testimony of Pee Wee's own daughter, delving into the details of her testimony regarding the presence of Dennis Bellamy and his younger brother at the trailer of Gaskins on the night of their deaths. In the manner and method of a southern evangelist at a tent revival, Summerford began to fix on a theme for his argument, a theme that would be repeated again and again like the chorus of a spiritual. "What kind of man are we dealing with?" rang his refrain as he raised his voice and several times focused on an individual juror, "What kind of man, Madam Juror? What kind of man, Mr. Juror?"

Following his theme, he reviewed Gaskins' testimony regarding the different women in his house who were supported by him and provided cars by him. He reminded them of the women, to whom Gaskins became married without regard for the fact that he had not divorced his previous wife, and of the women or girls with whom he slept without regard for their age. "What kind of man is this," he railed again and again. He wound up with the description of the Ford Torino hidden in the brush shortly before Gaskins had tried to escape to Mississippi, hidden in their community with weapons loaded and at the ready. He urged that Gaskins intended to somehow reach that vehicle, and asked them to consider the implications of the potential danger to dedicated lawmen that might have faced him, had he reached that car.

"Think about it, ladies and gentlemen of the jury. The keys were in his pocket and he was going there to retrieve his loaded guns and the sticks of dynamite. What kind of man?" he shouted, "What kind of man?" ending with his now familiar exhortation. "The kind of man who would have left one of our very own deputies dead in those weeds if he had gotten to those guns; that's what kind of man."

After the arguments were concluded Judge McEachern charged the jury, providing them with the formal recitation of the law as it applied to the case. He carefully charged the presumption of innocence, the burden of proof that lay solely upon the state to prove all of the elements of the case, and the lack of any requirement on the defendant to prove his innocence or offer any evidence. He distinguished his duty to determine the applicable law and the duty of the jury to decide factual issues. He covered the consideration of different types of evidence, explaining the particular nuances of circumstantial evidence. He explained that the state had the burden to prove malice whether actual or implied. Malice, he explained, is defined as involving a wicked heart and need not exist for any specific period of time but must exist before the person is killed. It may be implied by circumstances including the use of a deadly weapon. The judge explained that in South Carolina, the penalty for the commission of deliberate and premeditated murder was death by electrocution. Lastly, he explained that there were three possible verdicts: "Guilty of murder that was not willful and deliberate; Guilty of murder that is willful, deliberate and premeditated; or not guilty. He directed that the verdict must be unanimous and that it must be signed by the foreman of the jury.

The State had no exceptions or additions to the charge and the defense only reiterated the request for a charge of manslaughter which was denied.

The jury began deliberations at five twenty-five P.M. on April 27, 1976 on the fourth day of trial.

At six P.M., the jury requested that the testimony of the daughter, Shirley Ann Evans, the testimony of Marie Marlowe, and the testimony of Sherry Lee be re-read.

The repeated testimony completed, the jury retired for another ten minutes and brought back their verdict which was reviewed by the judge and then read by the Clerk of Court.

"Guilty of murder that was deliberate, willful and premeditated," the clerk read.

At the request of the Defense each juror was polled with the traditional question: "If that be your verdict so say you, Aye". Each juror replied affirmatively.

Sentencing was set for the following morning.

93

The next morning the defense argued various issues previously objected to during the trial, and then Judge McEachern pronounced sentence in the traditional and formal language ending with:

"...you, the prisoner at the bar, Donald Henry Gaskins, shall suffer death by electrocution at the hands of the officers of the law, and in the manner provided by the laws of the State of South Carolina. And may God have mercy upon your soul."

Monk Hinnant made a final objection to the constitutionality of the South Carolina death penalty statute arguing that it was cruel and unusual, and that as applied, it deprived defendants of equal protection under the law. Hinnant then asked that the defendant be allowed to see his sister, mother and brother who were present in the court.

The judge asked the sheriff if those arrangements could be made in the detention center and the sheriff replied that they would be.

CHAPTER FIFTY FIVE

Justice Marches On

Summerford immediately informed Query and Cantrell that the trial of one of their defendants would be called on the coming Monday. Pressed to disclose his intentions as to which trial he would call, he finally called their offices on Friday afternoon with the information that he would call the case against Walter Neely on the following Monday.

Before leaving Florence, Query went again to Assistant Solicitor, Saleeby, regarding the fact that he had not been allowed to see any of the state's evidence nor had he received any of the exculpatory material to which he was absolutely entitled.

"I'll pass it on to Ken and see if I can get everything to you now that the next trial is about to go," he replied. "You know I couldn't give you a copy of the newspaper without his OK."

"Just tell him that I will ask for a hearing on all motions. He may never give me anything but I'm going to make sure I paint this record full of the fact that I keep asking and he keeps telling the court that he will produce everything and then produces nothing," countered Query.

"Grady, I will tell him but I won't convey your threats. I'm sure he'll do what the rules require. If you want to start a fight you need to do that face to face."

"You're right. No point for you being in the middle. I'll fax him a letter listing my demands so that the record is clear."

Dudley stopped Query as he was leaving the detention center after Query had seen Knoy. He told Query the solicitor had relented to the point that he would allow Query to see the statement given against his client by an eyewitness. The solicitor told Dudley he would allow Query a chance to advise his client that the state's case against him was very strong, but the solicitor was offering him a plea to Common Law Murder which would allow him to avoid the death penalty. Realizing that Knoy Judy's case would be called with the same immediacy at the conclusion of the Neely trial, Query returned to Charleston to investigate the contents of the statement and evaluate its validity and potential for harm.

Query was shocked to see that the statement was given by Sandy Gaskins, Pee Wee's ex-wife or wife who was currently Walter Neely's girlfriend. He was even more astonished to see that Sandy had placed herself at the murder of Johnny Sellers and Jessie Judy. Amazingly, she had not been arrested nor charged with any crime. Unfortunately, the statement also put Knoy Judy at the murder and made him an active participant in the slaying of Johnny Sellers.

The statement was a horrendous blow to Judy's defense, but there were glaring inconsistencies in the statement. The lack of detail and the absence of any information about the burial of the bodies in shallow graves raised serious doubts in Query's mind about the statement. Remarkably, Sandy gave no description or acknowledgement of Jessie Judy having been killed or buried with Johnny Sellers despite the fact that they were found in the same grave. The young lawyer also recalled Tom Henderson saying that one of the witnesses had given more than one statement. The solicitor had refused to reveal the identity of the witness and Query had assumed that the reference was to the daughter of Gaskins, but now he wondered.

Query had talked with Sandy on a number of occasions. Oddly enough, Sandy and Donna Carrullo Gaskins and Donna's children were all living together. Query had contacted them early in his investigation of the case and Donna had asked him to keep her apprised of the events unfolding in Florence since she couldn't be there. Finding them both to be a wealth of information about the cast of characters rapidly unfolding before him, Query took full advantage of the invitation and visited them frequently to provide updates and to ask questions. Both women had expressed amazement at the charges against Knoy, describing him as nonviolent and easygoing. Remarkably, in view of the statement, Sandy had always disavowed any knowledge of any of the murders. Based on his conversations with Sandy, Query was convinced that she was a very weak and insecure person who could be easily influenced, particularly by someone in a position of authority.

Query went to the apartment in the West Ashley section where Sandy and Donna lived. Donna had agreed to an interview with North Charleston detectives Stoney and Green on the condition that Query could be there with her. While waiting for Donna to finish dressing to go to the police station for the scheduled interview, Query glanced up to see a picture of Christ on the wall directly across from where Sandy was sitting.

"Sandy", he asked, "did you put that picture there or did Donna?"

"I did, Mr. Grady."

"Is that because you believe in him as the Son of God?"

"I sure do, Mr. Grady, he is my Lord and Savior."

Query knew that he needed to be extremely cautious and very gentle with Sandy. He was well aware of her limited intellectual ability but she always seemed willing to talk to him. He had also observed that her most persistent defense mechanism was to withdraw and totally shut down, stubbornly resisting any further attempt at communication, if she became uncomfortable. He wanted to confront her about the accuracy of her statement that was the blockbuster condemnation of his client. It was the mysterious eyewitness account the solicitor had alluded to again and again and which the assistant solicitor had finally shown to Query earlier that day in Florence. He needed to avoid a shutdown by the timid young woman and he wanted to gather information by allowing her to tell him about the statement, not by cross examining her or challenging her about the statement. Her professed beliefs appeared to offer that opportunity.

"Do you think that Jesus would be happy with the statement that you gave to the police officers about the murder of Johnny Sellers?"

"No, sir, he wouldn't."

"Why not, Sandy?"

"Because it's a lie, Mr. Grady. I ain't never been nowhere where nobody got killed. You know me, you know I couldn't go with nothin' like that," she blurted, hesitating between phrases, her voice barely above a whisper.

"I don't understand, Sandy. How could you have told them all of that if it wasn't true, if you weren't even there?" he queried his voice gentle and reassuring.

"I didn't so much tell them nothin', Mr. Grady. They said they knew I was up there the night that Johnny and Jessie was killed. They said they had witnesses to me bein' up there and that I would have to go to prison. Then they told me that if I told them what Pee Wee and Walter done, they could keep me from having to go. They kept kinda tellin' me what they thought had happened and then askin' if I agreed with what they was sayin'. If I said no or I don't know, they'd just change it around a little bit and then ask me again. When they got it the way they liked it, they would write it down and then read it back to me, ask me did I agree and if I didn't they'd write it different. Then they started to tell me to just sign it and I could go home. It just got more and more messed up. Finally I just gave up and stopped talking to them. They said, well if this is the best you can remember, just sign it right here, Sandy, and you can go home. And I did."

"You mean they were trying to get you to lie?"

"No, not so much that. They thought I knew what had happened and they was just tryin' to guess what had happened. It seemed like they believed I was out there because somebody had told them I went up to Roper's Crossroads with Walter on the night that Johnny and Jessie was killed. I don't know if I went up there then or not. I don't know when they got killed. They even tried to say Donna was there but I told them no way, that she had a baby to take care of. So they would guess at what had happened and then they'd try to get me to agree to it. That's after they had yelled at me and told me they knowed I was there and that if I didn't quit sayin' I wasn't I was gonna be put in the lectric chair. And they would say this one was there or that one was there and that Pee Wee killed them and then they'd say Pee Wee and Knoy killed them.

"One lawman would say, 'It was late at night, wasn't it?' Another would say, 'Did Pee Wee shoot him?' Then another would say, 'Were the headlights on or did somebody have a flashlight?' And then, 'Walter had the shovels, right? So Knoy must have had the light'."

So I tried to go along with what they wanted, and they promised I wouldn't have to go to the 'lectric chair if I helped them get the people that killed Jessie and them. They told me that they knew who did it but they had to have someone who could say they seen it. They said they knew I was there because people had seen me leave with Walter that same night."

"Will you tell the truth now and swear it before Jesus? Can you look right at that picture, Sandy, and tell me what happened?"

"The truth is what I've said to you, Mr. Grady. I wasn't there. Some stuff Pee Wee has told me, but I don't really know nothin' about it. He would just say things like, 'We carried Johnny Sellers up to the country; he won't be causin' no more trouble,' or 'We won't be hearin' from him agin,' and I didn't ask no more about it. I was pretty sure what he meant and I didn't want to know any more than that. I swear before God, that's the truth, Mr. Query. I'll tell that to anybody you say as long as you'll stand by me and not let them put me in no 'lectric chair for somethin' I ain't done and barely know about."

"You just tell the truth, Sandy, I'll stand by you and so will plenty of other people," Query tried to assure the frightened girl who was struggling through her dilemma with her childlike mentality.

Sandy recanted her statement, both by affidavit and in a personal confrontation, with Solicitor Summerford where she stood her ground. In the face of threats of prosecution for perjury or as an accessory to murder, if not murder, she had found somewhere a new courage and would not acquiesce to his insistence that she had been present at the murder scene. As angry as their confrontations had become, Query could not fault Summerford for his frustration or his warnings to the frightened and challenged young woman in telling her that she could be subjecting herself to imprisonment if she was intentionally lying to the police and interfering with their investigation.

Query bolstered her by warning Summerford that intimidation by the police had already resulted in one false statement from the easily intimidated girl and that he seemed determined to replicate rather than rectify.

"This change in her statement really has the ring of truth, Kenneth. I'm telling you, she told me that it was not true after telling me that the picture of Christ on the wall of her little apartment belonged to her and that she believed in him as her personal savior. She recanted her statement implicating Judy while she sat there crying and looking at the picture of Christ."

"Well why would she have given that statement to begin with? How do I know someone hasn't threatened her and made her change it? She may not be afraid of your boy, but I'll guarantee that she is still afraid of Gaskins."

"Gaskins hasn't told her to recant. He hates Judy. I tried to talk to him about it with Monk present. Gaskins said that Knoy Judy had nothing to do with any murders but that he wasn't going to testify for him because he would have to incriminate himself. He also said that he didn't like Judy and didn't particularly care what happened to him. That's the problem, Ken. I can't produce any witness to prove he wasn't there because they would have to admit being there."

"I'm just not buying that she would give a statement like this if the boy wasn't even there."

"Damn it, Ken, let me threaten her with the electric chair and give me the authority to hold her and surround her with people with guns and she'll say you were there. She didn't give a statement to the police telling them what happened, she agreed to what they were telling her. According to her, she started out saying that it was what Walter had told her, not that she was there. Gaskins may have told her what to say thinking that Knoy would be able to prove that he was somewhere else and thereby cast doubt on what she said about Gaskins being there. That would have ruined her credibility in case she ever testified against Gaskins," Query continued. "Or maybe he wanted her to incriminate Knoy. Apparently, they've competed for two different women, Jessie and Donna, and with Gaskins locked up, if Judy's out, he wins. I don't think Gaskins likes to lose. I also feel sure that Walter has told her something about all of this, but I doubt that any of us will ever know what he told her or whether it was the truth or just something that Gaskins was setting up."

"The fact of the matter is the statement she gave you is worthless because of the affidavit she has given me, but I also know that the affidavit she gave me is equally worthless for the same reason. But, your threatening her with further prosecution is absolutely senseless. I think she is entirely under Gaskins control when she is in his presence. So in the long run, nothing you or I can do will determine what she does or says once you put her in a courtroom with Gaskins actually there.

This confrontation occurred more than once when Query was arguing that charges against Knoy Judy should be dropped since Sandy's patently unreliable testimony was the only hard evidence against him. The original witness who believed that she had seen Judy with Gaskins, Jessie and Johnny in the general area was the only other evidence. Although she had quit talking to Query after a brief interview early in the case, Query believed that it was extremely unlikely that she would make a positive identification of Judy.

The quandary for the lawyer and his client was that Summerford remained unchanged in his determination to pursue a murder conviction even after Sandy recanted her statement about Knoy's participation in the murder. Summerford also remained determined to call Sandy as a witness. Under normal circumstances the fact that she had varied the facts in her original statements to police and had ultimately recanted the statement altogether would have satisfied Query. He would have felt comfortable that a jury could be convinced that there was reasonable doubt of Judy's guilt. But in this case, the fact that Judy's association with Gaskins could be easily proven and the fact that the victims were Judy's estranged wife and her lover caused him grave concern.

"Kenneth, it is more and more obvious that this kid has just been sucked into this because he worked with Gaskins and because his ex was one of Gaskins' victims. His parents can probably establish that he was in Charleston when the murders occurred but since there is no precise time of death an alibi defense is very difficult to establish. Let him take the polygraph and if he passes it then let him out of this mess," Query literally begged of Summerford.

"If he can pass the test given by someone in whom you have confidence, then you will know that he was not involved. You can also satisfy law enforcement and the public by releasing the results of the test," Query continued.

"I'm not givin' him any damned polygraph. I've got a statement that says he was there holding the light for Gaskins to shoot his wife and I'm going to try him for the death penalty or he can plead to a life sentence. Everybody says Gaskins can beat the polygraph. Maybe he taught your boy his trick."

"Well, let me give him a polygraph. I'll have the guy come here to the detention center and give it to him."

"No way. No polygraph and I'll make sure the jail doesn't let you bring anybody in there to give him one."

"Still on the relentless pursuit of justice, eh?" Query scoffed as he walked away.

Summerford did not call either Judy or Neely for trial on May 24, 1976, but jury selection began on May 31, 1976, in the trial of Walter Neely for the murder of Dennis Bellamy. Cantrell and Staubes filed voluminous briefs on the issue of the constitutionality of the death penalty, already seriously in jeopardy in light of the Furman decision by the U.S. Supreme Court that found the death penalty unconstitutional in another state. Neely's lawyers filed similarly complex briefs on the failure of the solicitor's office to provide the defense with statements or evidence that might tend to prove the innocence of the defendant. Specifically, they pointed out that it was apparent that several witnesses had given multiple statements which were inconsistent with each other or had testified in contradiction to earlier statements and yet the lawyers had not been provided with the statements. Query either joined in these motions or filed his own versions of the same.

Motions were filed again by Cantrell and Staubes for a change of venue citing not only the earlier publicity but also the minute by minute coverage of the Gaskins trial during which Neely was mentioned over and over. Affidavits were filed in support of the venue motions pointing out, in addition to the matters covered in the motions filed by Hinnant, that during the earlier trial the answers of some of the potential jurors were not only patently incredible but utterly preposterous. People who lived within the Pee Dee area claimed not to have seen nor heard any publicity about the bodies or graves found in the Prospect community. In fact, it was hard to hear a conversation about anything else. It is not uncommon for an unscrupulous person fascinated by a high profile case to deny any prior knowledge in an effort to become a juror. Judge McEachern nevertheless continued to deny the motions and merely asked Summerford for his assurance that any statements would be provided to the defense and assuring the lawyers that he would carefully examine potential jurors for any bias.

Cantrell, Staubes and Query believed that it was highly likely that the judge had already committed errors in these rulings that were sufficiently egregious to warrant reversal of any conviction on appeal. Query was present during the motions and conferred actively with the Cantrell and Staubes since all of the issues were pertinent to his defense of Judy.

As jury selection began the attorneys argued that they should have the right to ask the questions of the jurors as is the practice in many states, a process known by its Latin name *voir dire*. Judge McEachern insisted that he would pose the questions and that the attorneys for the defense and the state could submit written requests for him to ask specific questions. Beyond name and address hardly a question was asked of a potential juror that was not objected to by the tenacious young defense lawyers who were emboldened by the advantage of not having to practice regularly before the now openly cantankerous judge. After questioning, they raised numerous objections to the qualification of each juror. Jurors and alternates were nevertheless eventually chosen.

The jury finally having been selected, the trial began with brief openings by the attorneys and then testimony. Even during Summerford's opening argument, Cantrell made objections that are normally avoided as a matter of courtesy during arguments by opposing counsel. He apologized as he objected explaining that the argument was so far outside the rules that it necessitated the interruptions. This clearly established the contentiousness that characterized the proceedings.

Glen Ard testified that Walter Neely had taken him to the grave sites and that while he had been either unable or simply reluctant to point out an actual grave, Walter had shown Ard a small area and pointed out the peculiarity of cut saplings that had been inserted into the ground. Ard said that Walter had denied knowing the identity of any of the people buried in any of the graves despite the fact that the bodies of his wife, his wife's lover, his wife's brother and her half-brother were among those discovered.

On cross examination Ard said that he had taken Walter and left the other officers and agents at the country store and driven with him to a wooded area. He denied having given Walter whiskey or having threatened him with a gun from his glove compartment. When Cantrell sarcastically posed the question as to why on earth Walter would have suddenly shown a stranger where the graves were located after two days of avoiding giving any straight answers to questions or circumventing the identification of any place, that he actually remembered. Ard replied:

"Let's just say two old country boys came to an understanding," chuckling slightly. "I think he just wanted to get something off his chest, but then he couldn't bring himself to finish it and admit he had killed them."

Cantrell urged that the second part of Ard's answer was unresponsive to his question and was intended to prejudice the jury. He moved for a mistrial. The motion was denied but the tone and tenor of the trial was re-confirmed.

Shirley Evans was again a major witness confirming that Walter Neely had been present at her daddy's trailer on the night of October 10, 1975, when she had seen Bellamy and Knight.

The pool hall employee identified Neely as the person who left North Charleston with Bellamy and Knight on October 10, 1975.

The defense began its case with a psychiatrist who testified that Walter had an IQ of 60 and that he functioned generally at the level of a nine or ten year old and would be easily led and dominated by an older person with a strong personality, such as Gaskins.

As is usually the case, the defense attorneys continued to attempt to negotiate with the prosecution, seeking a mutually acceptable plea to a lesser offense that would result in reducing the penalty to which the defendant would be exposed. Such negotiations continued on the part of both sides because a plea insures a conviction for the state, forecloses the possibility of an appeal and the incumbent risk of a new trial while the potential sentence is reduced for the defendant or as in the present case, the prospect of a death sentence is eliminated.

Following the mid-morning break on the fourth day of the trial, the prosecution and defense attorneys announced to the judge that they had a matter to take up outside the presence of the jury. Visibly tiring of the constant issues of law that demanded specific rulings by him on matters of evidence and law, the judge reluctantly agreed. An essential aspect of every criminal trial involving a serious crime is a sort of "trap the judge" by which the judge is forced by the defense to make one ruling after another in the hope that he will err sufficiently on at least one ruling to require a reversal by the appellate court. That strategy was certainly in play. After half an hour, the attorneys announced that they were ready to call the next witness. This was a clear message that the attempt at negotiating a plea had broken down.

Walter Neely did not testify but others testified to Neely's presence in North Charleston on the date that Dennis Bellamy and John Henry Knight were allegedly murdered.

The jury returned a verdict of guilty of the willful and premeditated murder of Dennis Bellamy and of Accessory before and after the fact of murder in the same case. Judge McEachern sentenced Neely to death by electrocution.

CHAPTER FIFTY FIVE

Knoy You're Up

The Furman decision overturning the death penalty cases in states with statutes similar to South Carolina had not been officially adopted by South Carolina but Query knew that it had changed the playing field dramatically and would soon be applied to South Carolina.

For Knoy Judy the death penalty was effectively off the table, Query believed.

After being advised that the solicitor was calling his case for trial, Knoy told his attorney that he wanted to plead.

That night in the detention center, after the guilty verdict in the Neely trial, Query suggested to Knoy that they embark on a dangerous tack.

"I've had all I can take, Mr. Query. Like you've said, when we go in there for a trial they'll find me guilty just because they can put me around Pee Wee. I want to give up. This is killin' me any way and it's killin' my daddy," he said barely able to mouth the words.

"Knoy, Summerford's never going to back off on a plea to murder. Sandy has admitted that her statement is absolutely not true. He can't threaten you with a real death penalty anymore and I think there is something that we can try that might move him off of the murder. It's a pretty dangerous and desperate move but I think we can trick him into giving you the polygraph test; otherwise my fear is that he'll try you for murder. With a jury just knowing that you lived and worked with Gaskins, coupled with the fact that the victims included your ex-wife and her lover, bolstered by the statement of that woman who thinks she saw you with Pee Wee, Jessie and Johnny, lays a stage for them. When you add whatever Sandy ends up saying at the trial, it will probably be enough to convict you.

Shoot, the way things are stirred up around here the prosecutor can pretty much get up and say to a jury: 'this guy is a friend of Pee Wee Gaskins and he is charged with murder' and the trial would be over no matter what we have to say."

"What kind of trick, Mr. Query? I thought you just said he would never get off of that murder charge."

"Summerford constantly operates in two different arenas. On the one hand he basically says to us: 'I don't care whether he did it or not I'm going for a conviction of murder.' While at the same time he is saying to the public: 'Oh my, if this boy is innocent, you don't have anything to worry about. I'll find out myself and be sure he is not wrongfully convicted.' If we can expose him to the public, let them know that the charge may not be true, we could change the odds. My thought is that we'll pretend to confess. I'll tell him that you are going to confess to everything in Sandy's statement except the part about Sandy being there. We'll have just enough differences that he'll demand a lie detector to prove that your version is the truth so he can profess to the newspapers and TV that he forced you to tell the truth and nothing but the truth by making you take a lie detector. Then, he can present it at your guilty plea and take credit for having solved the mystery," Query confided.

"I can't even remember what all she said. None of it is true and I just don't remember it," Knoy answered. "Mr. Query, I'm so scared I can't remember who they say was buried out there. I've never been there. Hell, I've never been here in this town before. How can they think I murdered anybody?"

"I have a copy of her statement or at least one of her statements with me. We'll go over it before I leave. After all this time of refusing you the lie detector, he's going to turn around and demand that you take one to prove that your confession is true and that he has been right all along. When he does he'll send you to SLED to take the test or have SLED come over here to give it to you. Before they test you they will go over all of the questions and talk to you about your statement. At that point you will tell them that the statement is not true, that you made it all up and that you are not guilty of anything to do with Gaskins. You'll tell them that you want to take the test to prove you didn't do it. They'll give you the test and the newspapers will plaster it everywhere."

"How will the newspapers know about it?"

"You don't have to worry about that. They've got people on the inside at SLED that call them before the ink can dry on a report. Look at all of the leaks that there have been since the beginning of this case. If no one leaks it, I'll tell the news people about it. I think Summerford will even back off after you pass the test. He is a strong believer in the polygraph, especially if the SLED guys administer it. He's really not out to convict you if you're innocent, he's just got a lot of conflicting evidence and he's convinced that you are guilty of something. He's too lazy to look at any other possibilities, but more than anything he doesn't want us to embarrass him before the public. He'll think that if he has a polygraph that confirms your confession, he can preach about how he was right about everybody in this case from the beginning. I don't think he can pass that up. The biggest thing about him is his ego."

This strategy was extremely risky and Query knew it but he was convinced that in a trial the prosecution would manage to link Knoy with Gaskins and equally importantly with two of the victims. Once the link was made, there was at least the appearance of a motive since Knoy's estranged wife, Jessie Judy, appeared to have been killed with her paramour Johnny Sellers. That apparent lovers' triangle constituted the most familiar motive known to man and one likely to convince a jury, particularly one that knew the now infamous Gaskins had been convicted of cold blooded murder. Either way, the worst result was a life sentence that Query saw as unavoidable in an immediate trial but believed might be avoided if he could create enough doubt of success in the mind of the now emboldened prosecutor.

The following day Query went to Summerford to announce the invented confession. Summerford immediately sent for Judy to be brought from the detention center to his office in the same building.

"All right, Kenneth, he'll talk with you but we have to agree, and I am recording this as you can see by the little recorder on the table, that what he says here today cannot be used against him and that it will be a statement made by him without having been advised of his rights against self incrimination and that this statement cannot be used against him in any way whatsoever. It is informational and hypothetical for the sole purpose of exploring a plea and a final resolution of this case. He may be willing to take a polygraph if you insist on it, but we'll have to ask him about that," Query baited.

Good fortune finally smiled on Judy in the bizarre conference. Summerford was attempting to extract every gory detail from the young defendant. In his exuberance, he confused the facts of another case with those of the Gaskins case. Recalling the details of an autopsy in an unrelated case, he suddenly demanded of Judy, "And after he killed that young girl, your wife, then he cut her heart out didn't he?"

Judy, totally confused by the question that inserted a bizarre fact that he had never heard before, denied it. Query, sensing an opportunity, asked for a break to confer with his client.

"Just agree with whatever he says, Knoy. He's talking about a different case. I remember people talking about it. It will just prove that you were making it all up when we take the polygraph."

They returned and Knoy agreed that Gaskins had cut out the heart of Knoy's wife when he killed her. He continued to agree with every other detail suggested with the notable exception of the identities of the people who were supposed to have been present. He denied that Jessie Judy was killed at the same time as Johnny and denied that Sandy had actually been present, alleging that she was merely repeating the story as it had been told to her by Gaskins.

"So you're saying Jessie, your wife, was killed at different time then Sellers," questioned Summerford.

"Later the same day and put in the same grave," interjected Query trying to avoid another stumble by his client over a new detail. "Ken, remember Dr. Sexton said there was a small amount of dirt between the two bodies indicating to him that Jessie may have been buried after Johnny albeit in the same grave."

To the delight of Query and Judy, Summerford demanded that the accuracy of Judy's statement be confirmed by a polygraph test. He further stipulated that the test had to be administered by the senior polygraph examiner at SLED headquarters in Columbia.

"I'm going to set it up for Monday, if you want to be there," Summerford snapped at Query. "No delays, I'll ask them to drop everything else and set it up," Summerford insisted.

"I'll be there." Query assured, "If I have anything in Charleston, I'll get it continued or ask someone to cover for me. Kerry Koon is a sharp young lawyer in my office and he'll cover for me."

After the meeting Query rushed to Charleston to explain the dramatic plan to Mr. and Mrs. Judy. They were alarmed to say the least.

"I can't believe it, Mr. Query. How can you let him say he did something that he didn't do," Mr. Judy asked, stunned by the prospect. "Especially something so horrible," Mrs. Judy lamented.

"Because we don't have any leverage. If Summerford just links Knoy to Gaskins and Jessie and Johnny, he's ninety per cent of the way home with all of the publicity about Pee Wee. They'll get a conviction. We just don't have hard evidence to exclude Knoy from the formula. All we have is his denial. We have to try something drastic. They won't be able to use this statement if the plan doesn't work, but it may keep him from being able to take the stand."

"How can you win if he doesn't testify?"

"Well, the burden is on them to prove their case against him and I would be very concerned to have him testify and face cross examination by Kenneth Summerford anyway. Cross examination is not just questions; it's an argument between the lawyer and the witness. The lawyer is continuously making statements and demanding that the witness admit that the statement is correct or the lawyer is pointing out differences between two things that the witness said and making a minor difference sound like a huge lie. Knoy can't win that battle. Kenneth does it every day and he is ruthless. He makes mistakes putting in facts that are incorrect but he just glosses over it and keeps on attacking. He would make Knoy look like Gaskins' best friend and full time criminal partner. This plan might seem crazy but I think it is our only chance to get Summerford to stop and really look at the fact that Knoy is not guilty."

"What if he still wants to try him for murder?" Mr. Judy asked quietly, barely able to control the tremors in his voice.

"I don't think he will, Mr. Judy. While I don't like him and don't like the way he pushes people around, I don't think that he would ever try to convict someone of a crime that he really didn't think they had committed. In a way, it's part of the reason he's so dangerous. He becomes so convinced that a defendant is guilty that he devotes himself entirely to proving it and that belief, right or wrong, allows him to bulldoze over a defendant without hesitation, completely convinced that he is doing the right thing and unmoved by anything not consistent with his theory of the case. I think if something slams him in the face that says this man is innocent, he will stop and re-evaluate. When he sees that Knoy is not lying, I think he'll reconsider, especially if he knows that I have the means to expose him if he doesn't."

"I think this will work, Mr. Query. We are doing one thing while pretending to do the opposite. It's a Cherokee thing. I like the feel of this. My heart tells me that this will work," said the mother.

"Well, I hope we're right. It's risky but I think we have to do something to stop this steamroller," Query replied.

"We're gonna go with what you say, Mr. Query. We believe in you," Mr. Judy confirmed.

Monday morning Query drove two hours to SLED headquarters on Broad River Road, on the side of Columbia opposite of Charleston. After he was admitted to the offices of the polygraph examiners, he was shown the examination room where the test would be administered. He was then taken into a small adjacent office where he was surprised to see that the examination room could be observed through a one way mirror. Even more to his surprise, he was told that he would be able to remain in the office behind the two way glass with the other examiner and watch and hear the legendary Lieutenant Faulk administer the examination.

More than fifteen minutes after Query arrived he saw Knoy Judy led into the small suite of offices used by the polygraph team. The dark haired young man was fully adorned in leg shackles and belly chain with an individual cuff for each hand permanently attached to each side of the belly chain. His hands were held at the top of his hipbones and the movement restricted to just a few inches. As Knoy shuffled along in jail coveralls and jail flip flops, Query could not help but be moved by the look of abject fear on the young face.

After short introductions Lt. Faulk directed that the chains be removed and escorted Knoy into the examination room.

"You want me in there to watch him?" asked the deputy escorting Knoy.

"I've been in this room with a few bad guys over the years," replied the white haired sixty year old polygraph expert. "I'll be just fine on my own."

Inside the smallish room Knoy was seated in a special chair with an elongated arm rest which allowed the blood pressure cuff to be comfortably attached at his bicep. Sensors were attached to his hand to analyze changes in galvanic skin response occurring as a result of perspiration. Sensors were attached to his chest with adhesives to monitor heartbeat and a bulky hose that looked like a small vacuum cleaner hose was wrapped entirely around his chest to monitor respiration.

All attachments in place, Lieutenant Faulk began to explain how the equipment worked and to outline the procedure. He then questioned Knoy about the statement that he had given to Kenneth Summerford. Knoy acknowledged that in his interview with Summerford that he had recited each part of the statement which had been modeled after that given by Sandy. He acknowledged that his statement was similar to the one given by Sandy Gaskins but pointed out that his statement contradicted Sandy's account by denying Sandy and Jessie had been present when Sellers was killed.

When he had completed reading the statement, the lieutenant asked if it was true just as Query had told Knoy to expect.

Knoy immediately stated, "None of that is true. I have never been to Prospect. I don't even know where it is." Knoy then directed the veteran examiner's attention to the portion of the statement that included the removal of the heart that had been mistakenly added by Summerford. He said that he had agreed with Summerford on that point to make it clear that he was just going along with what the solicitor was saying.

At the conclusion of this shocking disclosure the veteran policeman and polygraph expert instructed Knoy to remain seated, exited the room and came quickly from the examination room into the small office where Query and the other examiner were observing.

"Did you hear that? He is denying everything in the statement. He said he doesn't even know where Prospect is, that he has never been there. What am I supposed to do now?"

"Give the test, Lieutenant. This is what we have been waiting for since he was arrested," Query blurted out unable to restrain his excitement.

"Why would he say all of that, if none of it is true?"

"It's the only way that we could get him to the machine. The solicitor wouldn't let us take the test as long as we said he wasn't guilty but when we made up this story, he wanted it confirmed by the polygraph. I want you to give him the test. I've been asking for a test since the girl Sandy recanted her statement. She has totally recanted and says that the statement she gave was untrue. Best evidence is the stuff about the heart. The Medical Examiner did not find that her heart had been cut out. We want to prove that this boy wasn't there when anyone was killed, that he has never even been to Prospect."

"I'll be glad to give it to him. I've used the polygraph to show the guilt of a lot of people but I'm always OK when the test can show that someone is not guilty, the point is to find the truth. The polygraph is a good way of accomplishing that, if it's administered right. The machine is only as good as the operator. But this was ordered by the solicitor of Florence County to confirm the statement given to him. I can't give it without talking to him —letting him know what is going on here."

"If you call him, he'll say don't do it. We've been asking for this test for months."

"Well, I feel like I have to call him. I'll tell him I think we should go ahead with the test."

"Okay, but let me talk to him if he says no," Query added.

Query listened as Faulk described the events of the morning. Faulk listened intently for a minute and then said:

"I think we should give him the test, Solicitor, but I won't give it if you tell me not to. I understand, sir, but the lawyer says he wants to talk to you," and after a pause while he listened he turned toward Query. "He says no test and he doesn't want to talk to you."

"Tell him I'm leaving here and going to the TV station and then to the State newspaper."

The lieutenant repeated what he was told.

"Here, he says he'll talk to you but no test."

Query took the offered phone handset and moved close to the desk.

"Good morning, Kenneth."

"What the hell are you pulling," roared Summerford through the receiver with such force that the two polygraph examiners had to restrain chuckles.

"If you refuse to let him take this test, I'm going to call a press conference right here on the front steps of SLED and I'm going to tell them that as long as he was confessing, you were demanding a test but as soon as he professed his innocence, you were adamant in directing the examiners not to give the test. I'll tell them you refused even though they were willing to give the test and recommended going forward with the test. I can have a dozen TV people and a reporter from every newspaper in the state here within the hour and you have my promise that I'll do it."

"Come on back here and we'll talk about it."

"Not a chance. We're here, he's hooked up. Give him the test or turn on your television," Query said struggling to restrain his anger.

"All right, all right, give him the damn test, but it doesn't change anything and it's not admissible," Summerford finally agreed.

The test was administered and Lt. Faulk watched carefully as the multiple arms of his machine moved across the chart graphically depicting the measured reactions in different colors of ink. When the test was complete, he again hurried from the polygraph room into the small office.

"He's a very good subject," he said mostly to his associate, and then he turned to Query. "I mean he registers well on the machine. We start by asking test questions, having him be truthful on some obvious questions like where he was born or his mother's name and then having him be intentionally deceptive on some other equally obvious questions. We see whether the deception shows up on the chart. He registers very nicely. I'll study the chart carefully in a minute but I can say without hesitation that he shows no signs of deception. That is to say, that it appears he is telling the truth. According to the test, he did not kill anyone or assist in anyone being killed, he was not present when anyone was killed and he has never even been to Prospect, South Carolina."

"Will you call the solicitor in Florence and tell him?"

"I'll send him my report."

"Could you possibly call him now? You see what I'm dealing with. I'm leaving here and going straight over there. If you call him and tell him then I don't have to try to convince him that he passed."

"Let me do my complete analysis first and then I'll call him. You can stay here with me while I do it; I'll show you some of what we look for on the charts and what the actual questions were."

The elderly lieutenant was an ardent proponent of the polygraph and enjoyed teaching the art of the polygraph as much or more than administering the tests. He showed Query his preliminary questions and then the test questions, pointed out on the multilevel charts the variations in the different measurements that were depicted on the chart from the preliminary questions and then from the actual test. He pointed out the consistencies of the measurements when there was no deception and the reactivity when deception occurred with the test questions.

Finally he stated, "There was absolutely no indication of deception throughout the critical questions. He registers very distinctly on the test questions and shows no signs of deception during the real test and that's what I will report."

Lieutenant Faulk called Solicitor Summerford when he had completed his analysis of the charts. When he had finished the call he turned to Query and said:

"He just asked me if I was sure about the results. You heard what I said; I told him that I would bet my career on this one. That boy was really a good subject the way he registered. I think Summerford'll listen to you. I've done a lot of tests for that man and he knows that I know what I'm doing and that I don't hedge one way or the other."

"Thank you, Lieutenant. I really appreciate your making that call."

"Well good luck to you and to your client. The boy admitted that he'd done some stealing so maybe this whole thing will get him back on the right path."

"Yes sir, I hope so. Y'all take care."

Query drove at ninety on the way to Florence and found Kenneth a little after two PM.

"I know you'll want to get the official report, Kenneth, but I hope this will be the end for the case against Knoy."

"It'll be the end if your boy will plea to common law murder."

"What are you talking about? You've got a polygraph by the best guy in the state that says he's never even been to Prospect."

"That's the offer."

"This is unbelievable. Y'all have had this kid locked up all this time, now it turns out he's innocent and you're going to put him in prison to keep from saying you made a mistake?"

115

"You've got a lie detector test. They're not reliable, that's why they aren't admissible in court."

"So, they only work when they confirm what you think. Come on, Kenneth, this kid didn't kill or cause anyone to be killed."

"All right, I'll give you a one shot deal. Plead tomorrow and I'll let him plead to accessory after the fact. That's the deal and after tomorrow it's off the table."

"Where does that come from? What could he have possibly done to help somebody escape or cover up the crime if he didn't know about it? You're willing to go to trial because you know in this climate you can just get up and say this guy is indicted for murder and he knows Pee Wee Gaskins. The State rests."

"That's my last offer. If he had told us what he knew about all of these people, we would have gotten to the bottom of this a lot quicker. I think that amounts to accessory after. Besides, I'm not completely convinced that he didn't have Gaskins get rid of his wife and her boyfriend."

"There's something else I need to show you. While you were down there threatening me, we did a search of Judy's cell. This is what we found. A complete written version of his statement."

"That was written for me, Kenneth. I think that it is protected by the attorney/client privilege."

"It doesn't have your name anywhere on it. I think it's a confession."

"Oh bullshit, Kenneth. It's even got that crap about cutting out somebody's heart in it. He was writing this so he wouldn't forget the story," Query surmised.

"Doesn't matter why; if he doesn't plead in the morning, I'll use it in his murder trial."

Query met with Judy and explained the offer. Exasperated he yelled, "Why in the hell did you write that stuff down?"

"I couldn't remember the story. I had to write it down in order to say it again. I'd never heard that stuff before. I'm sittin' down here you know, I don't know what all is going on up there. I knew that you told me that I would have to be able to tell the same story when I did the test. I've never taken a lie detector test. I was afraid if I forgot something they would fail me so I wrote it all down."

"It was a stupid thing to do without asking me about it. There's nothing we can do but fight to get it suppressed because it was intended for me and no one else to see."

Query went on to explain the offer in detail: "It carries a maximum of ten years and you'll be sentenced to the maximum. There is no point in pretending that there is any chance of anything less than that. You'll be eligible for parole in three and we'll do everything we can to get you out on the first shot at parole. Otherwise, I think we can have a hotly contested trial and at the end you will be wrongfully convicted of murder and sentenced to life in prison. If we can cause them to make enough mistakes we might get a new trial, but that's what you get –another trial."

"Ten years. You're telling me to plead to ten years when I don't know anything about any of this."

"Knoy, if they try you for murder, they'll get a conviction. Ten years might be unfair but on the other hand you've got a string of break-ins that you got away with. Anytime you start getting all out of shape about doing time just pretend you're doing it for those. You've still got a couple of charges down in Charleston; I'll get them thrown into the deal. I know you weren't going to get any ten years for them but at least they'll be gone. I'm sorry, Knoy. I don't like it but I sure don't want to come see you in fifteen years to talk about how much time you have left. I've never told anybody to plead guilty to something they didn't do, but I can't let you get a life sentence out of this, Knoy. That's twenty years to do. We can't let that happen, but I don't see avoiding a conviction as long as they can link you to Gaskins. We can go to trial and at the end of it I promise you that you will say that I did a great job. But I'm afraid that the jury will convict you because of the connection to Gaskins and to Jessie Judy."

The following day, July 21, 1976, Knoy Judy entered an Alford Plea to Accessory After the Fact of Murder. The Alford Plea, named for a North Carolina case that approved the procedure, involves pleading guilty without admitting actual guilt. The court is informed by the attorney for the defendant that the defendant does not admit he is guilty of committing the crime but rather having examined the case against him concedes that it is likely that he will be found guilty if tried before a jury. The Alford plea was permitted only after another caustic argument with the solicitor.

"I don't believe in Alford pleas," boomed the solicitor in the anteroom outside the courtroom. "I want defendants to admit in open court what they did."

"How am I supposed to do that when my client says he didn't do it and I have a polygraph test given by the best examiner in the country that says he's not only innocent but he's never even been to Prospect?" countered Query in a voice sufficiently raised to assure that all of the courtroom personnel in the anteroom would hear.

"All right, he'll still go to prison for ten years and it gets treated the same as a guilty plea for sentencing," the solicitor said with undisguised menace. "I'll tell the judge we're ready and that it's an Alford.

The court does in fact treat an Alford Plea the same as an ordinary guilty plea and the potential sentence is the same. Knoy Judy was sentenced to the maximum penalty of ten years. After court the jailers allowed Query and Mr. and Mrs. Judy to meet briefly with Knoy.

"I'm sure we did the right thing, Mr. Query, but I don't want to do ten years," Knoy lamented, tears rolling down his cheeks which were no longer bright from the sun and which retained some color only as a result of his Native American heritage.

"I'm sure you'll probably hate me every day you're in there, Knoy. And you'll think, 'I wouldn't be in here except for Query's crazy scheme,' but I truly hope that we just saved you from a life sentence that you didn't deserve," Query replied.

"I'll be there when the time comes and we'll do everything possible to get them to grant you parole on the first try. You have my word on that, all of you do," Query said as much to the parents as to Knoy.

Slightly less than three years later Query would meet the Judy parents at the parole board in Columbia. Knoy was brought over and they were put in a hallway to await the call of their case. A member of the staff called Query aside and told him that there was not a full board.

"You have to get every vote if you go today but you have the right to wait for a full board and then you only need a majority," his friend told him.

"Well Knoy here we go again. There's always a strange wrinkle." He explained the procedural anomaly and they waived the hearing to come back the next month.

At that the next session Query appeared before the parole board and began by explaining that he had appeared before that board for the first time when he was still a law student. He said that he was told by his professor and by the board, that rule one was to never try to convince the board that your client had not been guilty in the first place. Not to re-try your case before the board.

"Well, Mr. Chairman and Members of the board I'd like to begin today by breaking that rule and telling you that my client did not commit this crime." Query then went on to relate the entire lie detector story.

A senior member of the board, Cotton Lackey, who had seen Query at his first appearance as a law student and at every appearance since, questioned him:

"Mr. Query, are you telling us that this fellow had nothing to do with any of the murders or the cover up and yet you pled him guilty to Accessory after the Fact of Murder?

"Yes sir, technically we entered an Alford plea and did not admit guilt but I am telling you I believed that was the only way I could prevent his being convicted of murder. I told him he had gotten away with some breaking and entering and he should just grit his teeth and accept that he was doing the time that he deserved for those crimes. Not only am I telling you he didn't do it; I'm telling you that Lieutenant Faulk of Sled confirmed it on the lie detector and in fact confirmed that Knoy had never even been to Prospect."

After a few minutes of deliberation the board granted parole to Knoy Judy.

CHAPTER FIFTY SIX

Query Associates Grisso

On the day of Knoy's plea on July 21, 1976, when Query was leaving the courtroom, he was approached by an attractive young woman whom he recognized as the sister of Pee Wee Gaskins. Blonde and shapely she was dressed in a conservative but nicely fitted suit, as had been her custom throughout the Gaskins trial. She wore spiked heels that accentuated her shapely legs and she was over a decade younger than Gaskins. She had been present for every single court appearance by Gaskins and every minute of his trial. Throughout she sat quietly with her mother and was at all times attentive to her. She worked in an office and during breaks utilized her experience to help the defense attorneys by making calls or taking papers back and forth to their office several floors below.

So much younger was she than Gaskins that she had known him mostly as the half-brother who came and went from the prisons of the south, but she had also known him as generous to her and her mother and always protective. Men of all ages who were attracted to the beautiful young woman approached carefully and minded their manners, well determined to avoid the wrath of her tiny protector even when his protection was from afar.

On that day at the court, as on most, she was straight to the point and focused on the business at hand. She asked Query if he would be willing to represent her brother on the remainder of the charges against him. She said that she was making the request on behalf of her mother and herself and that while they had very little money, she would be helping her mother and they would make payments.

"We think Mr. Hinnant and Mr. DeBerry are wonderful. It's not that. We just know that they have a lot of public defender cases. Mr. Hinnant said the court might even appoint someone else if Pee Wee is tried again. We just want someone who will fight for Pee Wee and we've seen you fight. I was in the court when Summerford tried to have you put out of court so you couldn't help Monk. That convinced me. I don't know what all Pee Wee must've done but I want him treated fairly," she explained.

The solicitor had asked to have Query excluded from the court because he was not an attorney of record for the defendant Gaskins and yet he was regularly conferring with Gaskins' counsel.

"Oh, I think Mr. Query has been admitted to the bar and if Mr. Hinnant wants to have him sit behind counsel table and if they choose to enter into discourse with him regarding their client or the proceedings, I believe they have that right. I will not, of course, allow it to delay the progress of the trial or create a distraction. Is that clear to everyone?" the judge had ruled.

Query was admittedly fascinated by the case and the strange little man who helped little old ladies, understood as much about courtroom maneuverings as many lawyers, brought an entertaining sense of humor to the most dire moment and yet appeared to commit murder with no more hesitation than when he discarded a worn part from one of the engines he expertly repaired. The case was already the number one news story in the state and was on the front page or first page, second section of every newspaper in the state week after week. Some of the high profile cases that Query had tried in Charleston had garnered significant media coverage and he was not unaware of the effect of media attention on the activity of his phone lines in the office. He was fresh from the clash with Summerford and his ego drove him toward another contest. Those considerations coupled with Query's determined battle against the death penalty and the sheer temptation to remain involved in such a fascinating and notorious case made the proposition too appealing and he agreed.

Query and Cantrell had talked openly about the possibility of a book about their experiences in the case and Query felt certain that Cantrell could be convinced to participate in the remaining cases against Gaskins since the Neely case had been concluded. Cantrell explained though that he was campaigning for the state senate and the impositions upon his time between the run for the legislature and his legal practice made the extent of his involvement questionable. He at first agreed to be co-counsel but then called Query to say that the reaction from his supporters was not good.

He said, "Look, I'm in but I don't want this to keep me out of the senate. If that appears to be where this is going, I'll bail. Just want to let you know up front."

"I understand perfectly," replied Query. "I think we're a good team but I would rather have you in the Senate for a long time than in this case for a short while. Just keep me posted."

Query then approached his good friend Bud Grisso about working together on the case. Grisso had recently completed four years as the U. S. Attorney for South Carolina. Before he was appointed U. S. Attorney, Grisso had been the solicitor for the Tenth Judicial Circuit. Query knew that Grisso would bring some political clout and that his face and trial ability would be well known to judges all around a state in which judges literally travelled the circuits. Circuit Court Judges were assigned by the state Supreme Court to travel from county to county for scheduled sessions of civil or criminal court. Grisso's skills and reputation would be invaluable in future confrontations with Kenneth Summerford.

Grisso agreed to participate in the representation and the two of them asked Cantrell to join them to the extent that he could afford the time. Cantrell initially agreed but later confided to Query that his hopes to take his political career to another level had caused him to conclude that involvement with the high profile murder cases would not be politically wise.

Query and Grisso filed appearances in the remaining cases, each of which Summerford assured them he intended to try. At that juncture a bizarre set of circumstances began to unfold. The North Charleston Police had made no further progress in unraveling the disappearance of young Kim Ghelkins since their investigation had led to the initial discovery of the gravesites in Prospect. Their frustration was growing exponentially. Gaskins and Walter were on death row awaiting the outcome of their appeals.

Detectives from North Charleston had traveled to Columbia to talk to Gaskins and Neely on several occasions but to no avail. Neely would not meet with them. While Gaskins would meet with them and carry on extraneous conversations about the prison, his trial and his new mortal enemy, T. Kenneth Summerford, he would avoid questions about Ghelkins and eventually tell the detectives to contact Grisso and Query.

When he went frequently to Columbia on other business, Query would always visit with Gaskins. While he had not been notified by Summerford as to when he intended to call the next case against Gaskins, he was certain that there would be limited time to prepare after notice. By these interviews he hoped to at least obtain as much information as possible in preparation for the potential trials.

When North Charleston Police Chief Linwood Simmons and his Chief of Detectives Mickey Whatley realized that Gaskins was now represented by Grisso and Query in all matters except the appeal of his death sentence from Florence County, they contacted Query.

When he was working as a detective with the Charleston County Police Whatley had been a detective in cases involving defendants represented by Query. Al Cannon, a young detective on the North Charleston force, had also known Query during the two years that he was a Charleston County Police Officer when they chanced to meet in the various courts of Charleston County. Cannon was hired as a detective by North Charleston in 1973. Cannon was a graduate of the historic College of Charleston and was pursuing his master's degree in criminal justice making him an obvious rising star in law enforcement. Cannon would go on to obtain his law degree in 1982 and after a brief stint as a private attorney he would be appointed Chief of Police for North Charleston and in 1988 he would be elected Sheriff of Charleston County. Whatley would also serve as Police Chief in North Charleston for a time before being elected to the South Carolina Legislature.

Both of the detectives felt that Query could be easy to work with and that it was worthwhile to explore any possibility of obtaining some form of cooperation from Gaskins.

None of the typical offers of leniency in return for cooperation had any application and the detectives and their chief knew that it would take a unique circumstance for them to be able to reach an agreement that would allow them to obtain any information from Gaskins. They also believed that Gaskins was highly manipulative and that his penchant for conning people might actually be turned to their advantage. Gaskins was already under a death sentence and was under indictment for seven other murders in another jurisdiction where the North Charleston Police had no authority therefore making the typical considerations of reduced sentence or transfer to lower security level institutions an impossibility.

Al Cannon called Query and told him that they would like to meet with him and explore the possibility of obtaining cooperation from Gaskins regarding the disappearance of the young girl from North Charleston. Chief Simmons, Chief Detective Whatley, Detective Cannon and another officer met with Query in the North Charleston Police Station. The meeting was during the evening hours to provide the best opportunity for a long meeting without interruption.

"Obviously we can't do anything about his current sentence and maybe not even the other outstanding indictments, but Al says that the two of you agree that the death sentence he's under is likely to be thrown out because of the U.S. Supreme Court case. So maybe there could be some incentive for him to work with us," began Whatley.

Query traveled to Columbia to meet with Gaskins and present the rather vague preliminary proposal from the police.

"What do you think they're up to?" Gaskins asked Query.

"Well they are certainly genuine about the fact that they would like to have your help in locating Kim Ghelkins or in finding out what happened to her," Query replied. "But you have to understand. Pee Wee, there may not be a lot that they can offer unless we can get the other judicial circuits involved."

"Let's hear what they got to say, Mr. Queury," said Gaskins. "Can't lose nothing' by that can we?"

Query told the police that Pee wee was willing to meet, but that he wanted to come to Charleston for the meeting.

"What's the point in that?" asked the chief.

"He says having the police come up and spend the afternoon talking to you at CCI is a good way to get killed," Query replied. "Besides I think he just wants to go for a ride. Not real exciting up there where he is."

"This guy has escaped from prison or jail several times, Chief," Whatley said. "He's certainly got a lot better chance at that riding up and down the highway then he does at CCI."

"No question about that," answered the chief, "but if we go up there and he doesn't want to talk to us then that's the end of it. Tell you what, Grady, let us talk it over and we'll get back to you."

"Well you have to give me pretty good notice, you know. They won't go get him and bring him to the phone when I call. I have to go up there to tell him anything. He can call me sometimes, but that's only about once a week at best and if he calls me they won't always let him call his wife or his mother, so he usually chooses to call them."

"Yeah, we understand, we'll give you plenty of time to talk to him, if we come up with something," said the chief.

A few days later the chief called Query and advised that he had decided that it was worthwhile to bring Gaskins down to Charleston in order to explore the possibility of his cooperation.

Gaskins enthusiasm was surprising to Query when he went back to Columbia to tell him about the latest meeting in North Charleston. Query had advised him that there was little or nothing in the way of a real offer but Gaskins was immediately ready to meet with the police.

"Pee Wee, we've got to be awfully careful about how we approach this," Query advised. "You still have a pile of cases pending in Florence and North Charleston can't bind Florence to any kind of deal. If you tell them anything that can result in charges up there you have to assume that Florence will pursue the prosecution."

"I understand that, Mr. Queury, let's just see what they can come up with. You see when you're in here, there can be things other than legal deals that can mean a lot. Just bein' allowed to get to the telephone or havin' extra time on visits can make a big difference."

"Okay, I understand. I used to work up here so I know how something that wouldn't mean anything on the outside can be huge in here. Just promise me that if you are going to talk to them about something that you will tell me what it is before you start and then I can at least bargain for the most protection that we can possibly get against future charges."

"Yes sir. Yes sir, I'll do that for sure, you tell them to bring me down there and we'll see where it goes," Gaskins replied, his usual banter even more rapid than usual and the tone of his voice rising with excitement.

Chief Simmons finally opted for a visit with Gaskins at CCI. He informed Query that they had decided that there had to be some assurance of obtaining some useful information before they could take the risk of moving Gaskins. He had also decided that SLED needed to be informed of their ongoing investigation and of their intention to interview Gaskins.

CHAPTER FIFTY SEVEN

Talks Begin

Arrangements were made for an interview with Pee Wee at CCI. He was taken in leg irons and belly chain to the main entrance where he, the police and his lawyer were locked in the maximum security visiting room. Chief Simmons and two of his detectives from North Charleston came up for the meeting. One of them was very young. He was slender and seemed friendly but very intense. The other man was Mickey Whatley. He was a heavy set career police officer that Pee Wee had seen come around North Charleston when Whatley was with the county. Pee Wee was told that Whatley was now Chief of Detectives for North Charleston. Chief Simmons had contacted Query and asked him to be part of any interviews that Pee Wee was willing to give. Pee Wee had been told by other inmates that the chief was a fair man and would stand by his word.

"We're not giving you any kind of immunity, if that's what you're looking for," Chief Linwood Simmons began.

"I know better than that. Y'all wouldn't give me immunity for illegal parking."

"Well the reality is that you have information that nobody else has. We think it can solve a North Charleston case. Maybe more than one. We won't ask about anything else if you don't want to talk about it but our cases are important to us and we would like your help on those," Chief Simmons continued.

"I've give it a lot of thought and what I want isn't that hard. I'll get with Mr. Queury and we'll come up with something that will make my life a little better in here and he'll get back to you on it. But that's it for today.

I've got to go back there and tell 'em y'all come up here to question me and I told you to git down the road. I got to stay alive up here you know."

"I can't imagine that you are in any danger in a cell by yourself on death row," Whatley wondered out loud.

"Somebody with enough power wants you dead up here –you're dead, Mr. Whatley. Ain't nothin' nobody can do about it but you. If you can't kill them before they kill you, ain't nothin' anybody else can do."

As they were leaving the visitation Query asked if he could have a minute with his client and Pee Wee told him what he had in mind.

"I'll only deal with North Charleston though," Pee Wee told him. "Those boys from SLED will run straight to Kenneth Summerford like he was their daddy and he won't have no part of doin' anything I ask for. That I can guarantee. What I want you to tell them is that I'd like to have private visits with my wife. That's all I'm askin' for. You can work it out with them. Get them to agree to something that's fair. Y'all make the deal and then I want to prove to them that when I say I'll do something, they can know that I will," Pee Wee directed his lawyer.

"Are you talking about just visiting with her privately without anyone else in here or are you talking about conjugal visits?"

"I'm talkin' about conjugal visits. When I was over at Walden and at Wateree they had a picnic area and even some tents and things. That was years ago but that's what I'm talkin' about."

"Pee Wee, I can tell you without even asking that there isn't a chance in hell of them letting you get in a tent or get anywhere close to the woods," Query told him unable to stifle a laugh.

"No, I know that. I just want to figure out some way to have some privacy with her. I know it will have to be in a jail or a prison. I wouldn't try any kind of break. Hell, I sure ain't gonna leave Donna standin' there naked. I ain't no fool."

"Okay, Pee Wee, I'll give it my best shot, but I have to tell you, I just don't see it happening."

"Well I guess we won't have nothin' else to tell them," Pee Wee told the lawyer. "Any way you look at it, it's pretty sure I'm gonna die right here, either in the chair or from old age, so if they want my help they're gonna have to figure a way to do this for me."

Query told Gaskins later that the first response was that they could not grant conjugal visits. Chief Simmons said that was strictly up to the prison system and that they would not allow it. Query said that after a lot of discussion the North Charleston Police had decided that it might be possible to allow the visits while Gaskins was in their custody and temporarily housed at the jail in North Charleston. Their position was that North Charleston had an ongoing investigation that gave them authority to bring Gaskins to North Charleston for questioning and to accompany him to other locations in order to search for bodies or other evidence. This might allow them to grant him the private visits with Donna without violating prison rules.

Query said that Chief Simmons had told his men that he believed it was more important to use everything available to them to solve the case of the young girl missing from their city and to live up to their responsibility to the family of that child than it was to worry about the technicalities of the rules of the department of corrections. He said the chief and his detectives had all agreed that they were not doing or allowing anything that was immoral or illegal. If the woman agreed that she was Pee Wee's wife and indicated that she wanted to be with him that it would not be immoral or illegal as long as they did nothing to pressure her to agree or to in any way force her to do anything she didn't want to do.

"I'm sure she'll be agreeable," Pee Wee told his lawyer. "You tell them to set it up."

The next time Query went to see Pee Wee at CCI he told him that the North Charleston Police were interested in talking more but they wanted Query to tell them what Pee Wee was willing to talk about. Pee Wee told him that he would tell him where to find a body that he knew about. Pee Wee told Query that he would not discuss anything about the body or how he knew about it but that he would tell them how to locate the body as a show of good faith.

CHAPTER FIFTY EIGHT

Striking a Bargain

"He says that he will tell you where to find a body to prove that he is going to keep his word," Query told the North Charleston Police Chief.

"Which body?" asked Chief Simmons. "You know which one we're interested in finding."

"He hasn't told me that," responded Query. "I've told you what he told me. That's as much as I know. You tell me that it's a deal and he will give me the directions to pass on to you."

"Is it here in North Charleston? He says he doesn't want other agencies involved but you know we can't go traipsing all over another jurisdiction without bringing them in."

"I've told him that. He understands that they have to be brought in at the point that you actually start looking, but he doesn't want to provide information to anyone but you."

"Okay, go see what he's got."

Query was back on his pony to Columbia. The meeting with Gaskins was nothing less than riveting. Gaskins coldly described a concrete tank located behind a wooden farm house on a paved country road in Florence County. Query misinterpreted the description and imagined some type of cistern. Pee Wee explained that down the back steps of the house the tank with a concrete cover could be found off to the right in the backyard. He estimated the distance from the nearest crossroads and the directions seemed sufficiently precise even though Query had not ever seen that particular road.

It was about eleven A.M. when Query called Detective Chief Whatley and reported the results of the meeting including the directions.

"I'm going to call SLED and Sheriff Barnes and see if we can meet them there today," Whatley said. "You want to be there?"

"I guess so. My day will be shot anyway," Query answered.

Three hours later SLED agents Tom Henderson, Ira Parnell and Tom Owens with detectives from North Charleston and a Florence County Deputy and Tom McJunkin, the Chief Deputy from Sumter County, stood by the little country road as Query re-read the directions from Gaskins a ninth or tenth time.

"It's just not here," said Owens. "We've gone a mile farther from the crossroads then he said it was located and there is still no house on that side of the road except that little one room block building beside the barn."

"That little bastard is probably up there laughing his ass off just thinking about us out here tramping up and down this road looking for a house that doesn't exist," someone volunteered.

"Now why would he do that, Tom?" asked Query. "He's trying to establish some credibility so that we can open some negotiations, so what could that gain him."

"Because he's crazy as hell and he loves screwing with us," said Henderson. "Besides there's not a damn thing we can do for him. Even if we would agree, Summerford's not going to go along with anything."

"Well there's a retired deputy lives right there at that crossroads," said the Florence County deputy. "We could ask him. Maybe we were supposed to turn at the crossroads. He'll know if there's a house looks like that anywhere in this area."

"Nothing to lose," said Owens.

The retired deputy lived in a small frame house on the opposite side of the crossroads from where the conversation took place. It was decided that Query and one of the agents would accompany the Florence deputy to the house. When they arrived they spotted the man at the barn slightly behind the house. The deputy shouted a greeting and the men walked down to the man. As they approached they were surprised to see a full grown deer prancing around a small paddock with high wire fencing. The deer ran over to the older man and rubbed its head against his hand as he held it against the wire.

"Found it in the swamp when it was a fawn, near starved," the man said before introductions were made. "I'm afraid to let it go. It ain't afraid of people and some SOB will shoot it, if I let it go."

The men were introduced and asked about the house Gaskins had described to Query.

"That house was right up there on the left less than a half mile," the man said immediately. "It burned down, been probably a year ago or so. Weeds have grown up over what was left. It burned clean to the ground. Nobody livin' there so it was about gone by the time anybody knew it was on fire."

"We think there is an old cistern or some kind of concrete tank near the house," Query said. "Are you familiar with anything like that?"

"I don't know of anything like that," he replied. "Wait, though, wait a minute, there is a big septic tank out in back. It ain't like most septic tanks. The cement cover on this one is above the ground. Just sits out there like a small cement slab."

"We didn't even see a driveway," said Henderson.

"All grown up," the retired deputy replied. "Just watch for where there's a pipe in the ditch. Turn in right there; that was the driveway. Just dirt, no pavement; just like mine. Head on up there you'll see where you can turn across the ditch. I'll come right up behind you and show you what I'm talkin' 'bout."

The men returned to the other officers still gathered on the roadside and led them back toward the retiree's house until they came to the barely visible vestige of a driveway. Once in the driveway the charred remains of some of the large timbers that had once been the farmhouse were visible in the high weeds. Tom Henderson opened the trunk of his SLED vehicle to get a small army style trenching tool and coveralls.

"Damn, Tom are you going to start a war?" joked Query looking at the assortment of weapons in the trunk. While they waited for the retired deputy to arrive, Tom displayed the guns one by one. Two high powered rifles one with telescopic sights, the other, a familiar looking military assault rifle, a short barreled 10 gauge riot gun, a Colt .45 automatic, a Smith and Wesson .357 revolver, a 9mm Berretta automatic pistol and a fully automatic short barreled gun with a clip that appeared to hold more than thirty rounds of ammo. Tom then showed Query the stainless steel .357 revolver that he carried in his shoulder holster and a very small .25 Colt automatic fastened to his right ankle.

"Nobody gets shot because he has too many guns. Can happen if you're one short," Tom laughed and turned to follow the retired deputy who had now arrived. They circled the charred perimeter and just five paces from what appeared to have been the back steps they found the cement slab. It was about three inches thick and approximately three feet wide by six feet long.

Tom Henderson bent and tugged at a corner.

"That thing weighs a ton. No way Pee Wee could have moved that and then put it back in place," Henderson said.

"Hell, Pee Wee would've thrown that thing off like a piece of plywood if he wanted to bad enough," said the old deputy. "I've knowed him all his life. Strongest man I think I've ever seen. Bunch of guys were messin' with a big ol' bailin' machine. They were tryin' to fix something and couldn't get to it. Pee Wee was half the size of the smallest one there and he backed up to that machine, squatted down, grabbed hold of the spokes and stood up with it. Little rascal stood there and held it while they got a block of wood under it. Pee Wee just walked off then and when they finished fixin' it they had to get a jack to get the block out. Everybody in the county has heard that story. They used to have an old country game called 'throw the horn' or catch it by the horn'. Don't matter the name. Idea was grab the anvil in the blacksmith's shop by the round part, the horn, and pick it up and try to toss it. Most men couldn't get it to budge. A few could pick it up just enough to throw it out a foot or so. Pee Wee walked in there, started doin' that starin' and breathin' thing he does, picks that damn anvil up by the horn and throws it out in front of the shed."

"Well that's a hell of lot different than lifting that lid," said Ted Owens. You need a back hoe or something. It's not only too heavy but there is no way to get hold of it. I think Gaskins is just jerking us around again. He's probably laughing like hell knowing we're out here trying to figure out how to open this up. Besides he never said anything about it being a septic tank and he hasn't said who is supposed to be buried out here. Let's get out of here. He can either tell us the whole story or we're done with this."

"Ted, what sense does that make. He gave us directions. It turns out they were correct and he described a concrete lid of some kind in the backyard. The least we can do is open it and see," Query urged.

"We don't have any way to open it. That's my point and I think he knew that," responded Owens.

"I've got a six foot pry bar at the house," volunteered the retired deputy. "We should be able to slide it off using that."

"What the hell, go and get it," suggested Tom.

The deputy was back within minutes and took the long steel bar out of his truck. He went to the corner of the tank, jammed the flat tip on one end of the bar in the ground and pulled it against the edge of the lid. The lid slipped enough for him to shove the bar down into the crack between the top and the tank. Using a lifting motion he was able to move the top diagonally to open nearly a third of the tank to view.

The other officers shined bright five cell flashlights into the bottom which held about a foot of black water. Although black in color the water was very clear under the lights. It had been darkened by tannic acid from the layer of leaves that lay at the bottom of the water. As the beams of the lights played along the bottom Query was shocked by the sudden iridescence of what he suddenly realized was an upside down smile flashing at him.

"Ever seen that before?" asked Henderson as he noticed Query's shocked reaction. "They call it the death grin. The teeth stay white while the rest of the skull turns gray and when the light hits them it's like a reflector. There you can see the rest of the skull clearly once you get past the glare from the teeth."

Just as Tom described, the skull was visible in the tea colored liquid. As they focused their lights more carefully, a blouse appearing to be in the shape of one supported by a mannequin could be traced with sleeves that led to skeletal hands. At the bottom of the blouse a white belt still held the top of blue jeans as though it was encircling a now non-existent waist. The patent leather belt glowed almost as brightly as the teeth. The blue jeans were intact and led down to skeletal feet. It was now obvious that the head was lying at a peculiar angle to the rest of the body.

Several officers returned to the cars and radioed the news back to Florence.

Sheriff Barnes from Florence and deputies from Williamsburg County arrived in a short time. "We'll just secure the area and post guards for tonight. I'm sure Dr. Sexton and the coroner will want to see the body just as you found it and they can't possibly get here before dark," Barnes told the others.

"We'll meet back here at eight in the morning," said Owens.

"I've got court tomorrow but y'all don't need me for this part anyway," Query said.

"We need to talk to Pee Wee as soon as we can," said the sheriff.

"I'll get up there as soon as I can," Query said. "I expect to be in court for the rest of this week. I'm not sure he'll talk to anyone anyway. That was what he said to me when he gave me the directions. He said he wanted to prove that he was willing to give you accurate information, but that he had nothing to say about the body, how it got here or how the person was killed or by whom."

"See if he'll at least tell us who it is," came Barnes's response. "You know how long it can take to make an identification without that."

"Do you think it's the girl from North Charleston," Chief Simmons asked.

"I have no idea. He didn't even say man or woman. Just appears to be a woman by the clothes, I would say," answered Query. "I'll be glad to ask him, but you know how he is when he says he won't do something."

"Any chance you could go ask him today?" pressed the sheriff. "I'll call the prison and get you in."

"I guess so. I understand that you don't want to go through the same thing as the bodies in Prospect, taking forever to be identified and the press and everyone else trying to guess. That'll put me home after eleven with court tomorrow. You guys are going to have to start being nicer to me."

"We're always nice to you," chuckled Henderson. "We usually shoot lawyers when we get them out in the woods."

Query drove straight to Columbia where he was granted much quicker access and found that Gaskins was already in the visiting area because of the call from the sheriff.

"I ain't tellin' 'em a thing about that body," Mr. Queury, that's what I told you from day one. I gave that up to prove to Chief Simmons that I do what I say I'll do. Now I'm waitin on them to do the same. I'm not talkin' to anybody but him and I'm only talkin' to him in Charleston."

Query called Sheriff Barnes on the home number that he had been given and told him what Pee Wee had said.

"Well I guess it's up to the chief," said Barnes. "Will you call him and let him know? I'll tell him we have no problem with them talking to Pee Wee without us there, if that's what it's going to take. I'll coordinate with Williamsburg as well."

That weekend Detective Cannon and another North Charleston officer walked out of the main entrance of CCI with the tiny man from Prospect between them. He was, as usual, fully restrained with a belly chain with the bracelet part of handcuffs on little one inch lengths of chain on either side at about the pelvic bones. His legs were manacled and a chain ran from his waist to the chain that ran between his ankles.

Gaskins managed to talk almost continuously for the entire one hundred ten miles without ever touching on the subject of murder or bodies despite efforts by the detectives to turn the conversation in that direction. Instead they got virtually minute by minute details about life on death row and long recitations about which police could be trusted and allegations of corruption about various others. They also got a complete description of several women who were corresponding with Gaskins and who had sent him pictures of themselves.

"One of 'em's buck naked and purty as a peach," he chortled.

"They let you get naked pictures of women in the mail? asked one of the detectives.

"You got to know how to get it in there," Pee Wee answered.

Gaskins was brought through the back entrance of the small North Charleston Police station where he was placed in the holding cell that was formed by bars on three sides and a solid wall in the rear. The officers were polite and told him that it would just be a short wait while they let everyone know they had arrived.

Chief Simmons was seated in the conference room when Gaskins was led into the room. The chief stood and after directing that his men remove the handcuff portion of the belly chain from the hands of the little man he asked him to take a seat. Present were Al Cannon, Rufus Stoney, Detective Chief Whatley, the chief, Gaskins and Query.

"Pee Wee, I appreciate the fact that you have done exactly what you said you would do. I am hoping you will help us now with the identity of the young woman."

"I think it's time for you to back up what you said," Gaskins replied.

"We're going to do that, but I'm sure it would mean a lot to her family to know. I hope we can accomplish that for them, but like you said I have to back up what I said. Can we discuss this after we make arrangements for you to meet with your wife?"

"Sure I understand that I have to do something every time you bring me down here," said Pee Wee. "But it goes both ways."

"Okay, Pee Wee, I understand. Now just a couple of things. First of all you are married... ? Uh, Donna is your wife, is that right."

"Yes, sir we were married up at Johnsonville."

"There has been some discussion that you were married to Sandy."

"I did call her my wife but the fact is she never divorced her first old man so we couldn't have never been married."

"Okay, let's be real clear on some things. First, this has to be totally voluntary on her part. If there is any indication that she is being threatened or forced in any way —it's over. Secondly, if you have any thoughts of escaping and believe me I've heard all of the stories about you being an escape artist, don't do it. I will shoot you and I have told my men to shoot to kill in that event. We will assume that your wife is a part of the plan and the same applies to her. That will be on you if anything happens to her. Finally, she will not be considered a hostage under any circumstances. She is coming here at your request and at her request. If you refuse to let her leave or hold her as a hostage we will consider that she is a part of the conspiracy and we will not be responsible for what happens to her in doing what we have to do to capture or kill you. Do you understand me?"

"Yes, sir, I wouldn't never let nothing happen to her —not in no way whatsoever."

Of the many strange occurrences in Donna's life the phone call from the chief of the North Charleston Police Department in mid evening on a winter night may have been the most peculiar. For starters she was not accustomed to receiving calls from police officers. Normally they just burst through the door with guns drawn yelling "Everybody on the floor, get on the floor you scumbags, face down, hands above your heads, do it asshole, down, get down now!" On those occasions, once she was allowed back on her feet, she was accustomed to seeing narcotics agents wrapped in Kevlar vests with police stenciled on the back and a large yellow badge stenciled on the left breast. Donna was not into drugs other than pot but she had lived in houses in California where marijuana and LSD were both used and sold. Hence the occasional less than polite entry by police.

Other times as she walked the streets in L.A. or San Francisco or a dozen other cities between that coast and Charleston when she had met suspicious police, they had told her to face a wall or a fence and put her hands on the wall above her head and spread her legs. In those instances a quick "pat down" for narcotics would inevitably result in an accidental but lingering touch of her normally unfettered breast, an undisguised grope of her butt or even the bold nudge of her crotch or pubic region under the guise of doing the pat down search. But never had she received a polite call with a kind and almost apologetic voice addressing her as Miss or Mrs.

"Miss Carullo or Mrs. Gaskins is it? I'm Chief Simmons, chief of police for the city of North Charleston. I'm sorry for calling you so late but I would like to speak with you for a few minutes, if you don't mind.

"Sure, I guess so, she replied," still taken aback by the fact that she had not been ordered to do anything or threatened in any way.

"Would you prefer that I call you Miss Carullo or Mrs. Gaskins", the chief asked.

She thought to herself, I guess either one is preferable to slut, bitch or cunt, which were the polite addresses she had gotten from most of the officers with whom she had dealt in the big cities, but she replied:

"Oh, either is OK –just Donna is fine."

"Thank you, I'm here with Donald Gaskins, he tells me that the two of you are married. Is that correct?"

"Yes sir, I'm his wife but I'm not sure how legal it is. I don't know for sure if he and Sandy ever got a divorce."

"Mr. Gaskins' lawyer, Mr. Query, is here and he says that it appears most likely that you are legally his wife by common law if not otherwise. He says that it does not appear that he and Sandy were ever actually married. At least that's his view of it. I've asked you these questions for a rather unusual reason, Mrs. Gaskins. We have asked Mr. Gaskins –do you call him Donald or Pee Wee?"

"Pee Wee"

"Well Pee Wee has agreed to cooperate with us in providing certain information that we believe is very important. This is information that will not only be helpful to us in solving some criminal matters but we think that it will be even more important in helping some people who are worried about missing loved ones. We asked him to help us for their sake and we told him that in return for his help we would do anything within our power to show our appreciation. Of course as you can understand we are limited in what we can do for him and he certainly understands that. Point is, he has told us that more than anything else he would like the opportunity to spend some time with you. Is that something that you would like to do?"

"Yes, I would like to see him; you know I have not been allowed to visit him at all."

"I can promise you that you will get to see him while he is here in North Charleston. But I must tell you that more than just a visit he has asked me to allow him to have a conjugal visit –do you know what I mean by conjugal visit?"

"Let us have sex."

"Yes, but I'm not asking you to make that decision at this point. If you want to see him I'm going to let you come down and visit with him. You can tell us at that time whether you would like for it to go any farther."

"When do you want me to come?"

"Could you come tonight? Could you come right now within the next hour or so? You know I don't have total control over how long he will be here in North Charleston. As you might know he is technically a Florence County prisoner. We have him temporarily as part of an investigation. So the sooner that you could come the better."

"I don't know. I'll have to ask Sandy if she can watch the children."

"Where is Sandy? Can you reach her?"

"Oh yes, we live together. She is Pee Wee's other wife –I mean his last wife. She's Walter's girlfriend now. I know she will babysit. I just need to ask her, but I'll have to get a cab. I don't have a car."

"Don't worry we'll send a car for you."

"Do you think you could send a cab? I mean we don't need any more police cars coming to this house."

"We'll send an unmarked car."

"In this neighborhood people know an unmarked car the same as if it had blue lights all over it. In fact that is usually the kind that comes to take someone away."

"Mr. Query says that he can come for you. Will that be okay?"

"Oh yeah, no one will think he's police. He drives a Porsche convertible and has long hair."

"All right its set. Mr. Query will pick you up in one hour. He tells me that he knows where you live. If Sandy can't keep the baby you call me back within the next thirty minutes. My private line is 555-3838."

The chief turned toward the group around the table, his broad shoulders and heavy chest alluding to the often tested strength from a lifetime as a street cop. "She says she's coming and she didn't seem to balk about the idea of a conjugal visit. She's fine with Grady coming to get her."

"Yeh, I think she's sweet on him", laughed Al Cannon.

"That's a compliment. She's a good looking girl, but I don't think it would be a good idea to cuckold Mr. Gaskins. Do you?" was Query's retort.

Attorney Query arrived at the duplex apartment in the West Ashley section of Charleston which was a good twenty minute drive from the North Charleston Police Station about forty-five minutes later. The apartment was one of a large group of refurbished World War II barracks or military housing that had been moved from the navy base and converted into low-income apartments. Attorney Query went quickly to the door. Donna answered with her jacket already on and after Query said a brief "hello" to Sandy they hurried to the car in the slow drizzle.

Once in the car Query spoke carefully and gently to the young woman:

"Donna you absolutely don't have to have any part of this if you don't want to. You have nothing to fear from the police or Pee Wee. They can't charge you for being his wife or for living with him. They can't even require you to testify against him as his wife, that is, if he's told you things about what he's done. Even if you aren't legally his wife, you certainly had every reason to be afraid of him and no one is going to prosecute you for not having come forward with information about him."

"I wasn't ever afraid of him. He's never hurt me. He's never even yelled at me. I've yelled at him, I've even hit him when I thought he was playing up to another woman. I can't help it. I'm a full-blooded, hot blooded Italian woman. It's how we act."

"What I mean is that knowing what he is capable of, you would naturally be afraid of him."

"I didn't know anything about all of these things that they say that he has done. I never knew anything about him killing someone."

"But you knew something about what he was capable of —you saw him beat Dennis Bellamy unconscious right in your front yard on Calvert St. I know you heard him tell Knoy that he was about to never be heard of again."

"Just the same I was never afraid of him. I'm not afraid of him now. He wouldn't hurt me. He wouldn't let anyone hurt me."

"But you had every right to be afraid of what could happen if you crossed him. That's my only point."

"Oh, I knew he stole cars and guns and that he always had stolen guns hidden around everywhere and stolen cars hidden up in the country and I knew people were afraid of him, but I mean, I never knew anything more than that. He never even told me that they were stolen but I would have to be an idiot not to figure that out."

"Good, but again my point is that you don't have to do anything tonight just because the police want you to. You don't even have to go to the police station with me. You don't have to see Pee Wee and you certainly don't have to be intimate with him, if you don't want to do it. Do you understand that?"

"Yes."

"But do you believe it?"

"Oh yes, I really do. I want to see him. I want to be with him. I think it's embarrassing, but I want to —you know, have sex with him to make love to him. And I know that he wants to make love to me. I love him, Mr. Query. I don't care what they say he's done. He has been the most kind and gentle person in my life —both to me and to my babies. It's embarrassing for you and the police to be sort of putting it together —arranging for us to have sex and all, but, I mean, I've been having sex since I was thirteen mostly for all the wrong reasons and all too often with strangers. I've been with truck drivers who expected it for giving me a ride; guys who expected it for letting me come in out of the rain or cold."

"When I was in California it was basically the way I got pot or acid to get high. Some of those guys I never really even met as a person; just met their drugs. When I finally decided to come back to Charleston I used my body as my ride and my meal ticket. When I got pregnant I quit the drugs. After my baby was born I never went back to it. Oh I don't mean pot. I started smoking that again after I stopped breast feeding. And then after I started living in Pee Wee's house not even that. He didn't allow it. I don't know why I'm telling you all of this. I guess I just run my mouth when I'm nervous. Besides you just seem easy to talk to and I guess it's important to me for you to know that I'm not a whore. I've never taken money from anyone but I've always used sex to get my way –to get something I wanted or needed. I was lucky to be pretty enough that someone would always get it for me either for sex or just for thinking they might get sex from me.

I guess I lived with some guys just to make sure I would get by and when something better came along or I got bored I just moved on. So anyway having sex to please someone is not exactly something that I don't understand. It's no big deal to me but I know that it is the most special thing that I can do for Pee Wee. And you know he never required it of me.

I lived with him in his house and he fed and clothed me and my babies for nearly a year and he never once asked me to sleep with him or even implied that he thought that I should. He treated me like we just somehow belonged there. I mean I helped cook and clean and do my share, Sandy lived there too and she was his wife, but I had my own room and he never came in it. There were four of us there all of the time plus the kids. Walter lived in the little trailer out in the back but he was in the house most of the time. He just kind of followed Pee Wee around. I finally went to Pee Wee. He never came to me. He had stopped sleeping with Sandy and made her sleep upstairs in the room next to me, so one night I just went to his room. After that I stayed in his room every night."

"After a few weeks he told Sandy that she should go and stay with Walter in the trailer. She didn't seem to mind. Pee Wee always said he gave her to Walter. I guess you've seen that Sandy is not the brightest light in the sky but she is sweet. We get along good and she always helps me with the children. She always has since I first moved in with them. Her baby is a teenager now and is usually in Prospect with Pee Wee's mother. She will spend hours just playing with mine."

"You've convinced me, not that you had to convince me, but I think you really do love Pee Wee. I'm also convinced that there is a pretty nice lady hidden behind all that tough girl talk."

The expectations of the cops who had been waiting for nearly an hour, which they filled primarily with speculation about Donna, were fully gratified when the young Donna Carullo entered the back door of the tiny North Charleston Police Department. She walked slightly ahead of the lawyer down the long brightly lit hallway toward the little assembly of police detectives. Brown hair with flashing highlights, the body of a young Sophia Loren and hints of an Italian movie star's face to boot caused all to stare and some to gape. Modestly attired in a white blouse, barely sheer enough to reveal the lace bra underneath and tight but not painted on jeans and ballet style shoes, she still scarcely hid the voluptuousness that virtually screamed to any man watching her easy strides as she walked the length of the hall toward them.

Her entry brought her directly past the big open holding cell, its size exaggerated by the presence of the miniature gangster who sat alone in the big space. The long bench that ran the length of each of the barred sides stretched easily ten feet on either side of the little man who sat dead center. When he saw Donna he dashed across the cell much more quickly than anyone could imagine possible given the constraints of the chain between his ankles and his prominent limp. Donna paused, leaned her face against the bars and kissed the little man as he stretched across the bench.

"Thanks for coming, baby," he said quietly. You talk with them with Mr. Queury in there and then you do what you want. I don't want you here to feel sorry for me. I want to see you, only if it suits you."

"I'm here because I want to be, honey, Grady told me I didn't have to come."

"We better get in there before they back out," said Query guiding her toward the hall by her elbow.

As she came closer to the assembled police officers the lights revealed a face that fulfilled the promise of loveliness that the body and the walk had evoked, complete with the full pouting lips, the softly rounded cheeks and the smoldering brown eyes of the Italian actresses that she so clearly resembled."

The murmurs from the waiting men were loud enough and sufficiently obscene to draw a "knock it off" from the chief.

Donna was invited into the meeting room and sat at the table beside Query, facing the U of cops formed around the head of the table.

"Mrs. Carullo —er Gaskins 'um well I believe you said Donna was Ok. May I just call you Donna? We sort of told you a little about what's going on here and I'm sure Mr. Query gave you a little more information on the way over," began the chief.

"Excuse me chief," interrupted Query, "just to give a little structure to all of this, I need to act like a lawyer and tell you that Donna has asked me to represent her and I am now here as her attorney as well as Mr. Gaskins' attorney. In that regard she has not been advised of her rights nor has she been identified as a suspect and it is our understanding that she will not be questioned in any manner whatsoever about anything while she is here or in the future about anything said here. Enough said on that; obviously she is here voluntarily and I have advised her that she is here by invitation only; that she is not obligated to do or say anything and that she can leave anytime she wants to. She understands fully and she is here because she wants to take advantage of this opportunity to visit her husband."

"She further understands that she and her husband will have the right to a conjugal visit if they decide at their sole discretion that is what they wish to do during their time together, but that she is not being asked by the police to consent to a conjugal visit and she is in no way obligated to participate in a conjugal visit if that is not her desire."

"I have also explained to her that you are limited in your ability to afford appropriate accommodations for their visitation' that you still have to give paramount consideration to security of the prisoner and the safety of your personnel. She understands that these priorities are particularly taxing in light of Pee Wee's reputation as an escape artist and the violent nature of the crimes with which he has been charged or in fact convicted."

"Please go ahead with your explanation I just wanted to be clear on her understanding. As is pretty obvious by my little recorder on the table, you all know that I am recording this portion of our meeting for Donna's protection."

"Donna, do you agree with what Mr. Query has told us," said Chief Simmons.

"Yes, Sir."

"Do you wish to visit with Mr. Gaskins."

"Yes, I definitely do."

"Do you wish to have the opportunity to have a conjugal visit with your husband if you both agree on that."

"Yes, Sir."

"We are going to meet for a few minutes with your attorney and we will try to make the best possible situation that we can without compromising security or endangering anyone. Now obviously you are the one person that we cannot protect to any great extent in the event that Pee Wee does something violent or tries to escape. You will be alone with him in the same room and he will not be restrained or under guard. Do you understand that?"

"Yes, sir."

"Do you understand that we cannot consider your safety if Pee Wee tries to escape or attacks one of my officers? What I mean is we will not be able to look on you as an innocent hostage. We have to consider at that point that you are with him because you want to be with him and that you are a participant in whatever is happening. We will have to use whatever force is necessary and take whatever action we think is appropriate. In other words you could be in great danger –you could even be caught in the middle of a shoot out."

"I understand about all of that, I'm not afraid, he would never do anything to hurt me or put me in any danger."

"OK, Mrs. Gaskins, please excuse us. Just make yourself comfortable and we'll try to set things up the best we can."

The police and the attorney left the meeting room and gathered in the hallway.

"Well, now that we've gotten this far, how the hell are we going to actually do this?" questioned Chief Simmons more of himself than of the others.

"Just hang up some sheets on the cell and let her go in there with him. They'll figure it out. Hell how long as he been without any? You could probably just put her outside the cell and he'd figure something," offered one of the Detectives.

"I thought about trying to use the holding cell but we've only got two and they are exposed to each other and to anyone entering that part of the building. Somebody on the street makes an arrest and is bringing the guy in and the guy gets violent, we can't ask them just to sit on him and wait outside while Mr. and Mrs. Gaskins have sex."

"Just let them use the conference room," suggested Query.

No, I don't like that at all," said Detective Cannon, the youngest of the officers present. "There are three windows in that room. We'd have to station one of us outside each window and I don't want to make the headlines for shooting Pee Wee as he comes out of a window naked and I happen to be right there because I've been waiting for him to have sex with his girlfriend."

"Chief, how about the interrogation room? No windows, one door and we might be able to get the fold up bed the extra duty officer uses in there. Tables fastened to the floor we can't move it, but we could put the mattress on the floor –cram it in there."

"Grady excuse us for one minute and let us talk about this. Are you okay with the interrogation room?" asked the chief.

"Chief, I think it is really very important that this not be any more demeaning for Donna than is absolutely essential for safety and security. Throwing a mattress on the floor of a room the size of a closet does not exactly imply that she has the option to either sit and talk with her husband or participate in a conjugal visit. Could they meet in your office? It's huge."

"I don't know if we can secure it. There is a window and there are letter openers, maybe even guns or knives that I haven't thought about in months. It would take us all night to search it thoroughly. But you make a good point about her feelings and for that matter public opinion, if this ever got out to the newspapers. By the way I hope that's not what you have in mind."

"Not to worry. I won't say anything. I'm just trying to obtain a benefit for my client in a situation that doesn't lend itself to any normal course of action. This is what he wants in return for his cooperation. I've asked him to let me go to Summerford and Sheriff Barnes about immunity, but he only wants to work with you and he says he wouldn't trust what Summerford said anyway. I've told him there are ways to enforce that but he insists that this is what he wants," Query explained. "He knows that even with immunity on the remaining cases, he still has at best a life sentence from the Bellamy conviction."

"Give us a minute. We'll do the best that we can."

Query walked down out of the hallway and over to the holding cell where he explained briefly to Gaskins that the chief was trying to make suitable arrangements.

"Seems like they woulda figured this out ahead of time," offered Gaskins.

"I think they are surprised that it got this far," said Query. "I'll go tell Donna what's going on. She's in the conference room by herself."

"Yeh, go ahead in there and stay with her. She's probably wonderin' what the hell we've gotten her into."

"I imagine you are right about that." She and I have that in common, Query mused as he walked back past the chief's office where the police were now gathered and stepped into the conference room. Donna sat alone at the conference table her hands in her lap.

"This is kind of weird isn't it?" she said rhetorically and then asked, "Have you done this for people before?"

"No, I've helped men get clearance to visit overnight in tents with their wives until some fanatic decided that was somehow morally wrong and pressured the prisons into stopping it. The people actually running the prisons realized that it was great for morale and a reward system for best behavior. It was also a good transition for men who were soon to be released."

"Well, I think it's a good thing," she said. "I can't imagine him being locked up by himself in a tiny cell."

"There are plenty of people who think even that is too good for him, so be careful voicing your opinions or letting anyone know about this."

"Don't worry. I don't talk about anything to do with him to anyone. I'm even very careful about what I say to Sandy. I don't think she would ever do anything on purpose to hurt him, but she takes what people say at face value. She has very little understanding of people having their own plan. Oh, why am I beating around the bushes? She's sweet but she's got the mind of a child. She's not innocent when it comes to sex or men but she can't think one minute ahead. She follows whoever she's with and that keeps her out of trouble most of the time. When things get too complicated she just goes back to Amusements of America with her mother and sits in that little booth selling tickets to kiddy rides until everything settles down. That's where she'd be now if the police hadn't told her she couldn't leave. At first she didn't think she could go to the store. That's how she thinks."

A knock interrupted their idle conversation and the chief and his entourage re-entered the conference room.

"I think we have an acceptable plan," said the chief. "Grady can we see you for a minute?"

Minutes later the little group reconvened in the hall.

"We're going to use my office," said the chief. "It has some problems but we think that we have a solution. We're going to divide the room in half with something like a clothesline and hang a heavy drop cloth that the painters have been using. It's a little dirty but it's so thick it'll be like one of those cubicle partitions. Behind the drop cloth there will only be a couch and we have room to put the fold up bed in there too. All of the file cabinets and my desk, anything that could be dangerous are on the other side. The part of this that you may not care for is that I will be in the room."

"Oh sure, that's being very considerate of her. Don't worry Ma'am we want this to be very private and respectful for you but I'll be standing over you with a flashlight and a machine gun just as a security measure," Query erupted. "Maybe you should film it; just to be sure they don't do anything inappropriate."

"No, no, just hear me out. I will be across the room behind my desk between Pee Wee and the window. The drop cloth is heavy canvas and it will completely divide the room. They will have the same privacy as if they were in a tent. In fact they will even have the light switch on their side of the room. I can turn on my desk light on my side. The more we talked about it; we just can't leave him alone in a room for an unspecified period of time with no one to even verify that he's still in there. I will stay seated in my chair across the room with a riot gun in my lap. I think that is the best that we can do."

"I mean we have a legitimate interest for this city and its citizens and I think it is reasonable for us to agree to this if it allows us to locate the bodies of the loved ones of people living in North Charleston. Prosecutors give up a lot more to get a lot less for sure. But we cannot set up a circumstance that results in him escaping or someone getting hurt. After all we are dealing with a murderer who has escaped more than once from a maximum security prison. I can tell you that he will not leave that room if I am in there with a sawed off shotgun and these officers are outside the door."

"I'll need to talk to Donna. This is a lot different than what we have been talking about," said Query.

"I know it's not great and please tell her that we don't want to embarrass her but she has to understand this guy has murdered several people and has escaped from the toughest prison in this state."

"Escaped more than once," Cannon offered nervously.

"Yeh, I'm afraid it's got to be this way or we can't do it," concluded the chief. "We are trying to keep up our side of this and I think he is trying to keep up his side of it, but this is the only way I can see to work it out."

"I'll explain your reasons," said Query returning rather hesitantly to the meeting room where Donna was still waiting.

"I'm not sure I can go through with it, but I'm okay to try. I mean he won't be watching us will he?" came Donna's reply.

"No as I understand it you'll be on the other side of this big canvas, sort of like in a tent and he'll be outside of the canvas and across the room. He'll be sitting at his desk."

"Okay, I'm going to try and if I just can't do it I'll just tell Pee Wee. I know he'll really want me to but he'll be okay with whatever I decide. At least we'll have some time together."

"She's okay," he reported to Chief Simmons and the others. Now we need to explain this to Pee Wee.

"Well, he can take it or leave it. I don't have the same concerns about his feelings that I do about hers. We're doing this to accomplish something that we have not been able to do with ordinary police work and that's it. I'm not trying to be his friend. Let's bring him in," said the chief.

"Why don't you let me explain it to him?" Query asked.

"Go," commanded the chief, far more accustomed to ordering than requesting.

Query went down the short hall and into the large area where the free standing holding cells were located. The cell measured about fifteen feet by twenty feet and was designed to hold a lot of people for a short time. A single toilet/lavatory combination of mottled stainless steel was centered on the only solid wall which was opposite the entrance in the front wall which like the sides consisted of steel bars. Metal benches about eighteen inches wide lined two of the barred walls and the door opened through the other. It had been constructed in the center of a larger room in the converted Piggly Wiggly grocery store. The building served as the police station and municipal court for the newly formed city of North Charleston.

"Well, Pee Wee, the good news is that Donna is here and she has agreed to a conjugal visit. The chief has agreed. The bad news is that the only way they are willing to go forward is for the chief to be in the room."

"No, sir, Mr. Queury, that ain't happenin' –I ain't goin' with that. No way, I ain't havin' Donna naked in front of some police chief or nobody else and I sure ain't gonna have us goin' at it in front of nobody. Is he some kinda pervert or somethin' or does he think I am?"

"Hang on, Pee Wee let me finish and then it will be up to you."

"I can tell you right now, it ain't no way. Let's get out of here, Mr. Queury. Tell 'em to haul me back to CCI. They just playin' with me. They lied just like every other police I was ever involved with. I shoulda' knowed better."

"Pee Wee they are afraid that you will take his opportunity to escape. That's the whole deal. You and I both know they are way out on a limb with this. They are trying to work with you, but they are also trying to protect themselves. If you escaped they would never work in law enforcement again and they might wind up facing charges. They have been polite to Donna and they have tried to figure out a way to give the two of you as much privacy as they can without risking your escape."

"I give 'em my word, Mr. Queury, you know I ain't gonna go back on that.

You can tell 'em that."

"Well, Pee Wee, they are not particularly accustomed to dealing with people who keep their word and I don't think that they are much more likely to take my word than yours. But let me explain it all before you decide."

"The chief is going to let you go into his office. That part I asked for. They're going to separate the room completely into two parts with a heavy canvas drop cloth. The chief will be on the other side of the canvas. He won't bother you or come on your side of the room. You can even turn off the lights from your side of the room. He says he will remain seated at his desk. Point is he wants someone in there with a gun so that they can shoot you right there if you try to escape."

"How do I know he'll stay at his desk?"

"I think we have to take his word on that. It's fair to believe that he's not going to all of this trouble and then blow it to sneak a peek."

"I reckon you're right, Mr. Queury, but he's gonna hear everything we say."

"Whisper."

"That'll work alright unless we start makin' love but I'm tellin' you now, Mr Queury, there ain't no way of makin' love to Donna quiet," the glee in his voice was now unmistakable.

"That's up to y'all, Pee Wee, I'm afraid this is as good as its gonna get."

"Well you know Mr Queury, I been locked up eight months. Nothin' I wouldn't do for a chance to be with Donna, but this has got to be all right by her too. I can't force her in ta somethin' she don't feel right about."

"She says that she is okay with it. She says that she will tell you if she feels too uncomfortable and she told me that you would honor her wishes if she just couldn't feel right and didn't want to go through with it."

"You can bet on that. I don't want her doin' nothin' that's not all right by her."

"The deal, Pee Wee, is that you two will have time together. What the two of you decide to do with it is up to the two of you. This has all been explained to Donna and she wants to be with you. If you get in there and you feel uncomfortable then just sit and talk or hug and kiss for as long as they let you stay. I'll tell the chief we want to at least visit and you and Donna will decide on the kind of visit."

"Yeh, just havin' time with her will be great. Whatever comes of it."

"Chief, we're on," Query reported.

Pee Wee was brought down the hall in the familiar waist chain handcuffs and leg irons, all three of which were connected, the waist chain to the handcuffs and a separate chain running from the waist chain to the leg irons. The result was a shuffling walk even more exaggerated than the familiar gait of men in leg irons alone. This was further amplified by Pee Wee's dramatic whole leg limp on the right side that resulted in a lurching movement that approached the movie versions of Dracula's assistant or the Hunchback in his slightly sideways track. Seated in the meeting room with Donna now beside him the conditions of the visit were again explained to him.

In a surprising moment of human compassion Chief Simmons brought out a bottle of medium grade bourbon whiskey and offered a drink to Donna.

"I know this is not very comfortable for either of you. And I want you to know even though we're doing this strictly to get information as a part of an agreement with Pee Wee; it does provide a unique opportunity for you to be together. We would like to make it as pleasant as we can within the boundaries. If a drink will make you feel more at ease than, please feel free to have one. I cannot offer one to you, Pee Wee, because it would be a violation of state law, but Donna can take the bottle with her and I'm not going to be checking on you."

"I'm not much on drink," replied Pee Wee with the mirthful smile seldom seen by law enforcement but nearly always near the surface around those close to him, "besides I wouldn't want to get you in no trouble, Chief."

"I think I would like to have just one," said Donna, I'm awfully nervous. Is that okay, Pee Wee?"

"You have whatever you want, honey, I just can't believe you're really here. How much time you givin' us Chief? I know that you ain't invitin' us to be present when the morning shift comes in."

"Well, I guess you're right there, Pee Wee. What do you think —an hour seem reasonable."

"I don't mean to be vulgar but I'll be a good bit more that a hour if we decide we're gonna do the conjugal visit," he grinned.

Donna blushed.

"Let's do it this way. You decide in the first half hour if you are going to have this as a conjugal visit. If that's what you decide than you take as much time as you need and tell me —let's say fifteen minutes after you're done. Have some time to just be together and get dressed at your leisure. But don't fake me out on this, Pee Wee, be honest about the time."

"That's more than fair, Chief, you got my word on it I'll be honest with you on the time."

CHAPTER FIFTY NINE

The Visit

It was purely weird. The cops were actually breaking rules to let me and Donna be together. We went into the room with the chief and he showed us how the canvas was hung to completely block one side of the room.

"I'll be right here at my desk, Pee Wee. I won't get out of my chair unless you make me. Turn around."

To my surprise he unlocked all of my chains and laid them on his desk.

"Make no mistake, Mister, I will shoot you. I'll unload this riot gun on you, if you do anything stupid and if Donna is in the way so be it."

"You ain't got to worry about that, Chief. I sure ain't goin' to be escaping' from Donna. That you can count on. Besides I've give you my word."

Another surprise; as the chief sat down behind his desk he turned on a small radio and music played softly as we went to our side of the canvas.

She was as beautiful as ever. Her skin was as smooth as a river rock and the color of homemade caramel. Her skin always glowed like you were looking at a rose through milk colored with honey.

She kissed me deeply at first just with her mouth and her hands on my face, touching me as though afraid that I might now be somehow different. And then she was kissing me with all of her. Her magnificent breasts came against me as her arms brought me to her. Full and heavy in their incredible softness they would stand on their own like excited puppies once they were unbridled. She had nipples that were actually hot through her blouse and her bra. I've never known another woman with such heat in her nipples when she was excited and the effect on me was beyond exciting. The fever was rising in me and my maleness was making itself known.

She came against me with her whole body. I felt the firmness of her pubic mound pressing hard against me in sharp contrast to the softness of her belly and I could feel the muscular smoothness of her thighs below.

In that little minute of closeness we forgot Chief Simmons perched in his swivel chair across the room and began unbuttoning each other. Soon I was kissing her breasts and pressing my face between them. I moved my face down her velvet stomach kissing and licking her as I went. I nuzzled and kissed her stomach around her bellybutton and around to the sides of her waist. This always brought a lot of giggling protest that really meant you're doing your job. I began pulling her jeans slowly down over her hips brushing my lips lightly over the protruding pelvic bones and around on the tops of her hips and then sliding down to kiss and breathe on the spot just over the black hair that marked the spot. I pulled the jeans off of her feet and kissed every inch of her thighs, her knees and her calves and ankles as I pulled them down and then I started at her feet and worked my way back up to the moist heat of her womanhood.

I kissed her there and stayed there even when she began to ask me to enter her. Insistently I continued to urge her on with my mouth and tongue until she began to raise and lower her hips finally shuddering in climax. Only then did I roll onto my back and bring her on top of me. As she slid on to me she threw her shoulders back and arched her back like a cowboy riding a bull. Her breasts pointed upward and her stomach hardened with the effort. She rode with more and more force in her movements, hips thrusting forward and then shoulders pulling up and back. I moved with her, a gentle but powerful bronco between her silk thighs. After ten minutes she leaned completely forward kissing my mouth and adjusting her knees to ride like a jockey with short rapid movements. I sat up and she wrapped her lovely legs around me locking them behind my back to gain leverage as we rocked together. Her excitement was so total now that she was moving without thought, consumed by her desire to achieve a final shattering orgasm. I laid back again and arched my back raising onto my shoulders with my legs thrusting my pelvis as far upward as I could. She threw her head and shoulders back resuming her bull riding position and moved harder and harder and faster and faster until she finally burst in a moaning gasping orgasm that caused Chief Simmons to drop something on his desk. Only then did I allow myself to release. As always she was completely mine as she collapsed into my arms and I gently caressed her back and kissed her breasts.

I had always been able to do that with women. Ever since the nurse at reform school, I could even satisfy women who said they had always hated sex, cause them to want it every day. I gave the women around me safety and kindness and sex that was how they wanted it to be not what I wanted them to like and they were mine forever. Even the ones who wandered off to find the fear and excitement they had known before were still loyal to me and I could have them any time. Jessie had been the only exception she was too much for one man to tame.

"Chief, I'd like to stay here all night, I know you know that, but I gave you my word. We're all dressed and ready to go back out. I would like to visit with her a little longer if it's okay."

"Sure Pee Wee, you've kept your word and you haven't caused any problem. We'll put you back in the cell and get a chair for Donna. She can sit there outside of the cell until we finish up here. We'll be planning to roll out of here before long so you might want to get some sleep."

"I don't sleep except when there's nothing else to do, y'all know that by now."

Donna and I were allowed to talk until sometime after two A.M. when the chief finally called out and asked Donna to leave. At three in the morning police, lawyer and convict, we were on our way to CCI.

"If y'all can go by Sumter County I can show you just where to find that colored girl Clyde," I told them.

"What are you talking about, Pee Wee?" asked Al Cannon. "We don't know about anybody named Clyde."

"Colored girl I killed for old man Kolb and some law enforcement people. I can show you exactly where to find her because it's by a road and a big drainage ditch. All that'll be the same as it's always been. Y'all done right by me and I want to deliver on my promise."

"We can't go digging around in Sumter County without getting them involved, Pee Wee. You ought to know that. We'll go by the place and let you show us where it is, but we will not search without contacting the local sheriff."

"Call 'em up, get 'em out there if they'll come. Get 'em up now. I can find it in the dark, it's that sure." They won't look. I'm tellin' you Kolb told me there was lawmen involved. They never even investigated when she was kilt. Said she probably just run off somewhere. I want to keep my word on this and give you another body. You swing by the road where I tell you and you can go straight back to the very spot. You'll be able to take them right to the ditch and then you just walk down that ditch until you find her."

"We're not calling anybody tonight," said Cannon. "We'll call them tomorrow and see if they know anyone by that description and name."

The police car followed directions given by Gaskins. Finally they turned off of the paved road and onto a well maintained farm track that ran through plowed fields. Where the road crossed a big ditch that appeared to be four or five feet deep Gaskins directed them to stop. Query stopped his car behind the squad car and walked up to the right hand side. Chained as usual Gaskins was helped from the car to stand on the edge of the farm track where it crossed a huge drainage ditch.

"Right down that ditch, right there," Gaskins squawked apparently excited by the moment. "Just head right down through there about two hundred feet. The body is up under the bank with rocks up against it. It'll be right there, I'm tellin' you. Up under the left bank."

The next morning the North Charleston detectives got a very cold reception from the Sumter County Sheriff's Department.

"Yeh, there was a girl around here. Black girl, called herself Clyde. She was a part time lesbian and part time hooker. Rumors were she was involved in dealing heavy drugs. Nothing for sure on that but enough rumors to say she was into something," said Chief Deputy McJunkin. "I'll tell the sheriff what you've told me and I'll get back to you."

McJunkin didn't call back until the following day.

"Sheriff Parnell says y'all are crazy as hell if you let Pee Wee run you around those woods out by the swamps with some wild story about that black girl. Plenty of people know she disappeared so that doesn't mean anything. Sheriff says you get that little culprit out there beside the swamp, he's only one step from gone. You'll never even know he's gone. Once in that swamp you're in his house. He can be ten feet away and you couldn't find him for hell. Sheriff says he ain't going to be the one gets made a fool of. We're not going out there tromping around in a field that gets farmed every season. No way there's a body in the ditch out there and it's never been found."

"Mind if we look?"

"I asked the sheriff about that. He said stay the hell out of Sumter County. You run your town and he'll run this county. He seemed real serious about that."

"Sounds like it," replied the detective and hung up.

Chief Simmons relayed the information to Query and he told Gaskins the following week.

"Just like I told you. The law was involved in getting' rid of that gal. They ain't about to look for her," Pee Wee reacted. "I can't give 'em to 'em if they won't go look for them. I wanted to give 'em that one because it was so easy to find. I'm gonna have to search for the others. There's no way just to tell somebody how to find them. I have to get out there and look around, try to find something I can recognize."

"Well of course North Charleston is most interested in locating the little Ghelkins girl. They'll probably take you anywhere if it's to look for her."

"I don't have anything to say about that just now. There's a lot involved there. I'm just trying to show them that I will do what I promise I can do," Pee Wee said finishing the conversation.

Query conveyed the message to Chief Simmons.

"I don't know what's going on with Sumter County but they aren't at all interested. According to them Gaskins has been telling wild stories in that part of the country for his whole life and they aren't going to let him make fools of them running them all over the countryside."

"The girl in the septic tank seemed pretty real to me," said Query. "Pee Wee says that girl's name is Patricia Alsbrook. He thinks she is from Kingstree. She was supposedly a runaway. Ran away from home with Pee Wee's niece."

"What about the niece? Where is she?" the chief asked immediately.

"He wouldn't say. Just claimed he hadn't heard from her since the Alsbrook girl disappeared. He wouldn't talk about what happened to the Alsbrook girl either. Just said he believed that's who it was."

"Okay, I'll notify Williamsburg and Florence County and the medical examiner. At least this should speed up their work. There's a big difference between verifying an identity and finding one from scratch."

"What about getting Pee Wee back down here?" asked Query. "That will be his only issue when I get back up there to see him. He says it will be more difficult to locate any other bodies because there are no landmarks like the tank or the big ditch that would not have changed."

"As far as I'm concerned we can schedule another interview down here. He was truthful and accurate about the girl in the tank and he very well may be telling the truth about the girl in Sumter. I can't see calling foul on him when Sumter County doesn't seem to care enough about a missing black girl to even go walk out into the field."

The next meeting at the North Charleston Police Department was again set up on a Friday night both to accommodate Query's court schedule and to move Gaskins around at a time that would draw the least attention. The detectives and their chief increased the pressure for Gaskins to provide information about the young girl from North Charleston, reminding him that she was the only true nexus for their department and the only justification for continuing the interviews. Pee Wee countered reminding them that six of the eight bodies found near Prospect were from North Charleston. Ultimately he agreed that he would attempt to locate the grave of the young girl which he said was near the farm where his daughter and her husband lived. That was also the location of his trailer. It was all referred to as Ropers Crossroads by Gaskins. He avoided questions about the manner of her death, claiming that he knew the general location only by virtue of information provided to him by someone else.

The description of the location ultimately given by Gaskins brought up the recurring situation in which the gravesite could very easily be in either Florence County or Williamsburg County. Chief Simmons had followed protocol and called ahead and Williamsburg deputies were waiting for them along with agents from SLED and deputies and detectives from Florence County.

"I gave my word on this and I'm going to back that up, but you all got to understand it's been a year and I can't necessarily just walk right up on something. A lot has changed even from what I can see from here. I'll have to see what I can find to go by," Gaskins said speaking directly to the chief.

An older deputy standing by Query murmured, "Now I can tell you that's pure bullshit, I guarantee you Pee Wee can look around here for an odd tree or a rock or even just a little crook in the road that we wouldn't even notice and five minutes later he'll know exactly where he is. He could show you where he caught his first rabbit. He's just going to drag us around out here hoping for a chance to make his break. He's also got us out here close enough to his old crowd from the Neck to get us all killed right out here in this field. Well you can tell the little bastard this much, a shot get's fired within a mile of here, I'm going to blow him in half with this sawed off shotgun and then empty all seven from this Smith and Wesson automatic into the leftover parts."

"I sure hope nobody is squirrel hunting anywhere around here," Query told the guy. "I'm not sure you're good enough to hit just Pee Wee with that cannon."

There was a ring of truth to what the deputy said, however. Pee Wee had told Query that he had made a lot of enemies and that he still had a few pretty rough friends around the Neck.

"I got no plan. I give my word on that, but them boys in the neck got a mind of their own. If we're out in those woods and some shootin' starts we want have no way of tellin' which ones it's comin' from –friends or foes. If it starts, I want you to get down –get under something if you can and stay there until it's over. I'll be takin' care of myself and we'll just have to see how I come out. One way or the other I'll likely get out of this mess, either in a box or on the run. I'd hate to see you kilt just for bein' there."

"Yeh, me too, Pee Wee. Me too."

CHAPTER SIXTY

Searching

The following morning at dawn the police drove Pee Wee down to his daughter's farm at Ropers Crossroads near Prospect. One of the police cars stopped at the house to tell his daughter that they would be on the back of the farm and that no one was to come out there until they left. The entourage consisting of Sheriff Barnes, one of his deputies, a deputy from Williamsburg County and detectives from North Charleston drove on to an old wagon road that entered the back of the property and continued down it for several hundred yards. Everyone emerged from the cars. Pee Wee was maintained with hands cuffed in front of him but not attached to the belly chain. Leg irons were removed after some discussion among the lawmen about his ability to go into the woods with his legs shackled. The waist chain was left in place and the chain that would normally run from the belly chain to his leg irons was left attached in the back and one of the deputies held the chain like a dog leash and walked behind Pee Wee. The little search party began to walk on the road and into the edge of the woods.

An area in heavy woods can change a lot in just one season and here a year had passed. Pee Wee appeared to be having a difficult time locating any kind of landmark from which he could get an accurate location. As he began to become better oriented he started to wonder if he was making the right move by finding Kim's body. Chief Simmons was the only person with authority who had agreed to the arrangement for conjugal visits in return for truthful information and the only case in which he appeared to have any real interest was Kim Ghelkins. He ruminated that if he located her body, there was a chance that the chief would pull out of the other cases or be forced out. It was very likely that no one else would agree to the same terms. Even though Chief Simmons and his officers had kept their word he couldn't help having the feeling that once they found Kim, they would just leave him sitting on the row at CCI.

After several hours of looking, Pee Wee asked to be allowed to speak to Mr. Query.

"Pee Wee is there something out here or are you jerking us around," Whatley asked.

"Just let me whisper something to my lawyer and I'll show you what's real," Pee Wee snapped back.

The lawyer leaning down and Gaskins stretching up to his ear as the law men stood around them, Pee Wee whispered:

"I can't find her for them so I'm gonna have to give them a different one," he told the lawyer. "Something has changed about these woods. They've timbered in here and it's throwin' me off."

"I've got to keep my word to Chief Simmons. He's kept his promise to me and I want to be able to keep up my visits with Donna. Since I can't find Kim I'm going to take them to a different grave," Pee Wee continued. He turned to the group and announced his decision.

"I'm just not seeing anything here that gives me a track on this," Pee Wee told the officers near him. "I don't want to give up on this but it could take us days to find something familiar and if they have cut any timber in here and it looks like they have, it could take even longer. I think it might be better to go up into the fields there and I can probably locate something else for you. I want you to know that I am being truthful with you and that I am cooperating completely. I gave you my word on that."

"What do you mean 'Give us something else', Pee Wee, you said you would locate the body?"

"I'm just not sure I can find it right here today."

"Well we're not interested in finding anything other than a grave."

"That's what I mean to find —I just can't find hers."

"You mean you want to take us to another grave —someone else."

"Yes, I feel sure I can find that one."

"Who are you talking about?"

"Well we'll get into that when I find it."

"We're here to look for Kim Ghelkins. Why don't we keep searching here until you find something you recognize?" asked Cannon.

"I just can't get my bearings here but I want y'all to know that I'm gonna do what I said. I'll go back and study on this one and I'll go over this location in my mind 'til I can get straight on where this one would be. But I'm sure I can locate Barnwell Yates. The landmarks there are much clearer and there won't be so much brush that's growed up around it."

"What are you talking about? What are you going to go back and study?" North Charleston detective Al Cannon asked obviously chagrined that the promise of locating the body of Kim Ghelkins had just evaporated. "It seems like you could come a lot nearer remembering while you're out here. You said somebody told you where to find her. What did they tell you to look for?"

"No, no, I've actually been showed the grave. It's my own marks I'm lookin' for, but I just can't get my remembrance just right. That's why I need to study on it for awhile. Just lie still and study on what I remember from bein' shown the grave and put that with what I seen here today and I'll figure it out. I'm plumb sure of that, but that's how I'll have to do it. Been doin' that all my life. I've been lost all over these swamps but never in the same place twice," the loquacious little outlaw rambled on.

"Okay, Pee Wee, if that's how it is, we have to just wait for you to figure it out. Who's this fellow Gates or Yates?" Cannon shot back, his suspicion not well concealed.

"Yates was a farmer from up this way that was killed," Pee Wee answered.

"Who told you about the girl from North Charleston?" Cannon shot back.

"I just can't go there just yet, Al; can't tell you who," he said to the much younger man. "My promise is to help y'all locate the bodies. I'm doin' that. We'll have to get into the rest of that later on. I've got to figure out how to protect myself once I give you more on that."

"Doesn't make sense to me, Pee Wee," Cannon replied. "Once the press puts out that a body was located by you, whoever you're worried about is going to assume that you told us everything about it."

"Naw, I don't think so. The paper'll be sayin' that the identity of the body hasn't been confirmed. That'll give me room to put out my own story inside the prison. I just haven't sorted through all that in my mind."

Pee Wee was determined to continue with his arrangement with North Charleston. He just wasn't sure where he was going with all of it. He knew it was pretty unlikely that he would ever be out of prison unless he escaped, so it wouldn't make any difference how many sentences he had. He knew that he could continue to reveal bodies hidden in remote graves for a long time and he surmised that he could then string out the long series of revelations regarding how the victims met their demise and at whose hands. As long as he could continue the conjugal visits he thought it was the best he could do under the circumstances. Of course he had not lost sight of the fact that there was also the possibility that an escape chance would come while they were wandering in the woods. As he tried to envision what would follow this latest revelation, his confidence was growing that Chief Simmons would keep his word about the conjugal visits. That was worth an awful lot to a man who might never see the outside again. He thought to himself that he had always been willing to risk a lot to lie with a woman and Donna was worth a lot more risk than most. Pee Wee suspected that as the police discovered bodies with his assistance that there would be a clamor to find any that remained. He believed that the North Charleston chief and his detectives would relish the limelight and continue the secret bargain with him as long as he continued to produce.

"I'm gonna show you where the farmer is. That's what I've been studying on."

"You saying you don't know what happened to Kim Ghelkins, Pee Wee?" snarled Whatley; angry with what he assumed was a lie.

"They's just a lot more to that. I have to sort through a lot on these things and y'all need to bear with me and I'll keep my word to keep showin' you what I can as long as y'all are keepin' your part," Pee Wee responded.

"All right as long as we're accomplishing something and locating the bodies of missing people, that's our mission here and we'll bear with it," said the chief detective.

"Whoa," Query said, "I need a minute alone with my client. I didn't know this was in his thinking and I'm not sure what all it involves."

Pee Wee was put in one of the police cars and his handcuffs were chained to the floor. His lawyer was then allowed to get in the back seat with diminutive killer.

"What are you talking about?" Query asked. "Whose grave is this, Pee Wee? What are you talking about?"

"I'm gonna give 'em Barnwell. I can find that one."

"The farmer? Is that the one you're talking about? The man they are saying you might be responsible for killing in Williamsburg county?"

"Yes, sir, that's the one."

"I don't like this idea, Pee Wee. We haven't talked about this. Just tell them you can't find it today that you'll come back and try again. I think they know you're really trying, but Pee Wee, you're opening up something all together different here. You don't want to do this without our having discussed it in detail. This will even bring in a different jurisdiction. I can't imagine anything but bad news coming out of this."

"I give 'em my word Mr. Queury, I can't go back on that. I'll have to do what I said or they'll never believe anything I tell them about anything else."

"That may be, Pee Wee, but I think everyone believes that you are trying, and I just think we need to talk this through before you go into something entirely new. You've just got to remember that while these people may be polite to you while we're cooperating; they still have every intention of killing you in the electric chair. You need to understand that Kirk McLeod is going to be a hell of a lot better at getting that done than Kenneth Summerford and we need to talk about that before you put yourself in the middle of a murder case in his jurisdiction."

"I'm going to go on with it. I want them to know I do what I say. I'm goin' to have to go this way, Mr. Queury. I'm not sayin' I can find Kim or not, but I can't do it today. That's what I'm tellin' you."

Pee Wee then directed the procession of police cars marked and unmarked along farm roads and then declared that they had reached their destination.

"Let's head up across them fields," Pee Wee directed as they took him out of the patrol car.

"I'm not sure about this," cautioned Whatley as he gazed across the plowed field at yet another dense stand of trees. "I don't like the idea of spending all of this time out in the woods and then moving into this open field," he said. "If I was setting up an ambush this is the way I would do it."

"Let's put Pee Wee in the car and spread out into the woods there and have a look," suggested Sheriff Barnes.

After assuring themselves that the woods were clear the officers again followed the little man in chains as he lurched and limped over the plowed field.

"I can't seem to get my bearings," Gaskins said to the group. "It just don't look right. I know I'm off somehow but I can't figure just how. Lookin' back over there, I seen something familiar. Let's go over to them woods by where we came in and I'll try and see if I can locate where Kim's at."

Query was completely confused by the reversal of his strange little client. He could only surmise that Pee Wee might have actually listened to his advice about the danger of the can of worms he was opening by revealing the body of the man from Williamsburg County. Pee Wee though was more interested in not losing the enthusiasm of his peculiarly disposed support group from North Charleston who were so motivated to find the missing girl that they were willing to accommodate this villain they despised. He had concluded that after the body of the missing girl was revealed to them, they would be totally invested in the mission to recover all of the bodies. Query had told Gaskins that once it was revealed to the press that he had given information leading to the discovery of any bodies, anyone opposing North Charleston's continued solicitation of his cooperation would be mowed down by the media, as long as the media didn't know the details of his arrangement.

Pee Wee was actually having some difficulty orienting himself but in less than an hour he saw a tree that he had marked. He was still unable to find his other landmarks but he began to circle slowly away from the marked tree and soon stepped down knee deep into a big track made by a log skidder. The gouge made by the twenty inch wide tires ran ten feet or so and the police dug several times in places that Pee Wee showed them along the tire trench. Hardened sides and bottom spoke to the age of the furrow and distinguished it from more recent marks of the same genre that retained a soft and wet appearance. Finally they found the heavy plastic sheeting in which the body of the young girl had been wrapped.

The officers cleared away a small hole less than a foot square and maybe eighteen inches deep. It was apparent that grayish colored flesh lay beneath the plastic. Only about a four by six section was revealed. To a man, the normally detached lawmen and the case hardened defense lawyer shuttered to themselves as they silently concluded by some subconscious calculation that what they were seeing was a small part of once living person's outer thigh.

Minutes after they were convinced that they were looking at part of a body, Pee Wee was whisked away to the police cars and securely chained. He was asked whether he wanted to make a statement about her disappearance and murder.

"Right at this time I would not be prepared to go there," he said. "As I've told you they is a lot involved and I am mostly just goin' on hearsay here."

"I guess it just never stops," said one of the officers from Florence. "He just can't bring himself to just tell it straight up."

"I found her for you," was the only reply.

Calls were made to notify different offices and within ten minutes Pee Wee was on another high speed ride back to CCI and SLED cars were racing in the opposite direction to the gravesite.

Not knowing how Chief Simmons and his department would react now that the last victim from their city that they knew about had been located, Pee Wee asked to be brought back to North Charleston. To his satisfaction Chief Simmons sent for him immediately. Just a few days after Kim had been located Pee Wee told them that he was sure that he could locate Barnwell Yates.

Both Query and Grisso met with Pee Wee and warned him against opening up the Yates matter.

"No I've got to stay on this. If I show them where another body is, it will be a feather in his cap for Chief Simmons. If I just quit he'll look bad and he might just quit this whole thing," Pee Wee told them. "Get 'em back over here, let's get this thing done."

Just an hour after beginning the search near the same location where it had ended just days before, Pee Wee identified the spot where he said the man was buried. A few more minutes and the officers had uncovered enough to know that there was in fact a body at that location. The area was roped off and the calls made to bring in the coroner. Sheriffs and their deputies from Williamsburg, Florence and Sumter counties soon arrived along with additional SLED agents from Columbia.

"You want to tell us about it, Junior," asked Sheriff Byrd Parnell of Sumter, using the name by which he had known Gaskins for many years.

"I was just told where he was buried, Sheriff, that's all there is to it."

"Don't play with me. I'll see that you never see the light of day and I'll see you strapped into the chair, you little liar," Fumed the grizzled sheriff

"That's all I'm sayin'. I got nothin' else to say to him, Mr. Queury, you tell him I ain't got to talk to him. This ain't even his county."

"Get him out of here, he's never given a truthful answer in his life," said the veteran sheriff. "Put him in a car. He's not needed for anything else out here."

"Ask him if they found that black girl yet," Pee Wee shouted back over his shoulder as he was led away.

"He hates me and I hate him," Pee Wee would tell Query and Grisso back in Columbia.

CHAPTER SIXTY ONE

The Yates Murder Investigation and Trial

Silas Barnwell Yates had disappeared from his home in February 1975. Early on the investigation had focused on his jilted fiancée, the beautiful twenty-nine year old Suzanne Kipper, with whom he had been involved in a continuing legal conflict following a particularly bitter breakup. While they battled through the courts over expensive gifts that Yates had given Suzanne, the svelte young woman had begun dating a younger man, twenty-two year old John Owens. Owens was from a well to do family but by comparison to the sexy and sexually experienced Suzanne he was extremely naïve. Owens and Suzanne were soon married.

When Barnwell Yates disappeared it was inevitable that sheriff's deputies would question Suzanne and to inquire as to whether she had any knowledge of his whereabouts. The breakup and the open enmity between the two former lovers had been the talk of the community. Because of her legal battles with Yates Suzanne was already represented by an attorney. Owens had provided her with the attorney and so he also had ready access to his advice. When they were approached by investigating officers they both declined to be interviewed or to provide any information. Since investigators were without a body, the actual fate of the man was pure supposition and the investigation stalled without development of any further evidence.

After the discovery of the body of Yates with the help of Gaskins, the investigation swung into full force fueled additionally by the ire of frustrated law enforcement. Frightened by the constant pressure of the investigation, young Owens hired other lawyers from a firm experienced in criminal practice and told his attorneys that he had knowledge of the murder. His attorneys rushed to the veteran solicitor Kirk McLeod and offered cooperation and testimony in return for immunity from prosecution. McLeod refused to offer immunity but advised that he would consider allowing Owens to plead to a lesser offense if he was completely truthful and if, as the attorneys indicated, Owens was not the trigger man, the person who actually took the man's life.

Owens gave a statement to police saying that Suzanne had hired Gaskins and another man, John Powell, known as Teadlam, to kill Yates. He said that at the insistence of Gaskins, he and his wife had accompanied Gaskins when Gaskins abducted Yates, handcuffed him, put him in the trunk of his car and took him to a remote farm area where he killed him. He said that he and his wife had remained in the car when Yates was taken into the field and murdered by Gaskins and Teadlam Powell. He said that Gaskins then forced Owens and his wife to go into the field to see Yates lying dead with his hands still cuffed. Owens said Yates appeared to have been stabbed in the chest and he thought that his throat had been cut. He said they were kept there in the field while Gaskins and Powell buried the man.

Powell and Suzanne Kipper Owens were arrested and indicted for murder. Gaskins was also served in prison with a warrant for murder and he was indicted at the same time. The solicitor's office moved swiftly to prepare for the prosecution of the case and it was called for trial against all three defendants in April of 1977.

Although Gaskins was still under a death sentence, the South Carolina Supreme Court had already ruled that the Furman decision by the U.S. Supreme Court overturning death penalties applied to those sentenced under the existing South Carolina statute. This did not result in the death sentences of those on death row being instantly changed, but rather each defendant had to petition the court for a remand to the circuit court for re-sentencing where a new sentence of life imprisonment would be imposed. There was therefore no valid death penalty statute in South Carolina when Gaskins and his co-defendants were arrested and indicted for murder in the Yates case. While they would be tried for premeditated murder, the only possible penalty was a life sentence.

Solicitor McLeod and Assistant Solicitor, Ken Young, would explain that their decision to go forward with a trial for the murder in their circuit was based primarily on three considerations. Firstly, even though Gaskins had already been convicted in Florence County, the Yates case involved the murder of a member of a prominent family in McLeod's circuit and the citizens of that county were entitled to the assurance that such crimes would be vigorously prosecuted by their solicitor. Secondly, the other people involved in the murder had not been convicted of anything and had to be tried. McLeod and Young knew that the conviction of the others would be more certain if they were tried with Gaskins. Finally Gaskins still had his Florence County conviction under appeal and if he were successful in the appeal beyond the automatic remand for a life sentence, he could be granted a new trial in that case. McLeod wanted another sentence on Gaskins to guarantee that he would continue to be under a life sentence no matter what happened in Florence.

The case was originally set for trial in Williamsburg County. After two brief hearings and having considered the voluminous examples of media coverage, affidavits from criminal defense attorneys and others opining that Gaskins could not receive a fair trial in that circuit because of the publicity, Circuit Court Judge Dan Laney changed the venue. The judge ruled not only that the case would have to be tried in a county other than Williamsburg, but also that it would have to be in a different circuit away from the Pee Dee area.

Judge Laney said privately to the attorneys for the prosecution and defense that anyone from the Pee Dee who said that he hadn't heard about Pee Wee Gaskins and the bodies in and around Prospect was either too dumb to be on the jury or lying. After consultation with the South Carolina Supreme Court about the possibilities available for the transfer of the case, he ordered that the trial be held in Newberry County in Newberry, S.C., about eighty miles to the west and on the other side of the state capital of Columbia.

The trial was commenced in Newberry by the selection of a jury from that county. The jury was immediately informed that they would be sequestered throughout the trial and told that they would be allowed to go home to pack for the rest of the week when court adjourned that day. Newberry was a small college and textile town and the only motel that could accommodate the entire jury panel and the court personnel from Williamsburg County including the Clerk of Court, court reporter, solicitor's staff, deputies who were to testify, SLED agents who were either witnesses or there to provide additional security and other witnesses was the Newberry Inn. It was a sixties style motel and restaurant located alongside Interstate 26 that runs east to west across South Carolina from Charleston to Greenville passing through the state capital before continuing westward past Newberry.

Suzanne Owens and John Owens were out on bond and stayed at another motel twenty miles away in order not to be under constant observation by the sequestered jurors.

Both Pee Wee and Powell were in custody. Powell was held at the Newberry County jail and transported the short distance each day by deputies. Pee Wee was as usual being held at CCI and was driven back and forth each day in a SLED car with three agents in the car. Pee Wee wore his usual array of chains and was locked to a special loop in the floor by chain and lock. Another SLED car drove ahead of the one with Pee Wee and a third followed. Four SLED agents rode in each of the other two cars and the three who were not driving rode with riot guns or sawed off shotguns lying in their laps or close at hand. Query and Grisso made a daily objection to being denied access to their client because he was taken back to the penitentiary in Columbia every day immediately following court. Judge Laney ruled each time that Gaskins was being held on death row as a result of the Florence County death penalty and had a record for escapes from custody and that the unusual security was therefore necessary.

Security in and around the old courthouse mirrored that of the motorcade as Sheriff's cars from both Newberry and Sumter counties seemed to be in every other parking space close to the court. Highway patrol cars were also scattered about and unmarked SLED cars were intermingled with the others. Every entrance was guarded by two or more officers and in the packed courtroom several SLED agents stood along each side of the courtroom and at the back of the courtroom.

Attorney Grady Query's sixty year old father who had driven down from Charlotte to hear a day of the proceedings asked Query during a break:

"Grady, who are the men in suits standing along the sides and at the back of the courtroom?"

"They are all SLED agents, Dad. SLED is like the SBI in North Carolina. They are all part of the extra security in case someone tries to help Pee Wee escape or in the more likely event that someone tries to kill him while he's in the courthouse."

"Do those agents all have guns?" he inquired further.

"Sure, usually more than one," Query answered thinking of Tom Henderson's arsenal in his car. "Why?"

"I'll tell you this, if someone drops a book, when it goes bang, they'll probably shoot half the people in the courtroom including each other in the crossfire," his father said sarcastically. "They ought to at least get on the same side so they're all shooting at the same thing."

"They're trying to make sure Pee Wee doesn't jump out the window like he did in Florence," Query said laughing. "There's also an agent on the roof with a shot gun," he added. "There actually is a guy that got out of prison yesterday or the day before who supposedly swore that he was going to kill Pee Wee for killing his brother. They are pretty jumpy about that." Query added deciding that it was better to leave out the detail that the convict had actually promised to kill both Pee Wee and his lawyer.

Query mentioned his father's observation in light conversation with Judge Laney as they returned from lunch. After a short pause the judge stepped just inside the courtroom, looked about and then summoned a SLED Lieutenant and told him to move the agents to one side or the other of the courtroom and to move the ones in the back to the front of the courtroom.

"Hell, those guys in the back would shoot me along with anybody else from where they are," he pointed out.

Query and Grisso had originally intended to stay in Columbia where Grisso could stay at home and Query could stay in a motel on I-26 a little more than thirty minutes from the court. They soon found that they needed to spend most nights at the same motel as the others because of the necessity to talk with witnesses in preparation for the next day. While every issue in the courtroom was rigorously contested by both sides, the evenings were congenial. Court officials, solicitors, defense attorneys, SLED agents and even the judge often gathered for drinks in the extra room rented by the solicitor's office for use as an office and witness interview room. They gathered there because of the need to be out of the way of the jury while the jurors had dinner and moved about the common areas of the motel. Jurors were permitted to have one glass of wine or beer with dinner and it was important for attorneys, law officers and other witnesses to avoid contact with the jurors during this brief period of relaxation. Jurors were instructed to avoid discussing the case with anyone or even among themselves since all of the evidence had not been presented. They were directed to avoid newscasts and newspapers, making this brief respite even more important to them.

At trial John Owens testified that Suzanne had been constantly enraged over the course of action taken by Suzanne's former boyfriend after their breakup. He said that Barnwell Yates had reneged on gifts to her including a car, a horse, jewelry and a number of other items. He said Yates had successfully convinced the courts that he was actually the owner of all of the "gifts" and had only allowed Suzanne the use of the horse and the car.

Owens further testified that Suzanne had somehow met Teadlam Powell who had introduced her to Pee Wee Gaskins and that she had paid Gaskins and Powell at least fifteen hundred dollars to "get rid of Barnwell Yates". He said that he had gone with her to meet with the two men without knowing the true purpose of the meeting. He said that he and his wife had asked the men about beating up Barnwell Yates in retaliation for his heavy handed actions toward Suzanne. He said that he was unaware of any discussion of harm greater than a beating. He admitted that by going along with his wife's plan to have the two men hurt Yates, he had become unknowingly involved in the murder of Yates which was carried out by Gaskins and Powell.

Owens testified about the abduction of Yates from his home by Gaskins and the subsequent ride to a remote area with Yates in handcuffs in the trunk of the car. Owens said that he and Suzanne had begged Gaskins not to kill Yates when they heard him praying for his life from the trunk of the car. He said that Gaskins had said that he had been paid to do a job and there was no turning back. Gaskins said that Yates had now seen him and had seen Powell and that he would be able to identify them. According to Gaskins he believed that Powell and he would both go to jail for life for kidnapping if they let the man go at that point and that they were not going to let that happen. Owens said that Gaskins threatened that he would not tolerate any interference from Owens or his wife.

His testimony continued as he described a horrifying scene in which he and his wife were left in the car while Gaskins and Powell dragged their victim from the trunk of the car and marched him off across the field with guns in hand. He said that he and Suzanne were told not to get out of the car until Gaskins or Powell returned. He said they were told that the two hardened criminals would hunt them down and kill them if they ran. Owens testified that they he and Suzanne sat mortified in the car awaiting the sound of a gunshot or a scream.

When neither came they were shocked by Gaskins suddenly opening the door of the car. He said Gaskins then ordered them to get out and go into the field with Powell and Gaskins. He said they asked Gaskins to just get in the car and leave and that he replied that they were going to see what they had paid for. Powell took a shovel and a pick from the trunk and carried them as Gaskins led the couple into the field still carrying his pistol by his side.

"We told him that we didn't need any proof. We said 'We just want to get out of here'," his testimony went on.

He said Gaskins replied:

"We're all in this together now. If anybody goes down everybody goes down."

Owens continued, testifying that they were taken to the place where Yates lay on the ground dead with his throat cut. He said Gaskins and Powell then dragged the body a short distance and buried him. Owens said that they were then taken back to the car and driven to where they had left their own car. Gaskins then told them that if he got even a hint of them talking to anyone about the crime that they would join Yates in the ground, the startling testimony of Owens continued.

Solicitor McLeod's young assistant solicitor, Ken Young, did a masterful job of navigating through the testimony of the handsome and wholesome looking Owens who was just twenty-four at the time of the trial. Young was careful to elicit the testimony that expressed the fear of Gaskins that Owens felt and the attempt that was made by Owens to withdraw or abandon the course of action that led to the death of Yates. Young had to accomplish this without overplaying the innocence of his witness, who had after all been deeply involved in the conspiracy to commit murder and who had come forward only when arrest was imminent.

Young had him conclude his testimony with the admission that he had not contacted law enforcement once he was safely away from Gaskins, that he withheld information and otherwise assisted in covering up the murder and that his failure to come forward no doubt allowed Gaskins to avoid being identified and arrested. He conceded that this was sufficient to make him guilty as an Accessory after the Fact of Murder. He responded to questions put by Young stating that he had already entered his plea of guilty to that crime and that he understood the maximum sentence was ten years. He said that he had not yet been sentenced and that no other promises of leniency or reward had been made to him by the solicitor or law enforcement.

On the second day of the testimony security seemed to have increased beyond the apparent overkill during jury selection and the beginning of trial on the first day. It now included another officer on the roof reportedly armed with a machine gun and additional officers around the entrances and parking areas. As Query cleared the guarded front entrance he commented on the build up to one of the agents that he recognized. The agent whispered that Carl Sellers, the brother of one of the Prospect victims, Johnny Sellers, had been released from CCI just the day before and that a fellow inmate had reported to prison officials that Carl was planning to go straight to the Newberry trial where he would end the necessity of any more trials by killing Gaskins and his lawyers.

Query had met briefly with Carl Sellers years before when Carl came to him about the possibility of retaining Query to represent him on a charge that he was facing in Charleston. After hearing the amount of the retainer, Carl had gone shopping and Query did not hear from him again. Query didn't think it sounded too much like Carl to have included the lawyers in his threat. On the other hand Carl was a hardened veteran of CCI and it was an important part of the outlaw creed that he seek personal revenge for his brother's death rather than rely on the courts.

Owens had returned to the stand during the morning session for cross examination. Owens waivered little during cross examination and although the believability of his self serving version about his own limited involvement suffered considerably, it did not change the effect of his testimony regarding the roles of his co-defendants. He admitted having provided the money to pay Gaskins and Powell but hedged, swearing as before, that he had no prior knowledge of the plan to murder Yates.

It was no doubt obvious to the jury that the state had made huge concessions to Owens and it is doubtful that they bought his equivocation about the ultimate purpose of the conspiracy. The solicitor would concede in final argument that Owens may have avoided admitting everything that he knew or suspected, but contended that the concessions made by his office were necessary to insure the conviction of the two hardened killers and the woman who had initiated the crime.

"Prosecutors seldom have available to them ministers, deacons and priests as witnesses to a terrible crime. It sometimes becomes necessary to make a deal with one criminal in order to convict other criminals. We always set out to convict the worst of the lot when we have to do that kind of thing," he would argue to the jury at the end of the trial. "We got two killers and the woman that caused the whole thing and the witness still had to plead guilty. We may have had to bargain with the devil but we got the best of the bargain and when you find Pee Wee Gaskins guilty they will all be sent to prison where they belong."

Court was adjourned for lunch for an hour and a half because of the extra time involved in getting the jury to and from lunch since they had to be transported by deputies, seated separately from others in any restaurant and accompanied and observed by deputies at all times.

When Query returned from lunch he entered the courthouse through the first floor which in the traditional layout contained offices for various county officials, and public bathrooms. He stopped at the men's room and then intended to turn down the small hallway granted access to the back staircase restricted to use by attorneys and court officials. As he walked toward the two hand sinks in the bathroom, the door opened directly adjacent to the sinks and a nice looking dark haired man of about one hundred seventy pounds and about five feet nine or ten inches came through the door. Query immediately recognized the man as Carl Sellers.

The two men were alone in the restroom barely a foot apart. For lack of a better plan Query spoke pleasantly to the man.

"Aren't you Carl Sellers, I'm Grady Query. We met down in Charleston. I guess this is damn bad luck for me, the cops say you're planning to kill me."

"Hell I don't have anything against you, Grady. Pisses me off that you're representing that little piece of shit when you wouldn't represent me, but I ain't gonna kill you for it. Hell, I hope you get him off. That way I can get to him without goin' back to prison to do it."

"Don't try to get to him here, Carl. There are as many guns up there as there are on a battlefield and the cops have them all."

"I'm not that stupid. I just came to hear what's said and to see what happens. It'll suit me just fine if he gets convicted. I'm not really planning to go back to CCI to get him, but I have plenty of friends there that will. I'm just here to watch just like all of these other people. I have a right to do that, don't I? Can they keep me out because I'm on parole?"

"No, I don't think they can, Carl but we have another problem. I think it could be a very serious problem. When one of these cops figures out who you are, the chances are good they'll shoot you before you get a chance to discuss your right to be here," Query told him. "That's what everybody is all jacked up about. They think you're coming up here hell bent on killing Pee Wee right here in the courthouse. Apparently some snitch who knew you at CCI told them that you were coming up here to kill Pee Wee. Me too for that matter. I heard that from one of the cops when I came in this morning. The judge confirmed it before we went into court."

"I figured it was this way every day. I just came in downstairs so I could go by the can. When I started in they asked me if I had any weapons and asked if I was coming back out to go up and watch the trial. I told 'em yeh, I was just goin' to the can and then comin' right back out to go upstairs. They let me right in. Never asked who I was."

"The problem is that somebody is going to recognize you when you go back out there. Let me go tell them that you are in here, that you are not armed and that you are here to see the trial not to cause trouble," Query suggested unconsciously assuming the role of representing the man.

Query quickly found a SLED agent with whom he was familiar and explained what was happening. If you come down to the men's room, he's in there waiting for me to tell him to come out. You stay outside the door and he'll come out with his hands up and you can search him and do whatever else you need to do as far as security. I think he does have the right to go into the courtroom, but that's up to y'all."

The agent quickly alerted the other agents with his radio and three of them soon joined Query and the first agent downstairs where they were waiting outside the bathroom.

"Let's get in there and take him down," one of the recent arrivals said hurriedly.

"Wait a minute guys, he's just standing in there waiting for me to tell him to come out. I've already talked to him. I told him it might cause a panic if he came out and someone spotted him before he had been cleared. I'll tell him to come out. He already knows to back out of the door with his hands up. If he doesn't, then grab him."

Query knocked then opened the door to the restroom, holding it wide open he told Carl to back out slowly with his hands in the air. Carl did as he was asked and was quickly whisked aside and searched as he stood with his hands on the wall. In the end Sellers was allowed to go into the courtroom with a female who had come to Newberry with him and the two sat on the fourth row wooden pew with a SLED agent on either side of Carl. Carl came for two days but did not return after that. He would tell Query years later that it was too much of a hassle to be searched and then escorted everywhere and even followed to and from lunch and the bathroom.

"Hell, I asked 'em to come on and eat with me since we were spendin' the day together," he would laugh as he told him about it.

When the trial resumed Owens testified briefly on re-direct and a final cross examination but did not add or change anything of substance. Since an attorney for Suzanne, Teadlam and Pee Wee would each have the right to cross-examine they were hopeful that one of them would find the soft spot in Owens's testimony and break down his credibility so completely that the prosecutor would offer everyone a plea to a lesser offense such as manslaughter. When a prosecutor's case depends largely on the testimony of a single witness and that witness fails to deliver convincing testimony or crumbles under cross, the prosecutor will often plea bargain for a charge carrying less time or with a quicker eligibility for parole in order to eliminate the possibility of a defendant being found not guilty.

McLeod and Young were satisfied with the performance of their stat witness and confident that the jury would convict. They remained wary, however, of the testimony of Gaskins that lay ahead. They expected that Gaskins would blame Owens and seek to exonerate Suzanne and Powell.

CHAPTER SIXTY TWO

The Infamous Plea Bargain

At the conclusion of the testimony of Owens the attorneys for Suzanne asked the court for some time to confer with their client. When the attorneys had met for nearly an hour and were begging the judge for additional time, the judge decided to adjourn for the day and allow the attorneys to continue their talks with their clients.

Up until this point the lawyers for the three defendants, Suzanne, Teadlam and Pee Wee had met together during all pre-trial motions, during jury selection and at every break in the proceeding during John Owens testimony. They had met at length the night before the trial began and every morning and evening after the jury selection began. Since Suzanne was out on bond she had insisted on being present most of the time. Their strategies had been the same and their interests coincided. Essentially they each had to attack the credibility of John Owens and emphasize for the jury that he was getting a "sweetheart deal" and had every reason to place the blame on the others and to downplay his own role in the crime.

Owens though had held up well under hours of tough cross-examination and it was likely that the jury would rely on most of his testimony even if they thought he was more involved than he had admitted and even if the jurors didn't like the leniency he was granted in return for his testimony.

Because of the strength of the Owens testimony, the attorneys now met privately with each of their clients. It was essential at this juncture that the clients understand the potential impact of the testimony on each of their individual cases. The attorneys had carefully pointed out the conflicts that existed between the individual defendants and the importance of protecting each of their individual rights throughout their representation. It was important at this juncture that the lawyers ensure their clients understanding that they might need to make decisions that would detrimentally affect the outcome for their codefendants.

Suzanne's lawyers were particularly concerned that she realize that her husband had somewhat minimized her role, testimony that privately the lawyers rather doubted, but that they were nevertheless obligated to use to her advantage if possible. Because Owens had testified that he and his wife didn't participate in the actual killing and had attempted to withdraw, it seemed that this was probably the most opportune time to try to bargain for a less serious charge. They emphasized that she would be required to testify if she were to receive any consideration and to testify truthfully regarding the leading role played by Gaskins.

Their suggestion to Ken Young that she be allowed to plead to the same charge as her husband and receive a ten year sentence was flatly rejected. Young made his rejection sufficiently vehement to discourage any further discussion of that possibility.

"Not a chance," he said. "She might have had a chance at something like that if she'd come forward when John did. But it ain't gonna happen now. I'll try her for murder and accept whatever the jury decides before I'll even think about letting her plea to that. You tell her she has until tomorrow morning to accept a plea to Common Law Murder for a thirty year sentence or we are going all the way on the murder charge."

"Have y'all even thought about the fact that I will be forty years old by the time I get out of prison on parole if I take this goddamn deal that you think is so great," she told her lawyer. "You don't give a fuck about me, you just want out of this trial."

Suzanne suddenly asked her lawyer to include Query and Grisso in the meeting to discuss the offer that had been made to her in return for a guilty plea.

"Suzanne asked me to ask the two of you to come and talk to her about this plea offer," her attorney said somewhat bewildered by the strange message his client had insisted that he deliver.

"I don't see how we can do that," said Query. "As long as we are all going forward in the trial our interests are essentially the same and we can withhold any confidences for our individual clients by virtue of our joint defense agreement, but once she is offered a deal they probably become too divergent," he continued. "If she turns it down we may be back on the same page but while she is considering it I think there are inherent conflicts. She has to weigh the value of what her testimony can do to Pee Wee as her greatest leverage. We also have to take anything that we might learn that hurts her and use it to his advantage. Tell her we'd love to help her any way we can but those conflicts seem obvious."

"I've explained the conflicts to her over and over," her lawyer said exhaustion apparent in his voice. "We've actually been on this off and on since we broke from court to talk to her. She just keeps coming back to it. Her last comment was that she doesn't give a fuck about any conflicts she wants to talk to y'all. Excuse my French but that's exactly what she said. She said she'll waive any conflicts and put it in writing if necessary."

"Well the conflicts don't just belong to her," replied Query. "Pee Wee has the same rights to be protected against any conflict of interest and against the dissemination of any privileged information that we might disclose during such a meeting."

"Well please ask him if he'll waive. She says she won't discuss this anymore until she can talk to y'all. I'm at a loss for what to do next. I want to get the best deal I can for her and I think she'd be making a big mistake not to carefully weigh what they have offered. I don't think she is considering that the judge can give her consecutive life sentences for murder and kidnapping plus another consecutive twenty-five years for armed robbery, if she's found guilty on all counts."

"I'll talk with Pee Wee if you are sure you are all right with this. She doesn't need anything from us. You are an experienced trial lawyer and you've told her everything that we could possibly tell her," Query said.

"She likes you, both of you, and she has watched you guys fight tooth and nail over every tiny issue and she's become convinced that you might get a mistrial or get this thing thrown out on appeal even if you can't win it here. She's very bright and she understands that is your objective. I've sort of quietly joined in everything you've done so that she has the same appeal rights, but I've also tried to hide behind y'all a little so that she might get a deal at some point. She doesn't understand that part. She likes it when you're accusing the solicitor of hiding things and the police of creating evidence."

"I'm sure it's hard for her to appreciate those nuances and to appreciate the difference in your approach and ours with Pee Wee for whom there will be no offers. I'll see what Pee Wee says. He'll probably waive. As I've already told you at his insistence, he intends to testify that Suzanne knew absolutely nothing about this plot to kill Yates and that she wasn't there that night. He says that Owens hired Powell and that Powell brought him into it. He claims that they will both say that Owens hated Yates for tormenting Suzanne after they broke up and that Owens wanted Powell and Pee Wee to get revenge on Yates for causing her all of that grief," Query said. "I don't know whether any of that is true and I don't know firsthand what Powell would actually say, but that is how Pee Wee intends to testify. Moreover I don't know whether that testimony actually helps her or whether it hurts her. Having Pee Wee Gaskins vouch for you is not exactly what you want to play as your Ace," Query continued. "But I will ask him if he wants us to talk to her and whether he'll waive any privilege that might be lost by virtue of that talk. Our joint defense agreement prevents us from waiving their privilege by conferring or even talking directly to them but I don't think that protects us once they might testify against each other."

"Pee Wee, Suzanne wants us to meet with her and her lawyer," Query began. "Obviously the prosecution is offering to let her plead to something and she doesn't know what to do."

"Meet with her. Go ahead by god and meet with her if that's what she wants," the little man replied his voice at high pitch with agitation.

"You have to understand that we might be waiving some privilege to protect information that we have gotten from you," said Grisso. "It could be pretty dangerous, particularly if she came out of the meeting and said that you told her something or admitted to something or even that we told her that you admitted something to us. Whether it was true or not she could really say a lot that could hurt you. That's why you have to be very careful to protect the privilege that attaches to anything you say to us."

"I don't give a damn about no privilege. I know y'all will do everything you can to win this thing or to get it thrown out and if that don't work you'll try to win it on appeal. Fellas, I also know that the odds are they'll get me on some of this stuff along the way. There ain't no death penalty here, we're just fightin' to let 'em know it's gonna be a hell of a go every time they come at me. I know all of that," Pee Wee said to the lawyers, who were somewhat shocked at the accuracy of his ten second synopsis.

"Tell her to fight it to the end. Tell her I'll put it all on Teadlam and her husband for hirin' me to kidnap him and beat him. I'll be admittin' I took him off but then I'll swear them two killed the man which I didn't know was gonna happen and which was never a part of what I was hired on for," Gaskins went on. It was the same thing that he had told his lawyers from the beginning, but in the face of the testimony of Owens it would now be "he said –he said" and the odds were pretty good that Owens would be believed over Gaskins.

"Pee Wee, I feel certain that her lawyer is advising her to make a deal. If we talk to her we can't promise you that we will tell her not to do that. She's going to ask us for our advice as lawyers and if we talk to her we have to give her the best advice that we can. That's why we're telling you that we will not talk to her at all if you don't want us to," said Query.

"No, no, Mr. Queury, I want you to talk to her and I'm fine with you tellin' her what's best for her. I just wanted you to let her know where I'm goin' with it all the way I'll go when I testify. She weren't there and when I was startin' to beat the man, Teadlam or John stabbed him and then John cut his throat."

"Okay, we'll talk to her and if it gets questionable we'll just tell her we can't talk to her anymore and I'll be sure to tell her how you intend to testify," Query said.

Grisso and Query joined Suzanne and her attorney in a small conference room behind the courtroom. Ken Young had advised Suzanne's attorney that he would allow her to plead to common law murder. If she pled to that she would still receive a life sentence but she would have an earlier eligibility for parole. As part of the plea bargain she would be expected to testify against Gaskins and Powell.

"If Pee Wee tells them I wasn't part of it, don't you think they'll find me not guilty?" she asked directing her question to Grisso and Query.

"I don't think you can count on the jury believing his testimony, Suzanne. They'll be able to ask him about all of his convictions including the one for murder in Florence. The solicitor will argue that he is a thief, a murderer and a liar and that he is lying to protect the person who set this whole thing in motion," Query said. "I would ask them to let you plead to accessory before the fact," he continued. It will still get you life or a thirty year sentence but your chances for parole and eligibility for reduced custody status will all be greatly improved."

"I don't believe they'll go to that," her lawyer answered.

"If you tell them what Pee Wee is going to say they might do it realizing that a jury could easily go to common law murder even if they don't completely believe him just because it's an easy compromise. They probably want her testimony against Gaskins and Powell," said Query. "Owens may have laid the ground work but Ken and Kirk know he's left some soft spots by trying to disavow any knowledge of the final plan to kill the man."

"I'm not testifying against Pee Wee," said Suzanne. "Pee Wee has killed a lot of people and nobody knows how many people have been involved with him. He'll kill me or have someone kill me. I know he will. See if they'll offer Accessory Before."

"I doubt if they'll do that," her lawyer replied.

"Will you ask them?"

"Of course," he replied.

"Will you all go to them?" Suzanne asked.

"We can't tell them that you should be afraid of our client, Suzanne. On the other hand I will tell them that I believe Pee Wee could screw up the case against you if he testifies. I think they know enough about what he said in Florence to know that he can be convincing. But even more than that, they know that there is no telling what he might say. One thing they don't want for sure is to have you get convicted and then have it come back on appeal and have to do it all over."

"Do you think it would be overturned on appeal?" Suzanne asked.

"Chances of that are very remote," said Query. "That's not something you want to count on. There's certainly not been anything yet. It always has some bargaining power because they would rather have the certainty of a plea and not have to face the possibility of a new trial. I think we can pump up the bargaining power a lot by talking to them about the unpredictability of Gaskins."

"This is going to be your chance to get the best deal that they will go along with," Grisso interjected. "I've been on the other side too many times. Even if they think they've got locks on convicting you, they know something can go wrong and they don't want to have to put all of this together again."

All three lawyers would go to meet with the prosecutors. McLeod and Young would eventually relent and agree to let Suzanne Owens plead to the Accessory Before the Fact of Murder charge. They also agreed not to require her to testify as a part of the deal.

"I'm not sure we would even want her to testify. Owens testimony went very smoothly and she could just screw it up, if she testifies differently. She's given earlier statements to the police and she'll be cross examined on that plus you know she's angry with Owens and she'll try to hurt him if she can. After all her need for revenge against her men who cross her, is what got us here. I don't see any point in taking the chance. I won't call her unless someone says she wasn't there or something just totally contrary to what we know the facts to be. We'll just have the judge tell the jury she has pled guilty," said Young.

"If you believe Owens, she tried to call it off at the last minute," said McLeod. I guess that justifies working something out on a plea.

"I don't think you're entitled to tell them that she has pled guilty," Query interrupted, seeing the potential for harm to his case. "That would be highly prejudicial. I think he can only tell them that she is no longer part of this case."

"We'll have to let the judge make that call," snapped Young.

Suzanne Owens entered her plea of guilty the following morning and the judge after thorough questioning as to the voluntariness of the plea, accepted the plea and postponed sentencing until after the trial. He would rule after learning that she would not be called as a witness that the jury would only be told that she was no longer a part of this trial. They would be instructed that they should not be concerned with that nor should it have any effect on their decision as to the guilt of the remaining defendants Gaskins and Powell.

Minutes later Powell's attorney announced that he wished to enter a plea of guilty to common law murder. The attorney advised that he had not agreed to testify and assured the solicitors that he would not testify under any circumstances even if they sought to compel his testimony after his plea. His lawyer would tell Query and Grisso that while Teadlam Powell was determined not to help with the prosecution of Gaskins by testifying, he did not want to put his mother or himself through the agony of continuing the trial. His attorney said that Powell was convinced it was inevitable that he would be found guilty in the end.

After the same questioning regarding Powell's full understanding of the consequences of his plea and after determining that the plea was voluntary, Judge Laney accepted the plea of guilty to Common Law Murder tendered by Powell with his attorney at his side. Sentencing was postponed and Judge Laney instructed the jury that Powell was no longer in the case and that the jury should not consider that information in any way in their determination of the facts as they applied to the one remaining defendant, Donald Gaskins. The judge then adjourned advising that the events of the day had been dramatic enough to exhaust everyone and that a fresh start the next morning would be best.

Attorneys for the prosecution and defense joked as they relaxed after court that the judge was probably staying at the lake and the beautiful day had determined the necessity of the early recess.

Trial commenced again the following morning. Officers gave details about having been taken to the gravesite by Gaskins and of the recovery of the body. Dr. Sexton testified that death had resulted from a knife wound on the front of the throat that severed the windpipe, voice box, and the carotid artery on the right side. There was also a stab wound to the chest that severed a major vein from the heart and would have probably been fatal as well. It was his opinion that the weapon was a sharp knife six or more inches in length and that it was most likely that the person wielding the knife was right handed.

Marie Marlowe was called and testified that Gaskins had approached her about luring Yates from his house.

Others testified about the angry legal battle between Yates and Suzanne Owens.

The prosecution rested knowing that they could pressure Suzanne to testify in reply if it became necessary.

Gaskins took the stand and shocked everyone by testifying that he had committed other murders, but not the murder Barnwell Yates. As promised he testified that Owens had paid Gaskins and his son in law Howard Evans to grab Yates at his house. He testified that Marie Marlowe had lured Yates from his house and that he was to beat and frighten Yates as revenge for what he had done to Owens's wife Suzanne. Pee Wee continued his testimony, swearing that Suzanne was not present on the night of the kidnapping and that he had threatened Yates and struck him several times and told him that he would kill him if he reported the attack. He said that they were in the field where Yates was buried and that Yates who was in handcuffs had suddenly tried to run away. He said that he had struck Yates across the throat with a karate chop and that Yates had fallen to the ground unconscious. He said that he believed that he had killed Yates with that blow and directed Evans and Owens to bury him. According to Pee Wee's testimony, Evans had told him later that Owens had stabbed the unconscious Yates twice in the chest and cut his throat when he began to move and make noises while they were digging his grave.

Gaskins next testified out of the blue about the murder of the young black woman Martha Ann Dicks, who was known as Clyde. Query asked the judge to grant a brief recess during which he warned Gaskins that what he was doing constituted a judicial confession admissible against him in another trial and virtually certain to convict him in a trial in the future. Gaskins told him that he understood and that he was going to testify about several things that might hurt him in future trials but would convince the jury in this case that he was being truthful.

Gaskins testified that the murder of the young colored woman had been ordered by the owner of Kolb's junkyard who had told him it was to protect highly placed law enforcement people. He testified about having taken officers from North Charleston to the exact place where the body had been left and about the refusal of Sumter law enforcement and SLED to even look for the body. Gaskins raised the tension in the courtroom when he suggested that the Sumter County Sheriff's Department apparently had little concern over the disappearance and death of a young black girl as compared to the intense investigation of the disappearance and death of the daughter of a white legislator that had turned the county upside down. Gaskins turned to the judge and asked the court to order a search for the body. Judge Laney asked Gaskins if he realized that he was admitting to having knowledge of the woman's murder and whether or not he needed to discuss this testimony further with his attorneys.

"I have discussed my testimony with them, your honor, and they advised me not to go with it. But I believe that if we are going to get to the bottom of this, I am going to have to go with it all and tell about what murders I have been involved with or have knowledge of. I'm doin' this so that you and this jury will know I'm tellin' the whole truth, just like I swore I would do."

Query and Grisso urged the judge to grant the request to order the search arguing that it would go directly to the credibility of Gaskins. If the truth of his assertions could in fact be established, it would bolster his credibility regarding his denial of the murder of Yates. Grisso also proposed that the confirmation that Gaskins had shown officers exactly where the body had been left and the refusal of the officers to search could give credibility to testimony given by Gaskins that he was targeted by law enforcement in this case because of what he knew about other murders.

Judge Laney inquired in open court outside the presence of the jury about the failure of law enforcement to investigate after they were given information about the whereabouts of the body. The sheriff's chief deputy informed the court that through the years they had been lied to constantly by Gaskins when they investigated crimes about which he might have been involved or have some knowledge. He said that the decision was made that information from him was so inherently unreliable that they would not waste the resources of the county to pursue it, absent something else to corroborate what he had said.

"Well if it's as easy as he says to just walk down a ditch and find the body, that doesn't seem too complicated to check that out," the judge commented in a conversation that took place in his chambers after he moved the discussion from the courtroom. "I'll tell the jury not to come in until 2:00 tomorrow afternoon. Can y'all get out there at daybreak and see if there is anything to this? I think his lawyers may be right that this goes directly to his credibility. If he gave this to law enforcement months ago, and now he is being made to appear to have lied about it when no one has checked it out, the jury could believe that he was a target."

"But he chose to bring this up," argued Young. "It actually has nothing to do with this case."

"It takes a lot to set it up to take him out there, Judge," offered Tom Henderson from SLED.

"I'm not saying take him out there," growled the judge. "He's made it look like we are willing to do anything necessary to convict him for killing this white farmer but we won't even walk down a ditch to find the body of a black woman that he very well might have killed."

"He'll deny killing her," said the chief deputy.

"Chief that's not my point. He's really set y'all up to look like you'll do anything and everything to convict him here but you won't even investigate the murder of a black woman. It makes perfect sense that you didn't believe him but now he's testified to it under oath and put it on the front page of the newspapers and I think you better have somebody in that ditch in the morning."

"We'll be there, Judge," the chief deputy answered. McJunkin walked into the hall and spoke to one of the SLED agents. "Let me talk to him before you haul him back. I want to be sure on the directions."

The following morning sheriff's cars, SLED cars and every imaginable type of police vehicle converged upon the field where Gaskins had directed them. They were, of course, followed by determined TV and newspaper reporters who ignored the speed limits to keep up with the speeding cop cars.

Sheriff Byrd Parnell strode along the dirt road in his ever present yellowish white straw cowboy hat. He leaned over to Query as he came up to him. "I won't forget you tryin' to embarrass my department like this," he said.

"Not trying to Sheriff. You know I can't control what he says or when he says it. Maybe you should have sent somebody out here before now," Query replied.

The searchers went down the four to six feet of ditch bank and moved along in and next to the small stream of water that flowed at the very middle of the bottom. After about forty-five minutes someone cried out from atop the bank.

"Yo, got somethin' here. You better have a look; this is the real deal."

Deputies raced to cordon off the area and photographers raced to beat them to the spot. Not one of the regulars on the search parties, the young officer had forgotten the instruction not to call out. First a bone from a human arm and then shortly thereafter other bones that appeared human were found along the banks of the deep ditch. The coroner and the sheriff would later explain that the body had most likely been disturbed either by animals or by the action of flood waters when water raced through the ditch filling it completely and often overflowing it for several feet on both sides. As a result the bones were found along the banks several feet from the ditch rather than deep in the ditch and under an overhanging bank as described by Gaskins. Light brush along the banks that separated the ditch from the field had further obscured anything along the banks from the view of someone in the plowed portion of the field. A human skull and other human bones were soon found in the edge of the brush farthest from the ditch. An earlier search of the ditch itself would no doubt have been fruitless since the bones were outside the ditch the sheriff's office proclaimed. The search had taken less than an hour.

The following day Gaskins testified that he had killed Peg Cuttino who was the thirteen year old daughter of a Sumter County legislator. He testified that he did so at the request of members of law enforcement. He refused to identify the police officers. Another man, Junior Pierce had confessed to the murder while being held in Georgia where he was charged with another murder.

Pierce was sentenced to life for the murder of Miss Cuttino and returned to Georgia to serve out his life sentence before serving the consecutive South Carolina sentence. He would recant the confession saying that he was tortured into confessing to various murders while in the custody of a Georgia sheriff. Some uncertainty about the validity of his confessions was unavoidable since he had confessed to murders in other states that occurred on dates on which he was actually in a state penitentiary. Gaskins would reveal one detail police had intentionally withheld from the public in order to test anyone claiming knowledge of the kidnapping and murder. Gaskins knowledge of that fact and his claim about the date on which the murder had occurred caused alarm for some of the investigators close to the case.

Gaskins would reveal months later that he had received letters from Pierce through prison mail. All of his mail though was censored and anything from another prison would have been given extra scrutiny. Such letters would have been read thoroughly and probably withheld from the inmate and turned over to police. No explanation was ever given as to how he would have gotten letters from Pierce or how Pierce would have known what detail to provide or how such information could escape those reading Pee Wee's mail. Gaskins was, of course, well known for his ability to get information and contraband in and out of the prison that had been so often his home. Judge Laney declined the suggestion by Gaskins that Pierce be brought to Newberry to confirm his testimony.

"He could come in and admit or deny his guilt but that wouldn't prove anything about this case or the truth of what you are saying," Judge Laney observed in denying the request which was never even made by the lawyers for Gaskins.

Gaskins next testified about a murder in Horry County that was committed just a few days before Yates was killed. Johnny McDowell was serving a life sentence having been convicted of the murder in part on the basis of his confession. He said he confessed only because of the threat of the death penalty and the absence of an alibi that he could prove. Gaskins testified that the proof of his own admission lay in faulty evidence from the investigating officers and the medical examiner as to the manner of death of the two men murdered at a bridge in Horry County. Their bodies were thrown off of a bridge into the river after they were shot.

The law enforcement conclusion was that the men had been shot after their car was stopped by blocking the roadway at the bridge. The men, according to the conclusions of the investigation, were shot first with buckshot and then with birdshot as they tried to run. Gaskins explained that anyone loading a shotgun for a robbery or murder would have loaded the smaller shot first, followed by double ought buckshot and finally solid slugs thereby giving greater spread for quick shots up close and better knockdown for a target that was farther away or running away. He said the final proof lay in wallets and identification taken from the men and hidden under rocks at an interstate overpass.

"Query and Grisso asked the judge to order an investigation since there was the possibility of hard evidence to substantiate the testimony. The judge denied their request. Court ran on until after six P.M. After sandwiches at the motel restaurant the judge, the defense attorneys, the prosecutors and several law enforcement people met in the solicitor's temporary office and war room in the motel. Query and Grisso again urged that finding the wallets would absolutely substantiate the claims of their client and also solve a crime for which the wrong man may have been convicted. Grisso's seventeen year old son had driven up after school and was acting as a runner.

Judge Laney said that he could not justify delaying the trial for another quest for the solution of an unrelated murder.

"If the solicitor has no objection I'll ask SLED to send agents to a specific location, if that could be provided precisely enough for them to go directly to the spot. If they find the evidence that he says is hidden there, I'll allow you to recall Gaskins if necessary to revisit the testimony and show the jury that he was being truthful," the judge added.

Solicitor McLeod said, "I don't have any objection as long as it doesn't cause any more delay. This thing is going to break my county if we don't get it over with and get all of these people out of this motel. It's a good thing we didn't do this during football season. We'd all be camping out," he added laughing.

"We can go see Pee Wee first thing in the morning and get the exact location," Grisso offered. "He claims to be able to lay it out within a couple of feet and one thing about that big rip rap they put under bridges, they don't move it around once it's there."

"That doesn't work for us," said a SLED agent who was present. "We pick Pee Wee up at seven A.M. We never know what all they'll go through getting him ready to go since he pulled that stunt with the handcuff key. We have eleven men tied up just getting him here and then they all have assignments here. We can't hold all of that up. We're gonna be in a helluva fix to get other agents out there to look for whatever he comes up with because of all the men committed to the security at the court. Chief's got the SLED plane standing by to take them, if they have to go. I think Pee Wee's just jerking our chain on this and the Cuttino case, but since we found that woman near the ditch we have to take it all seriously. There's no telling what will come next."

"Well I guess we can talk to him when he gets here, but that means no one is moving on it until afternoon," said Grisso.

"Go talk to him tonight," said McLeod. "That way everybody knows whether they have to set anything up tomorrow. Y'all are going back to Columbia anyway."

"You call the solicitor as soon as you know whether there is something to go on and I'll make sure he knows how to get in touch with me," the judge said.

"It's almost eight, Solicitor", said Query. "I doubt they will let us in to see him."

"Tell them the judge sent you", McLeod half laughed.

"How about if you call them," suggested Grisso.

"I don't know who or where to call," he replied. "We call the warden when we want something and you can bet he ain't there. But tell you what, when you get there, if there's a problem have them call me."

The lawyers drove to the visitor parking lot at CCI. The lot was actually across the street from the prison fence and they had to cross a pedestrian bridge to get to a street side landing directly adjacent to the high razor wire topped chain link fence and the pedestrian gate. A small guard house the size of an outhouse stood just inside the fence to the left of the gate. During regular hours a guard at that location would verify that someone was to be allowed inside by calling the main gate. He would then unlock the gate and check for identification and contraband or weapons and then enter the visitor's name in a log kept there.

On that night the pedestrian bridge was dimly lit and the little guardhouse was empty and dark. The lawyers had stopped at a truck stop and called every number available in the book for the prison but to no avail. Once across the bridge one of the men pressed the call button on the little call box located just above and beside the lock on the chain link gate. A man answered from inside the main entrance. After the men had explained their purpose in being there, including the proviso that the guard could call the solicitor for verification, the guard advised them to stand by while he checked for orders. The men waited for about ten minutes before the reply came that someone was coming to escort them inside.

Grisso, Query and Grisso's son made the familiar trek of over fifty yards across the tarmac to the main entrance of the prison buildings. They went through the glass doors and through the electrically operated sliding bars into the big crossroads of the entrance. As usual they were escorted to the maximum security visiting area on their left just past the barred entrance to the Admin building. The electric bars slid closed and they sat in plastic chairs to wait for their client. The door operator sitting behind thick glass in the corner cycled the five barred doors so that only one was ever open so the lawyers were accustomed to being locked in. After twenty minutes Query leaned close to the bars and asked the sergeant at the desk diagonally across the big room from him how long it would be.

"Warden's coming down to talk with you," the guard answered.

Query had worked under Warden Joe Martin when Martin was the assistant in charge of the prison school. Query was in law school and working as a teacher at CCI. They had enjoyed a good relationship and Query felt good about their chances once they explained the purpose of the visit and the fact that they had the approval of the judge and the solicitor.

An hour passed before the warden arrived. When he came into the waiting room accompanied by a guard, it was immediately obvious that he had been drinking beyond a couple of beers by his reddened face and his blustery speech, which was unusual for the normally quiet spoken man.

"What's this all about," he began. "What're y'all doing in my prison in the middle of the night?"

"Joe, the judge wanted us to come and ask Pee Wee about something that came up during his testimony. Judge wanted us to ask him tonight so that it would not delay court tomorrow," Query explained.

"Are you telling me you have an order from the judge?" Martin asked.

"No, but I am telling you that he and the solicitor wanted us to come and talk to Pee Wee tonight so as not to interfere with the trial. I have the solicitor's number right here. He said you could call him to confirm. He wants us to call him as soon as we finish talking to Pee Wee, so he won't mind you calling."

"You got any idea what it takes to move him around? I'm not doing that for you or the judge without an order."

"You can let one guard take me back to CB 2 and I'll go up and sit on the catwalk and talk to him," said Query. "We only need to get some directions from him. You don't even have to let him out of the cell."

"Not happening; you all are under arrest for trespassing. This prison is under the jurisdiction of the Columbia police for offenses committed by civilians. They are on the way."

"What the hell are you talking about, Joe?" Query yelled the question at his former boss. "We had to call from the gate to be invited in, then we had to be escorted to the main entrance, we had to have electric doors unlocked and opened for us and we waited under lock and key exactly where we were told to wait. Waited here for a damned hour for you to show up with this crap. Why didn't you just have them tell us to leave when they called you?"

"I came because you refused to leave."

"Are you crazy or just drunk?" Grisso jumped in. "We couldn't leave we were locked in this room after being told to come into the prison and go into this room."

"Seriously, Joe, you can't invite someone in and then arrest them for trespass. If you want us to leave we'll leave. We have been asking permission all night, not once have we demanded anything or refused to do anything."

"We'll see whether I can charge you," police are on the way.

Martin left the room and the two lawyers and Grisso's teenaged son waited until the police came. When the Columbia police arrived the officer listened briefly to the explanation of the lawyers and then said, "I got no call on this. If he says arrest you inside the prison, that's all I can do. Y'all aren't going to give me any problem if I don't cuff you, are you?

"Of course not," answered Grisso. "We know this isn't your call."

"Just walk straight out the front door and the wagon is right there. We drove all the way in. Just hop in and don't say anything to anyone. I don't know what's going on here but I know Bud Grisso. He tried to help me get on with the Marshals when he was U.S. Attorney," the officer said.

"Why aren't they cuffed?" asked Martin.

"They're my prisoners now, Warden. We are inside the walls of a penitentiary so it's not necessary."

They were taken several blocks to the Columbia City Jail where Query and Grisso were fingerprinted. When the officer turned to young Bob Grisso his father intervened.

"He's a juvenile. Don't fingerprint him and don't book him. Sit him down over there and call his mother."

The officer hesitated for a moment and then said, "Let's get a bondsman over here and get you out and I'll just release him to you."

"First I want you to get hold of Judge Dan Laney, he's the presiding judge in the case we're trying up in Newberry. We are acting entirely on his instructions," said Grisso.

"I'll let you call him, but I'm not calling any circuit court judge in the middle of the night," the officer replied.

Grisso had to call Solicitor Kirk McLeod who then called the judge. In the meantime Query and Grisso were ushered to a holding cell and Bob was left sitting in the booking office. After ten minutes an officer came for the two attorneys. Sergeant wants you in his office. He said to hurry.

They found the desk sergeant standing at attention with the phone to his ear.

"Yes sir, yes sir, I understand sir. You don't need to yell at me, Your Honor; I'm going to do exactly what you tell me to do. Yes sir, they will be released right now. Yes sir, here he is. I'll put him on," he spoke with military precision and then handed the phone to Query as he exhaled loudly in relief.

"What in the hell is going on?" asked the judge.

"I'm not sure I know. We went to the prison; they let us in and then told us to wait for the warden. He came in and said we were under arrest for trespassing and the city police were on the way."

"They let you in?"

"Yes sir. They keep it locked you know. We couldn't get in except for them to come and open the gate."

"Who is the idiot that did this? You can't trespass if somebody lets you in," the judge continued.

"Warden is Joe Martin, Judge. I've known him for years. He's usually a pretty level headed guy," Query told the judge.

"You tell him to be in my chambers at nine in the morning."

"I don't think he'll pay too much attention to what I tell him, Judge."

"You tell him like this. If he is not in my chambers by nine o'clock tomorrow morning, I will send the sheriff for him and the sheriff will take him out of his own penitentiary in chains and bring him up here and through the front door of the courthouse in chains."

The following morning Query called the warden at his office at CCI at the normal seven AM beginning of the day. When the warden refused to take the call Query gave his secretary the judge's exact message word for word. When Martin called Query back he said that he had a staff meeting and couldn't be there.

"Joe, all I can tell you is that he was yelling over the phone when he gave me the message for you, so if you want to test him just toddle on over to your staff meeting. I assume that it will be a Newberry Sheriff's car. My guess is that they'll be waiting for you when you come out."

In the judge's chambers at nine present in addition to Warden Martin were Query, Grisso and Solicitor McLeod.

"I can't imagine what you were thinking," said the judge. "They were escorted into the prison by your guards. You do keep the place locked don't you? How can someone trespass when you unlock the door –a bunch of doors and let them in and then tell them to wait?"

"They refused to leave," the warden replied.

"Bud, were y'all asked to leave?" asked the judge turning to Grisso.

"No, Your Honor, we were escorted from the pedestrian gate across the courtyard and into the main entrance. We were then shown into the visiting room where the door was locked. The same way it's done every time we go in there. Then we were told to wait until the warden got there and we did; not that we had any choice; we were locked in the visiting room. When Martin got there he'd been drinking and he had already called the police before he even talked to us."

"Tell me how they refused to leave when they were locked inside the visiting room?' the judge asked Martin. The judge was now red faced, leaning forward and visibly upset.

"Well I wasn't actually there when they refused," the warden stammered.

"That's ridiculous," said the judge. "This thing upset me as soon as I heard about it, but now you're lying to me and I'm not just upset. I am furious. You've falsely arrested these officers of the court and on top of that arrested a juvenile and now you want to take me for a fool."

"I'm not lying, Your Honor, I may have misunderstood what my people were telling me," stammered Martin.

"The hell you're not lying. You just told me two things that couldn't possibly be true. Not unless they broke into the damn prison and then locked themselves in. You knew Bud's young boy was there too. This is a terrible situation. I can't find you in contempt for what you did, but I can damn sure find you in contempt for lying to me. You want to see what it feels like to do a year in your place over there?"

"No sir, Judge. I'm sorry if I overreacted."

"Don't apologize to me. First thing you are going to do though is apologize to Grady and Bud and to Bud's son. Then you are going to see that these charges are dropped by lunch time today. If that doesn't happen, I'll find you in contempt. If the charges aren't dropped their case will be tried before me as soon as this trial is over. I think there is a good chance they will be acquitted and then they are going to sue you personally and the department for false imprisonment, slander and libel and whatever else they can think of. You're gonna be found in contempt of this court for lying to me and I'm going to sentence you to a year for the contempt. You could have refused to let them into the prison and that would have been the end of it. Instead you have embarrassed them, made a fool of yourself and delayed this trial and then lied to me."

"I understand, Your Honor, I'll see that the charges are dropped. Grady, Mr. Grisso, I apologize. I obviously overreacted," the warden stated with a modicum of sincerity.

That drama behind them, the trial began again at ten A.M. with Gaskins resuming his testimony. During the morning break Query and Grisso obtained the detailed directions to the place where the wallets were supposed to be buried and passed them on to waiting SLED agents who left immediately to check the spot under the bridge in Florence County.

At one point Pee Wee testified that he was working on heating and air conditioning systems for Fort Sheet Metal on a particular date. During the lunch break Judge Laney told Query that he thought Gaskins had worked on the system in his house and asked him to ask Gaskins. Gaskins told Query that he had worked on the system for several months to fine tune everything.

Before he brought in the jury Judge Laney asked Gaskins: "Were you the one from Fort that came out and kept working to get the thermostats working and the right amount of air flowing into the different parts of my house when the new system was put in?"

"Yes Sir, Your Honor, Judge Laney that was me. I made sure to git it right. At least two times you left a door unlocked because you and the Missus couldn't be there and I went in set everything up right and adjusted it and then locked her up tight. I'm sure you know I left everything just the way I found it."

"Yes, yes, I sure do. I remember being really impressed with how determined you were to get it just right," the judge laughed. "I don't think I'll tell my wife about this."

"This case never ceases to amaze me," mused the judge. "Bring in the jury."

On cross examination Gaskins was asked to identify the law enforcement personnel involved in the murder of Martha Ann "Clyde" Dicks.

"I'm goin' to take the Fifth on that one," Gaskins said.

"What do you mean?" Young asked.

Gaskins asked to be allowed to talk to his lawyers and then stated that on the advice of his attorneys he was refusing to answer the question on the ground that it might incriminate him.

"He's testified about it, Your Honor. He brought it up. I don't think that he can now refuse to answer questions about it," Young argued.

"Your Honor, he has testified to having knowledge of the place where the body was found. He has not made any specific admission of guilt with regard to that crime," Query argued.

The solicitors conferred briefly and then advised the court that they would grant Mr. Gaskins immunity from prosecution in the case of Martha Ann Dicks, provided that he would give honest and complete testimony about his knowledge of her death.

"We know that this is unusual, Your Honor, but he has alleged that a man who runs a junkyard played a role in this and more importantly, he has accused unidentified law enforcement officers. We think it is essential that we get to the bottom of this and if there is any truth to what he says, we will pursue it to the fullest extent of the law," stated Solicitor McLeod.

"Very well, Mr. Gaskins, the State has granted you immunity from prosecution in connection with the murder of Martha Ann Dicks. You are no longer in danger of incriminating yourself by answering the question. Go ahead, ask your question again, solicitor."

Young posed the question again.

"I refuse to answer that question based on the Fifth Amendment," Gaskins responded.

"Mr. Gaskins, I am directing you to answer the question. If you refuse, I will hold you in contempt of this court for directly disobeying my order and you will be sentenced to one year in prison consecutive to all other sentences. Ask your question, Solicitor."

The same question was asked and Gaskins again refused to answer.

"Mr. Gaskins, I find you in contempt of this court and I will sentence you at the conclusion of this trial and that sentence will be one year consecutive to all other sentences."

The same thing was repeated again and then a third time. Each time the judge went through the entire explanation and each time he promised another year.

When the question was posed again, Gaskins turned to face the judge.

"Judge Laney, Your Honor, Sir, I don't mean no disrespect. We can stay here as long as he wants to keep askin' me that question and I ain't goin' to answer it and you'll keep givin' me a year on top of everything else. But you know Judge, I've already got me a death sentence from Florence, they're workin' on a life sentence here and they's eight more waitin' in Florence. I don't see we're gonna get anywhere with you passin' out one year at a time, 'cause I'm not goin' to answer his question and I won't even be around long enough to do any of your one year sentences after either the death penalty or eight or nine life sentences," Gaskins said matter of factly showing a wry smile.

"He's probably right, Mr. Young. Why don't you go on to something else?" the judge said.

"Yes sir, Your Honor. Has he been held in contempt for refusing to answer those three times?"

"Yes, he's in contempt three times, but I expect he's pretty much right about the effect of those sentences. Move on, Mr. Young."

Young finished his cross examination and called several witnesses in reply. The reply witnesses included Kenneth Summerford who contradicted portions of Gaskins testimony on the basis of statements made to him during an attempt to negotiate a plea on the remaining charges in his circuit. Seizing the opportunity to drive a wedge between Gaskins and his attorneys, who represented Gaskins both in the instant case and in those that were still pending in his county, Summerford volunteered that he had spoken to Query after the negotiations with Gaskins.

Looking directly at Gaskins, seated at the defense table with Query and Grisso Summerford said:

"I asked Mr. Query why Gaskins wouldn't just tell us the whole story on all of the murders and quit making us have to drag one little fact at a time out of him. I told him, I said Grady you know he just drags some of these people into these killings to get even with them. Stop encouraging him and get him to come straight, I told him."

"Query said to me, 'Kenneth I have no control over what he tells anyone or what he is going to go into next. I have no idea from one minute to the next what the little son of a bitch is going to do, and half the time as soon as I can get back to Charleston someone is calling me to come back to Florence or over to Sumter or Columbia because of something he called someone and said to them.' Do you hear me, Pee Wee? He called you, he referred to you as that 'little son of a bitch'. What do you think about that, Pee Wee?" Summerford finished, his voice raised and his face flushed as he leaned toward the tiny defendant some ten feet away.

"I'm sure if he said it he had a good reason and I'm sure he was lookin' to watch out for my best interest, I can tell you that. Not that I believe a damn thing you say anyhow," Gaskins snapped back.

"Enough of that," barked the judge. "Mr. Gaskins, you may not respond to the witnesses. I will not tolerate such outbursts."

"He ast me a direct question, Your Honor, Sir," Gaskins replied.

"Kenneth, you know better than to address him. Just answer the questions put to you by the solicitor or Mr. Gaskins' attorney. Go ahead with your next question, Solicitor."

"I have nothing further," stated Young amused by the banter.

Grisso cross examined the solicitor who had been his counterpart and contemporary when he served as a solicitor in another circuit. In the classic manner Grisso crossed by making statements and asking Summerford to agree that they were correct. He went through several of the statements about murders in Florence County that Summerford had testified were made to him while attempting to negotiate a plea with Gaskins. He then asked Summerford to agree that if Gaskins satisfied him with his statements that he had been told that he could avoid being exposed to the death penalty. Summerford replied that he only asked for the truth not to be satisfied with what he was told. Grisso then asked Summerford to agree that he had promised Gaskins that nothing he said during their meeting would ever be used against him, if they were unable to agree to a plea. Summerford denied having made such a promise.

"Now Kenneth, you and I have known each other a long time, is that right? We were solicitors at the same time before I left the Solicitor's office in my Circuit to become the United States Attorney for South Carolina," Bud continued, seizing the opportunity to vouch his credentials before the jury and to let the jury know that he had also prosecuted criminals in their state, "isn't that true, Ken?"

"Yes."

"Well I regret to inform you, sir that I intend to contradict you by introducing a writing signed by you at the time of that meeting. Do you wish to correct your testimony, sir?"

"I think I did tell him that, but that was before he came up here and started lying."

"But that agreement didn't say anything about it being void if he lied; did it, sir?" Grisso finished, holding a document out toward the witness without actually handing it to him.

"No, I don't think so."

"So you lied to him, and then you came in here and lied to this jury about the agreement? Never mind, withdraw the question, your honor, I have nothing further for this witness," Grisso concluded and then threw the document on the defense table as he returned to his chair.

"Guess y'all won't be having cocktails at the Grove Park," Query whispered, referring to the annual solicitors' conference usually held at the luxurious Grove Park Inn in Asheville, North Carolina.

Howard Evans was called and he denied having any part in the murder of Yates. He further denied that he had ever known either Suzanne Kipper Owens or John Owens. He testified that he was married to the daughter of Pee Wee Gaskins but denied any knowledge of any crimes committed by Gaskins. On cross he admitted having known Teadlam Powell all of his life and admitted that Pee Wee had a trailer on the same property where Evans lived and that Gaskins was there often and frequently spent entire weekends.

The following day the attorneys for the prosecution and the defense made their closing arguments. McLeod in opening said that Gaskins was a man who showed no regard for human life or for the misery that his actions had caused the family of Barnwell Yates, who he described as a highly respected farmer in his community. He said the evidence was overwhelming and could leave no doubt as to the guilt of Gaskins. He told the jury that he had not seen a more cold blooded murder and that just as it was his duty to prosecute this case it was their duty pursuant to their oath to consider the evidence and to find Donald Henry Pee Wee Gaskins guilty of the premeditated and intentional murder of Barnwell Yates.

Query and Grisso found it difficult to fashion an argument for their client who had just gratuitously testified about his involvement in two other murders and who had admitted abducting and beating the victim not to mention having admitted to delivering what he initially thought was a fatal karate blow to the victims throat. In their arguments they each stressed the requirement that each and every juror had to be convinced beyond a reasonable doubt. They urged that the deal that Owens had gotten that allowed him to escape a life sentence, which he surely deserved by his own testimony, was the incentive for him to testify against Gaskins.

The two defense lawyers in their separate arguments suggested that the state was so anxious to convict Gaskins of the actual murder that they had made too sweet a deal with Owens and that Owens had colored his version of the facts to exonerate himself of the actual infliction of harm and to point solely to Gaskins as the actual killer. They pointed out that this testimony was without any other evidence to support it. They reminded the jury that Owens was first the lover and then the husband of the beautiful and sensuous Long Legs Kipper Owens and that John was the one who hated Yates for what he had done to his wife.

Each of them told the jurors that all of the testimony agreed that Owens and his ill-treated wife were the people that had put together a plan to hurt Yates and that common sense would tell you that Gaskins had completed his work when he beat the man up. They reminded the jurors that Gaskins had even candidly and honestly admitted to them that he thought he might have accidentally killed Yates when he struck him with a fierce karate blow and had only learned differently when his son in law, Howard Evans, told him that when they were about to bury the man, they realized that he was alive. Each of them asked the jury in different words to consider the likelihood that John Owens, the angry young husband who had paid to have Yates hurt and who believed that Yates was dead and was about to bury him, had suddenly realized that his nemesis and the tormentor of his beautiful wife to whom he was unconditionally devoted was not dead and would in fact be in a position to go again to the law and continue his persecution of Owens and his wife. Angry, hurt and now frightened of going to prison for what they had done, was it not likely that he had actually delivered the fatal injuries. Injuries that reflected rage and emotion, to both stab and slash the throat of the helpless handcuffed victim. Not wounds that would reflect the cold professionalism of a hired killer. They pointed out that the one person who could tell them what had happened had not been heard from.

"Suzanne Owens has not testified. Who would she protect, ladies and gentlemen of the jury? Would she protect this man Gaskins that she hardly knew or would she protect her husband who paid to set these events in motion because she asked him to? That ladies and gentlemen is the definition of reasonable doubt and where there is reasonable doubt you must find the accused not guilty. It is not sufficient for you to think he might have done it or even that he probably did it. You must presume that he is innocent, the same way that you would assume a friend was innocent if he were accused and you may not find him guilty until that presumption is stripped away and you are entirely convinced so that there remains no reasonable doubt. John Owens has lied to protect himself. Suzanne Owens stood silent to protect her husband. The real killer has cut a sweetheart deal and there most certainly is a reasonable doubt," Query concluded.

Young gave the final argument recalling the testimony of each witness. He pointed to Gaskins and said "…he has no soul."

The jury deliberated for over an hour before returning a verdict of guilty. The judge dismissed the jury and directed all defendants and their counsel to appear the next morning for sentencing.

As they were leaving Ken Young spoke to Query and Grisso.

"Good job. I can't believe you kept them out for an hour. Shoot y'all might have gotten a hung jury, if Pee Wee hadn't decided to tell them about the other people he'd killed," he laughed good naturedly.

"I don't think they liked your boy Owens and the deal he got. That plus not having anybody but Owens saying it was Gaskins and not him that did the killing," Grisso surmised.

"Not my boy," said Ken. "We needed a witness and he was all we had. I probably should have made Long Legs testify. See y'all tomorrow. Be careful on the road."

The next morning the judge pronounced sentence first on John Owens on the charge of Accessory After the Fact of Murder –ten years confinement in the South Carolina Department of Corrections. Next was Suzanne Owens on the charge of Accessory Before the Fact of Murder –thirty years confinement in the South Carolina Department of Corrections for Women. John Teadlam Powell received life in prison for common law murder.

And finally the judge pronounced, "Donald Henry (Pee Wee) Gaskins, I sentence you to the custody of the South Carolina Department of Corrections for the rest of your natural life for the willful and premeditated murder of Silas Barnwell Yates and that sentence is consecutive to all others." The judge looked down at Gaskins and said, "I don't know how a man who has killed as many people as you can lay his head down to sleep at night."

Deputies were about to remove the defendants from the courtroom in belly chains, handcuffs and leg irons. Gaskins would be turned over to be whisked away by his standard SLED escort and the court personnel was beginning to gather their things to leave the courtroom.

Query said, "Judge, I guess I should raise one objection to that sentence as being beyond the authority of this court."

Stunned for a moment, the judge said, "You want something on the record?" a definite "now what" tone to his voice.

"No we don't need a record. I just wanted to point out that Pee Wee already has a death sentence. I'm not sure you have authority to give him any sentence that's consecutive to that one."

"Yeh, maybe not. He can appeal if he's executed," the judge quipped.

In chambers the judge and the solicitors again expressed surprise that the arguments of Grisso and Query had kept the jury out for over an hour.

"I thought they'd walk into the jury room, look at each other and all say guilty at once," said McLeod.

"Well at least we got him immunity in Clyde's murder," said Grisso with a wry smile.

"The hell you did," said Young. "He refused to answer."

"We're not going to be in any rush to try him on anything else unless he gets relief on an appeal. Then we might have to. Otherwise another trial just gives him a chance to make a circus of it. He knows we can keep piling life sentences on him as long as somebody wants to try it. Without the death penalty I'm sure he could care less," McLeod said.

Query and Grisso congratulated McLeod and Young on their victory and complimented them on a well tried case under difficult circumstances. The prosecutors returned the courtesies and the four men shook hands and left the courthouse to head to their respective offices and some long hours of catch-up.

SECTION 5

CHAPTER SIXTY THREE

New and Old

During the interim from trial to appeal imposed by the lengthy appellate procedure a rather bizarre series of events began to unfold in the normally staid and austere world of appellate review in the South Carolina Courts.

After the Furman decision and before any of the remands for resentencing of the men sentenced to death could be accomplished or while they were in the process, the South Carolina Supreme Court took an unprecedented step. In response to a petition by the South Carolina Attorney General, the high court required each of the six men subject to the death penalty to file briefs with that court to show cause why their cases should not be remanded to the circuit courts for a new trial on the issue of penalty only. For cases in which the appeal had already been decided, the question of life imprisonment or the death penalty would be based upon their affirmed conviction of murder and a new jury would determine the sentence of life or death. In cases where the appeal had not been heard, the question was whether a new trial, if one were granted could be held pursuant to the provisions of the new statute to determine both the issues of guilt and penalty or where the conviction was affirmed, a new penalty phase could be ordered.

The court's action was based upon the U.S. Supreme Court decision upholding the Florida death penalty for a defendant named Dobbert. Dobbert had been convicted under the new Florida statute for a murder he committed before the old statute was overturned by the Furman case. Dobbert had fled the state after the murder and remained a fugitive during the whole time that the Furman case was on the path to be decided by the U. S. Supreme Court. Like the rest of the country, the death penalty in

Florida became unconstitutional. When Dobbert was captured Florida had already enacted a new death penalty and Dobbert was tried under the new law. The Florida appellate courts upheld the conviction and death sentence reasoning that Dobbert had committed murder while Florida had a death penalty and that by his own action of evading capture he had forfeited the benefit of the Furman decision and was simply being tried under a constitutionally valid death penalty statute passed during his absence. The court held there was no *ex post facto* application of the new statute since the penalty was the same for the same crime and the method of guaranteeing a fair trial had merely been reformed to his advantage. To the surprise of many observers of the U. S. Supreme Court decisions involving the death penalty that court upheld the Florida decision.

After the requisite amount of panic all of the different lawyers representing the condemned men began to cooperate in formulating a response. The constitutional prohibition at the forefront of their defense was the prohibition against the *ex post facto* application of any law. It is the constitutional protection from prosecution for an act that wasn't a crime before the new law was passed or where a law is changed to provide for the imposition of a new or different penalty. The doctrine of 'fundamental fairness' often cited by the courts in death penalty cases and other due process arguments was also raised.

A further action by the Supreme Court elicited strong protests from the lawyers involved in these cases. The court ordered that as to the Dobbert issue all of the cases would be argued at the same time and that twenty minutes would be allotted for the combined arguments. Protests were immediately lodged by most of the attorneys urging that on an issue as critical as life or death each appellant was entitled to have his case fully argued by his own attorney and not merely espoused by some representative argument for the group. Egos of trial lawyers were undoubtedly as motivating as their elegant sounding arguments.

Query and fellow Charleston attorney, Dan Bowling, were in daily contact with each other and with others involved in the truly unique battle.[3] Oral arguments allow counsel for both sides to defend positions taken in

---

[3] Prior to oral arguments appellate courts thoroughly review the written briefs and the case has usually been assigned to a judge or justice to write the majority opinion. Judges have usually formed opinions regarding the final decision.

their briefs and affords a final opportunity to convince the members of the court. In cases where justices have differing opinions it permits questioning of the advocates who are presumably most familiar with the issues and best able to assist the court in its ultimate decision.

Bowling and Query were further taken aback when the familiar printed agenda for the arguments issued by the court was replaced by a second printed program without any explanation. Both dockets set some of the cases in the morning and the balance of the cases in the afternoon. The second rearranged the cases scheduled for morning and afternoon. Analyzing this unusual action, the two young lawyers suddenly realized that the condemned men who had active appeals seeking new trials had been rescheduled for the afternoon while those who had already had their direct appeal to the South Carolina Supreme Court denied were now set for the morning.

Their recognition of the significance of the change was virtually simultaneous. Apparently the justices of the court were inclined to remand the cases in which appeals had already been denied for life sentences and were at least contemplating the possibility of granting new trials in the afternoon cases in which appeals were still pending. This would result in trials in which the new statute would be utilized in its entirety, providing for both a new determination as to guilt and in a separate second phase of the trial a determination by the same jury as to whether or not the defendant would be sentenced to death. This was an application that Query and Bowling feared might survive the scrutiny of the same U.S. Supreme Court that had decided Dobbert, since the condemned men were after all asking for a new trial and the South Carolina court would be granting that request.

The two attorneys advised their clients to withdraw their appeals, meaning that they would no longer contest their convictions by seeking new trials. This was a drastic move because it effectively ended the ability to complain about any errors that occurred during the trials. On the other hand they had been literally delivered from the death penalty by the Furman decision and to again expose them to a new death sentence in cases in which a jury had already found them guilty of murder and recommended death was much too risky.

Convicted murderer Jamie McPhee was a very bright young man and his years on death row had freed him from heroin addiction allowing him to think clearly. He understood completely the danger of testing the new statute and immediately agreed with Query that his appeal should be withdrawn. McPhee signed the required affidavit to accomplish the withdrawal of the appeal. Bowling's client did likewise.

Query called Monk Hinnant, the public defender representing Gaskins and then drove to Florence to discuss the withdrawal of the Gaskins appeal. Hinnant refused to believe that the court had decided to separate the two groups in order to consider granting new trials and thereby exposing those with active appeals to a death sentence under the new statute.

Query, Bowling and Hinnant were together in the gallery during the morning session and the justices were curt and dismissive and particularly impatient with those protesting the abbreviated time for individual arguments. No questions were posed by the justices making it appear that they had reached a decision on those cases.

During the midday break, Query and Hinnant discussed further the circumstances of the Gaskins appeal. Hinnant was alarmed by the morning session and he was deeply concerned that all other active appeals were being withdrawn on the advice of lawyers that he knew and respected. His dilemma was compounded by his sound belief that errors committed during the trial of the Gaskins case were so egregious that a new trial was sure to result. His personal mission was not only to have the Gaskins conviction overturned but also a reprimand of the trial court and the prosecutors that would serve Hinnant well in future trials.

His alarm grew though as discussion continued. He of course knew that a conviction of Gaskins in a second trial was a virtual certainty and that a long dangerous battle to overturn the new death sentence would ensue with a multiple murderer as the lead case.

Defendants who are incarcerated are not present for the arguments before the appellate courts and the condemned men therefore reposed in their familiar death row cells while the drama unfolded. Defense attorneys therefore had no immediate access to their clients. The high columned Supreme Court stood across Gervais Street from the copper domed capitol was just a mile up the steep hill from CCI and death row. Hinnant asked Query to accompany him in rushing to the penitentiary to explain the urgent situation to Gaskins. Gaskins recognized the danger, knew of the withdrawal of the other appeals and quickly agreed to the withdrawal of his appeal.

As was so often true in these grisly cases a comic moment occurred.

"We have to have an affidavit in order to withdraw the appeal," Query told Hinnant; "since the defendant is not present the withdrawal is ineffective without the affidavit."

"We can't possibly get one in time. We can't even get one typed here at the prison and get back in time. Even if we knew somebody to type it," Hinnant groaned.

"We'll just write it out, Monk. Pee Wee can sign it and I'll notarize it."

"We can't submit something handwritten to the Supreme Court, they won't accept it. They'll reprimand us for trying to file it. I'll verbally withdraw the appeal and ask to be allowed to file it later."

"Come on Monk you're panicking. This isn't like you; old Rumpole of the Bailey taking on all comers and fearing none. You gonna tell your grandkids they killed your client because we didn't have a typewriter. Let's write it out. Take it up to the clerk and file it. You can offer to substitute a typed original, if it pleases the court. They're not going to refuse to file it but they will rule the appeal is not withdrawn until the affidavit is filed and they might just give Pee Wee a new trial right there on the spot. There are enough errors to justify it."

"You're right. This whole thing has just sort of shaken me up. But I'll do what we have to do for our client. You know that."

"I know, Monk, I didn't mean anything by that, you've fought the hard battle and taken all the licks for a long time in one of the toughest circuits for a defense attorney in this state. This is even harder because you know you'd probably be rightfully granted a new trial, if you didn't withdraw," Query offered sincerely.

"One last thing, Monk," Query said as they returned to the august structure that housed the highest court of the state, "I don't think you should make any argument whatsoever. Tell the court that you have been directed to withdraw the appeal and if they ask you what the basis of the appeal is, tell them that you must respectfully decline any comment and you are compelled to follow your client's wish and to simply and finally withdraw his appeal. Now this court appears to have rescheduled all of this stuff and to be predisposed to grant every one of these guys a new trial and let them go back and get a new death penalty –a death penalty that they undoubtedly believe is deserved. If you tell them there is a reason for a new trial they may just grant a new trial *sua sponte,* on their own motion."

The arguments after lunch commenced at two thirty that afternoon. Bowling argued first for his client, the first on the agenda.

"Mr. Chief Justice, justices of the court, I have been afforded insufficient time within which to pose an effective argument on behalf of my client and I wish to object to this procedure."

"Mr. Bowling you have requested additional time and that request has been denied, if you have any argument to make before this court then argue. You have already wasted most of your client's time complaining."

"My client has directed me to withdraw his appeal and I have with me and file at this time his affidavit withdrawing the appeal. Our opposition to a remand for the purpose of having a new jury decide between a death penalty or life imprisonment is set out in our brief."

"So you just wanted to complain about not having time to make an argument that you did not intend to make. Isn't that rather disingenuous?" questioned Justice Ness.

"I felt that it was my duty to object to the procedure, Your Honor."

"Sit down, Mr. Bowling, the appeal is withdrawn," ordered the Chief Justice.

"The State versus McPhee," intoned the clerk calling the next case for argument.

"Very well, next argument, Mr. Query for James McPhee. And let me caution you, Mr. Query. Argue if you wish, but do not spend your time complaining about not having enough time to argue," the Chief Justice admonished.

"Mr. Chief Justice, Members of the Court, I would be remiss in my duty and in my sworn obligation to vigorously advocate for my client if I did not continue my objection to the time allotted for argument and I do so with all due respect for this court. I too have been directed to withdraw the appeal on behalf of my client and I will file at this time his affidavit to that effect. I do, however, continue in my objection to a sentencing phase trial under the new statute on the grounds set forth in my brief."

"Is it your purpose to try my patience, Mr. Query? You aren't making an argument so you can't have too little time," admonished Justice Ness. A tenacious legal scholar Justice Ness was a man not known for his gentle disposition.

"No Your Honor, but to stand silent would be to appear to acquiesce and I make that objection in the hope that this honorable court might find it convincing in application to future situations."

"All right, Mr. Query, I'll accept your self-serving description of your noble purpose, I suppose that it is after all the goal of all objections about procedure —to affect change in the future," countered the sardonic old judge, who was as well known for his wit and his love for the chess moves of legal procedure as for his toughness.

"The appeal is deemed withdrawn and of no further concern to this court," ordered the Chief Justice.

"Let's move on but let me be clear, the objection to time is well noted and this court will not tolerate further comment on that issue. We will note that each of you objects unless you wish not to be included," ordered the Chief Justice.

Another attorney withdrew the appeal of his client and then the Gaskins case was called.

"Mr. Chief Justice, Justices of the court," began Monk in his eloquent antebellum style. My client has directed that I withdraw forthwith and with finality his appeal before this Honorable Court and I offer for filing his affidavit, duly sworn, though handwritten, toward that purpose."

"Mr. Hinnant, what errors would you have argued rose to the level of reversible error?" queried Justice Ness.

"With all due respect, Mr. Justice Ness, I must decline any expansion of the withdrawal which I have been directed to make absolutely."

The justices seated on the left side of the raised dais huddled briefly, turning their elegant high backed chairs toward each other and slightly away from the courtroom and then leaning toward each other to confer privately. At the conclusion of the brief interlude Justice Ness, barely able to suppress an emerging smile persisted for a moment more.

"Justice Gregory is really curious to know what issues you intended to argue, Mr. Hinnant."

"I must respectfully decline further comment, your Honor," replied Hinnant, faithful to his purpose and now resolved in the stubborn advocacy for which he was known.

"I thought so," Justice Ness literally chuckled looking directly at Query seated on the first row directly behind Hinnant, "Just one more question, Mr. Hinnant," said Ness. Hinnant and Query both held their breath.

"Whose idea was it to submit the affidavit to withdraw the appeal and then not present any argument; yours or Mr. Query's?" Ness asked his voice now filled with mirth.

"Mr. Query and I did confer with Mr. Gaskins over the lunch hour, your Honor, but we concurred in the conclusion that no comment would be made beyond the withdrawal of the appeal. But I would give credit to Mr. Query for its origin."

"Give him the credit or subject him to my wrath?" Ness continued his jovial banter. The business of the court was essentially complete and Ness was merely showing his appreciation of the chess moves completed.

"Thank you, Mr. Hinnant. This court is adjourned, concluded the Chief Justice."

The court ruled that none of the men who had been sentenced to death under the old statute could be required to face a new trial for the purpose of determining the penalty of life in prison or the death penalty finding that to do so would constitute and *ex post facto* application of the new statute.

The South Carolina Court found the death sentence of Donald Henry Gaskins to be unconstitutional pursuant to the Furman case and remanded his case to the Court of General Sessions for resentencing to life imprisonment on February 15, 1978. On May 18, 1978 Walter Neely's case was similarly remanded for resentencing to life in prison.

Years later after his mandatory retirement Justice Ness and Query flew together from Washington to Charleston following a meeting with Senator Strom Thurmond in Washington. Ness delighted in recounting the thrusts and parries that permeated the entire episode over the interpretation of the bizarre and probably completely unique and inapplicable Florida decision.

"I doubt that we would have ever granted new trials under that crazy Dobbert ruling from Florida," he chuckled conspiratorially. "The present day court and the U.S. Supremes would probably still be trying to unravel that mess if we had," he mused, "but it sure was fun watching you young lawyers taking on the Court. Y'all were damn smart boys to figure out the new trial thing and withdraw the appeals. Pretty good set of balls on you boys too."

Justice Bubba Ness was well qualified to recognize courage. He was a wounded hero of some of the worst fighting in the Korean War.

CHAPTER SIXTY FOUR

The Harwell Trial

The South Carolina Supreme Court ruled that pursuant to the holding in Furman that the South Carolina death penalty violated the constitutionally guaranteed right of a defendant to due process and equal protection under the law. The court found that the existing South Carolina statute, like the one from a different state examined in the Furman case could result in the arbitrary and capricious imposition of the death penalty prohibited by the Fifth, Eighth and Fourteenth Amendments of the U.S. Constitution. The death sentences therefore had to be vacated and the cases remanded for re-sentencing to life in prison.

Gaskins had been sentenced to death after his first conviction for the murder of Dennis Bellamy and to a consecutive life sentence from the Yates trial in Newberry. After the withdrawal of his appeal in the Bellamy murder that case was remanded and Gaskins had been re-sentenced to life in prison for that murder.

Georgia and Florida had enacted new death penalty statutes. The first death penalty case under the new statutes was reviewed by the United States Supreme Court in Gregg vs. Georgia. That decision along with two others examining similar statutes found that the new statutes afforded the necessary protections to allow the imposition of the death penalty. The new statutes required a bifurcated trial that consisted of two phases, one for the determination of guilt and a second phase for the determination of the penalty –death or life in prison. South Carolina enacted a virtually identical death penalty statute.

The Solicitor for Florence County wasted no time in starting the process to try Gaskins under the new statute for the murder of Bellamy's young step brother whose body had been found in the same shallow grave in Prospect. Gaskins was brought before the court and arraigned for the murder of seventeen year old John Henry Knight and the case was called for trial on Monday April 10, 1978, before the Honorable David Harwell who was the resident Circuit Court Judge in Florence County. Gaskins was represented by his appointed attorneys Grady Query and John "Bud" Grisso.

The jury selection under the new statute was arduous, time consuming and for the most part boring. A huge jury *venire*, the group of potential jurors from which a jury is selected, was summoned for the session of court during which Gaskins was to be tried. A motion seeking a change of venue had been filed on the ground that the pre-trial publicity was overwhelming and an unbiased jury could not be selected. The motion was accompanied by affidavits from various individuals attesting that the publicity had been so extensive that it would be impossible to select a jury. The motion urged that jurors would have heard, seen or read so much about the case that it would be impossible for them to separate the evidence in the courtroom from the information received from the media. A newspaper article announcing that Gaskins had been named the AP story of the year the previous year was also filed along with a statement from a major television station that covered the area attesting to the hundreds of news items involving Gaskins.

The trial judge, David Harwell, would one day become Chief Justice of the South Carolina Supreme Court. Florence was his home circuit, but he was also chosen because he was highly respected as a first class jurist, knowledgeable on the law and insistent upon the enforcement of procedural rules. The Supreme Court wanted no mistakes in the trial of this case no matter what the jury ultimately decided. Bubba Ness was now the chief justice of the South Carolina Supreme Court. He had the authority to assign the trial judge and he was confident Harwell would deliver such a precisely correct trial.

Harwell ruled that an inquiry of individual jury prospects would be necessary to determine whether sufficient bias still existed to prevent a fair trial in that county. He reasoned that a year had passed since the Newberry trial of Gaskins and that there had been little attention to the case during that time

The new death penalty statute consists of twenty-five pages. It is a complex statement of the law that required a very precise method of trial. It bifurcates or separates the trial into two separate parts. The first phase of the trial is limited exclusively to a determination of whether or not the state has proven beyond a reasonable doubt that the accused is guilty of willful and premeditated murder. The jury's verdict is one of two forms: guilty or not guilty. The jury does not consider the possible penalty during the first phase.

Should a jury return a verdict of guilty there is a break in the proceedings and then the second phase begins during which additional evidence on the issue of punishment is presented by both the prosecution and the defense. The prosecution seeks to show circumstances of aggravation regarding the acts involved in the commission of the murder such as armed robbery, rape, torture, multiple victims or other acts of obvious brutality along with other evidence about the defendant, most particularly his criminal record, with emphasis on incorrigibility and other crimes of violence.

The defense seeks to introduce evidence in mitigation. At this point the defendant has been found guilty of the murder and therefore the defense evidence in the punishment phase does not address further the question of guilt but rather seeks to show circumstances and conditions that affected the defendant at the time of the murder or that greatly affected his life prior to the commission of the crime. Abuse of the defendant as a child is frequently raised as is evidence of undue influence of a codefendant and all relevant aspects of the emotional and mental health of the convicted person. While voluntary drug or alcohol use are not defenses such use and the attendant effects may be offered in mitigation. Unexpected side effects of legal or prescription drugs are mitigating and may even rise to a defense if the ability of the defendant to appreciate the difference between right and wrong or to control his actions is a consequence of the side effects.

The sole question for the jury in the punishment phase of the trial is whether or not the convicted person is to be sentenced to death or life imprisonment. The verdict must be unanimous and in the event that the decision is for the death penalty each of the jurors must sign the verdict attesting to their vote in favor of the sentence of death.

The new statute also affected the conduct of the trial making it different from other South Carolina trials from the very beginning.

The new statute permitted defense attorneys to conduct *voir dire*, the questioning of individual jurors during the process of selecting the jury. This was a dramatic departure for South Carolina where the practice in all other cases is to have written questions submitted to the trial judge who then poses the questions the judge deems appropriate to the jurors resulting in a necessarily very stilted process as the judge reads the questions to the assembly of potential jurors in the courtroom and asks the jurors to stand or raise their hands if the question applies to them.

Voir dire conducted by the attorneys flows much more like the normal examination of a witness with responses resulting in follow up questions that further clarify the response. The questions seek to discover any prejudices or preconceptions that the juror might have that would affect their ability to be impartial. Since a juror cannot be excluded merely because of opposition to the death penalty, as had been the practice prior to the series of cases that overturned the death penalty, the portion of the *voir dire* dealing with opposition to the death penalty was particularly crucial. Judge Harwell therefore decided that he would ask the critical questions involving this qualifying issue and then allow lawyers for the prosecution and defense to ask follow up questions on that issue along with their other questions.

In order to insure the strictest compliance Judge Harwell asked the questions using the precise language of the statute, asking each juror whether or not they were opposed to the death penalty. In the few instances when the response about opposition was in the affirmative the judge then continued his formal interrogation.

"Mr. Juror, is your opposition to the death penalty such that it would prevent you from listening to the evidence presented during the trial and making a decision based solely upon that evidence as to whether or not the state has proven the defendant guilty?"

If the prospective juror responded that they would be able to decide the issue of guilt based solely upon the evidence regardless of their opposition to the death penalty, that juror would be qualified to serve. Once a juror was qualified by the court and questioned by the attorneys, the prosecutor would have three options. He could ask the court to seat the juror as a part of the jury using the traditional phrase; "Present the juror" or he could strike the juror without giving any reason using one of a specified number of preemptory strikes or he could ask the court to excuse the juror for cause by stating a reason why the juror should not serve in this particular case. If the juror was accepted by the prosecution the defense attorney would have the same right to strike or to have the juror seated as a member of the jury for the trial of the case. "Swear the Juror or Seat the Juror" are the traditional phrases used by defense attorneys to indicate acceptance of a jury member. Jurors may be struck for cause when they have expressed an opinion about the case or a relationship to a party or a witness or to one of the attorneys or for some other articulable reason that would prevent them from rendering a fair decision. Jurors may also be excused at their own request if they are unable to serve for reasons such as an inability to hear or see or to follow the questions presented to them. Jurors who have close associations with law enforcement are usually excused. The judge makes these decisions and determines what constitutes sufficient cause.

Aside from the special determination regarding opposition to the death penalty and the examination under oath of each individual juror by the attorneys the selection process was the same as in other cases.

Juror after juror was called and brought individually into the court room. One of the attorneys for the defendant and one of the prosecutors questioned each juror. Much of the questioning involved the willingness of the juror to base the verdict on the evidence alone. Query emphasized acceptance of the duty to require the state to carry the burden of proving every element of the crime beyond a reasonable doubt without any regard for the identity of the person charged. He and Grisso asked each juror to accept absolutely that every defendant is presumed innocent and that on every issue of evidence sought to be proven by the prosecution they must begin with that presumption and maintain it and put the state to the test of overcoming that presumption with evidence so convincing that it stripped away that presumption. They stressed that the evidence the juror considered must be so convincing that it proved not only that the fact alleged was most probable but that it had been proven beyond any reasonable doubt.

"I'm going to ask you to promise me something," Query said to each of the potential jurors he questioned. "Promise me that you will take the fact that every defendant is presumed to be innocent so seriously and that you will require the state to prove guilt beyond any reasonable doubt so absolutely, that if the person on trial was hidden behind a curtain throughout the trial and when the curtain was lifted, if the person behind it was your close friend or relative you would not hesitate about your decision. That is a part of your oath as a juror. Will you promise me that?"

Other questions were similarly posed with the intention to enlist the juror to question the evidence and require strict proof as the state presented its case.

Solicitor Summerford emphasized carefully considering all of the evidence, taking into consideration the believability of the witnesses and convicting the defendant if convinced that the defendant was guilty. He urged that they listen carefully to the testimony and promised that it would prove guilt.

"What is going to happen to us and to our community, if we don't arrest and .." he was asking when Query objected.

"Sustained," said the judge. "Solicitor, you know you can't tell them to convict this man in order to stamp out crime in the community. They have to decide whether he's guilty of this particular crime based on the evidence in this case."

When Query objected to Summerford launching a similar line of questioning to another juror the judge minced no words in warning the solicitor that he would not tolerate another foray in contravention of his order.

The other main line of questioning by Query and Grisso focused on the issue of pre-trial publicity and whether the juror had heard or read about the case and most importantly whether prospective jurors had formed opinions about the case or the defendant. Amazingly many of the potential jurors swore that they had heard nothing about the bodies discovered in the little community of Prospect. Unfortunately a drawback to this process in high profile cases is that many of those called for consideration as jurors actually want to be involved and will maintain that they have heard nothing about the case in spite of withering media coverage.

For those jurors who admitted to having read articles about the subject matter of the case, to having seen television coverage, or to having heard about it on the news or even on the street, the solicitor would attempt to rehabilitate each of them by eliciting answers that averred that while they might have received information, may even have formed an opinion, they would listen to the evidence legally presented and make their decision based solely upon that evidence. This questioning was put to each such individual prospect by the solicitor in such a way that the person was in effect prompted to swear that they could disabuse themselves of any previously formed opinions. The implication was that any prospective juror who could not clear their mind of all that they might have heard or read was so entirely biased and prejudiced that they had lost their free will and were in fact sort of un-American.

The name of each potential juror had been carefully placed in a plastic capsule and the capsules in turn placed in a tumbler. The tumbler would be turned by the clerk of court and the small door on the cylinder opened for a blind man whose job it was to reach in and select a capsule which he would then hand the clerk. The capsule would be opened by the clerk, the name published to the courtroom. One of the ancient bailiffs would be dispatched to take the elevator to the courtroom on the floor below and call the juror for presentation and questioning.

As the procedure moved laboriously along, several jurors were questioned by the attorneys and by the judge, found to be qualified and officially seated in the jury box. Both the prosecution and defense were allotted a specific number of preemptory strikes. These are the strikes that the attorneys may utilize to exclude a juror without having to give any reason. In death penalty cases the number of preemptory strikes is greater than in less serious cases.

Each side had been provided a list of the names and addresses and in most instances the employment of each potential juror. As a result the attorneys would often have formed an opinion as to the desirability of many of the possible jurors. These impressions were usually generated by the information on the list and such other information as they might have been able to glean from other sources. For Query these other sources included, of course, Monk Hinnant and Johnny DeBerry, but it also included Hinnant's staff, Pee Wee's mother and sister and the owner of the deli where the defense team often gathered. This ad hoc advisory panel included every employee of the deli from manager to dishwasher. All of the employees were by this time on a first name basis with Query and Grisso and influenced by the dedication and hard work of the lawyers, they were committed at least to the proposition that Gaskins was entitled to a fair trial. This was true even though most were not convinced that there was not much possibility of his innocence.

The preemptory strikes are jealously preserved and protected by prosecution and defense alike so that they might be utilized to eliminate those jurors that they have decided in advance are likely to lean against them or in favor of their adversary.

Against this backdrop and with five good citizens of the Twelfth Judicial District already seated in the jury box, an attractive young black woman was called for consideration from the one hundred twenty who waited in another part of the courthouse. In response to initial questions by the clerk, she revealed that she was a junior at South Carolina State College, a school that was established as a black college and which was located in the small town where the "Orangeburg Massacre" of February 1968 had occurred. The school's reputation as a bastion of civil rights support and the alma mater of nationally known leaders in the civil rights movement had literally earned its reputation in blood. It was clear that the articulate but soft spoken student was well informed and thoughtful when she responded to Judge Harwell's death penalty questions. Judge Harwell put his carefully worded questions regarding possible opposition to the death penalty to the young woman.

Turning to face the trial judge she looked straight into his eyes as she said, "I am opposed to the death penalty."

This triggered the additional questions mandated by the statute, "Is your opposition to the death penalty such that you would be unable to listen to the evidence and make a decision as to whether or not the state has proven the guilt of the defendant based solely upon that evidence?"

"Your Honor, my opposition to the death penalty though strong is not such that it would prevent me from considering the evidence and making a decision based solely upon that evidence as to the issue of guilt or innocence," she replied with precision that amazed lawyers in the courtroom. Most could not avoid ruminating about their own rambling attempts to recite the cumbersome language and concepts of the new statute.

Questioning by the judge having concluded, she was asked the usual battery of questions by the solicitor and then by Query. She stated that she had heard news reports of the discovery of bodies in a small community near Florence but that she was not from that area and had paid little attention to the coverage other than to note the macabre nature. She did not recall having heard specifically of Gaskins but did recall references to the nickname Pee Wee in association with the story. Query was significantly briefer than usual, certain that the solicitor would use one of his "free strikes" to exclude the young woman.

Neither the defense nor the prosecution sought to have the juror excused for cause.

With a slight smile that presupposed the answer the astute trial judge turned slightly toward the solicitor and posed the formal question, "What say you for the State?"

This inquiry required that the solicitor accept the juror with the traditional utterance of "Present the Juror" or exercise one of his preemptory strikes by saying simply, "Excuse the Juror". This was frequently dressed up a bit to "Please excuse this juror from the trial of this case." This softening of the dismissal was intended to diminish the anxiety of other jurors who might feel that being excused constituted a slight of some sort. With the exception of the jury selection in death penalty cases jurors are usually all present in the courtroom during this process.

As impressed as Query was with the young lady and as much as he would have given to have her on this jury, he had already turned his attention back to the list of jurors as he awaited the "excuse the juror" drone from the solicitor whom he thought would be similarly engrossed in anticipation of the next prospective juror.

Astonishingly the solicitor called out in his most melodic and impressive courtroom voice, "Please present the juror."

Stunned as he was by the statement, Query scarcely allowed the solicitor to complete the final "-or" syllable of juror before shouting "Swear the juror." He hoped to preclude the expected exclamation from the solicitor that he had meant to say excuse the juror. When the attempted take back was not forthcoming, Query sat with heart pounding trying to comprehend the sudden change of events.

Gaskins who sat close at his lawyer's right side tugged insistently on the lawyer's sleeve. Query stilled him with a nudge of his hand to the side of his thigh not wanting anything to upset the orderly procession toward the calling of the next juror.

Looking on the proceedings with absolute incredulity the trial judge carried out his next duty by instructing the pretty young juror to take the next seat in the jury box.

Then barely able to contain his feelings of confusion and frustration Judge Harwell directed the clerk to call the next prospective juror. Finally, as the courtroom twittered, Query leaned toward Gaskins in response to his earlier sleeve tugging.

"What's goin' on Mr. Queury? Why'd he do that? Why'd Summerford let that girl on my jury? She's against the death penalty, Mr. Queury. What's he tryin' to do?"

"I don't know, Pee Wee, maybe he doesn't really want to kill you," Query replied sarcastically. "Actually Pee Wee, I think he just screwed up, but we'll see. Just stay cool and don't show any reaction."

Judge Harwell began his introductory instructions to the next prospective juror explaining the process of questioning by the attorneys and the court but just as he was about to commence the questioning he announced that it seemed to him to be an appropriate time for a brief recess. He quickly instructed the six people newly ensconced in the jury box that they were not yet sworn and that they would be escorted to the jury room for the break and that they were not to discuss the case.

Without any of his easy familiarity to the audience that usually included a pleasantry of some sort coupled with an explanation about the proceedings, he rose from his seat, turned and went through the door which was one step down and almost immediately behind the bench. The door led through a small anteroom. Besides the door the judge used there was an entrance to the courtroom near the clerk's table that was stage right of the judge's bench. The witness seat was on the other side of the judge's bench nearest the jury box and the clerk's table and was directly across the front of the court room from the jury box. Seven steps across that small anteroom the judge entered his chambers, a roomy office with a large desk several comfortable side chairs and a small couch.

The judge's chambers doubled as a conference room for the judge and attorneys with business for the court. And when the judge was not otherwise occupied it became the attorneys' lounge. Any time trial lawyers were not busily involved in preparation of arguments or witnesses, they could be found in the chambers. There, easy banter and war stories were occasionally interrupted by attorneys bringing orders to the judge for his signature or two adversaries arguing an informal motion or settling a disagreement over discovery. From time to time a court reporter would scurry in laden with her necessary equipment to record a more formal argument on some issue. During these times trial counsel for other cases would often stay in the room where fresh coffee and goodies in the form of donuts or other sweets were usually provided for the judge's comfort by the clerk's office. Legal arguments, after all, no matter how mundane, are somehow always interesting to lawyers.

The attorneys exited the courtroom into the same anteroom but through the clerk's door not the judge's. Incongruously for the size of the room, two separate doors led from the anteroom into the main hallway, one near the door to the judge's chambers and the other at the opposite end of the narrow room. Query and Grisso turned left to follow Judge Harwell into his chambers and Summerford went through the closer of the doors and down to the solicitor's office on the floor below.

"What in the hell is going on?" raged the judge as soon as the door was closed. "What in the hell is Kenneth up to?"

"I don't think he knows that the same jury that decides guilt is used in the penalty phase," Query volunteered.

"That's my read too," offered Grisso.

"Bullshit, anybody knows better than that," the judge roared.

"That's got to be it, Judge, there's no other way any prosecutor would have put that woman on the jury," Query continued.

"No way, I'll never believe that," the judge responded, "come on let's get back in there, I'm tempted to let them go for the rest of the day while I try to sort this out in my own mind."

Lawyers, jurors, courtroom personnel and audience sat for nearly ten minutes before the judge came back to the bench. Judge Harwell brought the new prospective juror back to the witness stand and completed his instructions. He then allowed questions by the attorneys. The process continued until the remaining jurors and an alternate had been selected but Judge Harwell was noticeably briefer with his examination of the jurors regarding their beliefs about the death penalty and its effect on their ability to serve as a juror. The final juror was selected at eight P.M.

The judge then spoke briefly to the remaining jury pool advising that the jury had now been selected and that they were excused from further service.

Judge Harwell returned to his chambers followed by Query and Grisso and the solicitor. As the two defense attorneys followed the judge into his chambers Summerford suddenly turned and went into the hallway and headed back to his own office. The judge quickly picked up a few papers stuffed them into the large leather trial case familiarly seen at the side of all South Carolina judges. He turned toward the door appearing exhausted.

Pausing briefly at the door of his chambers he said, "Grady, you know damn well everybody knows that you use one jury for both phases of a bifurcated trial."

"I think Grady's right, Judge," offered John Grisso who was a contemporary of the judge, "this is a brand new statute. It's long and it's complicated. It introduces a lot of new things for a criminal trial. They've been so hell bent on rushing this case to trial that I believe they just jumped to the conclusion that the statute required two separate trials with two separate juries," he added, as the three walked the short distance down the hall to the elevator.

"Well, I just can't buy it, this is the biggest trial in the state. Maybe the biggest murder case ever in this state, and I just don't believe they would start this trial without knowing exactly what that statute provides for."

They entered the elevator and Judge Harwell pushed the "one" button on the control panel. As the doors began to close, Summerford suddenly thrust both arms into the gap causing the doors to slide back open.

Only half into the elevator he blurted, somewhat out of breath, "Judge, I just wanted to ask you one thing."

In the same millisecond both Grisso and Query thought —here it comes.

Summerford continued, "You use two different juries, one for the penalty phase and one for sentencing or just one jury for both parts, Judge?"

"Just one, Kenneth, just one," said Judge Harwell utterly and completely exasperated and now suddenly showing extreme fatigue.

"I thought so, Judge, that's what I was tellin' 'em in the office. Just checkin'. See you in the morning."

The doors closed and the tall athletically built judge sagged visibly. Query and Grisso on the other hand inflated slightly but chose to hold their tongues and allow the eleven floors to pass in silence.

At the first floor Judge Harwell said simply, "I don't believe it. I don't damn believe it. Good day fellows, I'll see you in the morning. Come straight to my chambers. Y'all have a good evening."

"We will, Judge, Ken just made sure of that," Query replied and turned toward the main door.

Query and Grisso drove together in Query's car to the deli reveling in the moment and recounting over and over to each other in the few blocks the moment on the elevator. A number of the big mugs were emptied that evening as they told the story over and over to each of the regulars as they arrived, describing the perfect answer of the bright young juror and then laughing loudly as one or the other shouted, "Present the juror."

"This trial is over, Mr. Query," gloated Grisso, "we're done here. Congratulations young man, we just won the impossible case."

"I agree that we just won," said Query, "but it's not over."

"Of course, it's over. He knows now he can't get the death penalty. No point in going any further."

"Shoot, Bud, he'll go ahead with this trial. He'll try the whole thing, get another life sentence and pretend that is what he intended all along. And then three months later he'll call one of the other cases and try it right that time without any death penalty opponents on the jury."

"He's right," inserted Hinnant over a tall mug, "Kenneth will just keep going straight at it just like he knew all along and he'll say he wanted to go into the real death penalty case with two convictions and two life sentences in place to be sure that he could get a death penalty that would be hard to overturn."

"Geez, I guess you're right, Monk, we might be back making opening arguments in the morning," said Bud.

None of the regular affable demeanor was there when they greeted a decidedly grim Judge Harwell in his chambers the following morning.

After a very brief good morning without the usual good humored banter while everyone got coffee. This morning it was, "Good morning, have a seat. Tell me has Kenneth offered y'all anything?"

"No sir, Your Honor, I've told him that Pee Wee would plead to twelve murders and even the BS burglary case they keep threatening to try just to interfere with our preparation for the murder trials. In fact I told him he could throw in some other unsolved crimes and we'd plead to them as well. He told me to go to hell that he intended to put Gaskins in the electric chair."

"Go get him and you tell him to get down here and tell him I said he'd better think about what we're going to do with this mess," said the judge.

The young assistant solicitor came back with Query and asked the judge to allow the solicitor a few more minutes because he was on the phone with SLED in Columbia.

"Sure just tell him to get down here as soon as he is off of the phone. Tell me, why on earth did Kenneth allow that student from South Carolina State to get on the jury?"

"Shoot Judge, neither one of us had read the statute word for word on the jury selection part. We thought there were two separate juries for two separate trials. That's what it sounded like in the newspapers. Kenneth thought that I had studied the fine points of the statute and I thought that he had, so we were just cruising along thinking we would be able to keep anyone like her off of the sentencing jury. In fact we thought using someone like her in the trial phase would make them unavailable for the sentencing phase."

Kenneth arrived moments later and greeted everyone with rather obvious false bravado.

"Grady tells me they'll plead to all the murders and take consecutive sentences," the judge said immediately following a brief hello.

"I don't want consecutive sentences. I want the death penalty and I'll keep trying the little bastard until I get it."

"Well then you should have read the damned statute, Kenneth. Now y'all know I can't tell you what to do, but I can tell you that right now we are going to look like the biggest damn fools in the whole country. Well maybe I shouldn't include Bud and Grady; they are going to look like they pulled off the trial of the century, if you go through with this charade. If they avoid the death penalty, and we all know that is exactly what is going to happen. That South Carolina State student wouldn't sign that death sentence, if you showed her a video of Gaskins shooting that boy and then dancing around the body. She just told you that under oath. That jury is going to come back guilty and then after another three or four days they're gonna come out and say they can't agree on the sentence. I'll have to ask them if they think they can agree, if they have more time and they're going to say there is no chance. That means he gets a life sentence. He's already got two life sentences so all I can do is give him another consecutive life sentence."

"The press will eventually figure out what happened and they are going to say Bud and Grady were brilliant for sitting there and keeping their mouths shut while you put that girl on the jury. But I wonder what they are going to say about you for doing it. I am going to recess for the day and I suggest that you spend the rest of the afternoon sitting in a conference room with these lawyers and try to work something out. I damn well mean that, but like I said I can't make either of you agree to anything, but Grady says his client will plead to all of the murders. And I can tell you if you don't find a way for him to plead, the press is going to try to make you look like a fool when they figure out what happened and they're not going to let this thing go after all of the buildup about trying him for the death penalty," continued the judge.

"Hell, we'll plead to all of the murders we've been talking about and you can throw in any other unsolved murders," laughed Grisso.

"Seriously, Ken this is a new statute and it's difficult for any of us to get a handle on. The U.S. Supreme Court seems to change its mind every time we think we know where we're going with this and we have to start all over. But the public doesn't see all of that and what they are going to see is that you tried Gaskins again and you still didn't get the death penalty and of course it will get out that he was willing to plead and then the press will keep rooting around until someone realizes that there was no chance in getting the death penalty with that woman on the jury and that you could easily have kept her off the jury. They'll be all over you and all over the whole court system. Especially with the amount of money this kind of trial costs. I'm just suggesting that you sit down with Pee Wee's lawyers and see if there is any way to bring this whole thing to a final conclusion. There is a lot to be said for having the guilty person convicted and the victims identified and located for the sake of the families. And finally the state can't keep spending tens of thousands of dollars trying someone when he is already in prison serving consecutive life sentences. Just take today, sit down together and see if you can come up with something that makes sense for everyone," the judge added, his tone clearly more conciliatory.

"What about the jury?" stammered Summerford.

"The jury is my problem, I'll handle that. If you work this out they'll be happy to know it's over with."

Summerford turned to Query and Grisso, "We'll meet in the conference room in my office in an hour. I've got to get the sheriff and the SLED agents will want to be here or at least be kept up on what is going on by phone."

"We'll be there," Query answered. "Call us in Monk's office if there is any change."

CHAPTER SIXTY FIVE

Plea Negotiations

The meeting began an hour later with the solicitor and his assistant and the two attorneys for Gaskins. The sheriff and SLED had declined to attend.

"I'm willing to let him plead to this case and take a life sentence consecutive to the other one. We can do it this afternoon that way the jury can be notified not to even come in tomorrow."

"Sure Ken, and then week after next we start the <u>NEW</u> death penalty trial for Diane Neeley or one of the others. We either wrap all of these cases up or we continue with this trial."

"You can't force me to continue the trial. I can go in there and dismiss it right now and it's over."

"And I can go right out on the steps of the courthouse and explain in great detail exactly why the case was dismissed," snapped Query. "You're not going to shove me around on this, Kenneth. You screwed up and you need to work something out to avoid this whole thing being splashed all over the newspapers. This was the number one story in the Associated Press, if you recall. It won't be just here it'll be all over the whole country. You'll sure be able to kiss the state senate goodbye and maybe this job too."

"I'm not making a deal with you because of politics. Are you recording this?"

"No Kenneth, I have never surreptitiously recorded you or any other attorney. When I'm recording something I put the recorder right out in the middle of the table just like you have seen me do."

"Well I don't care if you are. I'm willing to try to work out a plea not for my benefit but in order to let those poor families of these victims know once and for all what happened to their children and their loved ones."

"That's very noble of you and we are certainly willing to join with you toward accomplishing those goals," Grisso jibed. "Our job is to try to keep Gaskins out of the electric chair. It's about as simple as that. We're not going to win any acquittals. You could probably try him for a murder that happened while he was sitting in the courtroom with half the county watching and get a conviction. Just say 'Ladies and gentleman of the jury there was a murder and this is Pee Wee Gaskins. That's our case.' He'll probably never get out with what he's already serving but you load him up with guilty pleas to the rest of these murders and a consecutive life sentence for each one of them and you can honestly say that you did your job. You can say that you served the state by assuring that he will never see the street again. You never know, somebody might even figure out something about what makes someone like him tick, if they'll go up there and study him while he's locked up."

"I'd like to see them dissect his brain and figure him out like that," Summerford retorted. "But you're right Bud, you've been a Solicitor and you've been U.S. Attorney, you've prosecuted plenty of people and you know how it is. You get a guy for something and you know he really deserves the death penalty, it's hard to give up on it. But you're right he'll never get out again and there does need to be an end to all of this. Besides there's other counties that might want to go after him for the chair."

"I'm afraid that has got to be part of it Kenneth. We have to wrap it all up. We have a job to do too. Capers Barr has already said that his office is not going to use their resources to go after a death penalty when we know this whole question of *ex post facto* application of the new death penalty statute would still have to clear our state supreme court and maybe the U. S. Supreme Court."

"That Dobbert decision upholding the Florida death penalty for a crime that was committed under the old statute and tried under the new statute was grounded on a very peculiar fact set. Dobbert had escaped and remained at large during the time that the old statute was declared unconstitutional by the U.S. Supreme Court. Before he was re-captured the new Florida death penalty statute that bifurcated the trial was enacted. An operative factor was the length of time that he remained a fugitive. It was an anomaly," added Query.

"On the other hand Pee Wee's been right here the whole time," Query continued. I don't think trying to bootstrap that decision with the provisions in our new statute is going to fly. Our court has already taken at least a partial look at Dobbert. As you know, they had all of the existing death sentences before them to decide whether inmates already convicted of murder under our old statute could be granted a trial on the penalty issue only under the new statute. Our court would not go that far although they were obviously tempted. I think the same thing will happen once this question gets there."

Query continued, "Solicitor McLeod says the same thing basically. He says they've tried and convicted Pee Wee of one murder and that he thinks it would be difficult to prove that anyone else was killed in Sumter or Williamsburg County. He's just not going to spend the money for another trial. He says that if Pee Wee confesses to an unsolved murder, he is willing to agree not to seek the death penalty, that it would be more important to solve the murder. He also has doubts about applying the new statute to murders that occurred before the statute was passed."

"How'd you get to be the expert on the new statute? I was told that Florida case made it clear that we could use the new statute to try him for these murders," Summerford replied.

"Ken, I represented one of the men on death row whose case had to be reviewed after the U.S. Supreme Court decided Furman and overturned death penalty statutes throughout the country. I'm not trying to be a smart ass about these statutes. I know that you have to turn appeals over to the Attorney General and get back to the business of trying cases in your circuit. I also realize you were handling hundreds of cases for everything from possession of marijuana to murder while these appeals were going on, but I was living those appeals."

"I wasn't representing Pee Wee on his appeal when that issue was before the court, that was still Monk, but I was representing a guy named Jamie McPhee who was sentenced to death in Orangeburg County. He and his girlfriend were hitchhiking from Charleston. She was a pretty little thing, wearing cut off shorts and a tee shirt with no bra and two men picked them up and gave them a ride. Jamie was high on crystal meth or something and jonesing for a heroin fix. He was probably going to rob them no matter what, but they apparently made a few comments to the girl that heated the situation up. Jamie pulled a pistol, made the men stop the car, marched them out into the middle of a cotton field, robbed them and shot them both in the head. By some miracle one of the men lived and testified. Jamie was sentenced to death under the old statute," Query said.

"After the Furman decision the change to life sentences was not automatic. Exactly half of the men on death row had active appeals so their cases were already before the court seeking new trials. If their appeals were denied their cases would still be remanded to the Circuit Court for re-sentencing to life imprisonment. The others had already lost their appeals for new trials but they had to petition our Supreme Court to have their cases remanded to the circuit court for re-sentencing to life even though it was just a formality for them."

CHAPTER SIXTY SIX

Query and Summerford

Query continued his little speech to Solicitor Summerford. "Kenneth, when the appeals were withdrawn, the cases were all remanded for re-sentencing and that brought us back here and that's why I know that statute word for word. I read it before Georgia passed it and at every stage from there through the U. S. Supreme Court and finally the statute passed by our legislature once it was upheld," Query concluded.

"In my opinion it would difficult to sustain a death penalty for one of these murders committed long before passage of the present statute, but Dobbert blurs that clear line, so our position is that we wrap it all up here. No death penalties period. That's our position plain and simple. No death penalty. No death penalty, not here, not in Williamsburg or Sumter or Charleston or anywhere else in South Carolina," Query added.

"I can't bind other Solicitors, Grady, you know that."

"I do. But you can confirm the positions they told me they will take. Capers and Kirk and the Attorney General all take the same position and the AG will say that is his position for the entire state. I'm not sure he can bind anyone but at least we would have the argument that the chief law enforcement officer of the state was part of the agreement and we put it on the record as part of the plea. You can tell the court that you have spoken to each of them and confirm that they have agreed not to seek the death penalty for any murder committed before the plea."

"I'll consider that, and he is going to plead to every one of these murders that we know about," countered Summerford.

"That's right, all of them. And you can throw in any old unsolved ones if you want to and a spitting on the sidewalk," laughed Grisso.

"I don't want him to plead to anything he didn't do but I want the truth about any that he did."

"I'm just kidding. I just mean he's not going to hold anything back. Now I don't know about some of the stuff he testified to up in Newberry. I'll have to let y'all make the call on those. But if he did it and you're satisfied that he did it then he'll plead to it. That's our deal," offered Grisso.

"What about the burglary, he gonna plead to that?"

"Jesus, Ken, he's gonna plead to eight or ten murders with consecutive sentences. What the hell do you care about a burglary, but, yes, okay, he'll plead to that burglary. Why don't we throw in a malicious destruction of personal property just to round things out?" Query retorted.

"Oh, knock it off. I just need to clear that up. I have a job to do here. There are two others charged, if he pleads, they'll plead."

"Okay, let's quit jerking each other around and get this done. Pleas to all the murders and the burglary and no death penalties, it's actually pretty simple," Query said.

"I agree. Let's meet back here at two-thirty. I've got a lot of calls to make before I can confirm. I have to talk to Sheriff Barnes and SLED, Capers and Kirk and the solicitors will probably want to talk to their sheriffs and the police chiefs and then the AG. I'll try to get through to all of them and give you an answer at two-thirty."

"Sounds good, just call us in Monk's office if you need more time. We'll be using his phone to threaten witnesses," Query finished, unable to resist the opportunity for a quick taunt.

Summerford did need until four o'clock but at that hour he confirmed that all necessary parties were on board provided that Pee Wee would submit to an examination under oath with any and all prosecutors or law enforcement that wanted to be present. The debriefing would occur immediately and Gaskins would submit to a lie detector test to confirm his answers and if he was not completely truthful the deal was off and he could be tried on any of the murder cases in any of the jurisdictions.

"We've met with Pee Wee while you were working on this and he is on board, but of course we'll have to meet with him and get his confirmation now that you have more details and more conditions. I don't see any problem but obviously we have to go through the process. One thing you could help us with; they say they are going to leave any minute now and take him over to Darlington or back to Columbia for the night and we'll have to talk to him there or wait until morning. If you could stop that and get them to keep him here until we reach an agreement it will be a big help to everyone."

"Well you know those guys want to get back to Columbia. It takes time to get him back in custody and they wind up seven or eight getting home," was Summerford's reply.

"You're breaking my heart now. Whenever I finish in the stinking jail, I get to go back to the motel, clean up and come back to the deli for a sandwich or the special if there's any left," said Grisso, who was clearly the person most in a position to ask for some consideration. He gave an involuntary rub to his tormented leg.

"Okay, I'll tell them they'll have to explain to the judge if they can't keep him here long enough for us to finish," Summerford offered.

"Thanks, we won't waste any time. That cell is not really a great place to hang out."

"Go ahead back to the motel and rest that leg, Bud. I'll talk to Pee Wee. He's already okay with this and we'll have to go back over all of it tomorrow when everybody gets here," Query urged his friend.

Grisso was recovering from chemotherapy for a melanoma on his upper thigh that had left his right leg alternately numb or extremely painful. The long days of walking, standing and sitting magnified the suffering.

Arrangements began early the next morning and all interested parties who wished to attend assembled in the Sheriff's conference room at ten thirty. The conference room was chosen because it was adjacent to the sheriff's private office and different parties could adjourn to that office as necessary. The entrances to the office and the conference room were almost side by side. The doors opened into a short hall. A single armed guard could sit in the hall and observe both doors and Gaskins could be taken through an internal hallway to and from the jail.

Present for were Tom Henderson, Ted Owens and other agents from SLED, Sheriff Barnes, Kenneth Summerford, Query, Grisso, Gaskins and a court reporter who said that she was scared to death the entire time. Various sheriff's deputies, an assistant solicitor and other law enforcement officers were present for portions of the interview for which they had questions or when they were privy to information that could confirm the truthfulness of the testimony given by Gaskins.

CHAPTER SIXTY SEVEN

Gaskins Reveals All

The interview began with the recitation and confirmation of the agreement that provided for a complete and truthful disclosure by Gaskins of all murders in South Carolina in which he had any involvement in return for life sentences and no death penalty. From that point Solicitor Summerford would question Gaskins and then any of the other officials present would be allowed to do follow up questions.

(Quotations in italics found in this section are directly from the transcript of that meeting and are taken from the excellent transcription by Ms. Peggy C. Fowler, Official Court Reporter.)

Mr. Summerford: All right, you don't have to worry about any such statement as that, as long as it is the truth. Now, you indicated to us that you would take sodium pentathol.

Gaskins: I did.

Summerford: That you would be hypnotized.

Gaskins: I did.

Gaskins: Well, I'm gonna start in 1970 in Sumter and uh, I guess the first murder would be Patricia Ann Alsbrook. Her and my niece had run away from home… And uh, the next night I went out where they was at, out there at the place and when I got out there, they was both under drugs bad. And I started in on em about it and uh we had a fight in there and I beat em to death.

Summerford: What did you beat em with?

Gaskins: My hands... I got mad about the drug deal, they was drugged, my niece was over drugged anyway and I just went out of my head.

Summerford: ...what was your niece's name?

Gaskins: Janice Kirby.

Summerford: How old was your niece, Janice Kirby?

Gaskins: I think around 15,16 somewhere in there.

Summerford: How old was Patricia Ann Alsbrook?

Gaskins: I think around 18.

Summerford: ...what did you do with the bodies?

Gaskins: Patricia Ann Alsbrook, I taken and carried over to the next house which nobody lived in and put in a uh cement pit.

Summerford: Why didn't you put them both in there?

Gaskins: Because I, I just, I just couldn't put Janice in there. After it was all over with, I just couldn't put her in there.

Summerford: ...you talking about a septic tank?

Gaskins: Right

Summerford: ...What did you do with Janice's body?

Gaskins: I brought her to Florence County, Prospect, and buried her there at Prospect.

Gaskins: The next one was in '71. It was also in Sumter. It was that black gal. ...the name that she used at the time was Clyde. ...Martha Ann Dicks.

241

Gaskins: Uh, she was originally there from Sumter. She did a lot of traveling and uh while I was beating Janice up and everything I kept screaming at her and asking her where'd she get that damn dope and stuff she'd been getting. Well, she used to go up there to Mr. Culp's junkyard all the time, Janice did. And uh, this black girl always hung around there and she was a drug distributor. And that's where they had been getting part of their drugs at and everything. And my understanding was, I found out later that a few times that Janice had OD on drugs, and I think had to go to a hospital or doctor on account of that and uh, that night that Janice and Patricia Alsbrook died, I promised after it was over with that, ... Clyde would never live a year after that... The old man that ran that camera shop right there at Mr. Culp's junkyard and that, ...he always kept a cabinet there with all kinds of stuff in it ... telling my nieces never handle this stuff up here, it would kill you if you did. And one day that I was in there and he was in his dark room doing some stuff and I stole some of this fluid out of there that he had in there that he had told em never to touch because you smell it and it would kill you... and give her that poison in that Coca Cola, I went back up there and got my car. ... taken her out there to a ditch and put her in the ditch where she was found at... Yes sir, she was dead... From the odors and stuff that was coming from her... Well she turned it up to her head and the next thing I knowed the bottle hit the floor. I left the bottle laying in the floor there and I went and got my car.

Questioning continued about the eventual discovery of the body in the ditch described by Gaskins. He had been to the scene with officers from North Charleston but after that the Florence solicitor had restricted access to Gaskins until his trials were complete since Gaskins was technically being held by the state in CCI as a "safekeeper", meaning that he was too dangerous for a county jail to try to keep him confined.

Finally, during the Barnwell Yates trial in Newberry, Gaskins testified about having shown the precise location to law enforcement officers. He asserted that Sumter County had made no effort to locate the body despite receiving that information and stated that he assumed that they were not very interested since it was just a poor black girl. The trial had been adjourned to allow an all-out search of the ditch and barely an hour into the search the skeletal remains were located.

During the debriefing Tom Henderson of SLED would question the accuracy of the placement of the body in the ditch as described by Gaskins countering that the body was actually found outside of the ditch. Query clarified that parts of the body were actually found on both sides of the ditch which was ten feet deep and that the most likely explanation was that animals or flooding had been responsible for most of the skeleton being found outside the ditch.

Gaskins recanted his accusation that a law officer had ordered him to kill the woman. He was also silent about any involvement of the owner of the junkyard whom he had implicated in his other version of the murder.

Gaskins: The next murder was committed in late 1973 …The two persons that died, was murdered, was Doreen Dempsey and Michelle Dempsey…she came to live with me and my wife there in Sumter…a child was born to us while we lived there in Sumter… Doreen was pregnant and she stayed with us for a few months…Doreen went to that house in Charleston for unwed mothers… left with the baby..came back to Charleston …and she moved in with me.

Gaskins explained that he had broken up with his wife Sandy and that when he went to get his son from her mother's house, the mother and Sandy had called the police and told them that he had threatened them with guns. Pee Wee had both Doreen and his old flame Jessie living with him at that time. Jessie had lived with Gaskins two years before but had left to marry Knoy Judy. When Judy became involved in using hard drugs and huffing glue, Jessie eventually left to come back to Gaskins. Gaskins promptly moved his wife Sandy out of his bedroom and took Jessie into it. As a consequence Sandy moved to her mother's house.

According to Gaskins, his angry mother-in-law and her son burned down his house and he had to leave. Making peace among themselves, his wife, Sandy, Doreen and Jessie all moved into Johnny Sellers apartment on Reynolds Avenue in North Charleston. After a short time Johnny sent all three of the women to Lake City to live with Gaskins.

Shortly after that Johnny's brother, Carl Sellers, got out of prison and Jessie and Doreen moved back to Charleston with Johnny and Carl. Everyone thought it was a good idea to get Doreen and Carl hooked up together. She was the best looking girl he had ever been around and he was pretty good at taking care of her. When Carl found out that she was pregnant and that the father was again a black man he said that he was finished with her.

Johnny and Carl came to the little apartment at the back of the store where Gaskins and Sandy were living in Prospect. They brought stolen televisions and motorcycles with them in an Oldsmobile station wagon. They also had Doreen and her baby with them along with all of her luggage.

Summerford: You said the latter part of '73.

Gaskins: Right, it had to be after June of '73 because that's when you know I moved into that apartment down there and uh, they brought Doreen and that little black kid down there to my house. I told em I wasn't able to take care of her.

Gaskins: Well, me and Johnny and Carl and so finally at last Carl and Johnny both said that they wasn't takin her back to Charleston with em, so they left her right there. Well now, my wife was in the house at that time. And so uh, I told em well, I couldn't take care of her and one thing led to another. So me and Doreen walked around the house. I was gonna talk with her and she was about seven months pregnant at the time again and so I asked her who the daddy of the kid was that she had at the time that she was carrying right then and it was another black kid, from what she told me. We went on round to the fish pond, started round there and we walked around to the edge and I just shoved her right in the pond and grabbed her by her feet and held her under and then I went back and got the kid and done the same thing. And told Johnny and Carl to go ahead and take the hot stuff on to Belton Eaddy's, that I'd keep her there at my house…they went on to Belton's. I took Doreen and the baby and put em in the back of the hearse that I had…Went down next to Johnsonville, went down a hill, back in and drove way back in the woods there and backed up a road in there and took Doreen and the baby out and carried em over there and uh laid em, I'll say maybe 25 yards from that road. And covered em up and left em down there. I have never went back to this day, to that spot no more.

Summerford: Are you telling me now that the only reason that you killed Doreen and this baby was because they didn't have any place to stay?

Gaskins: No, no, no.

Summerford: Well why did you kill Doreen and the baby?

Gaskins: Well, Doreen thought more of a nigger than she did a white man. She'd rather go with a nigger man than she did a white man and uh, well, I did a lot for her and everything and she had some words that I just didn't like.

Sheriff Barnes: She didn't struggle or anything when you tried to put her in the pond?

Gaskins: Well, she wasn't able to do no struggling or nothing. She was way gone again, you know, with another baby and all and she wasn't expecting that.

Barnes: She didn't scream?

Gaskins: No, she didn't. She didn't even make no kind of a sound or nothing...

Barnes: Did you hit the baby anywhere at all?

Gaskins: The baby was not hit, no.

Summerford: All right now, when was the next murder or killing that you were directly or indirectly involved in, that you can recall?

Gaskins: All right, we come back, we come to now, to '74. That would be the death of Johnny Sellers and Jessie Judy. As you know, Johnny and Jessie was living together to begin with, down there in Charleston on Reynolds Avenue and that this stealing and stuff was going on, right on. They stole a lot of stuff and they sold some of the stuff over at some pawn shops in Sumter. They was bringing stuff down to Belton Eaddy to sell... Johnny and Jessie and myself picked up, I'd say about a eight or nine thousand dollar boat... Belton bought the boat...Johnny had got locked up and I'd went and got the money and got him out of jail together....So Johnny was gonna pay me out of his share... we worked some other deals…Belton and I got together and Belton told me that he owed Johnny a bunch of money and he had made another deal on the side and the best thing that he could see that we ought to get rid of Johnny…Johnny and Jessie came down from Charleston together, went to Belton's…Belton told us to go to a place and he would bring us the money…Belton put the gun in the trunk of my car. Belton had the gun already and it loaded and everything for me…So me and Johnny left there. We went on back down to these woods. Me and Johnny walked around there in the woods and I pretended that I seen a snake and I asked Johnny did he have his gun with him. Johnny had a 38 caliber pistol but he didn't have no bullets for it. So Johnny says I ain't got no bullets for my gun. I went back to the car and got my gun and I shot Johnny down there in the woods.

Summerford: What kind of gun was this?

Gaskins: That I used, 30.30 rifle…Belton met me when I come back out… After I shot Johnny, I didn't put the gun back in my car.…hid it side of a tree…I went back to Belton's house. Jessie was at Belton's house. I told Jessie that Johnny said for her to come on with me. So I went, took Jessie, and carried her back there and killed her and then I buried em back there.

Summerford: What'd you kill Jessie with?

Gaskins: A knife…Stuck her in the heart.

Summerford: Where were you when you did that, in the car?

Gaskins: No sir, right there in about 25 feet of where Johnny was at.

Summerford: She didn't question what you were doing out there in the woods?

Gaskins: Jessie would go anywhere in the world with me, anywhere. She lived with me from Sumter, right on all the way.

Summerford: Y'all have any conversation before you killed her?

Gaskins: I just told her I was gonna kill her.

Summerford: You did, what did she say?

Gaskins: Not a word in the world.

Summerford: She didn't say anything?

Gaskins: Nothing in the world.

Summerford: She didn't cry?

Gaskins: No sir.

Summerford: Beg you not to kill her?

Gaskins: No, she didn't beg, cry.

Summerford: She didn't?

Gaskins: Didn't have nary a word in the world to say.

Summerford: Was it dark out there?

Gaskins: No, it was about I'll say eleven o'clock on Sunday morning....they left their car in Kingstree and we all come up to Belton's in my car the red Mustang...Johnny's car stayed there in Kingstree until the sheriff auctioned it off.

Summerford: Well, why did you kill her?

Gaskins: I had to after I killed Johnny.

Summerford: What did you do with the knife?

Gaskins: The sheriff's got it...Campbell soup knife. It's a special made knife that you bone chickens with. And it's a stainless steel blade on it and you just don't break em.

Tom Henderson: Is that it?

Gaskins: That's it right there, yes…the gun was in the trunk… it had one bullet in it and several laying in the trunk…it was a clip rifle but there was no clip…later I gave it to Teadlum Powell… his wife will give it to you… Johnny was shot right down there where they was found…I just dug the hole right there by him and just rolled him over into it…

Sheriff Barnes: How about Jessie?

Gaskins: I said Jessie, I'm going to kill you…she looked at me like she didn't believe me…I just took it, stuck it right through about here and she just wilted right down to the ground and I pulled the knife out.

Sheriff Barnes: Did y'all have any sexual relations?

Gaskins: At that time no we did not, no.

Barnes: Do you remember how she was dressed?

Gaskins: … a pair of shorts and a little shirt… her shorts come off when I put her in the grave.

Tom Henderson: Did you bury Jessie and Johnny at the same time?

Gaskins: Yes sir.

Summerford: Pee Wee what was the next time?

Gaskins: There's the two girls that was taken from the Amusements of America in Charleston. We'd been down there to hunt em that time and it snowed on us and we left and everything. We couldn't find em down there. Their names was Linda and Jeannette… October or November of '74… White. One seventeen and one eighteen.

Summerford: There were four of you?

Gaskins: No sir, there was me, Ricky Snell, Charlie Shealy and Walter Neeley and the two girls, six altogether.

Gaskins: We taken them on down there, carried em out on the beach and started down there. When we got down there, I shot both of them. We put them in the canvas and carried them up into the woods. I came back, got my rifle and walked up and down the beach. We carried the shovels down in there and they was buried down there, but I patrolled the beach the whole time that they was down there.

Summerford: Did you ever go back there?

Gaskins: With Chief Simmons.

Summerford: You were unable to locate the place?

Gaskins: Well, we couldn't find it. It was back in March when it was snowing that time and everything. We went in there and we looked around and all and it was so cold in there why, and I never did get a chance to go back.

Summerford: Now, were all four of the men present with the two girls when they were killed?

Gaskins: Yes, they was.

Summerford: Were they holding them?

Gaskins: No, I pulled it out and it was that quick…Well, it was so fast, Mr. Summerford. It was a matter of I'd say a second and a half apart, both of them was shot. It was unexpected. There wasn't a word said or nothing.

Summerford: Okay, and did either of you have sex with em before you killed them?

Gaskins: As far as I know, nobody had it before they was dead but I think there was sex committed after. I wasn't there. I patrolled the beach. They was in there with them…the only one I heard talk was Ricky did have sex with Jeanette.

Summerford: All right and nobody ever questioned you about that, the disappearance?

Gaskins: This was Amusements of America and they moved out right after that and you know, people working there, they in and out and they got people that works there maybe one night a week or what not and they're gone.

Tom Henderson would ask Gaskins whether Snell and Shealy were actually present or whether this was his way to get even with Snell for testifying in one of the trials and with Shealy for not taking responsibility for the burglary charge against both of them. Gaskins would reply and argue that he had no quarrel with Snell and that he had in fact told Shealy and their other co-defendant that he would plead to the burglary and exonerate them.

Henderson would opine off the record that if the murder Gaskins described happened at all, it sounded much more like a Gaskins-Neeley affair then anything involving others.

"And we all know Pee Wee knows exactly where that grave is, if there is one. That little control freak was not about to let Walter and/or those other airheads decide where to put that grave or how deep or anything else. It was said that when they were out there in the woods, Gaskins kept circling an area where a sapling had three distinct slash marks in it that had obviously been cut years ago. When asked about the marks he said they meant nothing to him, but that sounds just like him. He's not going to find anything until he's ready. Story is the assistant chief, a real smart assed yankee, came out there in a fancy blue flight suit with zippers for everything and a fancy embroidered badge and name tag —and get this, a silky looking ascot. Gaskins took them about twenty yards from the tree with the marks on it and had them dig a huge hole telling them that he was certain they were at the right spot. He was hopping up and down, all excited, telling them he was sure that was it. When Pee Wee said he saw a piece of one of the girl's clothes he got the assistant chief so excited that the man jumped in the hole with his fancy suit to help. Once the guy was muddy, Gaskins moved on saying he was wrong that it was definitely further in the woods. Someday he'll either walk in there and go straight to the grave or we'll never know whether there was a murder out there. When I ask Walter he goes pale and won't talk about it, so it may have happened," Henderson finished.

Back on the record questioning would continue by the various participants for the state.

Tom Henderson: Can you pin this down to a date?

Gaskins: It would be the last days of October or the first days of November.

Tom: 'Bout October of '74

Mr. Summerford: Okay, let's go to the next one then.

Gaskins: All right, the next one would be on the 10th day of April 1975. That would be on a Friday. That would be Diane Neeley and Avery Howard. …I'm the man that set the deal up where they was to be killed at and everything in this now. …Charlie had been staying with my sister-in-law, Wanda Snell… Charlie started moving in on uh Wanda, Wanda had been living … with a guy, Roy Lee Knight. You know him. He's Johnny Knight's brother.…. It got so they couldn't get along and they started fighting…Wanda wanted me to break it up … I went in and told Roy Lee that he had to stay away from Wanda… Charlie was wanting to horn in too with Wanda…In the meantime, Johnny he comes in and him and Wanda's messing around …so I let them stay together at my house.

Summerford: Johnny Knight?

Gaskins: Right, let little Johnny and Wanda stay together. Johnny is on parole from reform school.

Summerford: He wasn't but 15, how old is Wanda?

Gaskins: Bout 14 and a half, 15. They was about the same age, pretty close to same age.…Well, anyway, I liked Johnny pretty good, so I discussed this with his mother, Mrs. Knight that if she would sign the papers for Johnny to marry Wanda, I would sign for Wanda…but in the meantime Charlie started moving in then and broke Wanda and Johnny up. Diane got teed off about that and she started running her mouth about that she would have the law to get Charlie, to come there and raid Charlie in my house and get him because she could have him locked up for statutory rape. I says you can't do that Diane, because that's gonna put me in jeopardy then. See I was on probation myself. I said if the law comes there, they gonna get me for contributing to the delinquency of a minor. I said it'd automatically cause me to have to go do two years, Federal…And so I go to Charlie and tells Charlie, there ain't no way in the world we gonna be able to keep her mouth shut but get rid of her. …Well, she's messing around with Avery Howard too at this time. She's meetin Avery up at my house….So the next day I told Avery, I said you better watch yourself. You gonna mess around now and Walter's gonna kill you…Ricky had been going with Diane too…I had been letting them use the shop where I worked at to go in there…I told Ricky, Charlie and Walter that I'd set it up for Diane and Avery to use the shop on a Friday night. I would go to Sam's Club at Lake City and work that night in case something went wrong, that I would be out of this here deal, but he had better get rid of Avery and Diane because he was going to prison if he didn't…I gave Charlie the same knife that he showed over there right there. And I think if they check it and everything, they'll find the same stab wounds in Avery and Diane that that knife there will match, that Tom's got right there…after they was stabbed they was brought down to Lake City. I got with them there ..went out to my daughter's trailer…got a axe and a shovel, went with them to the place where they was buried at down there… Charlie stabbed them…Wanda was there and she's also give the statement that she was there already too.

Sheriff Barnes: And they were where now, when you shot them?

Gaskins: Right down there at the gravesites where I shot em at. They had been stabbed and I shot em down there at the gravesite, shot em in the head, both of em in the head.

Sheriff Barnes: Is that the way they brought them from Charleston?

Gaskins: That's the way they come from Charleston, laying over in the car, …

Tom Henderson: Pee Wee, what were they stabbed with again, now?

Gaskins: That knife that you've got right there. That boning knife. I call it the Campbell Soup knife, yes. …The only thing I done was put a bullet in each one of them after they were down there at the place.

Tom Henderson: With this Berretta, .32 Berretta?

Gaskins: Right and like I say, the bullet that come out of Diane, I think will match the gun if it can be checked. It will match it and show that it is.

Tom Henderson: Did you do anything to the graves?

Gaskins: Cut some switches and sticks and stuff and put up all over it. …where it'd look like stuff growing up on it.

(After a short break)

Summerford: Pee Wee, I understand now, you're saying that you made a mistake and you gave one out of date? …give me your next one then.

Gaskins: Well, its Barnwell Yates. That was on February the 13th 1975.

Summerford: There's no question but that you, did you kill him?

Gaskins: Yes sir. …Well, I've always said that I thought, I even said on the stand in the court that I felt that I killed the man. I said that in court. I always was satisfied that I killed the man.

Summerford: Did you pull the trigger?

Gaskins: There was no trigger pulled in that.

Summerford: What happened?

Gaskins: His wind pipe was busted in two and he was stabbed twice, they said. …his windpipe was crushed.

Summerford: With what?

253

Gaskins: With my hands. ...I can bust one inch boards with my hand. I can sit right here and split a board with my hand and I've done that many times.

Summerford: Where was Barnwell when you did that?

Gaskins: In about 40 yards of where we dug him up at down there in Williamsburg County.

Summerford: Wasn't he tied?

Gaskins: Was he tied, his hands was handcuffed behind his back.

Summerford: Who was with you then?

Gaskins: Uh, John Owens, Teedlam Powell, Susanne.

Summerford: Well, you told me one time before that Susanne paid you to kill Barnwell Yates. Why would she pay you and then go with you to do it?

Gaskins: Susanne and John paid me.

Summerford: You telling me the truth, Pee Wee?

Gaskins: Yes sir, I killed him. John Owens, Teadlam Powell and

Susanne was with me the night I killed him.

Summerford: Pee Wee, his throat was cut.

Gaskins: I told you I busted his throat.

Mr. Query: Wait a minute y'all, let's get that straight. His throat wasn't cut. I sat through Joel Sexton's testimony. He didn't say his throat was cut.

Tom Henderson: The throat was deteriorated too much, you couldn't tell. Testimony was given by John Owens that his throat was cut.

Gaskins: I know, like I say, I know I busted his throat cause blood was coming out of his mouth. I flat, I told them that I thought I killed him. I told the jury I thought I killed him. That's what I couldn't understand, any other bruises on him, besides his throat busted because I hit him hard enough that I figured I busted his windpipe and maybe probably broke his neck.

Summerford: Who did the stabbing?

Gaskins: There was me and John Owens and Teadlam there at the time. I busted his windpipe and I won't say who stabbed him because I can't be sure of whether it was Teadlam or John Owens. I busted his windpipe.

Summerford: Where was he stabbed?

Gaskins: Well now, the autopsy report said he was stabbed in his stomach.

Summerford: Nobody else had anything to do with it?

Gaskins: Just the four of us, that's it. …I told Belton Eaddy about it after it happened. … In fact, Marie Marlowe went up there with me one night to Barnwell Yates trailer. I parked the car side the road, stood out there with the shotgun about that long, went up there to get her to knock on the door to get him to come out and if he'd walked out the door that night, she was gonna tell him the car, … would he come out and there and try to crank the car and I was standing in the edge of the woods. …If he'd come out, my intentions was that night when he was walking up the road, I was gonna walk out there and I was gonna shoot him that night.

Summerford: Okay, let's go to the next one then.

Gaskins: I'll say it was in October. No; wait a minute. Seem to me like she died before Johnny and Dennis and they died on the 10th of October. Seem to me like Kim was before Dennis and Johnny and they died on a Sunday.

Summerford: This is in '75 right?

Gaskins: Right. It was on a Sunday. Kim was 13. Uh, she came up to my house that night and I was over there at the next house at 1805 Calvert Street. There was Thomas Wright and Joe Byrd sitting on the porch along with myself, talking that night. And uh, if I'm not mistaken, this must have been a Monday night or Tuesday night, something like that and she was wanting to leave home. She was wanting to leave home and I couldn't take her and carry her no where because if I'd have left there at that time, people would know that I took her off. Joe Byrd told me that he would take her and carry her to his house and he would keep her at his house till I got ready to wherever I wanted to go. She said she wanted to go to my daughter's house. …He kept her at his house until Friday night. I got off work and everything and took off and went by there and picked her up and took her on down to my daughter's trailer down there at Roper's Crossroads. Kim stayed down there two or three maybe four months down there. I don't know exactly how much but anyway uh, a week or a couple of weeks before she was killed, she made a statement to Shirley Ann that me and Howard Evans and my half brother, Charles Hanna, had raped her. To begin with now my daughter told me this here, that I come down, that she had told her that to begin with, that Howard had raped her and from what I understand my daughter said something to her about it and then she changed it and said that Charles and me had done it. And then she didn't believe it then. So, uh I got to talking this over with Sherry and Marie. So they said, well Pee Wee, you better do something about that because if she was to tell the law something like that, you know what they'd do to you about that. I said well, I'll tell my daughter and them that I ain't coming down next weekend. I said I'll stay down there and I'll work and I'll come down Sunday, but I won't let nobody know that I'm coming down. For them to get Kim away from my daughter's trailer and get her to meet me away from the house. And my daughter or nobody will know that I've been down. So that Sunday I came down. I was driving my red Ford and I parked it in the woods coming in from the back way, parked it back there in the woods. About dark, Sherry and Marie brought Kim back there where I was at and I killed her back there and buried her.

Summerford: How did you kill her?

Gaskins: I shot her and stabbed her.

Summerford: Shot her with your Berretta?

Gaskins: Yes sir. In the back of the head.

Summerford: Did you stab her first or shoot her first?

Gaskins: I shot her first and then stabbed her.

Summerford: Why did you stab her if you shot her in the back of the head?

Gaskins: Well, I had my knife with me at the time and I shot her and then stabbed her.

Summerford: Where did you stab her?

Gaskins: Uh, I think right in the middle, somewhere right in here.

Summerford: Was she on the ground when you stabbed her?

Gaskins: Yes sir.

Sheriff Barnes: You say Marie and Sherry brought her to you?

Gaskins: Brought her to me that's right, in the Duster. They were driving the Duster.

Sheriff Barnes: Let me clarify something. They left the trailer and went back through Roper's Crossroads and came around that way?

Gaskins: That's right they came in from the dirt road out, back in this way back next to the trailer and after they put her out where I was at, they went back up to the edge of the field and turned around and came back out and went the other way and back to the trailer.

Tom Henderson: Were Sherry and Marie there when you killed her?

Gaskins: No, they put her out and they went on and turned around and came back.

Tom Henderson: Did they know you were going to kill her?

Gaskins: Yes sir.

Tom Henderson: How'd you bury her, Pee Wee?

Gaskins: I just dug a hole with a shovel and buried her.

Tom Henderson: Okay, right there where she was buried, is that where you killed her?

Gaskins: Right where she was buried, she was killed there.

Tom Henderson: Did you molest her or anything like that, have sex with her?

Gaskins: No, she was not touched.

Henderson: Did she have all her clothes on?

Gaskins: Everything, right.

Tom Henderson: Did Charles and Howard know?

Gaskins: No, I ain't never told them nothing about it, no. The only three persons that knew it besides me, I had told Belton that I had got rid of her too. He didn't know it before I told him after that I got rid of the girl. The only thing I told Shirley was that she had probably left and went on up to her people. She had some people I believe in Indiana or somewhere.

Mr. Summerford: All right, Pee Wee, what next.

Gaskins: Then we come up to Dennis and Johnny. October 10, 1975.

Summerford: All right let's skip those for right now, Dennis and Johnny. All right, what else?

Gaskins: That clears it. That clears all the murders I had anything to do with.

Summerford: What about those five you told us, you remember in my office---

Gaskins: Those people is buried in there Mr. Summerford. I can carry you to their graves right there, but they're legally buried. That's back in the woods back there that Johnny Woods testified to that the people were dead back in there. Those people are buried legally back there.

Summerford: Well, how about those that you buried in the junkyard that you were telling me in my office?

Gaskins: There ain't nothing to that.

Summerford: How about the Cuttino girl?

Gaskins: Ain't nothing to that.

Summerford: How about the one in Conway or Horry?

Gaskins: Nothing to that.

Summerford: Well why did you say that you had killed the Cuttino girl?

Gaskins: Uh. Mr. Summerford, I'm not guilty of that in no way.

Summerford: Well, you said you were. Now we want to know why you said it.

Gaskins: … Well, I felt that if I went into it and said I killed her and everything, that would take some pressure off of Pierce. Pierce was wantin to get out from under that and uh---

Summerford: Did you talk with Pierce?

Gaskins: I got letters from him.

Summerford: You ain't in a position to hold back some things. Now let's get it straight. You ain't in no position to hold back nothing.

259

Gaskins: Well, I figured if I come up with enough to put it in there to make it look like it do, why I could make some kind of deal. I just felt that if I come up with something strong enough that I could make some kind of a deal.

Summerford: All right, sir, same thing true down to the death in Horry County?

Gaskins: That's right.

Summerford: Did you get a letter from that man too?

Gaskins: I talked with him personally at CCI.

Summerford: They let you get to him and talk with him.

Gaskins: Yes sir.

Summerford: All right, now how about the police officer in Sumter County?

Gaskins: I have already told Mr. Henderson and them that that was just a made up statement.

Summerford: Why?

Gaskins: Well, I had quite a few enemies in the police force over there, I figured enemies.

Summerford: Well, really and truly now, when you get down to it Pee Wee, you really haven't told us as much today then as you told me the two days that we were in my office. Isn't that correct? Isn't that a fair statement?

Gaskins: A lot of the stuff I told you in there wasn't true.

Summerford: Why did you not tell me the truth then?

Gaskins: Because I didn't intend to go through with it.

Summerford: Why not?

Gaskins: Under the circumstances that we was under, I didn't figure that you was gonna go through with what you said. Now, I'm being honest with you there. I didn't figure you'd do it. I figured you was lying to me. Now, to be honest about it. That's exactly what I figured that you was lying to me.

During the interim when the death penalty statute under which Gaskins had been sentenced in the first trial had been overturned and before the Dobbert case in Florida had led Summerford to conclude that he could try Gaskins under the new statute for murders committed prior to the U.S. Supreme Court decision, Summerford had agreed to negotiate with Gaskins regarding the status of his custody. Gaskins' attorneys were Hinnant and DeBerry on the old case and Query and Grisso on the new cases. Gaskins was still being held on death row pending his re-sentencing to life imprisonment, which prior to Dobbert, all considered to be imminent. He asked his attorneys to negotiate with Summerford and other authorities for his return to the general population and ultimately to a facility such as the department of corrections hospital where he could work as a trustee. Although CCI had an infirmary cell block located off the tunnel, the department had a general hospital located on other grounds just outside of Columbia. The premise of the negotiations was that Gaskins would reveal all murders committed in South Carolina in which he had been involved and assist in locating the bodies of any victims to allow families to finally have closure.

As a result he was transported in the usual manner to Summerford's office in Florence to make the disclosure that would form the basis for such an agreement. Summerford never indicated anything beyond withdrawing "safekeeper" status and return to the general population at CCI or another maximum security facility. Gaskins told his attorneys that he was willing to negotiate toward that end, telling them that he had managed to achieve a pretty good situation in the general population in the past.

At that meeting he acknowledged the murders of all of the people whose bodies had been discovered. He then described the murder of a man in Sumter County that he said was some type of law enforcement officer. The murder was supposed to have occurred at the landfill in Sumter County and the body buried there. Whether such a crime was ever committed remains an unanswered question and may have been part of

Gaskins running attempts to embarrass the Sumter County Sheriff and the Sumter police. Murders involving anyone associated with law enforcement draw intense investigation from police and usually attract similar inquiry from news media. It is unlikely that the person killed had any connection to the authorities if there was in fact such a murder. Gaskins would later deny that the crime occurred.

In that meeting Pee Wee claimed responsibility for the murder of Peg Cuttino. Miss Cuttino, a young teenager, was the daughter of a state politician. She had disappeared and her body was later found in a wooded area. An itinerant man by the name of Junior Pierce with a criminal history was arrested in a rural Georgia and confessed to the crime along with various other murders around the country. As it turned out Pierce could not have committed some of the murders to which he confessed and he later claimed that the Georgia sheriff had described murders of young women and then tortured him and threatened him with execution unless he confessed. He recanted his confession of the Cuttino murder along with others but there was no conclusive evidence to exclude him from that murder. Gaskins's confession gained some credibility as a result of his knowledge of some details never released by the police to the public. Gaskins later revelation of having received letters from Pierce may have explained this knowledge although the letters were never produced nor found in the numerous searches of the Gaskins cell. All mail to Gaskins was censored by prison authorities and anything from another penal institution would have likely been seized or at least carefully analyzed and logged by the inspecting officer. However, the period of time that was most closely indicated by forensic evidence to be the date on which Peg Cuttino was murdered did not coincide with dates during which Pierce, who was convicted of her murder, was in the Sumter area. The date given by Pee Wee meshed perfectly with forensic evidence. A book written about the murder explored the many inconsistencies that indicated Pierce was not her killer. Pee Wee again confessed to this murder during his trial for the assassination of Barnwell Yates.

Next Gaskins confessed to the murder of five people involved in drug dealing, possibly related to the drug abuse by his niece or affiliated in drug distribution with the black woman, Clyde, who was murdered by Gaskins. All five were supposed to be buried in the junkyard that was operated by the man he variously associated as an accomplice, the instigator who acted on behalf of a member of law enforcement to hire Gaskins for the murder of Clyde or as simply having owned the junkyard. No evidence beyond his statement was ever found of these murders and Gaskins refused to provide specifics about the location of the bodies unless he was taken to the junkyard.

Clearly Gaskins blamed those who had assisted his niece in her procurement of heroin and other hard drugs for her murder by him. This may have been the real motivation for the murder of Clyde and certainly others engaged in the drug trade would have been in danger, if Pee Wee discovered their identity. Gaskins asserted that no missing persons reports had been filed because the five people were engaged in the transportation of drugs all along the eastern seaboard and their location and activity would have been secreted from even their close family and associates. After he recanted during his complete statement Florence in 1978 no search was ever made.

Finally Gaskins would confess to the murder of a man in a robbery in Horry County. Somewhere in the vast rural area surrounding the resort area of Myrtle Beach, the man had been waylaid on a narrow bridge where he was shot several times with a shotgun loaded in a peculiar manner with first a round of bird shot, then three rounds of buckshot and finally with a solid slug. This was the murder for which Johnny McDowell had been convicted. Again Gaskins' knowledge of the details of the crime and the crime scene lent credibility to his claims. This claim and that of the Cuttino murder may well have been a bizarre scheme by Gaskins to create dangerous and unscrupulous allies. The possibility that Gaskins in fact committed the Horry County murder continued to have some plausibility because of details known to him and some questions that were raised by evidence that tended to exculpate the man who was convicted. By recanting in 1978 he effectively ended any further inquiry although the man convicted continued to profess his innocence and others confined with Gaskins at CCI attested that Gaskins continued to make unsolicited statements acknowledging responsibility. Again he confessed to this murder during sworn testimony in the Yates trial.

Gaskins would even vacillate on whether or not he had committed that murder during conversations with Query.

When Query pressed as to why he would continue to say he had robbed and killed the victim after seeing him with a lot of cash earlier the same day and then disavow any knowledge of the murder other than that gleaned from the perpetrator while in prison, he would simply revert to his old reliable, "I'm just not sure if I want to go there right now." A response that Query would take to mean negotiations might still be ongoing with the convicted man.

The man convicted of the crime continued to profess his innocence and to urge that Gaskins had spoken about details not known to anyone but him. He argued that he had never been known to possess a shotgun like the one used in the murder or to have loaded one in the unique way described by Gaskins. Gaskins on the other hand was known to have favored a twelve gauge shotgun sawed off just above the legal limit and to have loaded it in the precise manner used to deliver the deadly barrage on the isolated bridge. Whether the Conway man was guilty or innocent was not likely to have had any weight in the negotiations of the constantly scheming sociopath.

Summerford: Well, are you involved, either directly or indirectly, in any other killings or murders in the State of South Carolina other than the ones you have discussed here with us today?

Gaskins: No, I'm not.

Summerford: No other county in the State of South Carolina?

Gaskins: If it is any other county then I've got my county lines wrong and I don't think I have. And that's not saying that I may not know that some other people is dead that I have heard people talk about now. Now, I'm not gonna say that.

Summerford: All right, let me ask you this. I want to go back to the part about Knoy Judy. Uh, he didn't ask you to kill Knight?

Gaskins: No, he didn't know nothing in the world about it.

Summerford: Johnnie and Jessie?

Gaskins: No, no, at that time Knoy was living with Donna, the girl that I'm married to right now and he had no reason in the world for wanting Jessie killed whatsoever. No.

Summerford: And he wasn't with you that night, shining the flashlight?

Gaskins: No no, he was not.

Summerford: Why, I wonder why he would say he was if he wasn't? Do you know?

Gaskins: Yes, I can tell you why.

Summerford: Why?

Gaskins: He was scared he was gonna get the death penalty if he didn't do it. If he was tried, that's exactly why he pled guilty to that. I can tell you that.

Summerford: But he definitely did not hold the flashlight?

Gaskins: Wait a minute Mr. Summerford. I've told you there that they were killed in the daytime. You can go down there and get Belton Eaddy, you can go down there and get his wife and all and they'll tell you that Johnny and Jessie was at the house in the daytime the day they was killed and that Belton was sitting at the end of the road out there the day I shot with the thing.

Summerford: Pee Wee, all I'm telling you is what this man has told us.

Gaskins: Well, I can't help it. He was not there.

Mr. Query: Wait a minute. No sir; I'm gonna clarify something there because Knoy Judy has told everybody that's in this room that he was not there and he told you that he gave, exactly why he gave the confession. He went to Columbia to take the lie detector test in order to verify that and the minute he walked in to talk to the man that was operating the polygraph, he said no sir, that's not true. Can I still take the polygraph test. You said, no sir, he can't take it and I said by God, if he doesn't get to then I'm gonna shout it from the rooftop.

And then he took the polygraph test and the best known polygraph operator in this State verified that he had not been there, that he didn't even know where Prospect was and that was where we wound up. We came back and sat down and you said if he doesn't plead guilty, I'm gonna try him for murder. And I said Kenneth, if you do that you can convict him. There's no question I can't believe you'd do it. You said, yes sir, I certainly can. I said all right, I'll plead him, but I'll plead him only on the condition that I go in first and tell the Judge that I'm pleading him only to the fact that he had knowledge from another person and that he withheld that knowledge from the police. And I said if you can take the plea on that basis, I'll plead him. Is that right?

Mr. Summerford: I don't know, I can't argue with you.

Gaskins: He was not involved in this death in any way.

Summerford: Well, then what you're saying then is that we've got a completely innocent man up in CCI, then?

Gaskins: Yes, in that case, yes you do, Solicitor, you do. Knoy Judy had just as much to do with killing Johnny Sellers and his wife, Jessie as you did yourself. I don't like him, don't misunderstand me, I don't like Judy worth a dang, because at the time that he come in there and married Jessie, now this time, just before he married Jessie, and I think his mother will tell you this here. That was one of the times that me and Jessie went off and I told her, and I took that same knife that Tom's got there and put it to her and I told her, I said I ought to stick this plumb through you. Took her right down yonder in Berkeley County and told her, I said I ought to take this knife and stick it through and kill you for marrying the sorry son of a bitch, and I think she went and told Knoy's mother and them about that too. I didn't like it but then I turned around and told her, I says you go ahead and marry him and when you find out he ain't no damn good, come on back to me and by God she did too. She married him and she got tired of him, she left him and she come back. She called me to come get her and I went to Mrs. Judy's house and got her.

Gaskins' wife, Sandy, the one he had given to Walter, had made an elaborate statement to the police describing the murder of Johnny Sellers, had testified in the first Gaskins trial and had given a contradictory statement to Query during his representation of Judy. It is highly improbable that anyone will ever know whether the first statement was a concoction by Gaskins to distort the facts and create confusion or an attempt on the part of Sandy, a person of very obvious limited intelligence, to adopt statements made by police officers trying to piece together the events of the murder from bits and pieces of evidence. This is a frequent pitfall for the police that can occur when they are dealing with suspects or witnesses of limited intelligence who are highly motivated by fear and have learned through painful experience the benefits of acquiescence during stress laden conflicts.

Even though the polygraph had confirmed that Judy was not involved and Sandy Gaskins had recanted her statement placing him, or her for that matter, at the scene of the Sellers murder, Summerford continued to be troubled by the letter found in Judy's cell and sought to seek an explanation from Gaskins during his statement.

"I can't understand why anyone would ever write something like that down," mused Summerford aloud.

"We were trying to set you up for the polygraph in Columbia, Ken," said Query.

"Gaskins and Neeley had both told me that Judy was not involved in any of the murders. Sandy had recanted her statement under circumstances that I believed were motivated by her belief that she might jeopardize her immortal soul when I pressed her to affirm or deny in front of her picture of Jesus. Sandy, Donna and the two girls, Marie and Sherry, who are from this area, had all assured me that to the best of their knowledge Judy had never even been to Lake City or Prospect. Throughout my investigation, talking to dozens of people who knew most of the characters, not one of them ever put him in this area. Moreover, literally everyone including some of the victims' family members insisted that Gaskins and Judy were at odds and not having any contact with each other during the time that these murders occurred. The one witness that saw the dark haired, dark skinned man with Gaskins, Jessie and Johnny had met Judy and would have identified him by name and not merely by description, if it had been Judy with them," Query said.

Mr. Summerford: Pee Wee, now you know as well as I do, any man that's smart enough to do hound dogs the way you've done and all that sort of stuff, you know as well as I do, my primary concern is not necessarily your involvement in it, but who is involved with you and whether or not you're after revenge now. Let's put the cards on the table. Cause we've got enough to hang you by the yardarm, you know that as far as life sentence is concerned. There's no question about that. I'm not concerned about that. What I'm concerned about and what I want to get straight is how many people were with you, whether or not you're trying to pull our leg about, are you after this person or that person. Are you mad with this one and want to get hold of him or her. Now, you know as well as I do that Wanda Snell took the polygraph test and she was a good subject and it showed that she was lying when she said that she was with them when they killed, like she said in that lot, that they stabbed them. The polygraph showed, the test that was run was that she was lying. Now Grady, we checked it out this morning and that's what it said.

Gaskins: ...The polygraph works sometimes...

Summerford: Well, you beat it one time, didn't you?

Gaskins: Yes sir, I did. Like I say, I'm telling you facts that I know myself you see, too. Just like yesterday, let's go back to the Knoy Judy deal. You were so concerned about wanting him hung on the thing. I lay in there and thought about that last night. I know the boy's innocent of them. I don't like him because he had two of as good a women as ever lived and he lost both of them.

Summerford: You took them away from him.

Gaskins: He got one from me. I took her back. He had another girl and she left him and come and I'm married to her today. The boy is innocent, but if you want me to lie and hang him, if that's what you want, I'll give you a statement if you want to hang the man now, if that's what you want.

Summerford: All right, I want to hang him, what can you tell me?

Gaskins: Well, you claim he was with me on the Johnny Sellers deal and if you want me to lie to you now, I want this in the record, if you want me to tell you a lie---

Summerford: Was he with you?

Gaskins: No sir, truthfully he was not, no sir.

Summerford: You wanted to get back at Charles Shealey because he's agreed to turn state's evidence in that case against you.

Gaskins: What's a burglary charge to me? It don't mean nothing. I have a life sentence and a death sentence. That don't mean nothing to me.

Summerford: Didn't you tell him that if he opened his mouth that you'd get him?

Gaskins: I told him if he kept his mouth shut, I'd take everything on me. That's what I said up in the courtroom. I says keep your mouth shut and I'll plead guilty to the charge.

Summerford next questioned Gaskins about the 30/30 rifle that he said was given to him by Belton Eaddy to kill Johnny Sellers. Gaskins reiterated that he had given the gun to Teadlam Powell and that he believed Powell's wife still had the gun. Gaskins went on to explain that Teadlam was just keeping the rifle for him.

Summerford: Why didn't you give it back to Belton if it was his 30/30 rifle?

Gaskins: Because he wanted me to use it again.

Summerford: On who?

Gaskins: Russell Cox.

Summerford: Y'all had already agreed on that $3,000, hadn't you?

Gaskins: Well he offered me on that---

Summerford: $3,000?

Gaskins: Right and as I'm sitting here, I would never shoot a law man.

Summerford: Promise?

Gaskins: Under no circumstances. I'll run like hell from em but I ain't gonna shoot em.

Gaskins went on to explain that he kept the rifle simply because he had always wanted one but that he later acquired a nicer one and just left that one with Powell. Next he talked of trying to assist police in the investigation of some crimes in which he had not been involved.

Summerford: Why?

Gaskins: Chief Simmons asked me to. Chief Simmons asked me to try to find out all I could find out about that. And uh, I--- Whatever he promised me, he has always fulfilled his promises to me, I would go all the way with him. …put it right plain, that when I went down there, he says I will let you have privacy with your wife. I can't tell you what you can do or nothing like that and he kept his word to it and I have been with him a hundred per cent all the way.

Summerford: What else did he promise you?

Gaskins: Well, that's all he could. That's all he could do, he said that uh, if you'll help me and what not, you come down here. He says if you and your wife wants to have a private visit, why I can set up the private visit with you.

Summerford: Did he give you any liquor?

Gaskins: Well, let's say I may have had a drink or two. I didn't say who gave it to me, but I say I may have had a drink or two.

Summerford: What kind?

Gaskins: Well I took a drink of scotch. I didn't have but one cup.

Summerford: Now, Pee Wee, think about this a long, long time before you answer it. Did anybody in law enforcement down there in Charleston try to get you to say anything or suggest to you to say anything about any killing, where it occurred, how it occurred or anything of that nature? Suggest to you anything wrong whatever? Think a long time before you answer that because a lot depends on it.

Gaskins: Mr. Summerford, I've talked with a lot of law enforcement officers. That's a question, I have talked with let's say with a lot. I've answered a lot of questions with the law enforcement officers, but that particular question, would be hard to answer either way definitely. Now I'll be honest with you. Because like I say, now I've been, for the last two years, been into a lot and between a lot of law officers and everything else, State, County, City and everything else.

Mr. Query: Kenneth, let me clarify that. I don't know of any time that he was down in Charleston that he was not in the presence of at least two officers from Charleston County and at least two officers from the city of North Charleston. So if anything along that line is what happened, then it took the conspiracy of four experienced police officers from two different police agencies.

Summerford: So you're saying that they promised you visits, private visits with your wife and gave you some scotch liquor to drink simply to tell them what happened?

Gaskins: Well, go in with the drink. My wife was offered a drink. And uh, I was asked did I want one. Well, I don't drink and my wife says uh, Pee Wee has never drank with me. My wife drinks very little, but uh Pee Wee's never had a drink with me. And I said well, I don't drink but on second thought, I will take a drink with my wife because I've never had one with her whatsoever and I took that one time is all and I've never asked for no more, never wanted no more.

Summerford: But what I'm asking you is that they let you have private visits with your wife and they at least gave her or you a drink in exchange for you telling them what?

Gaskins: Anything that I knew about any murders or what not. And you know I went to Williamsburg County and told them that I knew that Yates was buried out in the field you here and uh, that Kim was buried up here in the woods.

Summerford: Wait a minute, you told me this.

Gaskins: I told Chief Simmons that before I told you.

Summerford: Oh, you did. How long before?

Gaskins: Well, uh, I went down there one day and told Chief Simmons that. He took me back to Columbia that night. I told Chief Simmons of three, three murders, that was uh, the Ghelkins, the Yates, and Clyde's in Sumter. The next day two detectives came up and picked me up from the penitentiary and took me down. We went out there in the field and tried to find Yates and we couldn't find it. But that evening just about dark we did find the Ghelkins. I were to come back following, a few days, I believe, it was right after that again, to hunt the Yates again and uh, word came to CCI up there that you had stopped it or the State Law Enforcement had stopped it, that they couldn't carry me out no more. And I couldn't go back out to show em nothing. Then later on, I think I wrote the Sheriff a letter and told him that we'd come down here and you and the sheriff and Mr. Query and all of got over there and made out negotiations and all at that time on the Yates deal.

Mr. Query: Pee Wee, let me get one thing squared away. You gave them the statement before you had any visitation with your wife or before you had anything to drink, is that right?

Gaskins: I did, right, I did. I give em the statement, during that day and then that night, I had my visit with my wife. I give the statement and told them I would produce. They took me at my word. I give the statement and told them

I would produce so that night I had the visit with my wife. The next day they come and got me and I produced. That's the way it was.

Mr. Summerford: All right, then what you're telling me then is, no one other than Chief Simmons had promised you anything to get you to make a statement or give evidence?

Gaskins: Nobody but what you and I discussed over yonder at the other place.

Summerford: All right, now, tell me what that was.

Gaskins: Well we negotiated that you wouldn't have nothing against my wife visiting me privately at the prison up there.

For the next several minutes Summerford and Gaskins quarreled over whether or not Summerford had promised private visits for Gaskins and his wife and the further promise of an opportunity to serve his time at one of the medium security institutions. Gaskins was particularly interested in serving his sentence at State Park, a medical facility and hospital for the Department of Corrections. It was obvious to all concerned that the hospital would afford the greatest possibility of escape.

It was apparent that both parties had allowed the other to assume an agreement where none actually existed. Gaskins did provide information and in fact led authorities to the grave of Barnwell Yates as part of the bargain. He was allowed two visits with his wife. The visits were then terminated on the basis of the conclusion on the part of the solicitor that Gaskins was not being completely truthful.

It is noteworthy that Gaskins continually referred to the negotiations as having been between the solicitor and Gaskins. Query had cautioned Gaskins several times during that meeting that Gaskins was negotiating for concessions not within the control of the solicitor's office since the Department of Corrections would exercise exclusive control over his placement and visitation. Query further cautioned that promises about those issues could be withdrawn even if the department agreed and that there would be no basis for Gaskins to enforce the agreement. Query urged that they should be negotiating for the disposition of all of the outstanding charges to prevent any South Carolina jurisdiction from seeking another death penalty on the remaining cases. Gaskins, however, had his own agenda and insisted on forging ahead.

Questioning by Summerford continued in reference to the two girls from the fair that Gaskins claimed he had killed and buried on the Isle of Palms.

Summerford: We're gonna get Neeley down here in just a little while, put Pee Wee in with him and let Pee Wee direct or ask him to take us to the gravesite and show us where they are in Charleston.

Query: All right, for that, I know there's been a day and a half search without success.

Summerford: Well I know this and you know it as well as I do, that if Pee Wee tells Neeley to go there and point out these gravesites, he's gonna do it. Now, you know that. His attorney says that.

Query: I agree with that. I just don't want our deal to fall through because Walter can't produce.

Query then raised the issues of inconsistencies between the findings of the Medical Examiner regarding the manner of death of Avery Howard and Diane Neeley and the effect of those inconsistencies on the agreement. Summerford stated that the issue of a missing bullet in the head of Avery Howard was not of great concern since the autopsy clearly established that the rigor of the bodies at the time of burial could only be consistent with the victims having been alive in Florence County and jurisdiction over the murders therefore lying in that circuit.

Agent Henderson then engaged Gaskins in a colloquy of several minutes regarding an offer by Gaskins to have a substantial amount of money channeled to Henderson in return for Henderson not opposing Gaskins being allowed to serve his sentences at State Park hospital prison as a maintenance man. Gaskins had denied the offer during testimony at his trial in Newberry, but now admitted it. The two disagreed as to whether the amount was twenty five thousand dollars or seventy thousand dollars as alleged by Henderson but otherwise the conversation was admitted by Gaskins and it was admitted that Henderson did not accept the offer.

Henderson also asked Gaskins about having killed a man in Charleston by shooting him seven times. Henderson did not appear to know the identity of the alleged victim. Gaskins denied that it occurred but there were reports that Marie and others had claimed that they witnessed that murder. When Marie was questioned by police she said that she had no idea what they were talking about. The rumors were unclear regarding the identity of the other witnesses.

(Walter Neeley brought into conference room)

Mr. Summerford: Walter, how about listen to me just a minute now. You are Walter Neeley, correct?

Neeley: Correct.

Summerford: Now, Walter, I have talked with your attorney, Mr. Paul Cantrell, in Charleston, I talked with him just a little while ago and I told him what we're doing here today. That we're talking to Pee Wee Gaskins. I also told him that Pee Wee had told us and given us some information. I asked him if he had any objections to my talking to you out of his presence. He said that he did not as long as Pee Wee was present. That he had no objections to you going to any sites and showing us anything that you wanted to show us after you conferred with Pee Wee. Now, Pee Wee has told us that on one occasion, that you and he and two other people took two girls that were working for Amusements of America, 17 and 18 years of age, one was named Linda. What was the other one's name, Pee Wee?

Gaskins: Jeanette.

Summerford: ...Now, Pee Wee says that he would ask you to go to these two gravesites because you were there when they were buried. Now, my first question is, number one, do you have any objections, first to talking to us without your attorney being present.

Neeley: I would like to talk with him first about it.

Summerford: Do you mind talking to him on the telephone?

Neeley: Or either I could talk to Pee Wee, it'd be all right with me.

Summerford: All right, how about you talking with Pee Wee, either one, whichever you prefer.

Neeley: I'll talk with Mr. Gaskins.

Summerford: You want to talk with him privately?

Neeley: It doesn't make any difference.

Summerford: All right, go ahead.

Neeley: You want me to tell them, Pee Wee?

Gaskins: Well, I told them that we was gonna agree, that we was gonna cooperate with em all the way and that uh I'd go with em to the woods. We've got another place we've got to go to and that we'd go to Charleston too and go down on the Isle of Palms down in there and that we'd do that. Now there is one other situation that you and I were talking about concerning Chico and them that I think that me and you ought to discuss further before we bring that in now.

Neeley: Okay, Mr. Summerford.

Summerford: Now, Walter, let me explain to you now that what we are negotiating with Pee Wee now is simply this. That uh if he tells us the truth, not any half truths but all of the truth, nothing but the truth about all murders that he's been involved in, either directly or indirectly, that he will not be tried in the State of South Carolina under the death penalty. Now under the Constitution, I'm required, if you are gonna tell us something, to advise you that anything that you say will be used against you in a court of law. You have a retained attorney. You have a right to have him present, any time during the questioning by anybody, if you want us to stop we will stop and ask you no further questions. Now, do you understand all of that?

Neeley: I think so.

Summerford: All right, now is there any question you want to ask me now before we start asking you some questions?

Neeley: No sir.

Summerford: All right, now Walter, we will not seek the death penalty against you if you tell us the truth but the whole thing is based upon you telling us the whole truth, you understand that?

Query could not help but ponder the dichotomy as the state through this prosecutor motivated only by his own error in the courtroom bargained not to kill the retarded man who sat at the table surrounded by law enforcement. Query kept his musings to himself as he continued to play out the bizarre negotiation that would avoid the execution of his client and now also that of the slow thinking confederate of his client.

Summerford: Now, the same identical agreement that we have with Pee Wee. We have the same agreement with you we will not seek the death penalty for any murder committed in South Carolina. Do you understand?

Neeley: Yes, Sir.

Summerford: Now, it's based upon the entire truth, if you hide anything from us, if you lie to us about it, then we have no agreement, do you understand that?

Neeley: Yes sir.

Summerford: All right Walter, can you show us where these two bodies are?

Neeley: Oh, I believe so.

Summerford: Who was with you when you buried them?

Neeley: Ricky Snell.

Summerford: And who else?

Neeley: And me and Charles Shealey.

Summerford: Anybody else?

Neeley: Pee Wee.

Summerford: You'll go down there with us?

Neeley: Yes sir.

Summerford: Do you know the last names of those girls?

Neeley: No sir, I don't.

Summerford: Do you know where they were from?

Neeley: They were from round there at the fair, that's all I can tell you.

Summerford: All right, now how did this thing happen?

Neeley: Well, we found out they was messing around with a bunch of niggers and me and Pee Wee didn't like that. So we decided that we'd do something about it.

Summerford: Okay, so what did you do?

Neeley: Well, Pee Wee went out to the fairground and got em and me and Charlie and Ricky was at his house. We come back by the house and he had the two girls with him and he said y'all want to ride over to the beach. Said yeh, we'll ride over there. So we got over to the beach over there and this little old road that pulls off, goes down to the beach, we pulled off down in there. We was walking along the beach. Pee Wee shot both of them, put em in the canvas like, and we dug a deep hole and put em in it. Out in the woods.

Summerford: Did either of y'all rape the girls before or after they were shot?

Neeley: Ricky Snell did.

Summerford: Which one? Which girl?

Neeley: I don't know which one it was. It was one of them.

Summerford: Ricky Snell, he had sex with her after she was shot?

Neeley: Yes sir.

Summerford: Who dug the grave?

Neeley: I dug a while and Charlie dug a while and Ricky dug a while, till we got it deep enough.

Summerford: All right now, I'm not going into Dennis Bellamy with you at this time and Johnnie Knight. I'm asking you if you were involved in any other killings or murders along with Pee Wee before or after this Walter.

Neeley: No sir.

Summerford: But you knew about several?

Neeley: Well, yes sir.

Summerford: Well, I'm not going any further into this with Walter at this time simply because his lawyer is not here. I don't think it would be proper. I've got permission for him to go in as it related to the Isle of Palms. Now, I believe it would be better if we confined our questions to that at this time, Sheriff. How deep did you dig that hole, do you remember?

Neeley: About six foot.

Summerford: It was a six foot hole?

Neeley: Well there's a lot of people around the beach out there walking around through there.

Grady Query

Summerford: Okay, do you think maybe you could walk up and show us right, without ---

Neeley: It's been a long time. It's been over two or three years.

Summerford: Both of them are in the same hole?

Neeley: Yes sir.

Summerford: Sheriff, you want to ask Walter any questions?

Sheriff Barnes: Walter, you didn't mark it in any way?

Neeley: No sir, there's nothing but a lot of sand dunes and hills and stuff down there.

Summerford: Tom, you got any questions. Walter, what did he shoot them with?

Neeley: A pistol.

Summerford: Is that his favorite one, the one he carried all the time?

Neeley: Well now he had two or three pistols.

Summerford: I know but he had one he called his baby.

Pee Wee: I ain't never had one called that Mr. Summerford what I called my baby. Let him tell you what I called my baby.

Summerford: What did he call his baby?

Neeley: He called Wanda his baby.

Pee Wee: Okay, people got my guns confused up and everything. Another thing you was talking about, me pulling a .38 on Johnny Sellers, you know you was talking about yesterday. I didn't even own a .38 at that time. Mr. Crabtree

280

at the FBI over here had my .38 been had it a long time when that Johnny Sellers deal come over here.

Summerford: Well, what did you pull on him then?

Pee Wee: A 30.30 rifle is what I used on him. But people's come up that I pulled a knife on him and stabbed him and put him under my arm and toted him and him about 175 pounds. And then a fellow saying somebody held a light and hollered shoot him, shoot him and I shot him two or three times. One shot was all that was fired. The rifle wouldn't shoot but one time. How was I gonna shoot him two or three times and the rifle wouldn't shoot but one time and you have to reload it and put another bullet in it to shoot it again. I didn't even have a clip for it at that time.

Mr. Query: Let me ask Walter one thing about that. In the same thing, Walter, do you remember if, after the first shot, did the other girl scream or run or anything?

Neeley: No sir.

Pee Wee: It was only a matter of a second and a half.

Neeley: That Baretta is a automatic. It fires as quick as you can pull it.

Sheriff Barnes: Where did he shoot them Walter?

Neeley: In the head.

Sheriff: Where was he when he shot them?

Neeley: Well, me and Ricky and Charlie was with the girls walking up front. He was walking sort of behind us.

Sheriff: You looked at the bodies after they were down didn't you?

Neeley: Yes sir.

Sheriff: Did the bullet come all the way through or did it stay in?

Neeley: It come all the way through.

Sheriff: You could see the hole in the face of both of them?

Neeley: Yes sir.

Sheriff: Where'd it come out at?

Neeley: Up in here somewhere.

Tom Henderson: That's on both of them Walte?

Neeley: Yes sir.

Tom: Both girls shot in the back of the head or what?

Neeley: Yes sir.

Tom: And the bullet come out in the forehead?

Neeley: It come out somewhere in the head up here. I don't know exactly where at. (Walter then carried back to detention center)

Summerford: Go ahead now, if you want to tell us exactly what occurred in the Dennis Bellamy and Johnny Knight situation, start from the beginning, where you first met them and the relationship with them.

Gaskins: Well, Dennis Bellamy, he comes first. When I first went to Charleston in 1971, me and Sandy and Jessie went down there together and I met Walter down there in town. Walter was separated from Diane at that time. (Pee Wee explained that he had tried to affect a reconciliation by assuring Diane that he would not let Walter hurt her and that he had finally succeeded. As a result they were together again with Diane well along in a pregnancy).

... so we moved from one place round to Rugheimer Avenue down there. We stayed there for a while. I hadn't met Dennis at that time and we moved from there to O'Hara Avenue there in Charleston. Dennis and Walter and some

other boy went over to Johns Island I believe it was and got in some trouble or something over there. They came back in and Dennis come in there and wanted to borrow my shotgun. I wouldn't loan it to him. I told him I didn't loan my gun to nobody and he got mad at me and told me if I'd get out of bed, he'd whip my damn rear end. And uh, I jumped up and put my britches on and grabbed him. He was about drunk at that time and I carried him to the door and I knocked him out in the yard. He started cursing and I opened the car and got my pistol out of it and told him that he could get out the yard or I was gonna shoot him right there. Well about that time his sister, which was Diane, came running out there and says don't shoot my brother. I said well you better get him away from here. So I went on round to the back of the house to get away from him. I still had my gun in my hand at the time. I got around there and Dennis come round there and started arguing with me again round there. Well I hauled off and knocked him down then. I hit him with my gun. I didn't hit him but one lick but I laid him out with it. Well Walter got him, took him out there and put him in his car and sent him away from the house. I told the other guys that come around there, that guy that brought Walter and them back round there, I told that guy, I said you better get gone while you can go now. I don't know who he was. Walter can probably tell you. So they left there. Dennis told that he was gonna pull up beside me on the road some day and blow my brains out. He went right on over to his step daddy's house, Mr. Knight's house, and this is quote what I heard. Went over there and jumped on Mr. Knight. Mr. Knight, I understand, beat him up pretty good with a piece of two by four or something. He had to go at the hospital and get some stitches put in his head and anyway, he told the police that I had pistol whipped him. The next evening when I come in from work the police come round there to my house and asked me did I pistol whip Dennis Bellamy last night. I said he came around to my house and wanted my shotgun to go shoot somebody with over at James Island and I told him I didn't let nobody have my gun like that.

Pee Wee recounted the whole story again as he had related it to the police adding:

And I said, he said that he was gonna pull up side me on the road one day and blow my brains out and I says, I'm gonna tell you right now, if he ever pulls up side of me on the road, I'm not gonna give him a chance to shoot me. I'm gonna shoot him. *That's the words I told the police man. The policeman said, pour it to him and he left and that was the end of it. …Well, my house burnt down and that's when I left Charleston. Well, when I came back on Christmas day of '73, I moved in a trailer with Mr. Price, the man I was staying with when this trouble happened. I stayed in a trailer there on O'Hara for a while, moved on up to St. John Apartments and from there on to Calvert Street. This whole time Dennis Bellamy had only attempted to come to my house one time but I had seen him several times away from round there and we didn't get along. We didn't have nothing to do, he always was drunk, running his mouth and I wouldn't have nothing to do with him. There's one thing that I reckon your investigations will show. I didn't allow people coming to my house drunk around the children, cause I kept a good many children around my house all the time. I didn't drink the whiskey myself, I didn't take drugs, I didn't let people come around there drunk, cussing and going on around the younguns. That's one thing I've always stood up about. Well anyway, Johnny now was a different deal. Johnny stayed at my house a lot. I think I told you about Johnny staying with Wanda and one thing and another. Well, Roy Lee Knight used to live with Wanda too. I think I've already went into that too with you. All right, in March of 1975, that's when Dennis jumped on Walter out there at North Carolina Avenue and beat him up so bad and busted him all up and everything. I mean beat him where his face was just about unrecognizable and everything. And he come staggering down next to my house and I met him before he got down that way and I said, Dennis you put your feet in my yard and I'm gonna blow your damn brains out, now take it whether you believe it or not. He didn't go to my house either. So he left there and I went over to the telephone. I didn't have no phone at my house, but I went cross the street over there and got on the telephone and I called Walter's mother and told her about what had happened to Walter. So after that, I told Walter, I says if that son of a bitch ever gets in a position where I can, I'm gonna shoot his damn head off. So I never did mess around Dennis or nothing like that until the night that Dennis and Johnny came down there to that trailer that night. But as far as having dealings and such with Dennis Bellamy, never. That night that they came down there to my trailer, they had stole a blue '69 Ford truck and that's what, just like I testified in that trial, that's what they drove down there that night.*

Query silently pondered the fact that this entire cast of characters was well known to the North Charleston Police. While Pee Wee and Walter may have had the worst records of felony convictions and hard time at CCI, they were on a day to day basis less trouble to the police than the hard drinking Bellamy who tended to look for trouble after the liquor was flowing freely in his veins. Thus the "pour it to him comment" allegedly made by the investigating officer was not as improbable as it might have sounded.

Query could not help but think about the mention by Pee Wee of his call to Walter's mother. The call was mentioned without any detail of the conversation and without any explanation of his reason for making the call. It was so typical of the many conversations between Query and Gaskins in which Pee Wee would lead right up to something and then skip over it, always protecting his potential allies in the event that he ever escaped. The call, Pee Wee had told Query, was actually to solicit payment for offered revenge against Bellamy for the beating he had delivered to Walter. But when Query pressed the question as to whether she had paid Pee Wee to kill Bellamy, Pee Wee would only say, "Well let's just say, Mr. Queury, that me and her never had no quarrel and we both always kept our word to each other and she sure never felt no grief over the loss of Dennis."

Summerford: They had stolen that truck that night?

Gaskins: They had stolen that truck that night and that's what they drove down there.

Summerford: All right, go ahead.

Gaskins: Well, Johnny now, I had had a lot of dealings with Johnny cause like I say, I was hoping that Johnny and Wanda would get together sooner or later. He wasn't old enough to marry Wanda. And that night they came down there, Dennis was drunk, staggering all over the place. He'd staggered in the mud hole, I done went through that with you and told you about him when he fell in the mud hole. He sat in my thing there and pulled his shoes off and throwed em in the back of my truck and I've already told you about, on the way back to Charleston, I threw em in the Santee down there. But anyway---

Summerford: That was Dennis's shoes?

Gaskins: Right, right.

Summerford: Well, who's shoes are those that we have?

Gaskins: That's old man Knights. I done told you about that. That scoundrel was wearing them two weeks after Dennis and them was dead and everything down there.

Summerford: They weren't in your trailer?

Gaskins: They ain't never been there. I don't know how the devil y'all got em. They claim that Ray Shupe brought em or something like that there. And another thing, why did Ray Shupe go in my trailer and take a television out and keep it two years. The sheriff had to make him carry my television back and give it to my daughter and he got mad about it.

Gaskins enmity toward Deputy Ray Shupe was long standing and their run-ins had been frequent. It was true that Shupe had taken the TV for his own use and kept it until the sheriff required its return but the issue of the shoes may have been one of Pee Wee's many uses of nonessential details as an attempt to discredit a member of law enforcement. Attention was originally drawn to the shoes because the bodies of Knight and Bellamy were found shoeless. Some members of law enforcement and the media had speculated that the shoes of victims had been kept by Gaskins as trophies of the grisly murders. This pattern did not continue to other bodies and was pretty much abandoned but the mystery of Bellamy's shoes being found at the trailer when Pee Wee was adamant about having thrown them in the Santee River and the fact that Johnny Knight was also without shoes would continue to surface.

Soon after his arrest Pee Wee even played on the macabre appeal of the shoe issue. A guard at CCI who had been assigned to death row where Pee Wee and Neeley were held in adjacent cells told police that Gaskins and Neeley had threatened to kill him. The guard said Pee Wee laughed and told him that after they killed him they would play a card game for his shoes and one of them would add them to his collection. He said that they frequently told him about the large collection of shoes that they had amassed. No evidence of shoe collecting ever panned out and it seems that this was merely an example of Pee Wee's morbid sense of humor.

Gaskins went on to explain that confusion had existed about some of the vehicles and that one vehicle referred to as having been driven by Gaskins was actually a similar blue Chevrolet that had been stolen by Johnny Knight and Wade Stone.

Gaskins: …Well, the night that Dennis and Johnny came there, I told Dennis, let's take a ride in the blue Malibu. Now, this is after midnight now. That's why I say, a lot of the testimony that you've got is conflicting but I'm gonna tell it the way it is. We left there after midnight, and I'm gonna give you a man in a minute that you can prove what I'm saying too because he's one as good a Christian man as there is down there in the country. I drove that blue Malibu all the way back there to where Dennis was killed at. I parked it back there. Me and Dennis got out and walked back there and I shot Dennis back there. Went back to crank the car up and the dang thing wouldn't crank. I walked from there out to the road. Now here is some vital information you need to get. I went to a man's trailer there named Julius Hanna. I woke him up. I told him my car, the alternator had quit on it and it wouldn't crank, that I had been hunting and that I needed him to take me back over to my trailer to where I could get a way to come get the car, that it was down the road and I needed somebody to do it. He took me in his car and it was so foggy you couldn't hardly see and carried me from his trailer back to my trailer to get my white truck. I give him eight dollars for carrying me that little piece from his trailer over to mine. I gave him eight dollars that night, or that morning before daylight. He left there, I went and got a shovel and a ax that I had at that time and put in the white truck. Walter and Johnny were sitting in the trailer all during this. I went in there and told them that the car had quit on me, that we'd drove it and went back to a place and it quit on me and Dennis was at the car. They got in the white truck. We left in the white truck and drove the white truck back there, I got a battery out of another car that I had sitting out there in the woods where I had all them stolen cars parked out there. I carried another battery with me. I had a chain in my truck in case the battery wouldn't crank the car, that I could pull the car away from there, went on back down there, me and Johnny and Walter and we walked out there. We walked about the length of this room from where Dennis was at and I shot Johnny then, Walter took a rifle that was in the truck and walked back round the woods, like he was going back out and I told him to keep his eyes open to make sure nobody come back in there while I dug the hole and buried them and that is what happened that night. And after we buried em and everything, Walter drove the white truck back and I cranked the blue Malibu up and went back. Now, here is some very important information too, now. They all claim that my wife didn't come down that night. Both of my wives came down that night just like I said they did. They went to Sam's Club and after Sam's club closed up, Marie and Sherrie did get with them and they come up to the Eldorado. They didn't get back in till the next morning, I say around 5:30 or 6:00 to the best I can understand. That's about the time they got back. They went in and laid down. I got back about 6:30 that morning and it was still foggy as it could be. Me and Walter came back in the blue Malibu and the white truck. I went in and woke Sandy and Donna up. They was the two that was in the trailer. They got up and they got the children and Sandy and Donna and Walter went back to Charleston and I stayed there at the trailer. And that's what happened that night.

Summerford: All right, now when you left Charleston, had you already arranged for Walter to pick up Dennis?

Gaskins: No sir, I had told him a long time ago that if he ever got that son of a bitch to where I could, I would shoot him. I did tell him that now, but it was not arranged, no certain time or nothing like that. I hadn't seen Walter that day.

Summerford: All right, what about the Mustang, there was no such thing as a Mustang then?

Gaskins: Yes sir, yes sir, the Mustang had been there for quite a while. It had been there and I had to put a starter on the Mustang. I had to go up there and cut the serial number off that Mustang which I did this in the back yard of Belton's junk yard.

Summerford: Who stole that Mustang?

Gaskins: Uh, Wade Stone and Johnny Knight.

Summerford: From where?

Gaskins: From uh, they said a restaurant over there on Remount Road in Charleston. At a restaurant over there, that's where they said they stole it at. They had tore the starter up on it. The only way you could crank it, you had to push it to crank it. It was a straight drive.

Summerford: Well let me ask you this now Pee Wee. Did you know that Johnny and Dennis were involved in robbing the Icehouse in Charleston? Got $216.00 from it that night?

Gaskins: I heard something or other about they had been a robbery that night.

Summerford: Well, you took the money when you killed them.

Gaskins: They didn't have but just a little bit of change on em when I got em. They didn't have nothing but change on them when I got em Mr. Summerford.

Gaskins: Between all of em there was about $27.00 in change.

Summerford: Did Walter participate in that robbery, Walter Neeley?

Gaskins: That happened before they come to my trailer. I don't know what happened down there. I just heard talk.

Summerford: Well it happened on the same night.

Gaskins: Right, that's what I'm talking about. I heard that they had robbed the Icehouse.

Summerford: You didn't ask Walter about it?

Gaskins: Yes.

Summerford: What did he say?

Gaskins: He said that they had robbed the Icehouse.

Query knew the Icehouse Restaurant well. It was a popular restaurant and bar in the Old Market in the center of downtown Charleston. He imagined that a robbery in the crowded Market would have been a very dangerous incident. Reflecting on the questioning he thought that in typical fashion Summerford had been forced to ask a dozen questions to get close to a straight answer about whether Pee Wee knew about the robbery and whether he knew who had been involved. Pee Wee worked for Picquet Roofing just a few blocks down East Bay Street from Market Street and the popular eatery. He would have known about the good crowds that assembled there for Happy Hour and then for dinner. It was very unlikely that Dennis or Johnny had ever been in or even around the somewhat upscale restaurant. Query surmised that it was most likely that Pee Wee had planned the robbery and dispatched Walter and Johnny to carry it out. A drunken Dennis had probably complicated the plan rather than aided it and the take indicated that they arrived after the owner or manager left with the night deposit, probably because they stopped to shoot pool. As usual, however, Pee Wee's penchant for duplicity intertwined fact and fiction without any apparent motive for doing so.

Summerford: Well, what happened to the money?

Gaskins: Well, I got $27.00, I don't know. But I'll tell you this here. When Johnny and them robbed the place or sold hot stuff, they carried it and give it to their momma and daddy. The money they always gived to the momma and daddy out of stuff like that.

Summerford: Well, they didn't go back home after they robbed the place.

Gaskins: I don't know, I was already down there. I was already down there. I don't know what happened. I'm just going by what---

Summerford: Well, did they tell you how much? Did Walter ever tell you how much they got from the Icehouse?

Gaskins: No, no. I don't know whether he knows or not.

Summerford: Well, he was with them?

Gaskins: Well, Mr. Summerford, I been with people and ain't knowed what went on and I've done a lot of things with people with me ain't knowed what went on. You take the Barnwell Yates case. People don't know what I took out of that trailer.

Summerford: What'd you take out?

Gaskins: I took out a bunch of money and a bunch of bullets and stuff out like that.

Summerford: How much money did you get out of that trailer?

Gaskins: I got 22 one hundred dollar bills out of it and I damn sure didn't tell everybody that till I went to court.

Summerford: Okay, well, anyway, they did rob it, and you were aware before you killed them that they had robbed the Icehouse?

Gaskins: No, they hadn't discussed that with me.

Summerford: When did you find out about it?

Gaskins: Walter told me that at the trailer. He asked me how much money did I get and I poured every bit of the money out there. There was $27.00 there is what I'm telling you, off of both of them, $27.00.

Summerford: I bet Walter thought you lied to him, didn't he?

Gaskins: Well, he never did say nothing about it. There wasn't a dollar bill or nothing, nothing but nickels and dimes and quarters.

Summerford: Was Johnny looking up in a tree when you shot him?

Gaskins: No, no, no.

Summerford: What did you tell Johnny you were wanting to do?

Gaskins: We was walking out there and I just shot him.

Summerford: Where did you tell him that you were going?

Gaskins: Well, now, I know what you have already said in court, that I told him, look up there in that tree and I shot him.

Summerford: I'm going by what people told me now.

Gaskins: Yeh, you going by what Walter's told you on that. There was nothing never said about no tree or nothing like that. We was walking and I told him, I said, Dennis must be somewhere around here, when we got down there and we was walking on out there. We was just walking on down there in the woods and like I say, when I figured it was getting pretty close to where Dennis was at, I pulled my gun out and shot him and that was all that was to it.

Summerford: You shot him in the back of the head?

Gaskins: Yes sir. That was all there was.

Summerford: Why?

Gaskins: Why did I shoot him? Well, I had already killed Dennis and there was no way in the world that I could let him walk out of there.

Summerford: He didn't know that.

Gaskins: Well, you know when his brother didn't show up, why he was gonna say, well him and Pee Wee left together. I wasn't gonna take that chance.

Summerford: You were looking for the money, were you looking for the money?

Gaskins: No, I didn't even know that they even had the money on them until I felt in his pocket and got the change Mr. Summerford. The money didn't mean that much to me, cause hell, I carried anywhere from a hundred on up into thousands all the time. Money wasn't no problem for me.

Summerford: All right now, did you sit down in that trailer, inside that trailer with some papers for Dennis Bellamy?

At the trial in Florence for the murder of Dennis Bellamy for which Gaskins had originally received the death penalty, Gaskins' daughter, who lived on the same property where Gaskins' trailer was located, had testified that Johnny Knight and Dennis Bellamy had been in the trailer filling out papers on a night when they brought a red Mustang to Ropers Crossroads. She had testified that this would have occurred near the time or on the night that Bellamy and Knight disappeared. She testified that she had seen Johnny before that night but had not ever seen Bellamy.

Gaskins: No, now I know what you're fixing to talk about. I can answer that before you do it. Signing papers and stuff, no. Dennis Bellamy had never in his lifetime, Mr. Summerford, had ever been to that trailer in his life before that night. Wade Stone and Johnny Knight is the two people that had been to the trailer that my daughter's talking about now. I know what I'm talking about. They had been down there. They came with me down there that night to bring the Mustang before then. The Mustang was brought down there and I sat down and wrote---

Summerford: By whom? Who brought the Mustang down there?

Gaskins: Johnny Knight and Wade Stone.

Summerford: What time did Dennis Bellamy and Johnny Knight come down there the night they were killed?

Gaskins: It was round midnight or somewhere long there. I took it to be around midnight. I stayed at my trailer that night.

Summerford: Why did they come down there, did they tell you?

Gaskins: To bring the truck down there, wanting me to buy the truck. They wanted to sell me the truck.

Summerford: And they had stolen that truck that night?

Gaskins: They had stole that truck that night. That's right and I think the records will show you, at the Hawkins Auto Sales, that on the night of October 10, 1975, a blue 1969 Ford half ton pickup was stole off that lot. And Belton Eaddy got the truck the next day. It was rusted out round and round the body of it. The body wasn't no good on it.

Summerford: What did Belton do with the truck, do you know?

Gaskins: He told me that he sold it to a man in Marion County and the man had wrecked it and total lossed it. That is the words that Belton told me.

Summerford: How much did you get out of that truck?

Gaskins: I didn't get nary a dime out of the truck. I give it to Belton and told him to get rid of it and if he got rid of it, we would split the money on it and likely you can get Belton in here right now and I'll face him on it. And he said, he told me, he said I let a man try the truck out and he total lossed it. I said well, forget about it then.

Also let me go into this here. A few weeks before that now, another 1972 white Ford pickup truck was stole from the same place and brought down there to me. I let Belton have that truck. I don't know what happened to that either. I never did get nothing out of that one. But that truck wasn't stole by Johnny Knight and them. Walter brought me that truck. I think records will verify just what I said on that. But the only one I can be positive on was the blue truck that was stole that night and brought down there. Like I say, the only thing the truck would have been fit for was the motor and transmission and the tires.

Summerford: How did you manage to get Dennis to go down in the woods with you that night?

Gaskins: He was about drunk and we tried the Malibu out. We drove it down there and I told em lets take a walk that I had to go down there in the woods.

Summerford: For what?

Gaskins: Well, to relieve myself.

Summerford: When you first saw him did you realize that you were gonna kill him then, that night?

Gaskins: Yes sir, yes sir. Now, I ain't gonna lie to you. When he walked up to my door that night and I looked at him. I said to myself, you made a mistake by coming here tonight. That's what hit my mind at the time and I got a chance and I asked Walter did anybody know that they was down there and he said no.

Summerford: So Walter knew what you were gonna do?

Gaskins: Well, I asked Walter did anybody know that they'd come down there that night and he said no.

Summerford: So you took him off by himself.

Gaskins: I took him and nobody but me and him got in the blue Malibu.

Summerford: Johnny didn't say anything to you about taking him off?

Gaskins: No, Johnny and Walter was looking at the little television up on the counter there and playing the radio on it, setting up there on the counter there in the trailer.

Summerford: And you told Dennis you were gonna ride down there to see a man about buying---

Gaskins: I said, let's take a ride. I'll let you see how the Malibu runs and we'll see a man about buying the truck. I said I got no use for it. It ain't no good to me. I can't use it. It's too bad a shape. The body was too bad on it. So I took him off down there and I killed him.

Summerford: That's the first time that you had been in the company of Dennis for some time?

Gaskins: That's the first time I had been in the company or had any conversation with Dennis since the deal where he beat Walter up, right.

Summerford: Now, what did you do to Dennis?

Gaskins: Shot him.

Summerford: Where?

Gaskins: Let me make sure now. I don't want to give you the wrong side if I can help it. Here, here and here.

Summerford: Three times?

Gaskins: Right.

Summerford: You wanted to make sure he was dead, huh?

Gaskins: Well, like I told you. I had a reason for it. Most of the time I shoot one but I told you why come I had it out for Dennis the way I did and everything and it ain't no use to lie. I shot him three times. I think that will match the report you got on it too, from what you said in court.

Summerford: Johnny had on that shirt that had 88 on it, didn't he?

Gaskins: I couldn't tell you. I didn't pay that close attention to it.

Summerford: And you don't know what Dennis had on?

Gaskins: No, well, I saw the stuff in the courtroom now, but I'm telling you, I didn't know what they had on, but after looking at everything in the courtroom I could tell you what I saw in the courtroom but I couldn't tell you that night what they had on, no because I didn't pay it that close attention.

Summerford: Let me ask you something, Pee Wee. After you kill somebody like that, did it bother you? The next day or at that time?

Gaskins: Well, you think about it.

Summerford: I'm asking you.

Gaskins: I say you think about, I think about it, that's what I'm trying to get across to you. I think about it, yes. I go over it, why I did it and try to figure out would I do it again if I had to go over it again and what not.

Summerford: What conclusion did you come to?

Gaskins: In Dennis, yes sir.

Summerford: You would have done it again?

Gaskins: I would have done it again.

Summerford: How about with Johnny?

Gaskins: Well, under the circumstances, if they were the same, yes, but if Johnny would have came down there by hisself, if Johnny came with Walter or if Johnny would have come with anybody else, no.

Summerford: You wouldn't have done it then?

Gaskins: No under no circumstances.

Summerford: Why didn't you kill Walter, if you killed Johnny?

Gaskins: That's one of the biggest mistakes I ever made in my life.

Summerford: You should have killed Walter?

Gaskins: Yeh, I should have done it.

Summerford: Is there anybody else you should have killed other than Tom Henderson?

Gaskins: Yeah, there's a lot I should have killed, Mr. Summerford.

Summerford: Who?

Gaskins: Quite a few of them out there, inside and everything else.

Summerford: Inside where?

Gaskins: In the penitentiaries and jailhouses and in the streets out there too.

Summerford: But you say Walter is the one that you regret not killing more than anybody else?

Gaskins: No, I don't reckon I really regret it. In other words, if he hadn't never carried them down there I'm liable to still been out there. I'm looking at it both ways.

Summerford: Did you ever kill anybody that you really were sorry after you killed them?

Gaskins: Oh, yes.

Summerford: Who?

Gaskins: Jessie.

Summerford: You loved Jessie didn't you?

Gaskins: Yes sir.

Summerford: Why did you kill her?

Gaskins: Well I had to.

Summerford: Why?

Gaskins: Well, I'd killed Johnny there too and she knew that I took Johnny away and if Johnny didn't show up, why---

Summerford: Who else did you kill that you were sorry about?

Gaskins: Well, my niece.

Summerford: Anybody else?

Gaskins: I reckon really down deep, when you get down to the bottom of it, why you have a little feeling towards everybody regardless of what, even though like I told you, I killed Dennis and would kill him again but going down deep, you get to thinking about it, why it still gets on your nerves and on your mind about it.

Summerford: Dennis, of course, you enjoyed killing more than anybody else?

Gaskins: Well, I feel that he was justified in it.

Summerford: He was justified in getting killed?

Gaskins: Yes, I do. He's the only one that I felt that was justified.

Summerford: How about these girls that were walking down the beach that had been off with the black men?

Gaskins: No, I feel that they're justified in it.

Summerford: You felt that strongly about it?

Gaskins: I'm strictly against any nigger going with a white woman or a white woman purposely going with a nigger. I just don't think that that's right, no way in the world.

Summerford: Of course, you'd do that any time that that situation occurred, Wouldn't you?

Gaskins: No, I see it, I've seen so much of it and everything and it's still going on. No matter what one or two men can do, can't change the world.

Tom Henderson then questioned Gaskins for more than a few minutes about the shoe issue. He raised again that the shoes that were found in Gaskins' trailer and identified by members of Knight's family as Knight's shoes with Gaskins continuing to insist that Johnny Knight was not wearing shoes on the warm October night and that Gaskins had no knowledge of how the shoes had gotten into the trailer.

Query thought it a real quandary. Was Gaskins again playing head games with the authorities over an insignificant detail? Was law enforcement again playing fast and loose with the facts? Had the shoes been planted? If so, then by whom? Could Pee Wee's daughter have put them there for some inexplicable reason? Had she or her husband, Howard, put them there to divert attention from Howard and Howard's involvement, as alleged by Pee Wee, in the Ghelkins tragedy? There were plenty of questions but answers seemed rare.

Mr. Summerford: Y'all didn't have any papers or anything on the table, Pee Wee, why would your daughter---

Gaskins: Mr. Summerford, I've told you time after time that my daughter has never seen Dennis Bellamy, saw Wade Stone and Johnny Knight. How many times do I have to tell you that. She has never seen Dennis now.

Summerford: Why would she get into court and testify against you?

Gaskins: Mr. Summerford, I don't know. I'm telling you like it is that she never saw Dennis Bellamy, she saw Johnny Knight and she saw Wade Stone down there.

Summerford: All right, did you have papers that night?

Gaskins: Yes sir.

Summerford: You did have papers?

Gaskins: Yes sir, yes sir.

Summerford: All right, now why would she come in and testify about your trailer and that those shoes were in your trailer when she cleaned it up right after that visit? Why would she come in and testify to that?

Gaskins: I have never seen them shoes in there.

Summerford: Have you ever done anything to your daughter that would cause her to come in and tell something against you in court that wasn't so?

Gaskins: I can't understand it myself. I can't understand it. But I'm gonna tell you this here, Mr. Summerford and I don't give a damn how you take this here, because I went and cleaned that trailer and took everything out of it except the white tv and the brown suit of clothes in November when I left and went on that spree and left my car. I took the dynamite out of the refrigerator and took the caps out of the dresser draw. I went all the way through that trailer and took the stuff out of it and they was not in there and Marie lived in the trailer after that and she also testified to the fact them shoes was not in there. In December, after I'm arrested, they go in there and Ray Shupe and it may have been, what's his name, McAllister or somebody but anyway Ray Shupe and somebody went in there and was supposed to got the shoes out the trailer at that time after I'm arrested. I know damn well them shoes had never been in that trailer up until the night that I went there and took the stuff out of it. From then on, I don't know what happened. But the night that I went down there, the policeman had brought Sandy down there that night checking on Kim and I got there. Howard Evans told me, he says, "you in a heap of trouble." I said why. He said well, they said that them cars was stole on you and they got a warrant or getting a warrant for you for Kim too, and from that night, I went in there and took everything out of my trailer but the tv and my brown suit and I hit the damn road and I went to Jacksonville then.

Summerford: For what?

Gaskins: I just went on down there took off. I was fixing to clear on out at that time but I came back. Came back right out of Florence here, spent the night here at my brother's trailer, hid the car out in the weeds. I took it to be the sheriff the next day or some of his men like to knocked the window out of my car with that plane. I took that same rifle that you got, went out there and said all right, son of a bitch, come back and I'm gonna put you on the ground.

Sheriff Barnes: Wait a minute Pee Wee, you were gonna shoot me?

Gaskins: I was going to shoot the plane. Now, whoever done it, I don't know who it was, the sheriff should know who done it. They made a dive in the back and they made a dive in the front of it so whoever it is can verify what I'm saying and they, when they made that second dive, it was coming back this way at the front of it and they went on back across the field. I come right in the trailer there and went back and got my 30.30 rifle and said all right son of a bitch, come back now. I sat there about five minutes, and he didn't come back. I got in the car and cranked it up and went to where they found the car at.

Sheriff: Now, you had already come back from Jacksonville at that time?

Gaskins: Right, right I had came back in.

Sheriff: Why did you have dynamite in that car at that time, what were you gonna use that for?

Gaskins: When I cleaned the trailer out, I cleaned everything out except the suit of clothes here.

Sheriff: Let me ask you one other question, nothing to do with this particular thing. Had you heard or were you running when they caught you going with the bus ticket to Tupelo? Or were you just going to see this girl?

Gaskins: I was running. I was running.

Sheriff: Who told you that you were being looked for?

Gaskins: Howard, now Howard done that.

Sheriff: Howard Evans?

Gaskins: Yeah, when I come down that night and cleaned the trailer and everything out, he says you in trouble. The law has been down here with Sandy. They got you for the hot cars and what not. Yes, he told me that and also now, when I got down here from Jacksonville, back down to my brother's down there, Marie and Sherry was there and they left. That was on, seemed to me like either Friday night, I believe it was on a Friday night I come in there and Saturday night they got arrested at Sam's Club I believe it was and they also told me.

Sheriff: You hadn't entered into a contract for a hit anywhere had you?

Gaskins: No sir, but I had the information then that the law was looking for me and I was already on Federal Probation and I knew that if I was arrested it was automatically two years for me. But when I was going to Mississippi—

Mr. Query: Do you know what kind of shoes Dennis had on?

Gaskins: Yes He had on a pair of black shoes with leather bottoms on them and the bottoms was just about wore slap out on em too.

Ted Owens: Pee Wee, some time yesterday in a conversation in here, I understand that you told some of the fellows that you had some type of acid or something buried in your yard in Sumter.

Gaskins: I believe they dug that up. I believe they've already dug that up, that sulphuric acid. I think they've got that already.

Owens: Well, which place was it in case they haven't?

Gaskins: In the front yard there where I used to live at in Sumter. I'm talking about out there in the block house.

Owens: In the cement block house?

Gaskins: Yeah, there was two people knew where it was at, me and the other man that worked there with Mr. Fort, Lloyd they called him. It's buried in double drums out there.

Owens: How big a drum?

Gaskins: I believe that's about a 40 or 50 gallon drum something like that.

Owens: How deep is it in the ground?

Gaskins: It should be under the ground about that deep. It was dug deep right down in that red clay out there you know. Me and Lloyd dug the hole and buried it out there in case they ever needed it again, it'd be out there. It's in plastic in that big cardboard stuff and that's the kind that burns you up.

All of the law enforcement officers in the room and Query knew that inmate informants had told of claims by Gaskins that a drum of sulphuric acid was the perfect way to get rid of a body. The innuendo may have been entirely braggadocios to enhance his status in the prison but he was said to have claimed that he always kept some close to him. There had also been an occasion when a man in the Moncks Corner area near Charleston had crossed Pee Wee in some manner and the two had talked publicly of their enmity. The man had been severely burned on his neck and arm with sulphuric acid. When hospital personnel asked how he had been injured he said that someone had intentionally thrown the acid on him but that he was unable to identify his assailant.

Summerford: Pee Wee, one last question, have you told us now about every killing---

Gaskins: That I'm connected with.

Summerford: And you've told us the truth about who was connected in every single, you're not hiding anything from us?

Gaskins: I'm not covering nobody up.

Summerford: You not hiding or you not keeping information from us as to who was involved, right?

Gaskins: Everybody that was involved, I've told you about.

Summerford: All right, now, every person that you said was involved was, in fact, involved and you're not trying to get revenge on anybody?

Gaskins: I'm not trying to get revenge on nobody and I'm also telling you that anybody you don't want to bring in it, that' your business. You're the solicitor. I have give you the truth. I believe when the facts come out, I don't even think you'll have any trouble or even have to go to trial because when its laid out like I told you here today and the people hears that involved, they will say yes and that'll be it.

(Walter Neeley brought back in and questioned again)

Summerford: One question we want to get out the way before we go down there and start trying to find those bodies, tell us about this Avery Howard and Diane situation. Now, it's my understanding that according to what Pee Wee told us, they were stabbed in Charleston.

Neeley: Yes.

Summerford: Now, who all was present?

Neeley: There was Wanda Snell, Charles Shealey and Ricky.

Summerford: And you?

Neeley: No.

Summerford: Just the three of them?

Neeley: Yes sir.

Summerford: Were both of them stabbed?

Neeley: Yeah.

Summerford: Now, where were they stabbed, do you know?

Neeley: No, I don't exactly know. I wasn't with Charlie and Ricky when the killing was done. They come by my house and asked me would I go up to Pee Wee's with em, and I went up there with em.

Summerford: Tell us everything that you can remember that occurred on that particular day.

Neeley: Well, let me start from the beginning. At the beginning of it, my wife's brother was messing around with Wanda Snell. That was before Charlie come to Charleston and when Charlie come to Charleston, he didn't like it so he made Roy Lee quit coming around. So my wife told Charlie if he didn't leave Wanda and Roy Lee alone she was going to the law on him. Well he left that weekend and come back the following week. Ricky and them was already in Charleston. So he asked me could he borrow my station wagon. Early that evening my wife asked Pee Wee could she borrow his Chevrolet and she went off, said she was going to her mother's. I don't know where she went. I was fixing the muffler on my station wagon, well Charlie and Ricky come down and asked could they borrow my wagon. I said sure, you can borrow it and later on that night, they come back. Diane and Avery was in the front seat of the car. Avery was laying over this way and I think Diane was laying over that way. And they asked me would I ride up to Pee Wee's with em and we went up there and Pee Wee went to the trailer and got a shovel and stuff and we carried em down there and buried em where they was found.

Summerford: All right, did Pee Wee shoot any of them while they were down there?

Neeley: I don't think so. Cause he just give us the shovel and stuff and he left. He was out at the dance out there.

Summerford: He didn't come down there?

Neeley: No, he didn't come down there.

Summerford: Are you sure?

Neeley: I don't think he did now.

Summerford: Well, I want it the way you remember it.

Neeley: Well, that's about the way I remember it.

Walter was universally considered by those involved in the case as being perhaps the least bright of all of the perpetrators and their associates, but when questioned he always managed to extricate himself from involvement in the actual murders while appearing to respond to questions. Any con having served as much time as Walter, regardless of how dull witted, knew the infamous death knell associated with being identified as a "trigger man".

As Walter recited the details with general consistency with those that had been recounted by Pee Wee, Query recalled the case that is discussed in the trial advocacy classes of every law school for the teaching of cross examination skills. In that case sweatshop seamstresses were crowded into a sewing room on the top floor of a factory building in New York. Because girls had been caught smoking on the fire escape landing, thereby depriving the owners of a precious minutes of sewing garments, the owners chained the door to the fire escape. When a fire erupted in the building they were trapped and many perished in the flames or jumped to their deaths from the high windows.

The case was of historic proportion in that it sought to hold the owners responsible for the manner in which they had controlled their own premises and for the endangerment of their employees. Both areas were considered outside the purview of the law at that time. The instructional utility however came from the skillful cross examination of a surviving seamstress. She testified that there were keys to chains on the doors and that they had panicked and forgotten about the keys. Although it appeared to those hearing her that she was somewhat limited in her mastery of English, when she told the story of the disastrous fire, she did so with precise phrasing and in great detail. The wily and experienced attorney who cross examined her picked up on the inconsistency of her stumbling responses to his early innocuous questions and then said simply, "Tell it again Sophie". When she had repeated her description of the events word for word he said simply, "Tell it again Sophie." And then he sat down while she again repeated her verbatim script with the precision of a professional actress. The jury immediately realized that she had been coached to memorize her testimony and was acting on behalf of or in fear of her employers. The employers were found to be responsible. Like Sophie, Walter had been well schooled by Pee Wee and varied his rendition only to minimize his culpability and that of his mentor. Query could not help but think that was why Walter wanted to "start at the beginning".

Later when Walter and Pee Wee were taken to Isle of Palms just outside Charleston to search for the bodies of the two young girls, Walter would ask to speak to Query and would relate his concern that finding the bodies would be a mistake and that if Pee Wee continued to give information to law enforcement, the graves in Francis Marion would eventually be discovered. Walter described the basis of his fear saying:

"If they find that place up thur' in the Francis Marion, Mr. Grady, it looks like Korea up there. They'll give us the chair for sure over what's up there, if they can find enough to see what went on up there. Why is he doin' this? Why's he keep showin' them where there is bodies?"

"Don't know, Walter, I've told him to stop talking to them. That goes for you too. I'm sure that's what Mr. Cantrell would tell you. You call him and ask him."

"I don't need to call. I trust what you tell me, Mr. Grady but if Pee Wee wants me to tell 'em somethin', I guess I'll tell 'em. It's just that they's a lot of bodies up there. A lot more than anybody has any idea about."

In the conference room in Florence the questioning had continued:

Summerford: But you do remember that Pee Wee was at Sam's when y'all got down there?

Neeley: He was at the club cause Wanda had to go in there and get him and bring him out there.

Summerford: Who drove the car down there?

Neeley: Ricky drove the car cause he had driving license.

Summerford: And where were you seated?

Neeley: I was sitting in the back seat with Wanda and Charlie. Me, Charlie and Wanda was in the back seat. Diane and Avery was dead in the front seat.

Summerford: You sure they were dead, you didn't hear them moaning or anything?

Neeley: I guess they was dead. They looked dead to me.

Summerford: Did you help get them out of the car?

Neeley: Ricky and Charlie toted them out. I think Ricky toted Diane and Charlie toted Avery, I think.

Summerford: Did you touch any of them, Walter?

Neeley: No.

Summerford: What I'm trying to find out is whether or not they were limp. Do you remember whether they were limp?

Neeley: I imagine they would be a little bit limp cause they ain't been dead that long.

Summerford: Well, you didn't know how long they'd been dead when they picked you up, though?

Neeley: No, I don't.

Summerford: Did they say how long it't been before they'd killed em when they picked you up?

Neeley: Well, it must have been not too long after cause they said they come right straight to the house. It must not have been very long.

Summerford: Did they say where they killed em?

Neeley: It's on East Bay Street down there by the roofing place. Down there where Pee Wee worked at.

Summerford: I see, were they supposed to be in a building committing sex, having sex?

Neeley: I knew my old lady was messing around, you know, running around with different people and she could have had a man down there cause she had the keys to his place. Pee Wee gave her a key to his place and she could have been down there having sex with somebody.

Summerford: But you didn't know that they were gonna do that though, Walter?

Neeley: No sir, I didn't.

Summerford: But it had been discussed though had it not?

Neeley: Well, Charlie threatened to kill her, yes.

Summerford: Now, that was your wife---

Neeley: That was my common law wife. I wasn't actually married to her.

Summerford: But didn't it upset you to know that your wife was gonna get killed.

Neeley: It didn't bother me.

Query, Cantrell and Staubes had often discussed Walter's seeming ambivalence to the most horrendous occurrences in his life. It was difficult to assess whether his time spent at CCI and other institutions had simply desensitized him, especially considering that a considerable time was as Pee Wee's sidekick and homosexual prostitute where he would have been exposed to Pee Wee's unconscionable violence. Pee Wee always dismissed the use of extreme violence as an orchestrated means to achieve his unquestioned authority within the prisons. It was both intentional and purposeful. Walter apparently observed the violence or participated dispassionately and without plan or purpose.

In another vein Walter would go to great lengths to please the women who paid attention to him, but he nevertheless appeared to have utter disdain for them. He valued Sandy as exceptional because she had belonged to Pee Wee before she was given to Walter. But it was as a possession and he loved to emphasize the fact that she had been given to him. Diane probably had his heart but her dalliances, which were flaunted before him, had hardened him toward her and probably turned to hatred or at least severe resentment after the severe scalding of their only child. At first Walter tried to defend Diane for those injuries and for her infidelity, but he ultimately came to blame Diane entirely for his child's death and to hate her for his cuckolding. Cantrell believed that abuse by his father had supplanted any feelings of kindness Walter might have felt toward those around him. This with the exception of his mother who continued to dote on Walter as though he were a child when she was with him and to ignore him otherwise.

Both Cantrell and Staubes were convinced that despite his near moronic manifestation in public moments, Walter was much more a consort of Gaskins than a mere lackey. His performance under this questioning seemed to bear out their conclusions.

Summerford: Well when you saw her and knew that she was dead, that didn't bother you either?

Neeley: No, I just felt sorry for her, but it didn't bother me.

Summerford: It didn't bother you, but you did feel sorry for her?

Neeley: Yes.

Summerford: Well, now, Pee Wee told us, think about it a little bit. told us that when y'all came down to Sam's to get him, he left long enough to go get the shovel and I think an ax or pick or something, I forgot, and went down to the gravesite and he got in the car with his gun and he shot both of them in the head. Do you remember that?

Neeley: I don't remember exactly. I don't want to tell you something not true.

Summerford: Just tell us the truth, Walter, the way you remember it. You don't remember him opening the door of the car and leaning in there and shooting twice. He shot each one of them in the head. You don't remember that?

Neeley: I don't remember. See I got out the car and I went on down there a little ways. I don't know what he done.

Summerford: Did you ever look at the bodies to see where they were stabbed, Walter?

Neeley: Well, it looked like they were stabbed right through here, to me now.

Summerford: Did you look at them?

Neeley: No sir.

Summerford: Well, how did you, if they were leaning over, when you got in the car, how did you see that?

Neeley: Well, I just seen the blood, looked like where the blood was coming out there.

Once again Walter had managed to avoid contradicting Pee Wee, tried to remain faithful to his recitation and yet sidestepped questions that might force him to commit to some fact that had to be one way or the other. And he had again managed to recite the events so that he was not present at the murder and walked away from the car at the critical moment when the bodies were removed from the car and when Pee Wee might have shot them.

It was unconceivable to Query that a man who had been exposed to the level of violence that Walter had seen and who had been present with the bodies of at least six murder victims according to his own accounts would not have been at least curious enough about the bodies of the woman with whom he had lived as man and wife and that of her paramour to have at least viewed them when they were taken from the car.

Some discussion continued between the solicitor and Walter about the cars and the trip from Charleston and then the solicitor went on to pursue further explanations of the roles of the various players.

Summerford: Well, what I'm trying to find out is, did Pee Wee tell them to kill them and bring em down there to bury them? How did y'all know? Do you remember that Walter?

Neeley: After they was killed, Charlie said he knew where Pee Wee would be at. He said Pee Wee would be at the dance.

Summerford: Did he say that Pee Wee knew that he was gonna have them killed?

Neeley: No, he didn't say Pee Wee knew anything about it.

Sheriff Barnes: Walter, when y'all got to the gravesite, you say you walked off in the woods a little bit. You didn't stay around the car.

Neeley: That's right.

Sheriff: It was right quiet down there, wasn't it?

Neeley: Yeah, it was. It was after twelve.

Sheriff: You didn't hear a gun shoot?

Neeley: No, I was drinking. I didn't hear it, if he did shoot, I didn't hear it.

Sheriff: Who dug the hole?

Neeley: Ricky and Charlie.

Sheriff: Where were you while they was digging the hole?

Neeley: Me and Wanda was out there walking around, messing around.

Sheriff: Did you help them put them in the hole?

Neeley: No.

Sheriff: What was talked about on the trip to Lake City. That's right at two hours you were riding in the car with two dead people, supposedly, what'd y'all talk about?

Neeley: We didn't talk about nothing, just mostly small talk. That's all.

Sheriff: With two dead people sitting in the front seat, just small talk?

Neeley: No, we just tried to get up there as quick as we could.

Sheriff: Somebody have to hold them up in the seat?

Neeley: No, one was laying cross this way and the other one was laying cross that way.

Sheriff: Were they laying down flat or were they sitting?

Neeley: Sort of sideways.

Sheriff: Was there a lot of blood?

Neeley: Well, Pee Wee had to take the front seat out of the Chevrolet. We put another seat in it. A blue seat come out of the junk yard. It come out of a Chevy II. It wasn't the right seat for that car.

Sheriff: Did you see the seat that came out of the car?

Neeley: Yes. It had a lot of blood on it.

Sheriff: Were you there when Pee Wee took it out the car?

Neeley: No, I took the seat out. He was working that day and asked me, if I could, would I pull the seat out.

Sheriff: You ever discuss this thing with Pee Wee before?

Neeley: No.

Sheriff: You sure now, Walter?

Neeley: I'm positive.

Sheriff: Y'all ain't never talked about it in all that time you were side by side up there?

Neeley: No, we didn't talk about things like that.

Sheriff: Did Ricky and them tell you anything at all about the way they buried them?

Neeley: No, they just said they buried em back there is all he said.

Sheriff: What'd you talk about on the way home?

Neeley: Went over to the place there and got us a bunch of beers and started back home.

Sheriff: Where'd you buy the beer?

Neeley: Over at Sam's place.

Sheriff: You went back to Sam's place. Did you see Pee Wee again?

Neeley: Yeah, he was out there.

Sheriff: What'd you tell Pee Wee?

Neeley: We just told Pee Wee we put his shovel and all back by the barn and we was going back to Charleston.

Walter might not have been the best communicator, but it was obvious to Query that this was not the cause for the lack of accurate detail in his story. It was preposterous to think that these three rowdy criminals who had been involved in burglaries, robberies and other crimes, who were now well lubricated with a "bunch of beer" would not have gone on about the murders and the burials. Certainly the shots delivered to the heads of the two victims by Pee Wee after they had lain dead or apparently dead in the car seat for over two hours would have led to some discussion. Similarly, the idea that the only information shared with Pee Wee after a double homicide was the whereabouts of his shovel was implausible at best.

Tom Henderson: Walter, they came by and picked you up down there and you said you were at the house?

Neeley: I was at my trailer, yes.

Henderson: When they came and picked you up now, who was in the car?

Neeley: Wanda, Ricky and Charlie and Diane and Avery.

Henderson: And at that time, they were dead right?

Neeley: I imagine they were.

Henderson: Okay, when they drove up, who came in the trailer and got you, or what happened?

Neeley: Wanda come up there and got me.

Henderson: So you went out to the car?

Neeley: Yeah.

Henderson: Okay, now, what was said?

Neeley: He asked me what was we going to do with them. I told him I didn't know.

Henderson: You walked up and you saw your dead wife and Avery Howard in there uh---

Neeley: I asked them what in the hell happened.

Henderson: What'd they tell you?

Neeley: He said they killed em.

Henderson: Why?

Neeley: Cause Diane was threatening to call the law on him, I guess, I don't know.

Henderson: Okay, so you got in the car with em and y'all come on up to Lake City. You say it took, way about two hours to get up here?

Neeley: I imagine so.

Henderson: Where'd you go when you got out here?

Neeley: We went out to Sam's place and saw Pee Wee.

Henderson: Okay, did Pee Wee know about this.

Neeley: Not as I know of, he didn't.

Henderson: Okay, and y'all left Sam's Club. Did Pee Wee go with you?

Neeley: Pee Wee went to his house and got the shovel and stuff and told Charlie where to meet him at.

Henderson: Okay, now, did Pee Wee lead y'all somewhere then or something?

Neeley: He carried us down to where they was buried at.

Henderson: Had you ever been there before?

Neeley: That time and with Johnny and them.

Henderson: Okay, did you look at Diane and Avery real good?

Neeley: No, I didn't.

Henderson: Okay, you could see -you said you could see they'd been stabbed or what?

Neeley: Well, it looked like they were stabbed. They could have been shot. I don't know.

Henderson: Okay, could you see Diane and Avery's face?

Neeley: No.

Henderson: You never did see their face?

Neeley: I didn't look at em that close.

Henderson: Okay, could you tell Diane and Avery had been shot in the head or anything like that?

Neeley: I didn't see none.

Henderson: If they'd been shot in the head, either one of them or both of them, you could have told that, couldn't you?

Neeley: Yeah, if I'd seen it.

Henderson: You'd have seen the blood and stuff?

Neeley: Yeah.

Henderson: But you didn't see no blood on the face or the head or anywhere?

Neeley: No.

Henderson: So y'all went on down there to the grave site and Ricky and Charles dug the grave, right?

Neeley: Yeah.

Henderson: Okay, You didn't hear no gun shoot?

Neeley: I didn't hear none shoot. I was drinking pretty heavy that night.

Again Walter had kept himself as far removed as possible from actual contact with the bodies, but he had forgotten the critical part of the story that involved Pee Wee shooting the victims. Unlike Pee Wee, Walter had no idea that his version of the story brought jurisdiction of the murder under the authority of Charleston County. Although attorneys for Gaskins had insisted that Charleston also agree to no further exposure to the death penalty, Walter had not received the same agreement. Since his attorneys were not present, they had no idea that Walter would vary from the story that had been told time and again in which the actual deaths occurred by gunshot in Florence County. While it served to keep jurisdiction in Florence at that juncture, the reasons for Gaskins insisting on the killing shots having occurred in Florence were otherwise incomprehensible. To increase the confusion both versions were both consistent and inconsistent with various aspects of the physical evidence.

Henderson: Walter, did you know that Diane had been shot?

Neeley: No, I didn't. Not till they said it up there in the courtroom.

Henderson: Okay, well, Diane was shot and she was shot in the head. Now, how did that happen?

Neeley: Well, I couldn't tell you, I don't know.

Henderson: If she had been shot in the head down there in Charleston before you ever got in the car, you would have seen that?

Neeley: Yeah.

Henderson: And you said you didn't hear no shot up there at the gravesite?

Neeley: No, I didn't hear none.

Grady Query

Henderson: Okay, did you know that in the past, oh, it's been a year or so ago, that Wanda Snell told me and several other police officers about this thing?

Neeley: I heard something about it.

Henderson: Did you know that Wanda Snell went up to SLED headquarters in Columbia and took a lie detector test on that?

Neeley: I don't know. I couldn't tell you.

Henderson: Well, she did and the lie detector showed that she was lying, that she wasn't there and after she took that test, she confessed that that whole story was a lie, that she wasn't with nobody when Diane and Avery were killed and she ain't seen em killed. She ain't been with them after they were dead. She finally confessed that whole story was made up. She said sure, Diane and Avery were killed. She said they wasn't killed down in Charleston the way you say they were.

Neeley: Well, if you don't believe me, I can't help you.

Henderson: Walter, how long you been up there in that---you been in that penitentiary with Pee Wee for about two years now isn't it?

Neeley: Yeah.

Henderson: Y'all been on death row together.

Neeley: Yeah.

Henderson: At one time y'alls cells were right beside each other weren't they?

Neeley: Yeah.

Henderson: And you and Pee Wee talked a lot about this thing, Walter.

Neeley: No.

320

Henderson: I want you to understand something now, Walter. You remember what the solicitor told you this morning when you first came in here. He was giving you your opportunity right now and of course, Pee Wee wanted you to tell it too, but the solicitor told you that he wasn't gonna seek any death penalty on you on anything that you told us about as long as you told the truth, the whole truth. Now I know that Diane and Avery are dead. There ain't no doubt about that Walter, cause I've seen their bodies with my own two eyes.

Neeley: Well if you don't believe me, I can't help it.

Henderson: But I don't want to see you put yourself in a position now, Walter, to where Pee Wee or somebody else has told you to tell it one way and its really another way and then you lose your agreement you've got with the solicitor.

Neeley: Well, I done said all I'm gonna say about it.

Neely's demeanor showed obvious signs of frustration and anger as a result of the confrontation by Agent Henderson. Walter's face reddened drastically, his eyes widened and he took audible breaths in gasps through his mouth.

Henderson: I'm not trying to get you upset, Walter. I can see you're upset.

Neeley: That's all I'm gonna say about it.

Ted Owens: Walter, let me ask you a question. What kind of car did Avery have?

Neeley: I believe it was a black T-Bird.

Owens: Do you know what happened to that car?

Neeley: I believe Pee Wee had it, and I believe Pee Wee sold it or Charlie had it or somebody had it. I think Charlie stole it for him and sold it to him, I think. I don't know exactly how he come about that car.

Owens: Do you know who Pee Wee sold the car to?

Neeley: No, I don't.

Owens: Do you know Belton Eaddy?

Neeley: No, I don't know him.

Owens: Was there any damage done to Avery's car?

Neeley: Now, he come by there driving a Malibu one time with the windshield cracked and said he hit a child or something with it. He come by Pee Wee's one afternoon. I think the car belonged to the car lot or something. He said he hit a child or something on a bicycle. The windshield was busted on one side of it but that wasn't the T-Bird.

(Walter taken back out, Pee Wee shown a picture of a black girl.)

Mr. Summerford: Is this the person that you call Clyde or Martha Ann?

Gaskins: That's her.

(Showing another picture)

Summerford: Are you familiar with this girl here, have you ever seen her before?

Gaskins: I don't know her.

(Showing another picture of body in a suitcase)

Summerford: You don't know anything about this do you?

Gaskins: My God, no. No.

Sheriff: You never put nobody in a suitcase?

Gaskins: No, all my bodies that you've found ain't been in no suitcase or nothing like that now.

Sheriff: Now that gal used to be with the Amusements of America, Pee Wee.

Gaskins: There's a possibility that I could have seen her but I don't think so.

Mr. Summerford: Let me ask you in regards to that. You said that you knew you hadn't seen her. Now, your second thought you said you could have seen her.

Gaskins: Well, I could have seen her because you know there's so many women that works with the Amusements of America.

Summerford: You never heard it from anybody other than law enforcement?

Gaskins: No, nobody.

Summerford: Now, let me ask you this. There was a considerable period of time that you and Walter Neeley were side by side up there on death row. Did you and Walter ever talk about this situation?

Gaskins: There's very little you can talk about up there. Mr. Grisso and Mr. Query has been up there at our cells and the only way you and you can't discuss such as that unless everybody in the building hears it Mr. Summerford. They understand the situation up there and there's always so much and everything going on up there.

Summerford: Now, let me go back and ask you a couple more questions. I think we're about to wrap this thing up. Getting back to Avery and Diane, when you went to the gravesite, did you see Walter Neeley and Wanda at that time?

Gaskins: They was down there.

Summerford: Where were they?

Gaskins: At the car. They was at the car because when I done the shooting there was nobody in the car but the two people in there.

Summerford: They weren't walking down in the woods?

Gaskins: I wasn't paying that close attention Mr. Summerford. I was there, like I say, right there and when I got in the car and I made the two shots, I left and went and got back in the Duster and went back to Sam's club. Whatever happened after that, I don't know.

Early on the morning of September 15, 1979 Gaskins had traveled with a caravan of SLED agents, Florence and Williamsburg County deputies, Sheriff Barnes, the Chief Deputy from Sumter County and his attorneys, Query and Grisso to the Prospect community. Gaskins rode in a SLED car with four agents. He was shackled hand and foot and wore a belly chain that was fastened to both the chain between his wrists and the chain between his ankles by a separate length of chain that ran through a ring in the front of the belly chain. Yet another chain led from the chain fastening wrists to ankles to a u-bolt in the floor of the vehicle. A SLED car with two agents drove immediately ahead of the car in which he was riding and another followed close behind.

Gaskins led agents down a dirt road into the woods and then walked with them to a heavily forested area near a small cemetery that Gaskins said was a family cemetery.

"This'll be my niece, Janice Kirby. I wanted to put her right over there in that little cemetery because she was family. So I just got as close as I could."

For more than an hour the search party wandered tortuously in a small area. Agents and deputies probed the ground with long metal rods. Another deputy swept the ground with a metal detector while yet another used a special sensing device that had been developed to locate bodies in Viet Nam. Gaskins meandered for a short while in a concise circle looking at the ground and then to distant landmarks known only to him. Finally he indicated a spot near a peculiarly twisted tree. One of the major low branches had been removed long enough in the past for the cut to have completely covered over leaving a circular scar. Probing with the slender metal rod a deputy located something solid buried three feet or so under the soft woodsy soil.

Moments later working carefully with a small shovel, deputies uncovered the skeletal remains of Janice Kirby. Gaskins said that because she was family he had placed her as near to the small family cemetery as he thought he could and still avoid discovery. The area was then cordoned off and secured. After the medical examiner notified Gaskins, his attorneys and his interrogators returned to the Florence law enforcement complex leaving behind a cadre of deputies and agents to assist the medical examiner with the exhumation.

(Saturday, April 15, 1978)

Mr. Query: I have told him that you have told me that some fellow named Jack, who is associated with Kentucky, who was in prison for safecracking was gonna escape and that Avery Howard squealed on him and that you have information that he killed Avery Howard for this guy Jack, or as revenge for this guy Jack. And I told him that y'all had information that Walter Neeley could not have been there the night that Avery was killed. He said, bullshit.

Mr. Summerford: Now, Pee Wee, I want to tell you something you're so close, we are so close, to getting this thing squared away and getting you a life sentence and getting it behind you. Now, damn it, I've told your attorneys and I'm gonna tell you and I can't tell you any harder and straighter than this. If you don't come forward with the truth now, come Monday morning, I want the truth. I want the whole truth and nothing but the truth, so help me God, or I'll try you Monday morning. I'll try you for death. Now, it's just as plain as that now. Don't mess up. I'm trying to help you. I'm trying to help you every way I know how but you're going to have to tell us the truth. Now you sat there and told us that Walter Neeley was with you or was down there, came down to uh---

Gaskins: Came down to Sam's Club that night with Wanda, and Ricky and Charlie.

Summerford: Now, you want to look Walter Neeley straight in the eye and let him call you a liar.

Gaskins: I sure do.

Summerford: Well, he'll tell you, in no uncertain terms, after we pressured him, that he wasn't there. We know where he was.

Grady Query

Gaskins: He was right there with em now, Mr. Summerford. I know and also Chief Simmons has got the word from other people too.

Summerford: Pee Wee, don't give me that crap. I'm not gonna take any more of it now.

Gaskins: Let's go. I've got enough. My nerves is shot as it is. Y'all are wrong, you've done me wrong now. I have to the best of my knowledge, told you what it is now.

Summerford: Walter Neeley wasn't there that night. He was at the Port Drive-In.

Gaskins: Walter Neeley was there now. Walter Neeley don't even go to movies. I know what I'm talking about now.

Ted Owens: Pee Wee, let me ask you this then. Didn't you tell us the other day that you shot both of these people at the gravesite?

Gaskins: Yes, yes.

Owens: Well I wonder why Walter didn't hear the shots?

Gaskins: If he didn't hear em, he was stone deaf now. Y'all messing with a man that ain't got the mind of a nine year old kid. They're a lot of things, I've told you everything and now you want to lay me around and screw me on it. I know what you're trying to do now. Why, if I wasn't telling the truth, why did I take you down there this morning and give you another body. I've told you I killed people all the way through that I didn't have to tell you I killed the first one if I didn't want to. I could have still been hollering I ain't killed the first one. No, I've laid it out. There's fifteen people that I've come right out and said that I've either stabbed or shot.

Summerford: Well, do you want to listen to me a minute then?

Gaskins: Yes sir.

Summerford: All right, number one you've got Dr. Joel Sexton who says there ain't no way. You've got uh, Walter Neeley saying I wasn't there. He told me to say this. Every time we went out in the yard, he told me how it was; he preached it to me. He said, I'll admit to what I did and he has admitted it.

Summerford: Well, if we just had that one, then I would go along with you but we got four different reasons to know that you are lying to us.

Gaskins: No, I am not lying. I wouldn't lie and me going all the way like I'm going with you, I wouldn't lie and give you the bodies.

Summerford: It doesn't make that much difference is what I'm trying to tell you. The thing that concerns me is, you've admitted these killings. Why would you come up here now and tell us a different reason for doing it?

Gaskins: I've told you the reason why I've done em and I've told you, and you can check it out and come with me and let me show you.

Summerford: You're so close to getting this thing closed once and for all, and yet you sit right there, knowing that you're lying to us.

Gaskins: Mr. Summerford, I am not lying to you and I've told you to let's go and check it out point by point. Let's check Avery Howard and see ain't he got the bullet through his head.

Summerford: He's double checked it. He's double checked it again. We've been back to him and talked to him.

Tom Henderson: I called the doctor myself.

Gaskins: Yeah, but you ain't looked at the head.

Mr. Summerford: He's got pictures of the head.

Gaskins: Pictures don't always tell the same thing.

Henderson: Pee Wee, calm down a minute. When Dr. Sexton does an autopsy, he doesn't just look at the outside. He cuts the head open and looks in it from the inside.

Gaskins: Then take the photographs of it and see if they can see anything. I'm telling you, the bullet come through and through the head now, I know.

Sheriff Barnes: He takes his hands and he does this all over. There's no hole there.

Tom Henderson: And then he takes a saw and cuts his whole head in half and takes it apart.

Gaskins: Somewhere they missed it. Well, the same way in the Kim Gelkin deal. He missed it in that too.

Mr. Summerford: What are you covering up Pee Wee? What is it you don't want us to know?

Gaskins: What is there to cover up? I told you I shot both of em.

Summerford: All right, but why?

Gaskins: Why did I kill em, or why did I shoot em? I told you, Diane, the whole time, that I wanted to get rid of her, the whole time out of the way. She was going with Avery Howard at the time.

Summerford: That wasn't the reason Pee Wee.

Gaskins: Wait a minute, let me go ahead. Avery Howard, up in the penitentiary, used to be a lieutenant's runner up there.

Summerford: And he squealed on your friend?

Gaskins: He squealed on a lot of people up there, yes.

Summerford: What's Jack's last name?

Gaskins: Hillman.

Summerford: Pee Wee, come on, let's don't, don't fool around with us now. I told you from the beginning that you weren't dealing with---

Gaskins: I told you that I shot those people.

Summerford: I know you did. I want to know why and I want to know why you said that you did it in Charleston, when you did it in Florence County.

Gaskins: You want me to tell you I did it in Florence County?

Summerford: I want the truth.

Gaskins: I tell you what. Why don't you give me a lie detector test and find out whether I shot em right down there in Florence County, right there by the gravesite.

Summerford: You know you beat it one time. Come on Pee Wee. You swore to this Jack Hillman that you'd kill Avery Howard for squealing on him.

(After a short break)

Mr. Summerford: We've shown you the report of the officer, Mr. Lewis White, what he said, he was the car dealer. Your lawyers have gone down to the detention center and talked with Mr. Walter Neeley. He told them exactly what we told you he would say. He denied having been there. Now, you told me a moment ago while we were waiting that you were gonna tell the truth. Now, Pee Wee, come forth with the truth now. Don't give us any cock and bull story, for God's sake. We have made an agreement. I want to live up to this agreement. I told you if I caught you in one lie that I was gonna try to put you in the chair. Now, I told you that. Now I've caught you in the lie but I'm backing down on what I told you.

Gaskins: Walter and Diane was living down there in Charleston, pretty close to me. I been going with Diane a long time myself and Diane was also driving some cars for me and what not around there too. I bought a 1975 Duster that was stole. I got Diane to drive it down along with my wife Sandy, at that time to my daughter's trailer down there and at that time, I didn't have my trailer moved up there. So I promised Diane that I'd get her a good car. She knew the car was hot and everything and uh, so Avery was going with Diane too. I didn't like Avery. I didn't like him when he was in the prison and never would have nothing to do with him. There was a lot convicts in there didn't like Avery and I told a lot of them in there that someday, that if I got a chance, I'd get rid of Avery. And uh, it came up to that night, I had filled up the car with gas and everything and I let Diane have it and told her that if her and Avery would come down there that I'd let them have a nice car, that I had em down there at my daughter's trailer. And they got down there, I told em I had a better one at another place. We got together. I had my gun in my pocket and I got the knife and had it stuck in my belt I got Diane to do the driving. Avery was sittin side of her and I was sitting on the outside. We drove back in there to where at the gravesite. But we didn't drive all the way in back there. Before we got back there, we stopped there as you run into where the woods starts to go around and got out, was gonna walk back there. I told em I had the cars sitting back there in the woods. I was keeping em back there to where nobody would bother them. And before we got to the gravesite, I got Avery just where I wanted him at and I eased the knife out and before he knew what happened, I stabbed him and before I could get my hands on Diane, she started running. I pulled my gun out and shot at her. I thought I hit her in the back of the head and she fell and I run up there and took the knife and stuck it in her breast too. Then I came back there and shot at Avery but I undoubtedly did not hit him because he didn't have no bullet in him nowhere in the world. Then I went back to the blue Chevrolet. I had a shovel in the back of it and took it out and went on down there and dug the hole and toted them on down there and buried them, where they was buried at. Avery was on bottom and I put Diane on top, shut it up.

Summerford: Why did you tell us then that Charles Shealey and Ricky Snell was involved? You got something against them?

Summerford and Gaskins then went through an extended colloquy about the statement Wanda Snell had given and her subsequent failure on the polygraph followed by the recanting of her statement. Gaskins professed to have no knowledge of her reason for giving the statement in which she incriminated not only herself but also Charlie Shealy, and her brother Ricky Snell. Gaskins denied having talked to Wanda after his arrest but Summerford confronted him with a statement by her mother regarding at least one collect call from the penitentiary to her home in Pennsylvania.

Gaskins: I sat down there and Wanda told word for word, that she sat in the parking lot and saw the stabbing and the killing and that later on I got up with them and that we brought em on to the grave and, uh, I believe she said Charlie or either Walter one made her look in the grave and everything. But anyway after hearing her testimony that she give Chief Simmons down there, I went along with what she said because a long time ago, I had a girl get up right up in Florence County courthouse and say that I had got in the bed with her, when it was my first cousin got in bed with her and I done six years for him and from then on, whatever the girl said, I went along with em. And I still do that just about.

Summerford: Why did you take Walter out in the yard and try to get him---

Gaskins: Now, wait a minute. We'd go out in the yard, a regular walk and all, and Walter would talk and discuss the thing over with me. I told him what Wanda had told me and told him that I felt it was best to go along with what Wanda had said.

Summerford: You told him it was best to go along with this and you told him what to say, didn't you?

Gaskins: I told him what Wanda had told me.

Summerford: Brainwashed him, time after time every time you went in the yard.

Tom Henderson: Pee Wee, if the whole thing was a lie and the only reason you went with it was a girl did that to you once before and you figured you got caught once before, then why, the other day when the solicitor sat you down and told you, Pee Wee, the only thing gonna keep you from being tried for the death penalty is the fact that you've got to tell the truth. Walter Neeley was down here and you knew that Walter Neeley would tell whatever the truth was that you told him to do. So why didn't you just sit down the other day and say, right then, that the whole thing was a lie. Wanda Snell wasn't there, Charles Shealey was not there, Walter Neeley knows the true story. He can tell you why and this is the true story. Why didn't you tell it then?

Gaskins: If I had a told it then---

Henderson: Wait a minute. I sat there yesterday and told you, pointed out to you where you were lying, we knew you were lying, told you it was impractical for them to be killed down there in Charleston and be brought up here and put in a grave like that. Why didn't you just tell it then? Your agreement was that you wasn't gonna lie.

Gaskins: If I'd told you that and you'd pulled Wanda Snell's statement out and says here's where Wanda said so and so, I was right back in it.

Henderson: I told you yesterday that Wanda Snell admitted the whole thing was a lie and she admitted she wasn't there.

Mr. Summerford: Pee Wee, forget about everything else. Forget about what Wanda said, what Walter said, what I said, what anybody---only you know the truth. Now, tell us.

Gaskins: I killed them, I killed them.

Summerford: We know that. We want to know why and how.

Gaskins: I don't see where you can say I'm lying. I killed the two people and I buried the two people there.

Summerford: You're telling me that Diane ran and you shot and the bullet just happened to go in here and come out here.

Tom Henderson: She was hit right up under here and the bullet come right on out. Dr. Sexton said that gun had to be, that gun barrel had to be laid right up against her throat and pointed up and out.

Gaskins: I don't know how it could have done it because I thought I hit her in the back of the head.

Tom Henderson: Pee Wee, the bullet came out of Diane at the right side of the midline at the upper part of the teeth, which would be right in there. The bullet goes in right there, comes out right here. Now, how you gonna shoot somebody---Dr. Sexton says, and Dr. Sexton has examined thousands of killings. He's had a lot more experience with killing than you have, Pee Wee, and uh, he says the only way he knows of that bullet wound could have got there is somebody stuck a gun, she had a halter top thing on, and said somebody had to stick that gun right up between her breasts or under that halter or something like that and right up under there and pull the trigger and the bullet come out right there.

Ben Thomas: Pee Wee, Isn't it true that you are mad with Charlie Shealey cause he has testified against you before? Wanda Snell has gotten on the stand against you before and Walter Neeley has given statements against you? Aren't you mad with those three people? Wanda got on the stand against you in your very first trial.

Gaskins: No, she did not. No she did not, Ben.

Ted Owens: Who did she testify against then?

Gaskins: Walter Neeley, not me.

Ted Owens: But you were implicated then, Pee Wee.

Gaskins: Wanda did not come up in court against me, no way in the world in my trial, no.

Ben Thomas: You're not mad with them at all. You're not trying to put them in this thing just to get even?

Gaskins: If I was mad with Walter Neeley I could kill him any day I wanted to at the penitentiary.

Thomas: All right, let me ask you one more question. Maybe I ought not ask this, but I'm gonna ask it anyway cause I won't know the answer till I ask. Did Linwood Simmons or any police officer in the county or city of Charleston or City of North Charleston try to make any deal with you to put a killing in their jurisdiction, tell us that there were some killings down there, even if there weren't?"

Gaskins: They was wanting some bodies down there in their district.

A long discussion ensued involving Gaskins, Ben Thomas and Tom Henderson in which Gaskins was asked over and over whether law enforcement officers from the Charleston area had asked him directly or by suggestion or insinuation to involve Charleston in the murders. The questioning seemed to ignore the fact that North Charleston already had jurisdiction over the abduction of Kim Gelkins, the case that had started the whole investigation, and that the work of Detectives Stoney and Green had resulted in Walter revealing the whereabouts of the bodies. All of this in addition to the two girls Gaskins claimed to have murdered on the Isle of Palms in Charleston County provided jurisdiction for Charleston over those cases, but apparently the Charleston Solicitor had no desire to join the spectacle when Gaskins was already convicted and serving consecutive life sentences.

Gaskins ultimately said that he had become convinced on his own that Charleston law enforcement wanted to be involved in the continuing investigations. He said he was glad to try to provide information that would keep them involved so that they would continue to allow him to have conjugal visits with his wife when they brought him to Charleston.

Gaskins further surmised that if he were able to continue to involve North Charleston and received the large sum of money he had imagined he would receive from book and movie rights that he would be able to go there frequently for visits with his wife. He also thought that was where there might be an opportunity for escape. He stated that it was well known that "people in North Charleston were on the take". However, when he was questioned specifically about any mention of money by anyone in law enforcement he denied that such conversations had ever occurred.

Finally the agents seemed to exhaust to their satisfaction questions about any actual impropriety or suggestion of impropriety on the part of Charleston area law enforcement and the questioning returned to the details of the murders.

Further attempts were made to discover how Gaskins had communicated with Wanda Snell regarding the elaborate ruse of the stabbing murder of Diane and Avery on East Bay Street near downtown Charleston with her as a witness, but these efforts were to no avail.

The frustration at Gaskins' avoidance of certain aspects of his crimes was exacerbated by the feeling of the law enforcement personnel that Gaskins had nothing to lose by being completely candid. Gaskins, on the other hand, was looking toward spending the rest of his life at CCI where his reputation provided him with privileges among the inmates that few there could ever hope to enjoy. His continued persona as the consummate criminal was essential to the status that he intended to resume as soon as he was released into the general population, and he did not intend to jeopardize it. That was the seemingly inexplicable reason for his wending his way carefully through the crime details without crossing some illusory boundary of hard time criminal etiquette. This most assuredly included not incriminating his former prison mate, Jack Hillman, as tempting as it must have been to allege that the murder of Avery Howard was a paid hit paid. Hillman, wherever he was serving his time, would still pay dearly for his statement given against Gaskins, if the opportunity ever arose.

Query ruminated that the search for what motivated Gaskins evasiveness was an effort in futility. He recalled the many occasions when Gaskins had talked about a conflict with one or another of the victims and then made a concerted effort to avoid the details. Gaskins would conclude a story about a victim with a declaration as vague as "and they was never heard from after that" or "and I never seen them again after that". In the years that passed after his exposure to the death penalty had been ended by the Florence agreement Pee Wee became more candid in his conversations with the lawyer. For no apparent reason he would tell in detail the story of his relationship with a victim from beginning to end. He would report on the friction that developed at some point and describe the point at which the person so offended or betrayed him that their life became forfeit. After that point was reached it was a matter of opportunity or necessity that would lead to their ultimate demise. Pee Wee would then divulge in lurid detail the manner of their deaths and the exact nature of their final moments. It was only during those visits that Query believed Gaskins finally abandoned every manner of subterfuge.

That day in Florence it seemed to Query that the verbal fencing with the police might in and of itself be the motivation. The temptation to mislead and deceive those who had hunted him and captured him was simply too much for Pee Wee to resist. Pee Wee's intentional machinations in combination with his abhorrence for any simple statement of the truth, made the quandary of distinguishing fact from fiction in the various versions related by Pee Wee an impossible quest.

Query, SLED Lieutenant Ted Owens and Agents Tom Henderson and Ben Thomas had developed a friendly relationship during time away from court. They often met for drinks after driving back from Florence or Newberry to Columbia. They spoke to Query during a break.

"Come on Grady, call him on some of this shit," said Henderson. "Just say that's not what you told me, Pee Wee, or anything to get him off of these crazy stories that don't match the damned hard evidence."

"Y'all know the attorney client privilege still applies and it belongs to him. I can't stand by while he lies under oath, but I'd have to know when he's lying and then I couldn't do anything but quit representing him. I know y'all don't believe it, but I'm hearing some of this stuff for the first time just like you are. Just like Newberry. He never told me that he was going to start confessing to murders I'd never heard of and giving details. A lot of the murders he's never admitted to committing. He talks in riddles about people never being seen nor heard of after a certain day or occurrence. He alludes to someone else's involvement, including law enforcement people but then won't identify the person he's talking about. Put him on the polygraph."

"Everybody says he can beat the polygraph," said one of the agents.

"Give it to him and find out," Query replied.

(After a short break)

Pee Wee: (Explaining how he killed Diane) All right, to begin with, I had it in my belt (Talking about gun). I either carried it here or either carried it in my back pocket. All right, I had it like this here and I had my knife like that. When we was going down there, Diane was walking and Avery was walking all together. When I stabbed Avery and she turned and she started to scream and when she started to scream, she started to run and when she did, I grabbed her in the head and I told her, I said, you goddamn stinking bitch, for a goddamn long time, I've been after you. I dropped the knife right down there where Avery was at at the time. She was gonna run. I had my flashlight in my pocket too and when I grabbed it, I meant to shoot her in the face with it and when I did, I just snatched her head back like that and said, I'm gonna blow your goddamn brains out, and when I pulled it back there to shoot her, I thought it was down in her throat, down here where it'd go up into the brain but it didn't. It come out and I didn't know that. I just throwed it, grabbed her head like that there and throwed it there and tried to blow her head off with it.

Mr. Summerford: Grabbed her by the hair?

Gaskins: Grabbed her in the hair. She had hair like this here. Just grabbed it and jerked it and of course, I was doing a lot of dirty cussing and everything.

Summerford: Well, the shot didn't kill her then, did it Pee Wee?

Gaskins: No, it must not of. She hit the ground and she tried to get back up.

Summerford: And you stabbed her after you had shot her?

Gaskins: After she got, she was trying to get back up. Avery was laying just about like that there and when she went down on the ground, I started to shoot her again and I didn't do it and I got the knife then and put it right.

Tom Henderson: Now you gonna say that you stabbed Avery and you dropped the knife down on the ground, grabbed her, pushed her head back out, shot her, she fell, put the gun back up and picked the knife up then?

Mr. Summerford: You already had the knife, why didn't you just use the knife on her?

Gaskins: I didn't want to get bloody all over. I didn't have a chance to stab her the way she was fixing to run. And I was scared, it was at night and if she got a step or two on me, she was gonna be gone. I didn't have time. When I pulled the knife out and she turned to run, I dropped it and I didn't have time to get it because in the woods there, you been back there where them woods is, how thick it is. Well a couple of steps in them woods and you can't see nobody. I know, I've run through them woods at night now.

Mr. Summerford: Let me ask you this, was there anyone else with you at that time?

Gaskins: I was by myself back there.

Summerford: No question about it?

Gaskins: No question. As I've told you Mr. Summerford, I did promise the woman a car, and I believe her mother will tell you, that I had promised to give Diane a car.

Summerford: Now, is Belton Eaddy the only person in Florence County that has committed a killing or a murder or asked that one be killed, indirectly or directly?

Gaskins: That's the only one. In other counties you've got some more. You've got Marie and Sherrie you know, in that other.

Summerford: We've got Charles Shealey and we've got Ricky Snell. All right, but Belton Eaddy is the only one in Florence County, is that correct?

Gaskins: Florence County now, that's correct.

Summerford: Any questions Sheriff?

Sheriff Barnes: No sir.

Summerford: Tom?

Tom Henderson: No sir.

When questioning concluded for the day Summerford informed Query and Grisso, the attorneys for Gaskins, that he wanted to have truth serum administered to Gaskins. He said Gaskins would be asked to confirm the answers he had given during the recorded interviews by law while on the truth serum.

Query and Grisso asked to talk with their client in private. They were allowed to go into the Sheriff's office where they conferred with Gaskins.

"I'll take truth serum, lie detector –anything else they want. I've told them everything and I'm glad to back it up. Tell 'em to hook me up right now."

"Well it has to be done by a doctor, Pee Wee. It is administered by IV. Are you sure you want to do this –to have them put a needle in your arm and place you under the influence of this drug called truth serum?"

"Yes sir. I'm ready for it. I want them to see what I've told them is the facts of it."

Query and Grisso returned to the room. "He says he's ready. He'll consent to the administration of the truth serum by intravenous injection by a medical doctor," Grisso advised.

The sheriff had been momentarily absent from the conference room when Gaskins and his attorneys were allowed to confer in the sheriff's office and the sheriff returned at about the same time that Query and Grisso reentered the conference room.

"Who's in there with Gaskins?" the sheriff suddenly asked in alarm.

"He's all by himself," said Query, "sitting right by the door in that straight chair. There's a guard right outside the door."

"There may be weapons in there," the sheriff said as he rushed through the door.

"Don't worry, Sheriff, I ain't moved. I'm sittin' right here. Even if I knowed there was a gun in here, I'd be the last person in hell to touch it. I'll tell you that. Be a sure way to get myself blowed all to hell," squawked Gaskins, laughing as the sheriff and others rushed into the room.

Returning to the conference room plans were made to set up the truth serum the following morning at a local hospital. Charles Shealy was also supposed to take the same serum at that time.

Query conferred again briefly with Gaskins who shocked him by asking, "Anybody ever beat that truth serum? You ever heard of that happening?"

"I don't know about that, Pee Wee," he answered, "oddly enough I recently read an article about CIA agents being able to resist the effects of the drug. It explained that the supposition was that their intensive training and their strong belief in the importance of the protection of their country allowed them to resist the effects of the drugs. I would have to say that you should assume that it cannot be overcome."

"I guess we'll see what it's all about tomorrow, eh?"

"You sure you're okay with this, Pee Wee? If you need to change anything do it now," said Query.

"No, I've told it straight."

Query continued to be totally perplexed by Gaskins stubborn refusal to admit to other murders to which both he and Walter had alluded in numerous conversations with Query and Walter's attorneys. Query drove to Columbia the night before to meet with Gaskins for nearly two hours much to the chagrin of the prison authorities, who finally yielded to requests from the accompanying SLED agents and allowed Query to see his client. The trip to Columbia had been at speeds near one hundred miles per hour. Query had often chided the agents on that he was at a disadvantage for Happy Hour since the agents in their Gaskins caravan sped to Columbia every night at those speeds while Query was trailing behind at something near the speed limit. On this night, when everyone had agreed that it would be advantageous for him to meet with Gaskins at the prison, they told him to stick close to the caravan and that they would advise any law enforcement along the Interstate 20 route that the green Porsche was in fact a part of their entourage. As promised, when the nose of a Highway Patrol car on the opposite side of the interstate dipped sharply and shifted to the left lane to turn across the median, it suddenly resumed normal speed and continued on toward Camden. Query then blew by the law enforcement caravan in a moment of foolish bravado enjoying the burst of speed. Owens often reminded him that his calls ahead were the only reason Query still had a license.

Because of the hour Query and Gaskins were the only occupants of the steel walled visiting room. This actually diminished rather than enhanced their privacy. The only door was composed of open bars and the steel walls acted like a giant speaker. On most occasions when others were visiting simultaneously, the conversations would merge into a garbled offering that afforded a unique privacy to all. Query had first urged then harangued Gaskins to reveal any knowledge or participation in any murders in South Carolina during this blanket exemption from the death penalty, reminding him that a solicitor in any circuit in the state might attempt to apply the new death penalty against him if evidence of a murder that he had not divulged came to light. Finally Query resorted to berating the dangerous little man, an interesting exchange, conducted in whispered tones, which for Query became deep guttural hisses of anger.

"Pee Wee, you're going to make every damn thing that we have accomplished meaningless because of your stubbornness. They know there are a lot of allegations about murders that we haven't covered and there are other police agencies and sheriffs who would love to follow up on something in their county and become the only cops that could finally put you in the chair. It's an insult to me as well, Pee Wee. You know that a lot of my hard work has been to force them to enter into a blanket agreement that ends your exposure to any version of the death penalty."

"Because of hard work and two incredibly lucky breaks, we're about to avoid the biggest slam dunk death sentence in South Carolina history, and you're gonna screw it up because of some secret reason that you won't even discuss. Do you want this whole thing to go south so we can have another death penalty trial for Jessie or Johnny or Diane and Avery or Doreen and Michelle next month? The Supreme Court might just let it stand if you get another death sentence. The U.S. Supreme Court might just say: 'Sure sounds like Dobbert to us'."

Gaskins would never actually acknowledged that he was withholding information about other murders. Instead he offered obtuse explanations for why one might withhold such information.

"You know, Mr. Queury, a man like me knows where he'll spend the rest of his life. Once this is behind me I'll be back out on the yard. They's things I have to get workin' and they's people I don't want lookin' for my back every single day and night. You put certain things out there, then it can become a racial thing and you've got all the black militants lookin' to put you down. You put some other things out there and you're seen as a rat and anybody might put you down. I've told them about everything they know about and that's the it of it. There ain't nothin' else needs tellin'. Mr. Queury, I know you wouldn't tell them anything to hurt me and that you can't even if you wanted to because of your oath, but if you ain't been told then it ain't on you to worry about. We'll talk another time when all this is done. For now you just tell them we're done and that's all there is to it, that there ain't nothing else to tell. If they'll give me a conjugal visit, I'll show 'em where those two little gals are on the Isle of Palms. If they won't, then to hell with them."

CHAPTER SIXTY EIGHT

Right Out of James Bond

The following morning Gaskins and Shealy were taken to a hospital in Florence where a psychiatrist administered sodium amytal. For Query the situation was nothing less than surreal. First Shealy and then Gaskins were hooked up for IV injections of the mystical potion. A bona fide doctor, lab coat and all, administered the serum through the IV. The drug was first administered to Shealy. He was questioned primarily regarding the burglary with which both he and Gaskins were charged. His answers indicated that both were guilty of involvement in the burglary along with a third defendant. He was then questioned regarding possible involvement in any of the murders that Gaskins was charged with committing. His answers indicated, as had already been confirmed by the polygraph examination, that he had no personal involvement in the murders. He was further questioned regarding any knowledge of those murders. Again his answers indicated no firsthand knowledge, but revealed that he had heard numerous stories and that he had known several of the victims, some casually and a few intimately.

Even the untrained eye could not help but observe that the syringe used for Gaskins contained more than twice the amount of serum as that administered to Shealy.

Solicitor Summerford began the questioning. He went through the murders that had been talked about in the recorded session, reciting the version of the facts that they had heard from Gaskins over the last three days. He asked Gaskins to stop him and correct him anytime he misstated anything. With few changes or alterations Gaskins affirmed that what the solicitor had related was essentially accurate.

Next in a turn strange even to this situation, which was already bizarre almost beyond imagination, Gaskins replied to a seemingly innocuous wrap up question from one of the law enforcement officers, that there were other heretofore unmentioned murders in Charleston. He named three women each of whom he described as having been "involved with other women" and described murdering all three on different occasions.

One woman, he said, was buried under a historic home on lower Meeting Street in the plush "below Broad" section of Charleston, where two hundred year old mansions rose three and four stories and were surrounded by beautiful formal gardens with azaleas shaded by spreading live oaks. The gardens were enclosed by elaborate fences of wrought iron, stucco or brick. He said that the house could be easily recognized because of the ornate pineapples on the gates and he believed it might be Number 2 or 20 or twenty something. It was built up several feet and the area under the house formed a sort of fully enclosed basement. Gaskins claimed that while working on the heating system he buried the woman in the basement area after having raped her.

He claimed that one of the other women was held on the verge of death in a small tin equipment shed near the shrimp boats on scenic Shem Creek in Mount Pleasant across the harbor from old Charleston. Gaskins said that he administered sufficient water and first aid to keep her alive while he experimented with gradually disemboweling her.

The other woman was supposedly murdered and buried in the historic Magnolia Cemetery in Charleston. Gaskins described the location in detail but even Query who knew the cemetery well could not visualize the location that he described. Gaskins provided sufficient information to identify the woman he claimed to have buried in the historic district of Charleston and the woman he claimed to have killed near the shrimp trawlers.

Finally Gaskins spoke of another body buried under the house he once lived in on Calvert Street in North Charleston. He provided no details of the identity or even the gender.

All around the gurney on which Gaskins lay, officers wrote frantically to get the details of the stories which were related in a sort of drunken slur. When the grisly details had been completed the officers sought to fill in gaps by asking follow-up questions. At that point Gaskins head began to lull from side to side and he began to babble unintelligibly in the image of one speaking in tongues. From that point on he would not respond to questions and was soon wheeled across the room where a hospital ward curtain was drawn around him and Query was allowed to remain with him.

After a few minutes he appeared to awaken, looked up at Query, winked once and appeared to return to a state of unconsciousness.

The police quickly verified the identity of the woman said to have been raped and killed and then buried underneath the historic home. They easily confirmed that she had moved away from Charleston at about the time of the murder described by Gaskins and was alive in another state. She confirmed a brief affair with the little bandit whose lawlessness had fascinated her.

The gory details of the disembowelment and torture of the woman on Shem Creek could not be confirmed nor was there any report that the woman he identified was missing. Interestingly Pee Wee would describe an identical murder in the book Final Truth that included the litany of his so called "coastal killings". Again no identity was provided nor was there any report of such a person having gone missing.

Police checked the house on Calvert Street and the adjacent houses and found only bones that proved to be the skeletal remains of a small animal.

Ultimately piecing together enough information to identify the woman supposedly buried in Magnolia Cemetery, the police were able to confirm that she was not among the over two centuries of graves but was alive and well. She acknowledged having known Gaskins but would not discuss the nature of their acquaintance.

Monday, April 17, 1978

Mr. Summerford: Pee Wee, this is the third day, and you've been given a drug this morning called sodium amytal, supposed to be a truth serum. You were given that drug this morning and it is now 5:15. There's a couple of questions we want to ask you about. To see what the story is. Now, during the period of time that you were under the influence of this serum, you mentioned a Rachel (last name intentionally omitted). Do you know a Rachel (last name intentionally omitted)? Do you know a Rachel (omitted)?

Gaskins: Yes, I do.

Summerford: All right, What about her?

Gaskins: She lived in a project down there in Charleston, in the City of Charleston. And uh, she used to be a girl that went with girls. That's about all I knew. She lived down there in the project.

Summerford: Did you ever do anything to her?

Gaskins: I never have had no intercourse or nothing with her whatsoever.

Summerford: Did you ever harm her in any way?

Gaskins: No sir, I think you can find her down there somewhere around that project area now.

Summerford: You never did hurt her in any way?

Gaskins: No sir, but I'll tell you somebody that may would know right where she's at. Barbara (last name intentionally omitted) is a girl that lived at Mount Pleasant that used to go with Rachel.

Summerford: Did you ever have the thought in your mind to kill both of those girls because they were queers?

Gaskins: No sir, I caught Barbara with another girl up in my apartment back in, if I'm not mistaken, back in '61 when I was working with the American tobacco Company.

Summerford: Did you ever do anything to her?

Gaskins: Never, she's married to a doctor down there now.

Summerford: How about Linda? Do you remember her?

Gaskins: Uh, I can't recall right off where I met Linda but I didn't harm her in no way.

Summerford: Was it uh, did uh, you remember a tin shed near a shrimp boat? Didn't you have it in your mind that you were gonna take her in that tin shed and do something to her because she fooled around with other women or that she was queer on men?

Gaskins: If she messed around with other women, I would have never hurt her. I can't recall the exact Linda you're talking about.

Summerford: But you never did hurt her?

Gaskins: No sir, not that I know of, that I can recall no way.

Summerford: Do you remember a 20 Meeting Street? Where is that?

Gaskins: I don't recall Meeting Street.

Summerford: Do you remember going in a basement at 20 Meeting Street?

Gaskins: No, I don't. Let me ask Mr. Query on which end of town Meeting Street is, which way is that up or down?

Mr. Query: Down, way down.

Gaskins: That's down towards the Battery. I worked in a lot of places on Meeting Street. Some of em was down in the lower part of town down there.

Summerford: You don't ever remember going into a basement down there on 20 Meeting Street?

Gaskins: No, I don't. I went in basements but I don't believe on Meeting Street. I don't believe I went in any on Meeting Street not basements.

Summerford: You never put a body or anything down there, did you?

Gaskins: No sir.

Summerford: All right, now Pee Wee, I am of the opinion now that we're talking about 13 bodies that you killed, is that correct?

Gaskins: That is correct.

Summerford: Is there any more?

Gaskins: To my best knowledge, no sir.

Gaskins: I have another charge on me here. Can I plead guilty to it too and get everything off?

Summerford: What is that, burglary?

Gaskins: Burglary.

Summerford: Yea, we can conclude that too. Now hear this now and hear me well, I know that you are under the influence, but your lawyers are here now. But I think you've answered my questions well enough to know, that I think you understand what I'm saying. Now, our agreement is that you would tell us the truth on all of these. We conclude now from taking this serum and from other facts that you have done just that. Now, the agreement stands as to the 13 murders that you committed in South Carolina. We aren't concerned with what you committed, if any, out of the state. If we come up with other murders or anything else concerning you, now, we have reserved the right to go forward as we may be advised. Do you understand what I'm sayin? I'm simply saying this, that our agreement relates to 13 cases and that's all.

Gaskins: This covers 13 complete cases.

Summerford: Thirteen complete cases, now if you have any other cases you want to get off your mind now, now is the time to do it because our agreement is for the 13 and no more.

Gaskins: If I am in any way connected with any burglary charges or anything why---

Summerford: Pee Wee, you don't have to worry about the burglary charges when we've got 13 murder cases.

Gaskins: Well, there won't be no more murder cases.

Summerford: We'd like to clear up any burglary charges or anybody that was with you.

Gaskins: Charlie Shealey is supposed to give you everything on that.

Summerford: Were you involved in all three of his or just one?

Gaskins: No sir, no sir.

Summerford: Just the one.

Gaskins: One burglary charge.

Summerford: Well, we know about that so we'll clear that up. Pee Wee there was one other thing that I failed to ask you about that you said this morning. You told us this morning that you put a body under where you lived at 13, something Calvert Street, under the bathtub where the bathtub was, that you buried a body under there. Of course, we've checked that out. Now, by any chance did you ever bury a body at the house next door, or do you know what I'm talking about?

Gaskins: The only thing I can remember was, is I buried the body of a dog down under my house where I lived at one time, one of my puppies, but I can't ever—human body, no sir.

Because of their discussions of the night before and Gaskins drug induced ramblings of the morning, Query was angered by Gaskins insinuation that he could recall burying the body of a dead puppy but might not recall burying a person near one of his many abodes. Query

Grady Query

nevertheless held his tongue and sat silently with Grisso as the dialogue wound down. He knew full well from his hundreds of hours of interviews with Gaskins that if Summerford was talking about something that Pee Wee did not want to discuss, Summerford could ask all day about Calvert Street and Gaskins would continue his denials. Gaskins would answer only as to the specific address while the house on Bexley or in Sumter or a different house number might have a virtual foundation of human remains and go unmentioned.

Summerford: Did you ever bury a human body at the house next door to yours on Calvert Street?

Gaskins: No sir, I worked under that house.

Summerford: But you never buried anything under it?

Gaskins: I never buried nothing under that now.

Summerford: Did not?

Gaskins: No.

Summerford: Okay, Sheriff any questions?

Sheriff Barnes: No.

Summerford: Tom?

Tom Henderson: No.

Summerford: As far as I'm concerned, gentlemen, that concludes this thing. Now, in the morning, we'll take pleas from you on all counts. Now, let me ask you one other thing, there is one thing I failed to ask. Janice Kirby, did you kill Janice Kirby here? The way her body was wrapped around, it looked like to me that she was in, her body was warm when it was buried.

Gaskins: She was in the thing and I brought her down and wrapped her up and kept her till the next night. That was the hard thing of me going back to find where I had put her at because I didn't go to her until after I had dug the hole.

Summerford: Did you kill her in Florence County?

Gaskins: No sir, she was killed right in the stone house in Sumter.

Grisso mused that Summerford had on his own theory without benefit of the Medical Examiner concluded that because the body was somewhat curled at the bottom of the tree where it was found, that it had not been in a rigid state. Grisso knew from his many years of prosecution and defense in state and federal courts that rigidity resulting from *rigor mortis*, familiar to most, reaches maximum intensity after approximately twelve hours and then begins to dissipate. Approximately twenty-four hours after death a non-rigid state could have returned. The time frame that Gaskins had described of having left the body covered the night before and then burying her more than twenty four hours after she was killed was consistent with the relaxation of the rigor or with the position having been merely a coincidence.

Summerford: In Sumter?

Gaskins: In the stone house up there along with Patricia Alsbrook. I toted Patricia Alsbrook over to the other house.

Summerford: Put her in the septic tank.

Gaskins: And then came back and toted Janice out to the edge of the road and went and got my car and came back, picked her up and she was in the trunk of my car until I put her under those bushes until the next night, I came back and stayed two hours or less at my mother's and then went on down there and dug the hole.

Summerford: Now, Pee Wee, when you had the Sodium Amytal, you indicated that what you had said about the killing of the girls at the Isle of Palms, you made it up because you were mad with Shealey and also mad with Ricky Snell and that you never had killed any girls down there at the Isle of Palms or buried any down there, is that correct?

Gaskins: Yes sir.

Summerford: Now, is that the reason that you made those stories up, because you were mad with Snell and you were mad with Charles Shealey?

Gaskins: That's partially the reason that I'm mad with Shealey because he came in and I couldn't get him to do nothing and then Ricky Snell was always breaking into places and putting the stuff under my house, something like that. It would make it look like that I was doing the stuff.

Summerford: What other reason did you have for telling that lie?

Gaskins: They always was doing things and they wanted to put it off to where if anything happened it would fall on me because the places was in my name and no matter what I tried to get them to do, to not do it at my house, they'd still do it at my house and laugh at me and said it was no skin off of their nose.

Query was again somewhat astonished by these answers. He remembered the abject fear on the face of Walter Neeley when Walter had asked police to allow him to speak to Query in the back of a police car at the Isle of Palms. He expressed his trepidation over the consequences that might follow the discovery of the bodies of the two girls and the possibility that it could somehow lead to the discovery of more bodies in the national forest. Query well knew from his representation of Gaskins and Judy and his numerous interviews of potential witnesses including Snell, girlfriends, wives and acquaintances of Gaskins, Judy and Neely, that Gaskins encouraged all of the various brigands with whom he was associated to bring their booty to him so that he could sell it through his connections for a percentage.

Summerford: Okay, gentlemen, that concludes it as far as I'm concerned.

In the days that followed the court reporter, Peggy Fowler, typed her transcript of the questioning of Gaskins and the others. She concluded with the traditional oath of accuracy and completeness of the court reporter.

The following morning Donald Henry "Pee Wee" Gaskins pled guilty to nine murders, confirmed his guilt to the murder of Dennis Bellamy for which he was already convicted and pled to one count of burglary. He received nine consecutive sentences for murder, each requiring that he be confined for "the rest of his natural life" at the department of corrections and a final consecutive sentence of life imprisonment for the burglary.

A rather relieved group, that included Grisso, Query, the young assistant solicitor, Judge Harwell, and Sheriff Barnes, gathered in the judge's chambers for a few minutes. Kenneth Summerford put in a head and a shoulder and said "Judge, I have to run; got a lot of work to do. Bud, Grady, y'all take care, hopefully we've finished up with this."

"Hopefully so," echoed the judge turning to the others as Kenneth closed the door and shaking his head, "God knows I'm ready to be done with it."

"Gaskins seems resigned to a 'quiet life' in prison, Judge, so maybe we've heard the last of it. It has certainly been a pleasure working with you and I can't imagine anyone managing this freak turn of events any better," Grady said, rather openly pandering to the judge.

"Thanks, Grady, pleasure working with you and of course with my old friend Bud Grisso here. Y'all did a fine job and kept it professional under some incredibly difficult circumstances," replied the judge. "Y'all have a safe trip back to Charleston and Columbia and I hope that you find something left of your law offices. It's always hard trying cases out of town, but I know that this one has really been a burden."

Grisso, Query, Monk Hinnant, Bud's son Bob, who had come over for the final pleas gathered with their faithful host at the deli for a farewell. Bob had worked hard throughout the trial and the pre-trial preparation. No funds were approved for an investigator and Bob had undertaken the role of runner and legal assistant without pay. Tales of the final days were told and followed by goodbyes and promises to gather in the future to reminisce.

Two weeks of hard work would pass before Query would travel to Columbia to see Gaskins.

"When they gonna put me in population, Mr. Queury? I been in this hell hole of a cell on death row for four years. It ain't right now. I'm a lifer now; I ain't a condemned man no more. Every other lifer is out there in population. Can you get me back out there?"

"I'll work on it as soon as I get back to Charleston, Pee Wee. I'll write a letter to the warden and demand that you be given the same treatment as anyone else with a life sentence. They may give us a hard time for a while on it, but I think they'll come around as long as you don't get into any kind of trouble."

"What the hell kinda trouble am I gonna get into from here? I'm locked in near twenty four hours a day; one shower a week and one or two hours a week walkin' in that little yard that's only for the row," Pee Wee lamented.

"Well, just don't get in any trouble, Pee Wee. I have a feeling that you get around here a little more than anyone thinks. I remember the stuff about telephone calls out of state and some messages that you had to have gotten to Wanda and some others," Query responded with a grin.

"You know me too good, Mr. Queury. Sometimes I can get word out on somethin' if I have to, but it ain't the same as being on the yard," Pee Wee continued making sure his tragic circumstances were well understood. He was giving the hard sell to his young lawyer in hopes of immediate action that would affect the changes he wanted.

CHAPTER SIXTY NINE

Quiet Years

Query continued to visit Gaskins from time to time seldom failing to see him when he was at CCI to see other prisoners or had additional time after some court appearance in Columbia. For the first few years Pee Wee would tell stories of crimes and murders in other states but seldom revisit any of the South Carolina murders.

Finally on one occasion about three years later Gaskins suddenly changed abruptly from talking about a car chase in Tennessee and asked,

"I could never figure why they wouldn't do the conjugal visit to find them two girls on Isle of Palms. Why you reckon they wouldn't go along with that?"

"Well, Pee Wee, you told Summerford at the end of everything that it never happened. No place for them to go from there."

"They shoulda knowed I was just backin' up on that because they wouldn't go with what I wanted," Pee Wee said.

"I don't know how they could have known that, Pee Wee. Hard to get people to investigate if you say it didn't happen."

"Get hold of North Charleston and tell them we'll take 'em to it, if they'll go back to our plan on the visits. Tell them I got some others I can find for them."

"I'll tell them, Pee Wee but I'm afraid you may have held your cards too long."

Query contacted Mickey Whatley, who was by that time Chief of the North Charleston Police Department, and made the offer. Whatley would reply that while he had a lot of questions that he would like to ask of Pee Wee Gaskins, there would be no more conjugal visits.

A couple of attempts were made by Whatley to arrange a meeting but Gaskins always had conditions that were unacceptable.

Realizing that bargaining was at an end Gaskins began to tell Query of the tangled relationships with his victims, of the various motives in his seemingly endless string of murders and of his obsession over interracial sex. He would never touch on the racial issue without assuring Query that he had always gotten along well with black people and continued to have black friends within the prison. He always asserted that it was only the mixing of the races that he found repugnant; so much so that he felt compelled to strike out against it.

On the other hand when he was angry about a confrontation with a black guard or inmate it was difficult for Query to give complete credence to his assertions about the absence of any racial bias, while Pee Wee ranted about the conflict.

"Nigger laid around until it was too late to get me to exercise and then wrote me up for sassin' him. I'll sass his black ass he gives me half a chance."

Or

"Way it is now the niggers get whatever they want. They get a little cough or a ache and pain it's right off to State Park to the hospital. I'm lyin' up here with hemorrhoids so bad I can't sleep and have to bite down on somethin' to crap and they say they'll get the doctor to check me in the infirmary, if I put in for it."

Or

"That nigger keeps me up one more night with his hollerin' and then playin' that nigger music, I'll catch him at exercise one day and we'll be done with that."

These were typical statements in every angry discourse about a black antagonist and probably provided a more precise view of the true thoughts of Pee Wee Gaskins where race was concerned.

Pee Wee would continue to write and call his lawyers about getting him off of death row. Pee Wee would tell a reporter:

"I had my life sentences and I was at CCI, but the ridiculous part was that I was still on Death Row. I asked Mr. Query to come up and see me and I guess he wondered "What the hell is up next?" but he came and I told him it wasn't right. He contacted the warden and made an appointment to see him (the same one that had him put in jail). But nothin' got changed."

When he contacted Warden Martin he was invited to come to his office.

"Be sure and take down the 'No Trespassing' sign," he chided when he accepted.

"Joe, I don't think that you can keep Pee Wee on Death Row for any reason –not even for his own protection" Query began. "As I've told you, he doesn't want protection and is happy to take his chances in the general population. I understand your position that you have a duty to protect any inmate, whether they want protection or not. My only point is that Death Row is designated for a specific classification of inmates –those under a death sentence. I don't think you can change that rule just for Pee Wee."

"What difference does it make? He'll still be in CB2 or are you trying to tell me that I can't keep him there either?" replied the warden matter of factly.

"No of course not, Warden, I know that CB2 is designated for protective custody and that you have the authority to designate which inmates require that special level of custody. But there is a big difference between the row and the rest of CB2, if you live there. The row is one man to a cell, it has a separate locked gate at the end of the catwalk, the exercise yard is twice a week for one hour and the guards decide whether a man walks alone or with whom he can walk and a guard accompanies each man to his shower. You know all of that. Anyone else in CB2 who is not on some kind of disciplinary or too crazy to be allowed to move around, can move around the cellblock during the day, sit at the tables in the common area, eat out there and use the phone out there. It makes a huge difference when you're there twenty-four hours a day, three sixty-five a year."

"And what makes you think you can require me to move him?" the warden asked.

"Come on, Joe, he doesn't meet the criteria for that level of custody. I can get a court order easily enough, but if you're going to make me do that, I'll bring an action against the department. They're not going to give Pee Wee Gaskins any damages but they may give me attorney's fees. It'll just be an embarrassment that accomplishes nothing. I am really not here to pick a fight with you. This is a legitimate request and I came to you to talk about it rather than file something and fire the newspapers up again. You run a good show here. It's run much better than when I worked here. I don't mind saying that to anyone. I know you're not going to let him loose in the general population. Of course I'll keep writing to you and asking for it, but you are probably right about the fact that he would probably get killed in a couple of weeks or kill somebody that was trying to kill him. I'm equally convinced that you can't keep him on death row and I think you know that too."

"All right, it's not worth getting dragged into court and wasting a lot of time. Give me two weeks and I'll put him in a regular cell on CB2," the warden said.

"Thanks, Warden."

Pee Wee was placed in another cell in CB2 but not on Death Row. He continued to implore Query to have him released into the general population but the administration continued to deny the requests on the basis of protective custody.

"Well by god tell 'em when somebody kills Walter then lock me back up. Anybody lookin' for me is lookin' for him and if they can't kill that dumb son of a bitch they ain't gonna kill nobody. They damn sure ain't gonna kill Pee Wee Damn Gaskins."

"That's got nothing to do with it, Pee Wee. We both know they're not protecting you from anybody. They don't want you out there because they could never explain it if you escaped or killed somebody else out in the general population. Protective custody is just a good excuse for them. If we got around that, the next time it would be a new classification: 'extremely dangerous inmate' or 'escape risk'. They'll just keep doing that as long as they want to keep you in CB 2."

"Sue 'em in federal court for violatin' my rights."

"I can't do that, Pee Wee. I just don't have the time for that and I think their classification system would be upheld as soon as they went to the trouble to write one out. You can file it in federal court."

"I'm sure you're right. They'll keep classifyin' me 'til they find one the court likes."

"Maybe I can get made a run-around. At least I'd be out of this damn cell. You tell 'em again that I'll give up some more bodies if I can get my conjugal visits back. They can set it up right here in the penitentiary. I think Donna'll go along with it. And if she don't I'll find one that will. I got women writin' to me every day, Mr. Queury, tellin' how they'd like to be with me. They send me naked pictures of their selves. I bet I got a hundred of 'em. When they say they want to send me a picture I tell them to send it on, but if it's naked I tell them a person outside to send it to and then they get it to me. You just set it up I'll get the women," Pee Wee laughed.

"I doubt they'll do it, Pee Wee. Besides I thought there weren't any more bodies."

"Oh they's plenty more. I just got to have a reason to talk about 'em. On another thing I've wrote to the president and outlined my plan to kill Castro. I told him I would use leather tannin' chemicals and turn myself brown as any Cuban and then they could put me off on the beach. I'd bury my rifle and stuff and then I'd start to find my way around Havana pretendin' to be a mute and beggin' on the street. When I got everything the way I wanted it I would take my rifle and go down into the sewer and work my way around for as long as it took to find me a manhole within range of where he makes all them speeches. Ease the cover up about two inches, pop a shot off and slip right on back out through the sewer. They got a expert right here and I'd rather die tryin' to do it then rot away in here."

"Sounds like a pretty good plan. I don't think they'll go for it, but I guess you never know. Good luck on getting the run-around job. I'll try to come by the next time I'm in Columbia."

Pee Wee would in fact land the coveted job as "run around" or "block man" which involved primarily running errands for guards but frequently included carrying messages or items from one inmate to another. Many residents of CB 2 remained confined in their cells twenty four hours a day with the exception of exercise, showers, and occasional time in the small common area. As a result the "run around" became a very popular person among his fellow inmates and with the guards. Pee Wee with his usual industriousness and his talent as a fix it man soon endeared himself even to the guards and staff of CB 2 by making quick and effective repairs within the block.

After Pee Wee achieved that special status, Query found him to be much more at ease. While he still expressed a desire to be in general population, he was generally relaxed and jovial. Pee Wee began to go back over the various crimes with which Query was familiar and tell him what had actually transpired. In addition with gentle urging he told the lawyer about the experiences of his childhood and youth. He also began to outline the many crimes, including murders, about which Query had no prior knowledge. Query frequently made recordings or notes but when the potential harm to his client was so great and the information was so dangerous to his client that he needed to avoid any possibility of it falling into the hands of police, prosecutors or prison officials, he relied exclusively on memory.

"Now you keep all of this, Mr. Queury, and if we can ever trade it to get me a conjugal visit or to get me relocated, you use it when the time is right. If that don't come about and you decide to write your book, then you go with it. I owe you that. Hell, I owe you a lot. I reckon I wouldn't be here to tell you or nobody else wasn't for you and all you've done for me. Don't put none of that race stuff in there, if I'm alive. They'd kill me sure. And I don't think it would be purty," Pee Wee said to his long time advocate. "If I'm dead, then hell, put it all out there however you want. They got that new law says I can't get none of the money for a book or a movie but I'd be glad for you to have something' out of it."

"Your communications to me are still protected by the attorney-client privilege. As long as you are alive I won't disclose anything without your express permission. Some of this involves crimes or even murders in other states. You don't have any deal with them."

CHAPTER SEVENTY

Doing Life Over and Over

I put some of my old connections back together even while I was on the row but what I could do was very limited. I was feared and recognized as a major power man, but in reality I couldn't enforce anything except through favors. Not that there weren't plenty of people who wanted to gain favor with me. I was the most famous man in the penitentiary and in the whole prison system for that matter. My reputation for power plays inside CCI was still well known but I still didn't have an organization that could make things happen exactly the way I wanted them to happen and that was what I wanted. As soon as I hit my new cell in CB2 I started putting my crew together. I sent messages to old associates especially those who had a lot of freedom of movement around the prison. I sent for old timers who I knew to be stand up men and put them in charge of recruiting enough people to set up our operations. I had some money hidden on the outside and I had it smuggled in to me. Money is in very short supply in CCI and I turned five hundred dollars into a thousand in just two months and then kept doing it again and again. Because I didn't do drugs gamble or drink it was very easy for me to hold on to money and use it to make more money. For the most part even the men who knew how to make money had their own weakness and they got rid of it as fast as they could make it. I kept my money and that money meant power. As runaround I had some freedom of movement and the money got me other benefits.

The men who worked with me made good money and enjoyed many privileges. Often we ate our own food that was smuggled in by the guards. It was cooked in the prison kitchen but not with the regular slop they were preparing. Those working for me enjoyed that more often than I did because it was harder to get things in and out of CB 2, even for the guards. We had people who cleaned our cells and did our laundry. It was washed separate from the rest and ironed the way we wanted it.

The prison bounces back and forth between requiring uniforms and allowing inmates to wear some of their own clothing. This was a time when you could choose the uniform or just wear the prison pants with the white stripe down the leg and what they called a polo shirt or a golf shirt. A lot of my men wore nice golf shirts and good shoes. It was before the time that the niggers started killing each other for hundred dollar tennis shoes so tennis shoes were allowed. Men who could bought their own Levi and Wrangler jeans until they got pricey enough to get killed for. Tennis shoes and jeans went on the blacklist as the price went up in the stores and we were only allowed to wear store bought shirts and prison issued pants. Most who could afford it wore the shoes like doctors wear, made of soft leather with soft soles that are good for walking on concrete floors. I chose good solid work shoes and work shirts of strong cotton or lightweight short sleeved cotton shirts that buttoned up the front and could be worn out of the pants with a straight hem all around. Those were the coolest in the summer when CB2 turns into an oven and they allowed easy access to something carried in the waist band of my pants. I had to pay the guards a fee to wear those shirts. Everyone was supposed to wear prison pants but blue or khaki work pants were usually allowed.

As always sex and drugs were the highest priced produce and the most dangerous items for sale. I still stayed clear of the use or sale of drugs. The one exception was to sell the valium and other tranquilizers and sleeping pills that I was given by the infirmary. Anyone on death row can get enough of those drugs to keep them in a sort of daze. My daily allotment had been established when I was on the row and I had five tranks and two sleeping pills to sell or trade every day. The prison authorities had learned a long time ago that tranquilizers make for tranquil inmates and tranquil inmates make their jobs easier. This was particularly true of the violent men on the row and in maximum detention. My prescriptions alone would have kept me supplied with sexual favors, but of course I always had cash and my reputation for those needs.

I never wanted to be slowed down by the drugs. There were others like Jimmy McPhee who had been through addictions to almost anything known to man. After Jimmy cleaned up and became a fitness nut he wouldn't touch anything –not even aspirin. There were others who stayed away from even legal drugs because they didn't like the fuzziness and some seemed to get meaner the more they took. Timmy Blenkhorn was in a class by himself. Timmy would take as many and as much of anything available but seemed completely capable of mayhem whether he was high or clean; up or down; or just for no reason or any reason. Timmy would wind up as the only man to serve almost as much time in the Maximum Detention and Retraining Center as I did.

Timmy was from the rough part of Boston, the south side I think. I loved to hear him talk with that funny Boston accent. He liked to tell stories so it was easy to get him going. Once when we were both in MDRC, I was on the second tier and Timmy was up on the third. The food cart would come around at mealtime and they would place your square metal plate with the separate sections for beans and rice and mystery meat in front of the slot at the bottom of the cell door and a trusty would come along with a long slender piece of bamboo like a short fishing pole and push it across the space to a similar slot at the bottom of the inside door made of bars. You could then reach it through the slot and pull it inside your cell.

Timmy saved his drinking straws until he had made a stick about eight feet long, several straws thick and glued together with glue made from biscuits and water. When his tray was put down and before the trusty came along to push it in to him, Timmy pushed it out to the edge of the gallery. When he heard a guard walking along the bottom level he counted the steps and timed it to push the tray off to fall on the guard. I don't know whether the tray actually hit the guard but he at least got splattered. I think Timmy was bored. The word quickly spread and the building roared with laughter.

The guards swarmed up to Timmy's cell. When they move you in MDRC two guards come through the solid steel door and stand at the bars to your cell. You have to turn your back and back up to the cell. One of the guards reaches through the bars and cuffs your hands behind your back. You turn to face the bars. The guard then reaches all the way around your waist and puts the belly chain or belt around you while the other guard is fastening the leg irons around your ankles. The handcuffs are removed and you turn to face the guards. Depending on the type of belly chain either the handcuffs are put back on in front where they are fastened to the belly chain or each hand is placed in a separate cuff permanently fastened to the belly chain at each side. When they went for Timmy he wouldn't come to the bars and so they blasted him with the fire hose and then rushed in with billy clubs flailing and beat him to the ground where they could chain him.

The guard who had been hit or splattered walked behind Timmy as they marched him down the main corridor of the lowest level which is halfway below ground level with concrete walls that are always a little wet. The guard was so furious that he swung the big cellblock key that's about six inches long, weighs about seven ounces and is carried on a leather or chain lanyard in a big overhead loop and hit Timmy in the head with it.

Timmy was knocked to his knees and yelled out for everyone in the building to hear, "That all you got? My momma hits harder. You'd be totally worthless if your old lady didn't suck such good cock. Tell her to come see me again."

With that he got three more smacks with the big key with each one cutting a slash half the length of the key in Timmy's scalp. He was locked in a bare cell and considered too violent to move so he didn't get any stitches but he did eventually get some peroxide and a box of band aids. Even as the guards moved away to leave him lying on the bare concrete floor with blood pouring from his head Timmy yelled out to the offended guard once more.

"Hey, little dick, your old lady really does suck great cock. She said your mother taught her how to swallow it. I told her to bring yer mom with her the next time she comes."

*　*　*

The taunts echoed through the cavernous openness that rose through the center of the concrete and steel and momentarily every man was at his cell door and each of them was calling out his own insult. The frustrated guard was so enraged that he ran back to Blenkhorn's cell and struggled to open the solid steel door, his stick raised high even while he tried to turn the key. The other guards recognized his loss of control. The guards were mindful of the cardinal rule that a guard never goes back into a locked cell to hit an inmate with whom he has had an altercation that required other guards to control the inmate. The other guards got him under control and led him all of the way out of the building into the protected area within the wall that formed the prison within the prison. Timmy was injured, still in chains and helpless. Allowing the guard to attack him under those circumstances could have cost them all their jobs.

Query had represented Timmy when he was convicted of several armed robberies of drug stores. CCI eventually solved their Blenkhorn problem by taking advantage of the opportunity to transfer him to a new prison being opened in the western part of the state. After the food tray incident Pee Wee would tell Query that Timmy Blenkhorn was the meanest man he had ever met. Query thought that was a lot coming from Pee Wee.

Blenkhorn was transferred to Perry, a prison near Greenville. A number of violent inmates in his maximum security building overpowered guards and started a riot. Timmy didn't want any part of it. He was carefully maintaining good behavior and was trying to get moved to a medium security prison. Timmy stayed in his cell even though it had been unlocked by the rioting inmates. The men involved had taken several guards hostage and he knew that the fact that he had remained in his cell would be reported when it was all over and done. The other prisoners were afraid of Timmy and even in the excitement of the revolt; they did not consider it wise to confront him over his decision not to participate.

As the hours wore on the prisoners became frustrated with the failure of anyone to meet their demands for a written list of rights and access to a TV reporter. One of the guards with whom a couple of the prisoners had beefs was badly beaten. As the violence increased one of the ringleaders decided to up the ante. He threatened to kill the unpopular guard if the warden refused their demands. At this point Timmy emerged from his cell.

"Ju muttafuckas gonna get us all da chair. Ju kill one o' dese fuckas we all get electrocuted, don't matta who did da deed. Hand of one is da hand of all. I've done a lot a time on dat little bit o' law. I ain't gonna die by it. Ju gonna kill him ju got me to go tru'. Don't nobody here want to try dat. Lemme talk to 'em. I'll get 'em to call my lawyuh. He'll get your shit to da' TV people."

Timmy talked to the warden over an in house telephone line in the seized guard station. He told them the rioters were seriously into killing

365

one of the guards. He said that they all hated the man anyway and that their fear of Timmy was the only thing stopping them. It was two A.M. He asked the warden to call his lawyer Grady Query in Charleston and let him talk to the prisoners. The warden got Query on the line and over the next two hours he negotiated a plan between the two sides that ended in the surrender of the prisoners, no further harm to any of the guards and a full airing of the prisoners' grievances to the press through Query.

As a prime example of the gracious appreciation of the Department of Corrections to an inmate who does the right thing, Timmy, who had risked his life to save the guard, was charged with participating in a prison riot. The guards all testified on his behalf at the trial and Attorney John Delgado and Query represented him. Query had to become a witness and the rules of court required him to disqualify himself as an attorney at that point. Delgado finished the case and the jury quickly acquitted the oft convicted felon. Timmy was thereafter a devoted fan of both lawyers. The trial judge minced few words in expressing his disapproval of the decision of the prosecutors to try the case against the unlikely hero.

In another late night call to Query, Timmy, then back at CCI and in CB 1, inquired out of the blue as to whether Query's Mt. Pleasant home had ever been burglarized.

"Yes, Timmy, once when we were visiting my wife's family in Michigan, we came home to find that the house had been broken into. How did you know about that?"

"Dey get some old coins, a shot gun and a bunch of movies of jour kids wit da projecta?"

"Yes, Timmy, what is this about? That wasn't you was it?"

"No, no! We was just here on da block playin' some cahds tonight and dis guy, Goldberg or Goldstein somtin' like dat, he starts talkin' about breakin' inta dis house and gettin' like a tousand dollars worth of old coins, an antique shotgun and a fancy movie camerer and projecta. And then he says the case with the camerer had all dese movies of da guy's kids. Den he laughs and says he didn't know it when he broke in but it turned out de guy was a lawyah. Said de guy once got him off on a jewelry store heist. So he laughs and says I guess I just got back part of my fee. Hell old man Uricchio charged me a fortune and then Query did all the work."

"Sheit, I hit him before he finished sayin' your name. Knocked his ass cold. But I'm callin' you because we got him up on the fifth tier now and we'll trow his ass off, you want us to."

Query had to pause. Every movie of his young son and daughter were gone and the shotgun and coins had been gifts from his grandfather and probably had a value of ten times what the creepy little burglar had gotten for them.

Finally though, he said, "No Timmy, don't throw him off, that's just trouble for you and no help to me. I'm glad you hit him but please don't throw him off the balcony."

"Whatevah ju say, boss. I'd be glad to do it and nobody would evah know. People fall off dese galleries all da time."

"No let him go, Timmy. Thanks though I appreciate you having my back."

Several weeks later when Query went to the prison to see Pee Wee he had Timmy brought in after they had finished.

"Timmy, you didn't drop that guy five floors did you?" Query asked holding his breath.

"Nah, ju said not to and so I din't. Dumbass broke his leg though when we was helpin' him back over the rail. Jus clumsy I guess," Timmy laughed beaming with pride.

*   *   *

At the time I was setting up in CB2 Timmy was in CB1 and I let him run part of my stuff over there, but he was too crazy and it was OK by me when they moved him out to Kirkland Correctional off Broad River Road. I liked for my power men to be calm and easy going. They were all capable of doing what needed to be done when it came down to it, but the last thing I wanted them to do was to cause trouble when there was no reason for it. Timmy could get whacked out on drugs and go crazy on somebody or Timmy could just be Timmy and go crazy on somebody. I didn't need that. I wanted people to understand my rules and to understand the harm that could come from breaking my rules, but I wanted them to feel safe when they didn't break any.

I was now the unconditional head of CB2 and one of the three most powerful men in CCI. Being restricted to CB2 limited my ability to run the entire place but the other two power men didn't make any moves without my OK.

I soon got my wish or rather soon bought my wish and I was moved to the first cell on the second tier. This was the best cell in "Two" because it was up away from the common area but right at the top of the stairs. The second tier also caught any breeze through the high windows and it was warmer in winter. On the ground where I was before the move everybody walked right by your cell and the tables where the guys who weren't on lockdown sat around during the day were directly in front of the cell.

Any time I heard any of the guards complain about anything on the block being broken I would offer to fix it. As long as they had the tools there wasn't much that I couldn't figure out and repair. All of the cells had bars all the way across the front and solid steel walls on the other three sides. On the right side as you faced into a cell there were two bunks made of steel more like two shelves than beds. A steel toilet and sink combination was attached to the rear wall and the left wall was empty. There were two armored lights in the top of each cell about midway between the bunks and the left wall. The cells fronted on a steel mesh floored gallery and faced in opposite directions essentially stacked back to back. Between the backs of the cells there was an open space about four feet wide that was the mechanical race. All of the wiring for the lights and all of the plumbing ran up the solid steel backs of the cells in that space. Heat ducts carried hot air to the single vent in each of the cells. Death Row cells were the same but in addition there was a steel mesh gate at the top of the stairs and that blocked entry to that entire gallery. Death Row was immediately behind my cell on the same level.

Some inmates had small tables and a chair, some had makeshift cabinets or trunks and some had shoeboxes and big envelopes. Many of us had worms, a small bent metal rod with an electrical cord for heating a single cup of water for coffee or soup. I had a single burner hot plate and everyone had a radio. Many in CB1 had their own TV. Only a couple of us in CB2 had our own because it was illegal and there were TVs mounted on the outer walls of the building, although they usually couldn't be heard for all of the noise. Arguments over which channels were constant and so the guards just left them on whatever channel they were on except for ball games.

There were trusty couriers throughout the prison. They went from cellblock to cellblock, to administration and to prison industries carrying papers, work orders, special requests from inmates, leave requests from guards, disciplinary reports, disciplinary sentences and anything else someone could think of to put on a piece of paper. These men were the messengers for the prisoners as well as for the guards and administration. The good ones were delivery men for their fellow inmates. In addition there were inmate workers and repairmen who were in and out of every cellblock and up and down the tunnel. These were the freight carriers generally. They had carts and toolboxes and boxes with parts. They brought the packages that one inmate sent to another whether harmless or illegal. Guards and visitors were the windows to the outside and they brought in everything that could be imagined. Drugs came in candy boxes that appeared to be sealed from the factory. The drugs were hidden under false bottoms so that even when unwrapped, it all looked good. Sometimes the candy had been replaced and was actually the drugs.

Women brought drugs, money, shanks, hypodermic needles and even an occasional gun in their bras, under their skirts and in their vaginas. Women with babies were the toughest for the guards because there is so much stuff that comes with the baby that can look perfectly legitimate but be one hundred per cent contraband. Baby Powder could be smack or coke or some other drug. Baby's bottle might be full of dilaudid or some other potent drug and the diapers may have anything concealed between the layers. I paid the guards to let me have a TV and I kept a cardboard box that it would fit inside and stuck it quickly in the box with legal papers on top of it when there were visitors on the block or when I left my cell.

When the guards found that I could fix almost anything in the mechanical chase, keep the showers operating and keep their wall plugs making their coffee and playing their radio or TV, I was given free run of the entire cellblock. I volunteered to be the "runaround" or the cellblock runner. The runaround carries messages to the inmates, gets snacks from the canteen for those who aren't allowed to leave their cells, passes out food, razors at shaving time, books, pencils and medicine. He is everyone's servant but he is the only man who moves about whenever he wants without asking permission. I frequently sat by a barred window that looked out into the tunnel and could ship and receive as well as communicate right there. No one was supposed to go near that window except the guards. It was one of the most important benefits of the job because it gave me direct contact with the whole prison.

There were some low windows next to the common area that opened onto a small vacant space between CB2 and the death house. Men on outside work details could slip into that area and not be seen as they brought items smuggled in from outside. The other main spot for passing information or goods was the exercise yard. Because we had our own small separately fenced yard complete with its own razor wire topping, the guards paid little attention to the one or two men exercising. The little yard ran from the building toward the main drive that ran along the front between the prison buildings and the recreation fields. Someone out in front could throw things over the fence or pick the right moment to run over and pass something through the fence.

My situation continued to improve financially and power wise. Most men willing to take a chance considered it an honor to run errands for me and were well paid to boot. I had women writing to me and asking me to marry them every week. I sold cartoons that were actually traced from the newspapers and then filled in with prison humor. I had young boys who were my pussy boys and a line of others wanting to be. Women who could convince the guards that they were related to me or that they were from a church doing prison ministry or whatever would sell that week came to see me. I got hand jobs and blow jobs in the visiting room and a few times talked a guard into letting one pull up her skirt and sit on my lap. I tipped the guards every time I had a visit and paid plenty extra when the visit included any of the above. I sent men to hurt or kill other men when it was necessary but remained almost entirely outside the violence myself.

One man in CB2 was jealous of my freedom of movement and began to make trouble for me. He tripped one day as he was going past me on the second gallery and fell more than ten feet to the concrete below. A couple of guys were waiting down below and did more damage than the concrete. He was no trouble after that but he spent all of his time trying to get moved without telling anyone why.

Things continued to cruise along. Mr. Query would come and visit fairly often and since there was no limit on legal visits he would usually stay for an hour or two. A friend of his Jim Beaty, an English Professor and former preacher, came about once a month and talked and took notes and recorded so he could write a book.

There seemed to be no realistic possibility of escape from CB2. There was an assistant warden just for that cellblock and two people, the warden and a guard had to give permission for anyone to even leave the cellblock and then they usually had to be escorted by a guard. I wasn't allowed to leave period. Sometimes I would be allowed to go to the infirmary but I was in chains and with two guards. Visiting was in the high security visitation area that had been created for death row. It was a series of cages that used to be used for intake. We were taken one at a time into the back cages and strip searched. Then we were taken into one of the two small cells at the front that were all bars and we sat at a table in that cell with our visitors, not more than two at a time. The one advantage was that we were separate from all other visitation and there was only one guard sitting outside the cages. If he was sympathetic to a man's needs or well bribed, the visit could be extremely pleasant and well worth all you went through to get in and out.

At the end of visitation we were taken back through the back cells and strip searched again. The cages were inside a big room and a guard stood out there the entire time. Like everything else the strip searches could be managed with the right guard and some money. I had also mastered the ability to swallow things and then bring them back up so as long as it was smaller than a yoyo I could get by whatever search they wanted to try. Even money in a balloon or a condom can go in or out that way. If it was too big to get by the search I would leave it for a cooperative guard to pick up and send to me later. During visits an inmate would take your picture for a dollar. I always got the picture and had him make copies. I sold a lot of the pictures in the mail and sent others to the many women who wrote to me. Theirs were without charge.

I used everything I could think of and offered all the money I had or expected to get in the next few years to get to general population but they blocked me every time. I had a pile of life sentences, was in secure lockup and there were other cases they could try me for if it looked like I was going to get out. Escape was my only hope and I had to get enough money to buy my way into population or to find a way to escape CB2 which would take a lot of paid help.

I was working hard to keep things repaired in the cellblock so I could keep my free movement. I was sending out my photographs and cartoons and doing every little errand or favor that I could for the guards and the warden. One job that everyone hated was feeding on Death Row or any of the cells where men weren't allowed out. You had to carry all twenty or thirty some odd plates and cups up the stairs and put them on a food cart that could be rolled along the gallery. A tray of food and a cup of tea or juice or coffee would then be delivered to each man as you went along the gallery.

I offered to do it as part of my job as runaround. That rounded it out so that I needed to be out of my cell most of the day. There was a man in the second cell on the row who acted crazy all of the time. He was always reaching out trying to grab people going by and screaming crazy stuff that didn't mean anything. When I volunteered to do the feeding the inmate who had been doing it told me to watch out for him.

"He'll try to grab you," he told me. "But worst thing he does, he'll piss in his toilet and then dip it out in a cup and when you roll by he'll throw it on you or on the food cart.

"Why don't they close off the front of his cell?" I asked. "They've done that before."

"They say he's too crazy that they have to be able to watch him."

For the first two days that I took the food he threw piss water at me.

I went to the CB 2 Warden. "Sir," I said, "this is not something that anybody can put up with. Why don't you move him to the last cell and then he can only dirty his own food and nobody will care?"

"Can't do it, Pee Wee. He causes trouble every time they have to take him out for something. I can't have my guards exposed to the danger of having to wrestle with him for the whole length of that gallery. That's why we have him near the front. They say he's crazy but not crazy enough to be declared insane. He's on Death Row and there's nothing I can do to change it. I'll ask the kitchen to give you wax paper to cover the trays and you can try to protect the food."

"Yes Sir, Warden, I'll think of something."

The second night that I was doing the feeding a guard that I knew well was on duty. I told him if I could be out of my cell that night and I'd put a stop to it. The guard was glad to look the other way since they occasionally got a dose of the piss water.

The man was sleeping on the bottom bunk like most men who have a cell to themselves. I climbed up on the bars like a monkey and woke him to a sound he'd never heard on the row but somehow recognized as he came awake.

It was a sort of "Wokka wokka wokka."

He looked up still half asleep to see me pumping away squeezing a quart sized can of lighter fluid –wokka wokka wokka. In the same instant he felt the cold stinging wetness in his bed. I dropped the can and flipped open my old fashioned Zippo lighter.

"I know they all think you're crazy and maybe you are, but me and you are going to come to an understandin' right now," I told him. "Either you promise me you won't never throw no more piss water on me or the food trays or I'm gonna light you up. You understand me."

"Yes, sir, I understand you, Mr. Pee Wee. Ain't never gonna happen no more you got my promise."

"Crazy or not? Next time no warning. I'll just barbecue your ass. You understand me."

"Yes, sir. Ain't no more problems, I promise."

We never had any other problems and I used to take him a Snickers bar from the canteen every week. He never had enough money even for that but I would just tell him: "You can catch me next week." I think he was crazy, but even crazy people can think and they can enjoy a Snickers bar.

My good work and willingness to do repairs day or night got me put in charge of most of the cell block maintenance. I was made the "building man" and could go anywhere in CB 2 day or night. My cell was left unlocked at all times so that I could go where I was needed without a guard having to come let me in or out. I kept my tool box in the cell as well as a soldering iron for doing electrical repairs. I not only kept the worn out wiring in the block working but I also fixed radios, worms and even televisions for those who had them. I had a guard who brought in sandwich meat, cheese and bread so that I could make and sell sandwiches. Another brought candy bars that I sold. Still another brought the ever valuable cigarettes that were sold one at a time. I had a regular percolator and made the only real coffee in the block. Guards and inmates paid twenty cents a cup and I sold at least two pots every morning.

I ran a loan and pawn from my cell and was allowed to use an empty cell on the row to keep pawned items in. I made loans and did pawn for inmates and guards. I was allowed to have my own chain and lock on my cell and the pawn cell to protect the things stored there. There were one hundred and seventy five prisoners living in CB 2 and I kept asking for and getting additional help for the maintenance. I soon had nine assistants who were allowed to move around the block helping me. They were known as "workouts" and when I needed one of the assistants the guard would just give me the key and I would go and let him out of his cell to work with me. I could always have several men in any one area slamming and banging on things doing a repair when contraband needed to be brought into the block.

I didn't put up with much on the block. Quiet and orderly made my business run smoothly. Trouble brought a lot of looking. Years later a CB2 warden would tell people that the block never ran as smoothly as it did when I was the building man. He wasn't just talking about the equipment.

CHAPTER SEVENTY ONE

Cheating Death Row

An old timer named Pop McCormick who had been a friend through the years came to visit me with the weirdest plan I had ever heard. Pop had done some time with me at CCI before but he had finished his sentence and moved back to the area around Conway or Georgetown. He had gotten into trouble again and was back at CCI with a lot of time to do. It wasn't unheard of for someone outside to pay an inmate to kill another inmate. Men who were convicted because of a co-defendant's testimony would be sent to a different institution to protect the rat. Friends of the person convicted by the testimony would hire someone where the rat was serving his sentence to take him out. Men on the inside were killed over women on the outside and the other way around. But this thing from Pop was really different.

An older couple, Bill and Myrtle Moon, had run a little country store near Conway, South Carolina. Rudolph Tyner was a drug using, drug dealing nigger from New York with a long string of convictions. He was connected with groups that hated white people and wanted to take over the country. He was on the run and on his way to Florida but he ran out of money and drugs. He swung east off of I 95 or west off of US 17 to rob somebody. That took him to the Moon's little store. Tyner robbed the store, made the old couple get on their knees and beg for their lives and then shot them and killed them dead for no reason except to watch them die. It was the coldbloodest murder I had ever heard about.

Tyner was caught and convicted of the murder and armed robbery and sentenced to death. He was put on death row in the cell directly behind my cell. Even though I was off the row now, my cell still backed up to the death row cells that faced in the opposite direction. The barred side of the cells on the row basically faced the outer windows of the Cell Block 2 walls on the north while my cell looked out toward the south. Through the windows I could see the small building known as the Death House that I had cheated out of my visit. Because of my work I was on death row at least three times a day with the food carts. There were fifteen men on the row at that time—fourteen white and one black. Tyner was the one black. I'm sure that was the first time there was ever that many whites to blacks. I reckoned the solicitors were trying to even things up so they could keep their death penalty.

Tyner was a loud, smart mouthed Yankee nigger and I hated him from the first day that he was there. There was generally not much point in acting on your hatred toward death row inmates. They were locked up full time and the state was going to get rid of them for you as soon as they could get around to it. Tyner was an exception. He bragged about killing the old couple. Just as bad for me he bragged about the white girls who came to him with sex to trade for drugs. Most of all he liked to talk about the ones he said were the best. They were college girls and clean rich girls that he said came to him because he was in the movement. They were white girls. They didn't come for drugs. He said they screwed him to prove they weren't prejudiced and to make their own statement in favor of integration. He liked to talk about their rose colored nipples and how he loved the ones with light colored hair around their little pink pussies. I would have liked to set his black ass on fire but it's very hard to get to a man who stays locked up twenty-four hours a day. If I lit him up with lighter fluid, they would know it was me, especially after what I had done to stop the piss water boy.

The Moons had adopted Tony Cimo and raised him. Tony believed that they were his absolute saviors and the best people who ever lived. According to Pop, Tony had wanted to kill Tyner from the time that he was arrested. During Tyner's first trial Cimo had jumped over the rail in the courtroom and tried to kill Tyner, beating and choking him until deputies were able to pull Cimo off of the man. Which with it bein' Horry County, I'm sure they took their time about doin'. Most of them old courthouse deputies probably pullin' for Cimo to kill him.

* * *

Although Tyner was convicted and sentenced to death, his conviction was overturned and he was granted another trial. Tony Cimo's frustration grew and he was overwrought with the fear that the man would avoid execution. The second trial was moved to Marion County because of all of the publicity. Cimo hid on one of the few multistory buildings in the small town of Marion with a high powered rifle. It was his intention to shoot Tyner when he was being taken into the courthouse. Unfortunately Tony was not very familiar with the little town and didn't realize that prisoners were actually brought into the back entrance of the courthouse on the opposite side from his perch. After the trial began he again attacked Tyner in the courtroom and was again restrained and arrested.

Tyner was convicted again at the second trial and was once again sentenced to death. The conviction, however, did little to assuage the debilitating anxiety that Tony Cimo suffered. He was completely obsessed with the belief that Tyner would successfully appeal and be granted another new trial. He was utterly convinced that Tyner would ultimately escape execution.

By the time Pop contacted Pee Wee, Tony Cimo was totally convinced that Tyner was somehow going to escape the death penalty through his legal appeals. Tyner's execution had become the most important thing in Tony's life and he was determined to see that Tyner did not manage to avoid the death penalty. The more he heard about appeals and cases being reversed and people being re-sentenced to life, the more convinced he became that Tyner would somehow be able to avoid the death penalty.

It was because of this fear that he contacted a man named Jack Martin who had been a close friend of the Moons in October of 1980. He told him he wanted to find someone in prison who could kill Tyner.

Nothing more occurred until a year later when Tony again asked Jack to find someone at CCI who could kill Tyner. Jack was finally able to contact Gerald "Pop" McCormick who said that he might know just the man.

Jack Martin knew Pop very well and Pop finally called him at his home. Pop told him it wasn't hard at all to get somebody killed in CCI but he had never heard of anyone being killed on Death Row and frankly was not certain that it was possible. He said he knew the man who could do it if it could be done. Martin introduced Tony to Pop and as the discussions continued Pop advised Tony that if anyone could kill Tyner on the Row, it would be Pee Wee Gaskins. At Tony's insistence Pop went to Pee Wee about the possibility of killing Tyner.

* * *

I talked to both Martin and Pop and told them that I would give it some thought and that if I decided that it couldn't be done I would tell them that honestly and that would be the it of it. But if I decided that it could be done, then it could be. I surely did want to find a way. I had wanted to kill Tyner for a long time but now with outside help it just might be possible with money to boot. Killin' Tyner and getting' paid for it was a double your pleasure deal.

I thought it through lots of different ways and kept studying on it until I came up with a plan that I was sure would work. I rehearsed it in my mind the way I had done whenever I had the time before I killed someone, going over every step of how I would get them where I wanted them and exactly how I would kill them. I would then think about whether I needed to get rid of the body and how I would go about that. In cases where I wasn't likely to be connected to the murder in any way there was no reason to get rid of the body and trying to would just increase the chance of being seen or of leaving something that might link it to me. In this one there wouldn't be any question of getting rid of the body but nothing should connect me to it, if I did it right.

Finally I got back to Pop and told him to tell Jack Martin to let the man who wanted Tyner killed know that it could be done and that I could do it. We started to make a plan but I was not satisfied going through Pop. I was going to talk directly to Jack Martin and the man who wanted Tyner dead. Too many men had eased their load by putting something on me. I was going to be sure I was at least dealing one on one, that I would get paid and that I could take Jack Martin and whoever he was talking for down with me just as surely as they could take me down with them. I was in the end somewhat mistaken about that. I hadn't considered that the reputation I was so proud of in the joint would make my hide a lot more valuable than any of the others when the prosecutors made their decisions about who they would try for what.

Arrangements were made and Jack Martin and I began to talk directly by phone. I decided to record those calls. I wanted to be sure that I could collect for the work I was being asked to do and I also wanted to be sure that if somebody got the urge to confess for me and paint themselves out of the picture, I could at least keep the guy who started it all in the picture. When I called Jack I always told the operator that it was a collect call from Pop, just in case somebody got the tapes. Tony didn't have a lot of money and we agreed on two thousand to me and some money for the others involved. Of course the money wasn't as important to me as the chance to get Tyner and to do what had never been done. I also knew that those tapes would turn this into a retirement plan. I would be able to call Tony up for the rest of our lives and play a few words and ask for some cash. We must have talked fifteen or twenty times.

We were getting down to the nitty-gritty and I told Jack that I thought poison was the way to go. I could poison the guy since I handled all of the food for the row and even delivered snacks. Nobody would ask any questions about me taking him his regular food or even extra snacks since I got paid for taking people snacks. My guess was that they would never even test for poison. It was more surprising that people didn't die every day from prison food then when somebody did. I thought they'd probably just do some kind of half-assed autopsy and even if they found that he was poisoned they would probably decide that either the food killed him or he killed himself. Who cares would be the unwritten part of that autopsy.

To set Tyner up I took him some pot. I told him that I had gotten some good stuff in and that I would be selling it full time. It was well known that I didn't use so I told him I needed him to try it and tell me if it was really as good as the supplier said. I told him if it turned out good I'd sell to him on the cheap for checking it out. I knew he didn't have any money to pay for it but I pretended that I didn't.

He went crazy over it. Dynamite he said –best ever. I took him some more.

"Bring me some smack next time, little man," he told me. "I might get to like you after all."

Ordering me around like I was a waiter. It just showed again what an uppity nigger he was and how stupid he was not to know who he was fucking with. But I played along. Told him how glad I was he liked it and that I would see what else I could get hold of for him.

We had some good luck at that point when Pop was moved. It gave him freedom to move around the prison during the day and to go to the yard and to the athletic fields. Jack was responsible for getting the poison. I told Jack to get a cheap radio and then remove part of the speaker and put the poison under there. I told him how to reseal the package so that it looked like it had never been opened. I told him to send the radio to me. I also gave him the address of Dr. James Beaty, who was writing a book about me, and told him to put that as the return address since I received mail from him all of the time. We were on go.

The radio came as planned and I put some of the poison in a soft drink and told Tyner it was a new drug that would make you trip like crazy. I told him there was enough for at least three trips and that he should be careful to save part of it. I told him I had a friend that did just a tablespoon full and said he had seen shit he'd never seen. As I expected, Tyner drank the whole thing. The next day Tyner was sick all day but the son of a bitch didn't die.

"I don't know, Pee Wee, that shit really fucked me up and I didn't see shit —no colors, no wild shapes, crazy women or nothin'," he told me.

"Shit, Tyner, you chugged the whole thing. I told you it was good for three rides and you drank it all down. You overdosed. Instead of seeing the universe you knocked yourself to the ground and made yourself sick."

"Okay, man, just get me another hit. I'll try to stick to little tiny hits and see where it goes. Thanks, Pee Wee, I thought you were just blowin' smoke."

I gave him a double dose this time in a sandwich. I watched him eat the whole damn thing and the next day instead of dying he was there ready for breakfast.

I told Jack, "This shit ain't workin'. Hell it didn't even make him sick this time. You got to get me some real poison in here or I'm done. I'll call you in a week."

"Jack, it's me, did you come up with anything?" I asked him when I called.

"Oh yeah, we're good. The man promised me this new stuff would kill a horse. I told him I had coons all over my place and they were killing my chickens and tearing stuff up to get into the buildings. I told him rat poison didn't have any effect and that I couldn't leave the stuff out because of my dogs. I told him I needed something that would get them the first time. He said this stuff was guaranteed," Jack said, excited about his find.

"Well a guarantee don't mean much to us. We can't bring him over here and show him the nigger still walkin' around and ask for our money back."

"I'm just sayin' this is supposed to be really powerful stuff. I think you'll get him this time if you can get him to eat it," Jack told me.

"All right, same thing. Put it inside the speaker of one of those cheap radios. This time mail it to Pop and he will get it to me."

I told Jack that I would put the poison in some capsules and tell Tyner it was dope. I told him that I would also add a bunch of Thorazine to it. I knew enough Thorazine by itself could kill somebody. We called it "drop jaw" because they would give it to inmates who were violent or just causing problems and the next day they would be walking around with their mouth open and their jaw hanging down. It was all over the prison and easy to get because the men that were supposed to get it hated it and they would pretend to take it and then hide it.

"That won't work. It's tablets. I don't know how to hide it."

"I'll have a woman call you. You give it to her. She'll know how to get it in," I told him.

"I'll grind up the tablets and put it in some capsules. I'll put the thorazine in the capsules with it and add some ground up tranquilizers. If that don't knock his dick in the dirt nothin' will," I told him.

"Do it," was all he needed to say.

I got James Brown to take it to Tyner since James was the tier man for death row. The tier man is picked by me for each tier and he takes the food trays, picks up the empties, delivers razors for men to shave and waits to pick them up. He takes brooms, mops and cleaning supplies and runs general errands on his tier. A tier is all the cells on one side of each level. The first level is the rock and then level two and three with tiers A through F. Death Row was on tier C. I could go to any tier to do any of those things but usually let the tier men handle it. That made it seem natural for James to deliver something for me. It would also not be noticed by anyone that he went to the row for something, if they were asked about it later. The door to the walkway in front of the row was supposed to be locked at all times but it was usually left unlocked so that the tier man could go back and forth without a guard having to go up and unlock the mesh door.

Every man on the row was locked in his cell anyway so it really made no difference for them.

James delivered the capsules and Tyner took them all that same day. This time Tyner had to be carried to the hospital. He was real sick and semiconscious as they wheeled him out. As usual they didn't check to see how he got sick. They just kept him for a couple of days and then brought him back to the row. He was walking slow and weak and looked kind of gray, but he was still walking. He was one tough nigger to kill, I had to give him that. Some of the guards started to think he was trying to commit suicide and said they were going to put a suicide watch on him. Tyner kept assuring them that he might kill one of their honky asses, but that he had no interest in killing himself. All of the attention did mean that the next time we had better get the job done.

Jack got gun shy about me calling him and I told him I wanted to talk directly to the man behind it all. He told me he wanted out of the deal and that I should call Tony. From that time on I talked directly to Tony and again I made some recordings for my protection and for my retirement.

"We can't fool around with this poison shit anymore," I told Tony when I called him after Tyner came limping back. "I want you to get hold of some dyneemite. I want at least a half a stick of it. I'm not takin' no more chances. This is it; I'll blow his damn head off."

"I'll see what I can do, Pee Wee, I don't know if I can find dynamite. They keep that under lock and key," Tony replied.

When Tony checked his sources on the outside he learned that he could buy some C-4 plastic explosives easier than he could get dynamite. I think Jack was still helping him and he or a friend of his had used C-4 in the marines. I read up on it. It was easier to hide and a lot more stable than dynamite. You could change the shape of it to be able to hide it in an odd place. With dynamite it was a stick. You could cut it into pieces but it would still be pieces of a stick and any fool would know what it was. The other thing was that the C-4 would only blow when you used a detonator. An old stick of dynamite can go if you drop it. I told Tony to contact the source and buy four ounces of the explosive.

"Are you crazy? How the hell we gonna get four ounces of plastic explosive into the penitentiary. Some powder in the bottom of a box of candy is pretty easy but I'd have to send in a dozen boxes with the C4 lining the bottom to get that much. Why don't I just send you in a machine gun or a hand grenade?"

"Careful son, remember who you're talkin' to. Don't never call me crazy again. It might be hard to kill a man on Death Row but it wouldn't take me but a few hours to have somebody teach you who you're dealin' with. You understand me?"

"Yes, sir, I didn't mean any harm by it. You just took me by surprise. I don't have any idea how much I can even get. I've got this lead on it of course, but I'm sure you can't get any amount like you were at the hardware store."

"I'll set it all up to get it in. You just go to the man who has it and tell him we need four ounces. He'll have what you need. C4 won't just blow up. It ain't like dynamite. You can bang it around, make it into any shape and jump up and down on it. It won't blow up until you fire it with a detonator. Your man will have the detonator, the plastic, the wire —everything you'll need. I'll call you in three days and tell you where to take it. Be careful some people think I'm a little crazy and you know how us crazy people are."

"I'm really sorry about that. I know you aren't crazy. You're a professional just like you told me in the beginning and I know you know what you're doing. I've let you down not gettin' ahold of the cyanide or arsenic that you wanted in the beginning."

On the third day I called Tony and gave him the contact information for the people that would bring it to CCI. The next day he called to confirm that he had the plastic.

Five days later I called with the plan. Two people, a man and a woman, would bring the C4 in to the visiting room to two different inmates. It would be hidden in the heels of their boots —one ounce to each boot. It could be easily pulled out by taking a little strip of rubber off the front of the thick heel. The inmate who was visited by the woman just had to pretend he was rubbing her legs as he slipped open the heels and pulled out the plastic plugs. The other visitor just crossed his legs with his ankle on his knee and slid out the small plug of plastic, one foot and then the other. Over the thirty minutes of visiting it looked real natural.

The men inside brought me the plastic on two different days. The first one just carried it flattened out in his pockets and slipped it to me while he was leaning on the window talking. It was a common hand off that we had done again and again. Usually the items were a lot harder to hide. The other man brought it in his mouth on two different days. He said puttin' it in your mouth wouldn't hurt you that he had used it in 'Nam. I didn't know, but I wasn't puttin' it in my mouth.

The wire and the detonator were wrapped around a speaker and covered with electrical tape in a little boom box kind of radio that we were allowed to have. The radios had to be brought to the main gate or mailed in. They were carefully examined but there was nothing unusual looking about the speaker since there is always a wire coil as part of a speaker.

That was also sent to a different inmate. The radios were regularly sold and traded and I worked on them for inmates and guards or took them in hock, so the guards made no objection when someone brought it by and asked one of them to give it to me.

I told Tyner to bust loose one of the pipes under his sink so it would leak and I could come talk to him when they sent me to fix the leak. He thought I had more pot for him and so he did what I asked. I was in his cell the next day. I took him a small amount of drugs, just some ground up valium and painkillers and a little more pot which made him very happy. I told him that I was working on a plan to put some little radios in the cells so that people could call me when they needed something. I told him that now that I had access to the mechanical area behind the cells, I could run wires wherever I wanted.

"There's still a lot to be worked out," I told him, "but since our cells back up to one another, this is the easiest place to test it out. I've already got enough wire for that and I've got a little speaker that I think I can rig up to make it work."

"See if you can get me some smack," was all the dumbass had to say to me.

"You want to try the radio?"

"Oh yeah man that would be cool," he said, already messing with the powdered mixture I had given him. I told him to report another leak the next week.

David Carter, an inmate I had known through the years was moved into CB 2, he had been busted for something and came in broke and with no job. I bought a little radio from him for seven dollars and some canteen items –candy, crackers and other little stuff. I now had a speaker exactly the size that I needed.

CHAPTER SEVENTY TWO

The Tyner Solution

I used a large unbreakable plastic cup that is specially made for use in prisons. I placed the C-4 and the detonator inside it and then I glued the speaker in the top so that you could see the speaker. I thought that it felt solid and heavy like a radio or telephone. The weight came mostly from the quarter pound of plastic explosive and the little detonator in the bottom of the cup. I used my soldering iron to melt a hole in the plastic on the side of the cup near the bottom and put a female plug through it that was exposed on the outside. The female plug was connected to the wires of the detonator buried in the plastic explosive inside the cup.

When I went to his cell I told Tyner I would be sending him a cup that had a speaker at the open end of it and a microphone down inside it.

"This thing will be like a direct phone to my cell," I told him. "This way when you want to order a sandwich or something or just need to pass a message, you can call me on this and I'll come right around or you can tell me what you need to tell me right then like a telephone. Like I told you this is the first one I'm tryin'. Since my cell backs up to yours and it's such a short distance, it's a good place to try it out. If it works, I'll run 'em all through the row with the wires hid back in the chase between the cells where all the plumbin' and wirin' is run. Once we know it will work, I'll make 'em look like regular radios so there's no trouble keepin' 'em in the cells."

"I'll run a wire through my vent and then go into the chase and put it through your vent so there's just enough to grab hold of stickin' out. When you get the cup with the radio in it pull out the wire that I fished through

385

the vent. All you will have to do is just plug the wire into the female plug at the bottom of the cup when I tell you we are ready to test," I said.

I told him that we would test it in three days and gave him the exact time for the test. We checked our watches and I told him:

"When the time comes I'll bang three times on my back wall and tell you to test. Then you hold it close to your ear, plug the wire into the cup and say, 'Testing, testing, testing' into the open end of the cup. Then you say 'This is Tyner over to you, Pee Wee'. If I can hear you say 'Over to you, Pee Wee,' then I'll answer and we'll know it is working both ways."

I waited three days and then I had James Brown take the radio cup to him. I wanted it to be known that I hadn't been on the row for three days when the thing went down. James Brown was an inmate that I used for sex and I had made him tier man for death row. I had him take the homemade radio over to Tyner on the pretext that he was checking on the repairs to the sink. Brown was a tiny little fellow, the size of a girl.

"He thinks it's a homemade intercom," I told James. "I told Tyner if the thing works I'll be sellin' them to anybody can afford it. They'll be able to talk to me like in a fancy office."

I went to the back of my cell and fished a regular electrical wire through the vent and pushed it as far as I could. I went inside the chase and pushed it just barely through into Tyner's cell through his vent.

After he had delivered the radio James came back by my cell.

"Did you give it to him?" I asked.

"Oh yeah, he seemed real pleased. He said he was expecting it. Said you run errands for him and do stuff for him all the time. Didn't sound much like you. You his bitch, Pee Wee?"

"You'll see what all I do for him. Don't worry about that. And you'll still be my bitch when I'm finished with the stuff I'm workin' on, if you learn to watch your mouth. What did he do with the thing?"

"He turned it over and around and looked at the plug on the bottom. He seemed to like the idea. He pulled the wire out of the vent like he said you told him."

I waited until the time Tyner and me had set for the test. Then I banged on the wall hard with a wrench from my tool pouch. Right on schedule Tyner said:

"Testing, testing, this is Tyner over to you, Pee Wee."

Next I plugged my end of the wire into the electrical socket in my cell. An explosive roar went through the cell block that nearly knocked me down. It temporarily deafened everybody on both tiers and all of the guards. I quickly pulled what was left of the wire through the vent and hid it in my mattress until I could get rid of it.

I was standing in front of my cell with a couple of workouts two seconds after the explosion went off. It was louder than I thought it would be and the eleven workouts were soon running toward my end of the tier to find out what had happened. I ran down the stairs and met Officer Jones and told him I needed to go into the tunnel chase to see what had happened. I reminded him that there was a big electrical box at the far end of the tunnel that handled all of the power coming into the building and told him that it might have blown. For some reason it had sounded like the explosion came from the rock.

Carl Chaplin, another old time Charleston con, and me went into the tunnel chase that was always unlocked on the rock and went to the other end. We came back and reported that the box had not blown up and told the guard that we needed to get into the chase on the third tier to find out if the huge exhaust fan might have blown up or fallen. As we were starting up the stairs, someone called out that it was Tyner and he was hurt bad or killed.

We ran to his cell and found him half on the floor and half on his bunk. His left hand had been blown off along with the left half of his head. One finger had been blown off of his right hand and there was a hole in his shoulder. I thought he was dead on the spot but one of the workouts said he saw him move and the canteen man and somebody else put him on a stretcher and ran off to the infirmary with what was left of him. They claimed he lived about forty-five minutes. Like I said he was a hard nigger to kill.

I had done the impossible. On September 2 1982, seven years after they locked me up on death row for the first time and seven years after the last kill on the outside, I had just become the first man to murder a death row inmate while we were both on death row. I had done it while I was being held at the highest level of security in a special section of the toughest prison in South Carolina. And I got paid for it.

I told James we had blown Tyner up as a favor to the man whose momma and daddy he killed. I told James he ought to be real proud of bein' part of it. He said he was.

The investigators originally thought that Tyner had blown himself up trying to blow his way out of the prison. When the FBI experts determined that he had been holding the explosive up to his head, some thought that he had committed suicide, since there had been suspicion of that earlier. But they kept on digging; not because anyone cared that much about what happened to Tyner, but instead because they genuinely wanted to discover how he had gotten explosives into the prison and on to Death Row.

I knew the heat was rising fast and I took my blackmail tapes and recorded over them from the TV. I picked the show Hogan's Heroes and put it over the tapes. It had been about two or three weeks and they came to my cell and to several others. They made us strip naked and then walked us out of our cells and put us in empty cells. They checked our clothes and gave them back to us. They tossed our cells taking absolutely everything out of them. They then told us that we were being taken to Maximum Detention and Retraining Center. We could only take a few things to MDRC and the rest of our belongings were to be stored in the Property Control Room in the admin building.

In my cell they found some razors, a little bit of the pot I had for Tyner and some other things that were contraband. Those things went to the Contraband Room. Of course they took all of my tools and the tapes, but I don't know which room they went to. Eventually they seized David's radio with no speaker, some of the wire and the tapes as evidence. I think that was after Pop McCormick had run his mouth to a couple of people who went to the law to trade their little bit of info for a break of some kind on their sentence. The little bit that the two snitches had picked up from Pop was enough to turn the investigation in a different direction and all of the focus was on me and on Pop. It turned out the FBI was helping and, to my amazement, they could even go back and take the Hogan's Heroes off the top of the tapes and leave the stuff I had recorded between me and Tony Cimo and Jack Martin.

They started to turn up the heat on everybody on the block. They also began to make promises of rewards or special treatment or transfers and even early release for anyone that could provide information. A snitch gave them enough to get to James Brown and when they told him it was now a murder investigation and the death penalty was on the line he caved like a school girl. After it happened he was put in lock up along with me but he claimed he had no idea what he was actually taking to Tyner when he took him the cup with the speaker. In the end the law let him out by saying he was just delivering the radio for me without knowing anything about the plan to kill Tyner. Of course they only came to the conclusion that he didn't know anything after the little rat testified against me. He knew just enough to help them put most of the story together and their search for the proof began in earnest after he started talking.

When they arrested Tony Cimo, probably based on what James or Pop had told them, he cooperated immediately and got a sweetheart deal. I think he wound up doing less than a year out of whatever time they gave him. Everybody felt bad for him and he was written up like some kind of hero for getting revenge for what Tyner had done to his parents. Nobody mentioned that I was the hero that blew the son of a bitch to kingdom come.

They came up with enough on Pop for his part in the plan and told him they would be going for the chair against him under the "hand of one is the hand of all" doctrine. He hung in there as far as I know. The one guy I had been sure I could count on was Pop. He was an old timer who had built a lot of time. He had done a lot of it with me and I knew he lived by the convict code, but he had never looked down the barrel of the death penalty. They put us all in MSC –me, Pop, James Brown, and a guy named Lee and some others but it was hard to talk to each other over there with the double cell doors.

I always thought it was kind of funny the way they would come to you on death row or MSC and read you the arrest warrant and then tell you that you were under arrest for the murder of Barnwell Yates or Rudolph Tyner. I would always laugh and ask them if that meant I had to go to jail.

They noticed me for the death penalty for the third time. This one would be in Richland County and they brought Judge Laney in to try me again. I guess they owed that to him since he could only give me life up in Newberry.

I asked Judge Laney to appoint Mr. Query, but the judge said he turned it down. I figured he was pissed at me for doing another murder after what he had gone through to get me out of the death penalty. That wasn't it though. He came up and told me that he would like to represent me but he had another death penalty case down in Charleston and several civil cases that were ready to go to trial.

He said, "That's where I make a living, Pee Wee, trying those civil cases. This thing will take weeks under that new statute and I'm sorry I just can't leave Charleston for that long to do it."

"Well I sure wish you could try this one for me, Mr. Queury, they got me trussed up pretty good with everybody turnin' state's witness and all."

"Seems to me like the best defense in this case is that the state had him up here to kill him and you just gave them a helping hand. You know Buster Murdaugh who's been solicitor down in Hampton, Jasper, Beaufort and that area for about a hundred years always said 'There are three defenses to murder in this judicial circuit: Self defense; I didn't do it; and the son of a bitch needed killin',' Mr. Query laughed. Seems to me like you ought to go with the 'Son of a bitch needed killin' defense', Pee Wee. Ask them to pay you the fifty dollars the volunteer gets for pulling the switch when they put somebody in the chair."

"Seriously, Pee Wee, Judge Laney said he is going to appoint Jack Swerling and John Young to represent you. They're both as good as you can get. They're smart and they've got plenty of experience," Query said.

"What about these solicitors? Harpootlian or something like that and Anders?" I asked.

"Jim Anders has been at it for a long time and he's a real trial lawyer. He'll know his case and he knows the rules of the court and the law. Dick Harpootlian –he's awfully good too. That's the bad news. They're as good as Swerling and Young. But Young and Swerling will fight them as hard as I would and they'll know the best way to try the case."

He was right. Swerling and Young were damn good lawyers and they put up one hell of a fight, but Harpootlian and Anders were good too, and they had all of the ammunition.

At the trial expert witnesses explained how the explosive worked and described in gory details what had happened to Tyner. They put up guards and inmates to talk about the layout of CB 2 and Death Row. They even had a model of the cell block. They showed the jury how my cell was first on the right side of the second tier as you entered the cell block and Tyner's was through the mesh door to Death Row in the same place on the left. They described the mechanical chase that ran up between all three tiers giving access to electrical, plumbing and mechanical for all the cells on the left and the right and showed it on the model. Guards swore the entrances to the chase were always closed and that the entrance to Death Row was always locked. The inmates testified that they were left open and unlocked most of the time. All agreed that I was never locked in my cell and that I had access to the mechanical chase at any time and that I frequently went on Death Row.

James Brown was called and while he denied knowing everything about what was going on he admitted that he had helped me try to poison Tyner. He testified that although he wasn't aware that the homemade cup radio contained explosives, he had in fact delivered the cup to Tyner for me. Not satisfied with the facts he added a lie, saying that right after the explosion he had run by my cell and seen me pulling the wire back through the vent. I had jerked the wire back through my vent but I had hidden what was left of the wire and run out onto the walkway with all of the workouts by the time that little rat got to my cell.

On cross examination Jack Swerling was making some points with James about him knowing Jack Martin and also having a grudge against me. He had already admitted to taking the intercom to Tyner and it was beginning to sound like he had killed Tyner and then set me up.

Harpootlian had promised James he wouldn't say nothing about him being my pussy boy because James's momma was at the trial, but he got real worried about how Swerling was making it look like James had done the whole deal. Swerling kept pushing questions that suggested that James was trying to put the murder on me because of an old grudge and because he was jealous of me being so famous. So old Dickie, the Harpoon, broke his promise to James and on cross examination Harpootlian forced him to admit that far from being enemies we had been very close.

"What do you mean close, Mr. Brown?" Harpootlian questioned.

"We were lovers," said Brown almost in a whisper.

"I didn't hear your answer," Harpootlian said, and as he was saying it he walked all the way to the far corner of the jury box, so that James would almost have to holler for him to hear. "What did you say?" he boomed from that distance.

"We were lovers," James squeaked plenty loud but with his voice cracking and tears on his face.

"Lovers, hell," I told Mr. Swerling. "Ask him who was on top." He objected in just as loud a voice as the 'Harpoon' had used asking his question, but the damage was already done. On cross exam he wouldn't ask my question but would try to return to the idea that James had been angry with me and was acting out for revenge.

We called a lot of witnesses from CB 2 and they all testified that I had been out in front of the cells at the time of the explosion. They all testified that I ran down the stairs to the rock and went into the chase to see what had happened as soon as the big boom was over. They said I appeared as confused as everyone else about where it had come from. Other inmates testified that James Brown had gone to the row that day. Death Row inmates stated under oath that I had not been anywhere on the row. It was proven by guards and inmates that I could not leave the cellblock except in chains with a guard, but near the end it came out that I could go into the little exercise yard for CB 2 whenever I wanted and that there was a place where it was next to windows for one of the wards. One workout said he had seen pop get something and pass it from the walkway to the exercise yards into a window at CB 2, but he couldn't say what it was. David Carter confirmed that I had gotten the little radio from him and that it still had his name carved in the bottom. He testified it was intact when he brought it to me but that now the speaker was missing. I didn't blame David. He didn't have no idea why I wanted that radio.

They played the tapes of me talking to Jack Martin and to Tony Cimo and Judge Laney let them see the pictures of Tyner all blowed up. That put the icing on the cake.

The blacks who testified for the state or the defense all said that I always treated everyone the same without any difference because of race. The witnesses told the jury that I always tried to help people who were in the cellblock and especially the ones on the row who couldn't leave their cells.

Like I told Mr. Query over and over, I didn't have nothing against blacks, but I hated the niggers like Tyner who messed with white girls and him killing that old white couple for no cause just added to it.

The jury found me guilty and then after a day's break they went into the penalty phase of the bifurcated trial under the same statute Summerford had screwed up when he tried to death penalty me over in Florence. In that second part of the trial they brought out all of my record on top of all of the other murders that I had pleaded guilty to. They even brought Kenneth Summerford down to talk about what I had told them about those murders and on top of that Summerford threw in details of my statement about the murders of Janice Kirby and Patricia Alsbrook, Kim Ghelkins when I hadn't even been convicted for those murders, but it all came in as evidence of my prior bad conduct. Summerford said that I didn't show any remorse for any of the murders, not even the children. Swerling yelled objections and the judge said he couldn't give his opinion about me showing remorse, but as Bud Grisso used to say about tellin' jurors to disregard something, " there's no point in strainin' the milk after the cow has pissed in it". Ken Young came in to tell them about my conviction for killing Barnwell Yates just to add to the list of people killed.

In their closing arguments Harpootlian and Anders told the jury that all that information about other murders proved that I was the most dangerous man in South Carolina or even in America. They said that I had proven that it was impossible to hold me in a way that would keep me from killing again. I wanted to agree with them on that one.

Swerling and Young put up one hell of a fight, never giving in on any issue and putting up a come-back to everything Harpootlian and Anders could throw at me. It was in all honesty one fine trial. There was good lawyers on both sides who knew the law and went hard with it. They went at each other from start to finish, but they did it with the real evidence, not by cooking up stuff the way Summerford did. I'm not saying that Anders and Harpootlian weren't just as ambitious as Summerford, but they weren't going to break their own rules to put me in the chair just so they could put themselves in the Senate or the governor's office. In the end the State just had too much against me. They made a strong case with the recordings and the testimony from the other people that had been involved. The other murders were probably all it took for the jury to decide on the death penalty.

The jury didn't take a whole lot of time to come back with the death sentence and I was hauled off back to CCI. The SLED cars stopped way before the main entrance though. They stopped in front of the Maximum Detention and Retraining Center. I was hauled into MDRC, searched about three times, including my mouth, my ass and between my toes. I told them if they had one more of 'em stick his hand up my ass I might start to like it.

I was expecting to be walked up the stairs to one of the cells on the second level but instead they marched me down the short set of steps into what was known as the dungeon. I was walked all the way to the end and I knew that the cells got worse the farther you went. They put me in a cell with a concrete bunk fastened to the wall. It came with a thin mattress, but there wasn't much between me and the concrete. The cell did have a toilet. I had once been thrown into the end cell that only had a hole in the floor.

When lights out came my light didn't go out. My little cell was lit twenty-four hours a day and there was a camera outside the bars that they said covered the whole cell. The cells were six by eight and there was a window up about six feet from the floor. On the outside of the building that window opening was about a foot or two above the ground. I was actually in a cage inside a cell. The outer concrete walls front and back were a foot outside the bars of my cage. Then another set of bars separated me by about two feet from the solid steel door in the wall. You couldn't see out of the window unless you stood on the bunk and then just barely. Nothing to see anyway. The outside wall to the prison within the prison was only twenty feet away.

When they wouldn't turn out the lights after about a month, I went on a hunger strike, but as I started to lose strength and get woozy they told me they wouldn't take me out to the infirmary. They said they were going to bring people in and feed me with a tube right there in the cell. I wrote to all of my lawyers, Swerling, Young and Query and they all promised to call, write and sue if necessary.

They finally let me call Mr. Query in the hope that he would convince me to eat something. I told him that the light and the camera were still going.

I said, "They got me lit up day and night with a camera stuck right at me. Hell, Mr. Queury, I can't even jack my dick without them watchin' me on TV."

I don't know which lawyer finally convinced them but they did start to turn out the light for a few hours every night. I started to eat again but

I wrote every day to everybody I could think of, including the governor. I was telling them all that I had a right to be housed on Death Row just like every other condemned man.

It seemed like they were about to transfer me to Death Row when they stumbled on to a plan I was trying to put together to have my son or some of the boys from the neck kidnap Harpootlian's kid. Sheriff Barnes had arrested a guy in Florence who had heard about the plan. Barnes called Harpootlian and alerted him. I was going to have the kid hidden and then I would make a deal that if I was taken to Harpootlian's office, I would leave the office by the back door. James Brown had been transferred to Tennessee, where his mother lived, as a reward for his testimony against me, but not before he gave me some good information. Since James had been taken to Harpootlian's office many times in preparation for my trial, he knew all about the office, including a secret back door. He was so mad about what Harpootlian had asked him about being my pussy boy during the trial that he had told me about the back door to get back at him. Old Dickie couldn't figure out how I knew about the back door for the longest time.

My kidnapping plan was that after I walked out the secret door, I would hook up with my son and we would head for South America. As soon as I was free we would call them and tell them where to find the kid who would not be harmed in no way whatsoever.

My son was arrested on some other charges in Richland County. He was questioned about my plan but he was never charged on the kidnap plot because they realized that either he hadn't even heard about the plan or that he had no intention of being any part of it. Just the same they used the plot as a reason to keep me in MDRC and we had to start all over with the fight to get me moved.

None of it did any good and I was only transferred to the row after MDRC was permanently shut down as being unfit for human habitation in 1986.

The stay on the row didn't last very long because a new Death Row had been included in the new Broad River Corrections Center that was built over next to Kirkland, Wateree and the other corrections facilities near department headquarters on Broad River Road in Columbia. The new row opened in 1990.

CHAPTER SEVENTY THREE

New Room Old Chair

Broad River was as new as CCI was old. Narrow windows of unbreakable glass set in the reinforced brick walls replaced the big windows filled with iron bars. Everything was sparkling clean and there were actually some colors. Death row was now a square with cells surrounding a central operations room of bullet proof glass. All cell doors which were solid steel with single small glassless windows could be locked or unlocked from the panel in the control room. There was a nice visiting room. It was carpeted and there were tables and chairs and there was no glass or screen separating the visitors from the inmate. There was even a microwave oven. Visitors could get sandwiches or pie or cake from vending machines located inside the prison and have lunch with the inmate they were visiting. A large window allowed the control room a full view of the visiting area and only one prisoner at a time could have visitors.

My cell was like a room and had some bright colors in it and no bars. Of course I was the brightest thing in the room, all dressed up in the bright colored suit that designated Death Row inmates. The nicest thing was that my cell was big enough to have some room between the bed and the opposite wall. I was allowed to have boxes for my papers, pictures and art supplies and there was even a drawer under the mirror for my toothbrush, soap and hairbrush. The toilet was pretty much the same as those in all prison cells but it was not one of those terrible combos that made you feel like you were brushing your teeth in the toilet. The sink was separate and under the mirror. Of course toilet, sink and mirror were all stainless steel and fastened tightly to the wall.

They let me use a little recorder that Mr. Earl, who was writing a book about me, had left for me. I spent many hours talking to that machine because he had promised to write what I said. He would carry my final message of "Screw you!" to the cops and prosecutors that had plagued me all of my life. I put some truth in it and I put a lot of bull in it just to be sure I gave them some stuff to wonder about for the rest of their lives.

The bad news about the new row was that "old sparky" had come right along with the rest of us to where they had a brand new room all set up for it. I don't know if it got new switches or not but it was the same old chair. I had never given it much thought, but I have to admit I had a bad feeling in my stomach when they announced that it was being moved and set up just around the corner from us. It was a huge straight back chair made of solid oak and it had been waiting for me for a long time. Over two hundred men had taken their last seat in it. The leather straps that would keep you from flying out of the chair when they hit you with the voltage were thick and wide. They looked like something that had been made in the prison workshops with awkward heavy buckles and rods the size of my little fingers to go through the big eyelets used to fasten the straps.

I had thought with all of the modern look to the new prison and the new row that there would probably be a space ship looking chair of plastic and steel with hydraulic clamps to tighten around arms and legs and maybe even your body. I thought they might even be able to shoot a deadly beam of electricity to you from one ultramodern conductor to another without even touching you. Instead it was the same old chair that had stalked me for thirty years with the gruesome leather mask and the sponges soaked in brine to increase the flow of electricity from the cup on your head to the plate on your leg.

My appeals were denied one after another. The lawyers said the South Carolina Supreme Court has a policy called *in favorem vitae,* which they say means when the answer isn't clear, they are to decide in favor of life. It requires the appeals court to look for mistakes even if they aren't raised on appeal by the lawyers. The new statute also requires that all death sentences be compared to see that the penalty is being fairly and evenly applied. Again and again the decisions in my cases would say in so many words, that I was proof that there needed to be a death penalty and that by any comparison to other death cases my sentence could not be considered unfairly severe. I guess Tyner was proof that it was hard for me to stop killing and impossible for them to stop me from killing.

As the time approached for my sentence to be carried out, all of the people working on the row were very polite and nice to me. The other inmates on the row started to treat me with a sort of special reverence. I guess I represented all of their futures and they wanted to see me get through it without having some kind of breakdown. Some of the men I've known on the row have been too simple minded to be able to imagine what was going to happen to them. I don't think they could picture how it might feel or how they would want to look on the final walk. A lot of them sort of went from minute to minute and so I guess they didn't have to deal with it much until they were shaved, walked down the hall and strapped in the big seat.

A lot of us, including me, were stand up men who had reputations throughout the prison system. I had told Mr. Query that I would fight to my last breath when they came for me and see if I could add one more to my total, but he told me they would just zap me with something or pop me with a tranquilizer dart and then shoot me up with some powerful drug like Thorazine, so that I would just stumble down the hall and flop into the chair. I thought he was probably right and so I made a plan that I would try to cheat them once there was no other way to go. If that didn't work I wanted to walk out of my cell by myself and lead the little procession down the short hall where I would take my seat without anyone touching me or helping me. I wanted to look the witnesses right in the eye and take the hit without shittin' and pissin' myself in front of them.

The word came that my last appeal for a stay of execution had been turned down by the U.S. Supreme Court. Shortly after that I was moved to the death house. It was actually part of the same building but it was a separate room where I was to spend my last three days.

After I was moved into the death house I was allowed family visits inside the room and chaplains or preachers and lawyers could come inside and sit with me if they wanted to. I met with a chaplain and he prayed for me and I prayed with him. I wasn't sure I was eligible for consideration but I did say I would accept Jesus as the Son of God and my only hope for salvation. Of all people Mr. Query had come to visit me just a few weeks before and while we had never spoken about God or our beliefs, he told me that it was an important part of the Christian belief that no matter what you had done, if you accepted Christ and asked for his forgiveness you would be forgiven, if you truly believed. I thanked him because I knew he had always tried to care about me as something other than a monster, which was how I was being described by everyone else. I didn't know if that was what he believed or whether he was just trying to give me one last chance, like he always did.

I had told him about the book I was doing with Mr. Earl and that it would be let out as soon as I was killed in the electric chair. I told Mr. Query that he knew what the truth was and that he shouldn't believe everything I said in that book. I told him I weren't no kind of a pervert. I knew that he knew better because of all the time we had spent together and because of all of the people that he had talked to that had been around me in and out of prison. I had put some stuff in the book that sounded like I was a pervert and a homicidal maniac because I wanted the law to think they had never figured me out. Some of it was a lot like the stuff I told them under the truth serum, when I made up all those murders of women down in Charleston.

"I want law enforcement to know they never solved a damn thing. Either Walter solved it for them or I took them to it myself," Pee Wee said. "There's plenty they never came close to. Some of it's in Earl's book and they'll have to guess at what is and what ain't," he continued. "You can tell 'em the truth if you decide to or if you write a book. That'll be up to you now. I won't be neede no more protectin' or privilege," Pee Wee laughed.

Mr. Query said, "Got to mess with 'em just one more time, eh, Pee Wee."

We both laughed as the lawyer shook his head smiling at me.

I told him that I would like for him to be there for my execution but he told me that he wouldn't do that. He said that he had fought against the death penalty for as long as he had been a lawyer and that he would feel like he was somehow being a part of it and condoning it if he came to my execution.

"Pee Wee, I think that it is the most bizarre notion of our society when we expect to stop people from killing people by killing people. Even those in favor of it know that it has never been fairly administered. For a long time it was mostly for blacks. Now it is mostly for the newspapers or somebody's political ambitions," he told me.

"I understand that and I know how hard it was on you when they put your client Terry Roach to death," I told him.

Terry was a retarded boy that committed a bad murder and rape when he was sixteen or seventeen. He had done it along with a much older man that the court found had dominated over him, but they still executed him.[4] It tore that man, Mr. Query, up pretty bad. I had spent years on the row with Terry and he seemed like a quiet, simple minded sort of boy who would go along with what somebody told him to do. Mr. Query said the boy had some kind of Huntington's disease that would've killed him anyways in a very bad way. I told him maybe Terry had been better off having it quick in the chair instead of drawed out.

I had Mr. Query to contact Whatley at North Charleston, Sheriff Barnes in Florence, McJunkin in Sumter and anybody he could talk to at SLED and tell them that if they would put off my execution or change it to life, I would show them the location of additional bodies connected to their jurisdiction. I even wrote some letters to officials myself, but there were no takers this time.

The death house room was set up to be completely visible to someone in an adjacent area and then there was another space just outside the room where someone could sit to watch you even closer.

I had heard the final walk was supposed to be thirteen steps. I never could figure how they could know how many steps a man would take to get there. On the day before they would take me on that final walk, I played my last card.

I had swallowed some razor blades using the trick I had learned and I slowly brought them back up. I wrapped up tight in the blanket and then I cut both arms following the big blood vessel up from my wrist, which according to what I had heard and read is supposed to be the best way to

---

[4] Thirty-six years later the U. S. Supreme Court would revisit the very argument presented by Query, Mike Farrell and Grisso regarding the constitutionality of applying the death penalty to a person incapable of understanding the relationship between the penalty and their actions. They had asked that court to consider that premise in the case of Terry Roach. The new decision by that court found their argument to have merit.

be sure you will bleed out. I rolled completely up in the dark blanket so that the blood would not be visible on the sheets and wouldn't run out onto the floor.

I guess I was always meant to have that final ride with "old sparky" because the person that was assigned to watch me noticed that I wasn't moving at all and when he called out to me I didn't answer or even twitch. He decided he had better check on me and called the guards to go into the room. When they spoke to me and then shook my shoulder and I still didn't move they pulled back the blanket and saw that the bed was full of blood. I was barely conscious and I was rushed to the hospital part of the prison which was still there inside Broad River Correctional and they stitched me up.

I was taken back to the death house room and they moved a guard right outside my room. I would be under "close watch" until they came for me. My sister and my daughter came and spent most of that last day. That day I was also visited by my death penalty lawyer, Mickell Branham, who with the other people at the Death Penalty Resource Center had done everything possible to get the death penalty set aside for me and every other poor bastard scheduled to be murdered by the state. I do mean poor bastard. White or black, that's the call. Rich killers do life. Poor killers get electrocuted, gassed or injected.

I hadn't asked the governor to stop the execution. He ran on being in favor of the death penalty, so I wasn't going to give him the satisfaction. I hoped Mr. Query's theory was right and if there was some answering to be done that the governor would have to answer for me and the others the state killed, just like I would have to answer for the ones I had killed. I never knew whether Mr. Query really thought that or whether it was just one of those little quirky things he would come up with when we were talking. I definitely wasn't expecting any last minute call, even though my lawyers continued to try to get a Justice of the U.S. Supreme Court to issue a stay.

The date of September 6, 1991 had been set by the South Carolina Supreme Court by what was called the "death warrant" on the row. They had set dates before but stays had always been issued for an appeal to one court or another. This time the day had come and no stay had been issued and my lawyers said it was not likely that one would be.

CHAPTER SEVENTY FOUR

Dead Man Walking

Sometime that last night they told my family to leave my cell. The chaplain came again and stayed. They brought me the famous last meal right after my family left. It was a tradition on the row to ask for pizza, so I followed the tradition and ordered pizza, even though I never cared a damn thing about pizza. I wasn't going to eat anything anyway so I just kept up the tradition.

The most gruesomest part of it all started then. I was seated in a straight back chair with two guards facing me a half step away in case I caused trouble. I was not chained but of course that would happen if I didn't cooperate by sitting still. My head was buzzed with clippers and then lathered and shaved by a guard whose hand shook so bad I thought he'd probably finish with his razor what I'd tried to do with my own razors. Next they split my pants legs up to just below the knee and shaved about a five or six inch section between my ankles and knees.

A doctor or somebody that at least dressed like a doctor came in to talk to me at that point. He told me I could pretty much have all the tranquilizers that I wanted. He said I could start then but that I had to wait until just before I walked to take the big dose. He told me that I could also have a strong painkiller just before they came to get me. He said that there shouldn't be any pain involved, but I could have the painkiller if I wanted it.

"I wonder where they get that little fact from," I said. "I wonder who they asked about whether it was painful."

"I guess you're right about that," was all the doctor had to say.

"I'm not into drugs," I told him. "It sounds like most men take the walk so stoned they don't care what happens. I'm not going that way. I want to walk in on my own and sit down. I don't want to be helped into the chair because I'm so drugged out that I can't walk. I want that clear; I ain't stumbling in there too scared to move on my own or so high on drugs that I can't move on my own."

"Well it's here if you want it," he said. "No shame in being nervous and it will help keep you calm."

"Thanks, Doc, I appreciate it but I'm going to look it right straight up. There is one thing worryin' me, Doc. I don't want to shit myself or piss myself in front of all those witnesses. Anything you can do for that?"

"I'll get you a diaper. The body usually eliminates both ways when somebody passes, so I can't stop that, but the diaper will keep anyone from seeing that it happened. If you'd rather you can use these just before we go," he said, handing me some tight rolled cotton like a big tampon and a heavy rubber band. "You'll be given a chance to go the bathroom just before they come to get you. Put the cotton in your anus real tight and it will probably stop any feces elimination and wrap this wide rubber band around your penis as tight as you can to keep you from wetting yourself."

"I'll take the tampon and the rubber band," I told him. "A diaper just don't seem like the right thing to die in." I put them in my pocket until time to go to the toilet.

"I can get an orderly to help you with it if you want," he offered.

"I think I can stuff something up my butt and tie off my own dick," I told him, getting tired of the phony kindness as they got ready to kill me. I knew that he would be the same person who would step over and put the listening thing on my chest to check for a heartbeat when they had cooked my brain and fried my innards. So I sure didn't think of him as a gentle man of healing.

They came for me right after midnight. Each of the guards who had been with me for the final three days said their goodbye and told me they didn't bear me any bad will. A couple told me they were glad to get to know me better and wished that it had been stopped. Mr. Query had told me that a lot of the guards who go through the final watch and the execution come out against the death penalty after their experience with it.

The preacher blessed me again and we started the walk. I don't know who all went. There were guards all around me and the warden walked behind us with the preacher and the doctor.

"I won't cause no problems. Let me walk on my own," I said to the guards who were on either side of me holding on to my arms, holding me like you would a person who might fall out any time. It was obvious they were prepared to carry me and let me move my feet or not.

Some old timer, I never knew if it was a guard or somebody back on the row, even yelled out "Dead man walking". I guess tradition is real important to some people.

As I stepped into the death chamber I saw the chair ahead of me. It looked like it was made for a giant. Heavy oak with a high back with leather straps and wires all over it with the awful skull cap mounted at the top of the back. It was a mean looking thing and I guess it had earned that look. About two hundred men and two women had taken that seat and not one had walked away. At the door to the death chamber they asked if I needed help to get to the chair.

"I'll git in on my own steam," I told them.

And I did. I walked over and climbed up into that big chair and sat my stuffed up ass right down. They opened the curtain and I looked out at the witnesses. I saw my lawyer, Mickell Branham, that I had asked to be there, and I recognized Sheriff Barnes. My sister had asked him to be there for my family. He was listed as being there for the victim's family since that was the only slot open, but he came because my sister and my daughter had asked him to be there. Nobody from Tyner's family had responded to the notice that they could come or name someone to be there for them, so that had left the opening. Billy Barnes was a tough sheriff, but he was a good man, and he knew my sister and daughter had never done anything to bring any of this on and he had been kind to them through all the years. It was mighty big of him to honor their request.

They strapped my bandaged arms to the big wooden chair arms with two or two and a half inch wide heavy leather straps and then put the same kind of strap around my chest. At the same time others were strapping my legs or putting them inside in the ankle cuffs so the conductors were against the shaved part of my leg. Because of my size they taped it to be sure it stayed in place for the whole show. Before they put the plate against my leg they smeared on some goo that was there to make the juice flow better from my brain to my ankles. Two metal cuffs went around my ankles and were tightened down with the same goo smeared on first. The cuffs had wires running to them.

The warden asked if I had anything I wanted to say.

"I'll let my lawyers talk for me. I'm ready to go," was all I had to say to him.

A man behind me put a wet sponge soaked with salt water for good conduction of electricity on my head and then lowered the metal skullcap on top of it and pulled it down with a strap under my chin. This device would deliver the huge electric shocks through my brain and down and out through my calf and ankles. It was right at one o'clock in the morning.

They put the leather mask over me. The mask covers your whole face. They won't let you refuse it. I know they won't, because I told them I didn't want it. It ain't for the benefit of the man in the chair; it's not for you, it's to cover up your face so the witnesses don't see it if you bite off your tongue or your eyes pop out or burst. I had talked to guards who had been in on executions through the years and they had described what they found when they took off the mask. It sure wasn't anything they wanted the witnesses to see. I wanted to refuse it, so they could really be witnesses and see the horror of what was going on in there.

They strapped the mask on. The three men who were to throw the switch stepped in, somebody counted to three and that was the it of it.

CHAPTER SEVENTY FIVE

The Most Delicate of Processes

Sheriff Barnes said that Pee Wee looked like a small child crawling up into an oversized ladder back chair when he climbed into the big oak electric chair. The chair had been used in South Carolina for decades and over two hundred men had preceded the little man who had been labeled the "Redneck Charles Manson" and "the meanest man in America" by the press.

It was September 6, 1991, when the three volunteers, each of whom would be paid only a nominal fee, simultaneously pushed the button in front of them. No one of the three would know which of the buttons actually activated the electrical switch. That switch started an automatic sequence that would deliver a first jolt of two thousand volts for five seconds to be followed by one thousand volts for eight seconds and then two hundred fifty volts for two minutes.

As the first of the blasts of electrical current coursed through the body of the tiny condemned man his body arched and bucked against the leather constraints and then slumped against the straight wooden back of the enormous chair. No one could know whether any life remained for the subsequent electrical surge but certainly most of the eight seconds of one thousand volts had no further effect on nerves that no longer carried transmissions from a living brain. The subsequent smaller current produced only mechanical jerking consistent with the effect of the electrical impulses. Many would say that if there was ever a person deserving of the death penalty, it was this man, but the horror of the process gives pause to any observer. Many prison guards who have participated in the final days of preparation and the execution itself have emerged from the experience as vocal opponents of the death penalty.

The ashes of Pee Wee Gaskins were scattered by his daughter at Ropers Crossroads.

MATTERS OF INTEREST

I was only five years into the practice of law when I began the representation of a Gaskins co-defendant, but having appeared on the scene prior to the public defender system in South Carolina, I found myself at all times appointed to dozens of criminal cases. I had already represented men accused of capital murder who were facing the death penalty. As a young lawyer I was fortunate to have the benefit of the mentoring and tutelage of two of the finest criminal defense attorneys ever to practice in South Carolina. I brought to my cases the benefit of their counsel and relied at least as much on their experience as I did on my work in law school to earn the degree of *juris doctor*.

One of those mentors, Arthur Howe, had served as the chief prosecutor for Charleston County in the elected office entitled Solicitor and as the chief federal prosecutor for the lower part of the state of South Carolina in the appointed capacity as U. S. Attorney. His prowess in the courtroom and his knowledge of the law were well known and few wanted to face him in trial. The occasional exception was a young advocate who like a devoted student of the martial arts appreciated that there was much to be learned from defeat when it occurred at the hands of a master.

Howe's partner and long time friend was Paul N. Uricchio, Jr. Their friendship had grown out of their years as adversaries in the battlefield of the courtroom. While Howe was the product of privilege and fine educational institutions, Uricchio was a second generation Italian immigrant and the son of a tailor. After completing his service in the Navy, Uricchio landed one of the real prizes of his generation, a job at the naval shipyard in Charleston. He was not satisfied though and studied the law at night by correspondence course. Ultimately he stood for the bar, buoyed only by the correspondence course. Having passed the bar he was admitted to practice.

Like Howe, Uricchio would become known as a master of the courtroom. His adversaries preferred to dismiss his skills as a trial lawyer and emphasize his mastery of negotiation and compromise, but these were merely excuses for the defeats they suffered at his hand. He and Howe excelled not only at the trial level but also as skillful writers and advocates in the appellate courts. A man of the people, Uricchio frequently knew the police and the witnesses in a case and he used the familiarity to his advantage. But those who underestimated his courtroom abilities were often stunned by the verdicts that he won and many a judge who doubted his recitation of the law would see the opinion of the Supreme Court begin with the term "Reversed".

Uricchio and Howe had been young lawyers in the law firm of Major Meyer, a legendary practitioner in Charleston, South Carolina. The firm was known as the League of Nations because of the diversity of the associates so rare in those times. Besides Howe, the aristocrat and Uricchio, the Italian, Louis Lempesis carried the Greek banner for the firm and I. M. Goldberg represented the Jewish community. The back door of the firm was open to a courageous young black lawyer for his use of the library and for the clandestine association of the firm in cases of substantial value that could not be successfully brought by a colored lawyer. That young black attorney, Richard E. Fields, would ultimately become a Circuit Court Judge serving for many years in the highest trial courts of the state. Sharing Meyer's German heritage in the firm was Fritz Hollings who would become Governor of South Carolina and then United States Senator.

Although I was no longer with the Uricchio firm at the time of my representation of Judy and ultimately of Gaskins, the doors of Paul and Arthur remained open to me and the wisdom of their vast experience remained freely available to me. Often I would return to Charleston from representing Gaskins in Florence County some two hours away and spend hours with Arthur and Paul at their Broad Street offices long after the office had closed. I would recount the day's events and I expressed growing concern over the vitriolic attitude and approach of the solicitor in Florence County. While trials in the Ninth Judicial Circuit were hard fought and usually won by the staff of young solicitor Robert Wallace, the trials and the negotiations were conducted with courtesy and civility. Wallace had trained as an assistant solicitor under Arthur Howe. I was alarmed that the attitude of the Florence county solicitor became openly hostile and threatening when the two young lawyers from Charleston representing Neeley and I showed an inclination to fully assert the rights of our clients.

I later convinced my good friend and frequent associate in trial work, John K. "Bud" Grisso, to become co-counsel for Gaskins. Grisso was a former Circuit Solicitor in Greenwood, South Carolina and had then been appointed as United States Attorney for the State of South Carolina. He was a seasoned and highly respected trial lawyer of the highest order and brought to the team a reputation for toughness, for shrewd courtroom tactics and an expansive knowledge of criminal law and procedure.

Entering the cases at the same time I did was another experienced attorney, Earnest Hinnant. Hinnant was the first part-time public defender for Florence County and was appointed to represent Gaskins as a regular part of the responsibility of his office. He would continue for a long time as public defender but ultimately return to full time private practice. The epitome of the southern trial lawyer, he was dapper despite his somewhat rotund figure and eloquent and polite in his courtroom presentations. His gentle nature masked a tough litigator who normally faced overwhelming odds in the defense of his indigent clients.

Two other young lawyers from Charleston, Paul Cantrell and Chris Staubes appeared on behalf of Walter Neely. Paul was known to the family of Walter Neely, and they were retained by that family. Paul Cantrell would later be elected to the South Carolina State Senate and while serving in the state senate and continuing in the practice of law, Paul would die tragically in the crash of his single engine airplane. Chris Staubes would go on to become a founder of one of the most successful civil defense firms in the state.

After the trial of one case and the sudden conclusion of a second trial, I continued to represent Gaskins for many years. Ultimately I would decline the appointment for representation of Gaskins in his final trial for the murder of a fellow death row inmate, but I nevertheless continued to visit with Gaskins until his execution by the state shortly before one A.M. on September 16, 1991.

AUTHOR'S NOTE

We will not ever know how many people died at the hands of Pee Wee Gaskins nor will we ever know his true motives for the many that he killed. While I have attempted to portray Pee Wee's life as accurately as possible from what I observed and the hundreds of hours of conversations I had with him and with others depicted in this book, this is nevertheless a work of fiction. The conversations that are not part of a transcript are from my imagination or from my best recollection of conversations with Pee Wee.

Where no record exists and where events and conversations occurred that I could not have seen nor heard, and which were not specifically related to me by Pee Wee Gaskins, I have filled those voids purely from my mind's eye and they should not be considered accurate or even factual. The thoughts, conversations and actions of characters named for the sake of establishing some of the imagined scenes cannot actually be attributed to them, but rather are my thoughts on what they might have said or done.

Many events and many of the characters are depicted as Pee Wee described them and his perceptions should not be viewed as accurate or unbiased. These scenes, conversations and characters are depicted for any insight they might provide into the workings of Pee Wee's very different and unusual mind. He has been variously described as depraved, deranged, disturbed or demonic, and other characterizations of similar ilk. He was probably all of those things, but he was above all else truly unique.

ACKNOWLEDGEMENTS

I am thankful to my friend Pat Coil and his lovely wife Deborah for their diligent reading and re-reading, for their wonderful ideas and for their indefatigable mettle. Also to my friend Wally Seinsheimer for his willingness to struggle through a rough draft and for his encouragement and brilliant mind. I am forever indebted to my legal assistants Tracey O'Brien and Ashley Kay, who printed and bound numerous copies, uttered never-ending words of encouragement and without whom this work could not have been completed. I am grateful to my partners, Mike Sautter, Saul Gliserman, Bentley Price and Michele Patrao Forsythe, who made it appear that I was still at the helm despite my toiling with these words in the galley below. They are truly great lawyers who make my practice a pleasure. I need to also thank my long time associate, Kerry Koon, a brilliant lawyer who truly had a baptism by fire when he covered for me back home during the Gaskins Trials. Jane Gliserman who is one of the most creative people I have ever known read my first pages and gave me the green flag. Finally I am forever grateful to retired Sheriff William "Billy" Barnes who shared pictures found in this book and who more importantly spent hours talking about the events and answering endless questions. If my memory was as sharp as Billy's this could have been non-fiction.

I offer my apologies to the great lawyers, Dick Harpootlian, Jim Anders, John Young and Jack Swerling for having failed to more thoroughly and accurately depict their brilliant work on both sides of the case in the Tyner trial. It was the epitome of our adversarial system at work featuring vigorous prosecution within the rules and the tenacious defense of the rights of an accused in spite of all of the indications of his unfettered depravity.